PROSE STYLE

PROSE STYLE
A HISTORICAL
APPROACH
THROUGH STUDIES

JAMES R. BENNETT
University of Arkansas

CHANDLER PUBLISHING COMPANY
An Intext Publisher
SAN FRANCISCO • SCRANTON • LONDON • TORONTO

Library of Congress Cataloging in Publication Data

Bennett, James R.   1932–   comp.
    Prose style.

    Bibliography: p.
    1. English language—Style—Addresses, essays,
lectures.   2. English prose literature—Addresses,
essays, lectures.   I. Title.
PE1421.B38   1972   808.04′27   69-11256
ISBN 0-8102-0395-2

Previously published and copyright materials are reprinted with the permission of
authors, publishers, or copyright owners as identified at the pages where they are
reprinted.

CONTENTS

PREFACE

Because the history of English prose style is a large and tangled field, the intent of this anthology is not to survey its many dimensions, but to suggest directions for explorers. For those who wish especially to investigate historical and critical approaches, the usefulness of this collection is, I hope, self-evident. Each chapter contains Suggestions for Research, and Chapters III–V conclude with Selections for Analysis, critical commentaries and excerpts from the works of major writers of the period surveyed by the chapter. In addition, the book contains General Suggestions for Research, A Contextual Method for the Description of Prose Style, a Glossary of Historical and Critical Terms, a Bibliography by Period, and an Annotated Bibliography.

For those who are beginning their studies in English and are truly venturesome, even though lost in the thicket of freshman composition, this book might be a guide to a more mature style. For those who would create in English fiction, perhaps the book will offer some examples of prose and criticism which will lead them out of personal stylistic deserts.

To those students of modern linguistics who view the historical field as territory which either should never have been charted at all or should not be charted any farther, it is my hope that this anthology will help them find paths which will converge with the traditional rhetorical ones. Linguistic analysis isolated from the historical approach produces fragmentary results. Equally, a historical approach alone is partial. Historical categories such as Ciceronian, Senecan, and plain, for example, need careful linguistic analysis and definition if they are to become reliable critical terms. A fixed compass is of little help to an explorer or a straight road.

Nor is a fixed view of style; see, for example, the various definitions summarized in "On Defining Style" in Enkvist *et al.* (1964) or the analysis of divergent theories in "The Problem of Style" in Milic (1967b). While a good style is always individual, if the artist is to project the vision that is uniquely his, at the same time it is always conditioned by his culture, the choices available in his language in his time and place. Through the mating of a writer's individual style with styles of the past, a "new" style is born. Inescapably, because all men are part of the historical continuum, the "new" style has drawn, either consciously or unconsciously, from the continuous history of English prose.

Thus, it appears that the critic's and writer's tasks are not far removed. It is the critic's job to assess uniqueness within tradition. It is the writer's job to assert uniqueness within tradition. If the reader of this anthology accepts these premises, I trust that they will help in developing his critical criteria and his own style.

I am indebted in many ways to many people for the completion of this book. Professor Marjorie Ryan conceived of the idea with me. Western Washington State College and especially the University of Arkansas assisted me with funds and typists. To Betty Brigham, who helped for more than a year, I am particularly grateful. Professor Newell Ford has always been encouraging, and so have my colleagues. This book is dedicated to students of style everywhere.

INTRODUCTION

A good critic of style must be able to perceive both the uniqueness and the tradition which have mated. Lack of this fusion can produce dramatic mistakes, as in Sir Arthur Quiller-Couch's description of the Authorized Version of the Bible as a "miracle":

That a large committee of forty-seven should have gone steadily through the great mass of Holy Writ, seldom interfering with genius, yet, when interfering, seldom missing to improve: that a committee of forty-seven should have captured (or even, let us say, should have retained and improved) a rhythm so personal, so constant, that our Bible has the voice of one author speaking through its many mouths: that, Gentlemen, is a wonder before which I can only stand humble and aghast. (*On the Art of Writing*, pp. 122–123, as quoted in R. W. Chambers, 1932, p. cxxxv).

But to a man like R. W. Chambers, who knows history better, the composition of the Bible of 1611 is quite another thing indeed:

Looked at in isolation, the Authorized Version *is* a miracle. But, in fact, there was such a tradition of English prose behind those who drew up the Authorized Version that even a Committee could not spoil it. All their lives the translators had been repeating or listening to the words of the Prayer Book. All the forty-seven must have known by heart large sections of the Psalter in the already seventy-years old version of 1540. And if it is retorted that this is only pushing the miracle back from Jacobean to early Tudor days the answer is that the prose of early Tudor days had in turn been nourished on the Fourteenth-Century English of works like *The Scale of Perfection* or *The Cloud of Unknowing*. What that means, any passage taken at random from the *Cloud* would suffice to show. . . .

    And, if we wish to go behind that, we may turn to the noble eloquence of many a passage in the *Ancren Riwle*, or of Aelfric, or Wulfstan, or Alfred (R. W. Chambers, 1932, pp. cxxxv–cxxxvi).

This view is seldom denied today. One recent historian of English style, for example, understands English prose history as "a series of adjustments ... each of which ensured that English prose did not deviate too far from ... a continuity of the native line" (Gordon, 1966, p. 32). One way to de-

1

scribe the continuous "adjustments" of English prose is by the recurrent conflict between the impulse to be expressive and the desire to be useful. Critics of the seventeenth century, for example, have explored the intricate variations of "ornate" and "plain" styles—Senecan, Ciceronian, metaphysical, Puritan, scientific, journalistic—and the gradual ascendance of the "plain." They tend sometimes, however, to lose sight of the larger history. I believe with Hugh MacDonald that after the Restoration there was

less a change in prose, though a change there undoubtedly was, than an almost universal disappearance of a certain kind of prose. For there had existed ... from the days of Chaucer, or for that matter King Alfred, a straightforward prose in which it was quite easy to say plain things plainly (MacDonald, 1943, p. 34).

Chambers illustrates concisely the Elizabethan elaboration, "He fell into a fantasie and desire to prove and know," of Alfred's direct and simple, "He wished to search." But Chambers also reminds us that we often forget how many people in the sixteenth century wrote a "straightforward, vivid, simple" prose (Chambers, 1932, pp. lix, clxxii). And if the eighteenth century was one adjustment toward maintaining the "native" line, it also possessed writers expressively innovative and individualistic.

That these terms "expressive" and "ornate," "plain" and "utilitarian" are imprecise should not deter us from using them. We need both a theory of style and an inductive procedure. Although too many stylistic studies have lacked sufficient illustration and denotation, there has gradually accumulated a body of evidence that, with further study, will lead us to an understanding of the expressive and the useful in English prose, and their countless individual variations, until someday we will be able to speak reliably of writers as representatives of their time as well as individuals speaking in their own unique voices.

The critical essays in this book, which I have retitled for the sake of brevity, are intended to stimulate further exploration of the continuity of prose style. In Chapter I, Ian Gordon defines the "native tradition" (normal S-V-O order) in syntax from Alfred to the present. Edwin H. Lewis and Virginia M. Burke sketch out the gradual emergence of the unified, well-proportioned paragraph.

Chapter II is devoted to the Old English and Middle English periods. R. M. Wilson represents the doubters about continuity. Norman Davis broadly weighs the influence of French and conversation on the formation of Late Middle and Early Modern prose, while Samuel K. Workman focuses on the improvement of construction during the fifteenth century through French translation.

Chapter III tries to suggest both the enlarged variety, experimentation, and richness of the sixteenth and seventeenth centuries, as well as the continued and later increased strength of utilitarian writing. Walter F. Staton, Jr., explains the importance of the doctrine of the three "characters" or levels of style (low, middle, and high) in the sixteenth century and after. Gilbert Highet offers a broad summary of the Ciceronian and Senecan styles in the sixteenth and seventeenth centuries and later periods. Jonas A. Barish gives a close analysis of Ben Jonson's "curt" and "loose" styles in contrast to Shakespeare and Bacon. Harold Fisch outlines the importance of the Puritans in the simplifying of seventeenth-century prose, while Joan Bennett stresses the influence of experimental science in this simplifying process. As a conclusion to this chapter, Hugh MacDonald reminds us of the continuation of the old straightforward tradition throughout the period.

In Chapter IV the Restoration and eighteenth-century standard of modern writing is emphasized, but expressiveness is not overlooked. Robert Adolph offers concrete analysis of that gained clarity by comparing an early seventeenth-century writer with a Restoration author. An excerpt from one of Richard F. Jones' essays dramatically reveals the effect of science, especially of the Royal Society, on the simplicity of English prose. Jan Lannering examines Addison as representative of the "neo-classical" prose style in its "first stage of maturity." W. K. Wimsatt, Jr., specifies the eighteenth-century correctness in an analysis of Johnson's parallelism (with comparison and contrast to Addison and Hazlitt). In contrast, J. M. Stedmond identifies the Shandean "loose" style.

The experiments and consolidations of the nineteenth and twentieth centuries are presented in Chapter V. Josephine Miles discusses the continuity of late eighteenth-century with nineteenth-century American prose, and both with the Renaissance. William Minto describes the continuation of two traditional styles—De Quincey's "periodic" prose and Macaulay's "pointed" style. Francis X. Roellinger traces the change in Carlyle's style from that of the polite, impersonal, and anonymous reviewer to the highly personal and idiosyncratic style of *Sartor*. Richard Ohmann compares Burke and Arnold and stresses the individualism of Victorian prose writers. Harold C. Martin describes the steady development in narrative technique from Cooper to Crane, and Richard Bridgman surveys the development of the "colloquial" style in the United States. Two of America's most significant writers, Hemingway and Faulkner, receive special attention. Walker Gibson describes Lieutenant Henry's "tough talk," and Irena Kaluza isolates the role of parallelism in giving order to Faulkner's "subjective" style. And, finally, David Hayman scrutinizes one of Joyce's sentences in "progress."

THE CONTINUITY OF THE SENTENCE AND THE PARAGRAPH

THE CONTINUITY OF THE SENTENCE

Ian Gordon

... It is a commonplace to observe that the meaning of a modern English sentence depends on word-order—disrupt the order and ambiguity or nonsense immediately ensues—whereas a fully inflected language like Latin permits a relatively free choice of word order. Latin verse permits even greater freedom than prose: Ovid can write 'Nec amara Tibullo tempus amicitiae fata dedere meae'—'Nor did bitter fate grant the time for my friendship with Tibullus', where object precedes subject, the qualifying adjectives are both separated from their companion nouns, one adjective precedes its noun, the other follows it, and the verb occupies a position unlikely in Latin prose. Yet the firm links of concord in gender, number and case leave no opportunity for ambiguity.

Old English was like Latin an inflected language with similar concords. In theory, something like the same freedom should have been possible. In fact, it did not have this freedom. The movement towards a relatively fixed

From Ian Gordon, *The Movement of English Prose* (English Language Series; Bloomington: Indiana University Press, 1966), Ch. 3, "Continuity II: Sentence-structure," pp. 24–32. Reprinted by permission of Indiana University Press and Longmans, Green & Co., Ltd. Notes have been omitted.

(and sometimes rigid) word order both in prose and in verse was well established in the earliest extant documents, and even in the still earlier Runic inscriptions. Certain of the most-used sentence-structures of modern English go back as far as the English language can be traced. This does not gainsay the subsequent enrichment and embellishment of sentence-structure that followed from the study of French and Latin and mediaeval and renaissance rhetoric. But as with vocabulary, so with the sentence. The struetures embedded in word-order, the bones of the language, make their appearance early.

Here is a sentence from the late tenth-century prose of Aelfric:

þes foresæda halga wer wæs gewunod þæt he wolde gan on niht to sæ ond standan on þam sealtan brymme oþ his swyran, singende his gebedu

literally

This aforesaid holy man was wont that he would go at night to the sea and stand in the salt water up to his neck, chanting his prayers.

The Old English contains one idiom discarded in modern English, which today would have 'wont (or accustomed) to go'. But apart from that, the remarkable thing about the sentence is precisely that it is not remarkable. The word-order is the order of the present. Subject precedes predicate; prepositions occupy their modern position, the auxiliary verb immediately precedes the past participle, the final participial phrase is common modern usage, the adjectives precede the nouns, and they precede them in a hierarchy of proximity that follows precise rules still valid in contemporary writing.

If we examine the principal clause of almost any Old English sentence, we find there firmly established what has turned out to be the dominant sentence-structure of English. It is the subject-predicate sentence (what Bloomfield calls the actor-action sentence) with a rigid subject-verb-object (s v o) order. This order is so regular that extensive illustration is unnecessary. The following principal clauses from Aelfric, arranged in ascending order of complexity of modification, will show how accurately Old English word order foreshadows the word-order of the present day: *Se halga andwyrde*, 'the saint answered' (s v); *se halga ða sona andwyrde*, 'the saint then speedily answered' (s v); *se halga ða het him bringan sæd*, 'the saint then commanded to him to be brought seed' (s v o); *se halga wer ða sona het þa heardnesse swiþe holian onmiddan þære flore his fægeran botles*, 'the holy man then immediately commanded the hard surface to be swiftly pierced in the middle of the floor of his fair dwelling' (s v o *plus* adverbial modifier).

This is normal order, and it provides the structure of the main statement in Old English prose, and finally of all statements, principal or dependent, in later prose. It is the order of what might be called neutral narrative. The demands of rhetoric and emotion in any period of English can disrupt this normal order, bringing emphatic elements to the beginning or the end of the sentence—Blessed are the poor in spirit, say the Beatitudes; *Gode ælmiehtigum si ðonc*, 'to God almighty be thanks', writes Alfred with some emotion and a conscious reversal of normal order. But as soon as the voice drops and the narrative or the exposition continues, this sentence-structure forms the staple of all narrative sentences in English of all periods.

This establishment in Old English of a fixed order, corresponding to the order of the present day, extends beyond the S V O order of principal clauses. Adjectival modifiers early settled into structural patterns which, though un-recognised until recently, are nevertheless an essential feature of the 'gram-mar' of modern English. There is a precise sequence of modifiers in English —one *must* say 'many holy words', 'in all fine arts', 'a very beautiful bone', 'to no other business', 'in this same year'.

No reshuffling of the order of these modifiers is possible. The contrast with Latin is again significant 'hoc genus omne' can be written with the three words in any order without loss of meaning or idiomatic usage.

The 'rules' for the order of attributive adjectives in modern English can be determined empirically. They are fairly complex, and only a few of the main principles need be noted. Briefly, adjectives of description come closest to the noun (good men); 'determining' adjectives like 'this' and 'other' precede adjectives of description (these good men; other good men); where the determiner is definite, numerating adjectives follow it (these three good men); where it is indefinite, the numerating adjective precedes it (three other good men). Where there is more than one descriptive adjective, the pattern of proximity follows strict and describable conventions (good old black men). Where there is a series of modifiers, each occupies its fixed position (all these three good old black men).

It comes with something of a shock of recognition to discover that the fixed order of adjectives is nothing new. It has been fixed for well over a thousand years. The empiric 'rules' for adjective order in present-day English are substantially the 'rules' for their order in Old English prose. The phrases given in the last paragraph but two have their precise equiv-alents in the Old English of Alfred, Aelfric and the *Chronicle*, from which indeed they are taken—*monig halwende word; on eallum godum cræftum; swiþe æþele ban; to nanre oðerre note; on þyssum ilcan geare*.

The Old English inflexional bonds of noun with verb and adjective with noun were thus reinforced by a rigid structural grouping. The adjective modified the noun and 'belonged' to it as much by proximity as by gram-matical concord. Position as well as case identified the subject and the ob-ject. Position was probably the more important; certainly this rigid struc-tural pattern, established so early in the language, goes a long way towards explaining how inflexions could weaken without resultant loss of meaning. It is usually assumed that a fixed word-order took over the task of the lost inflexions. The truth is more likely to be the other way round. The fixed word-order made the inflexional endings redundant. They were losing their force before the end of the Old English period.

A full comparison of word order in Old English and modern English lies outside the scope of this study; it is a task that has not yet been at-tempted. But one further comparison will illuminate how close Old English structure can be to that of the present day. In a narrative sentence in modern English adverbial modifiers (words or phrases) tend to occur in a fixed order. A very common sequence in written prose is time-manner-place:

He took off his shoes and *then* (1) crept *silently* (2) *across the room* (3). *The previous night* (1) he had slept *peacefully* (2) *on the bed by the window* (3).

This sequence was well established in Old English, as can be seen in two sample sentences from Wulfstan and Aelfric:

Dæghwamlice (1) man unriht r*æ*rde *ealles to wide* (2) *gynd ealle þas ðeode* (3).

Every day they have committed injustice all too widely in all this nation.

Se halga wer *ða sona* (1) het þa heardnesse *swiþe* (2) holian *onmiddan þære flore* (3).

The holy man then immediately commanded the hard surface to be swiftly pierced in the middle of the floor.

Much work remains to be done on the sentence-structure of Old English. But two strong impressions emerge from a study of our early prose. They are well summed up by Quirk and Wrenn in their *Old English Grammar*, 'First, that there are in O E considerable areas of conformity to describable patterns; secondly, that these patterns to a great extent coincide with modern usage'. The heavy concentration of most grammars of Old English on phonology and accidence (in which the older language differs most obviously from the modern tongue) has tended to divert attention from the considerable areas of coincidence. In its essentials the structure of the Old English sentence is the structure of today.

Differences there are, and it is interesting to watch in the period between the tenth and the fourteenth century the inexorable shaping of the modern sentence. In early writing the position of the pronoun-object ran counter to the normal s v o order. Old English often put the pronoun object *before* the verb. This older order is still possible in poetry—'Him the Almighty Power hurled headlong' is common Miltonic usage. In the late *Chronicle* (AD 1137) usage wavers—'þe biscopes *heom* (them) cursede' appears within a few lines of 'me (i.e. they) smoked *heom* (them) mid ful smoke'. By the fourteenth century the order is that of today. It is possible that one of the factors that assisted the change, bringing pronoun-order in line with noun-order, was the development of accusative forms for the pronoun with the full phonetic weight of monosyllabic nouns. Some of the Old English pronoun-object forms, notable the overworked 'hie' (which had to do duty for 'she', 'her', 'they', and 'them') were phonetically 'light'. They could barely carry the stress expected of a noun in the object position. When the phonetically 'heavier' forms 'her' and 'them' were developed, alongside the emphatic monosyllables 'him' and 'it' and the older 'me', 'thee' and 'you', English had acquired a full series of pronoun-objects that could carry the required stress for the object position, and from the late Middle English the pronouns conform to the normal s v o sentence order.

One common Old English sentence-structure, often met in the *Chronicle*, was early discarded in narrative prose. This was the sentence that begins with a demonstrative word like *þa* 'then' or *her*. 'Here, at this point in the narrative'. In such sentences the order is verb-subject (v s) or verb-subject-object (v s o)—'Her for se here'—'at this point advanced the raiding army' (v s); ' aþbesæt sio fierd hie'—'then besieged the army them' (v s o). Although this order vanished from narrative prose, as later writers grew more skilful at subordination of clauses, it has remained alive in more elevated contexts—the 'here lies' of the epitaph, and the 'then shall the curate', 'then shall the Bishop' of the Prayer Book. Keats, with his sure instinct for the language, relies on it for subtle reinforcement in his line: 'Then felt I like some watcher of the skies.'

The s v o structure of the principal clause became the structure for all clauses. The process took some time. Old English dependent clauses tend to have their object before the verb (s o v). A sentence from Ælfric shows two instances:

Cuþbertus þam folce fægere bodade, þæt hi *wære* wæron wið deofles syrwan, þylæsðe he mid leasunge heora *geleafan* awyrde

literally

Cuthbert to the people fairly preached, that they *wary* be against the devil's snares, lest he with deceit their *faith* corrupt.

The displacement, to modern ears, of the complement 'wære'—'wary' and the object 'geleafan'—'faith' remained a feature of Old English prose down to the late *Chronicle*, where we can often find constructions like: 'þa the suikes undergacton ðat he *milde man* was'—'when the traitors discovered that he a *gentle man* was.'

In the thirteenth century, the s v o order of the principal clause finally asserted its dominance and it became the standard pattern for clauses of all types. The modern practice—normal order in both principal and dependent clauses except for deliberate rhetorical inversions—can be seen beginning in R. W. Chambers' twelfth-century touchstone of continuity, the *Ancrene Riwle*. By the fourteenth century we read a sentence like Rolle of Hampole's 'Bot thou sall witt þat no man hase *perfite syght of heven*' or Chaucer's 'I prey meekly every discreet persone that redeth or hereth *this litel tretis*' and recognise the completely modern shape of the sentence. A further area of coincidence has been established.

This discussion has been confined to the clauses as isolated units. They are the bricks from which the sentence is built. The bricks have changed little over the years, though ways of building have altered. . . . [E]ven in the midst of development the instinct for continuity is remarkably persistent. Modern English differs most sharply from Old English in the greater flexibility and subtlety with which it can link clauses together. It has resources for expressing relationship in varying levels of subordination unknown to the earlier tongue. In general, however, the process of development has been addition without much subtraction. English learned new devices without giving up the old.

Two of the commonest methods used in Old English for linking clauses are co-ordination and parataxis. In co-ordination, the sentence consists of a series of main statements joined by 'and' or a comparable linking-word:

Ic   arise, *ond* ic fare to minum fæder, *ond* ic secge him.
I will arise, *and*   go to my   father, *and* will say unto him.

In parataxis, the linking-words are absent. The main statements are set down side by side. In place of the linking-word, there was in speech a firm pause or juncture:

> Drihten, hæle us; we mote forwurþan.
> Lord,   save us: we perish.

This kind of structure is generally called 'primitive'. The term is hardly accurate, if primitive carries its normal connotation of something rudimentary and archaic which is discarded by an advancing culture. English discarded neither type of sentence-structure, and the Old English procedures of writing principal clauses joined by 'ands' and 'buts' and of paratactic construction, buttressed if need be by the most obvious and unsophisticated dependent clauses, have remained permanent features of good prose, and not merely the good prose of 'simple' writers.

A few examples will suffice. Milton, expert though he is in the complicated periodic sentence of later times, frequently writes with telling effect sentences of pure Old English structure:

And yet on the other hand unless wariness be used, as good almost kill a Man as kill a good Book; who kills a Man kills a reasonable creature, God's Image; but he who destroys a good Book, kills reason itself, kills the Image of God, as it were in the eye.

Alfred's vocabulary did not include 'reason', 'image', 'destroy', or 'creature', but he would have given this sentence exactly the same shape. Much of the essentially conservative prose of the Authorised Version is based on the Old English uncomplicated co-ordination and parataxis of clauses:

And his disciples came to him, and awoke him, saying, Lord, save us: we perish.

A century later Defoe can write an effective paratactic series:

I stook like one thunderstruck, or as if I had seen an apparition: I listened, I looked around me, I could hear nothing, nor see anything. I went up to a rising ground to look further; I could see no other impression but that one.

Across two further centuries Virginia Woolf can turn aside from the complexities of interior monologue to echo the same movement:

She held up her hand. She stopped the cab opposite a little row of posts in an alley. She got out and made her way into the Square.

In language, as in other things, England discards little of its past.

We can now ... reassess the question of continuity. After the publication of Chambers' study, it was generally accepted that Old English, not the Renaissance, should be regarded as the real starting-point. English prose of every period is continuously illuminated and explained in the light of what has gone before. Innovations are always possible, and cannot be ignored, but they never form more than a minority element in the usage of any particular time. New elements have been constantly introduced: in every period, enrichment of the vocabulary from foreign sources; in the Renaissance, a longer and more complex sentence-structure modelled on classical Latin; in Middle English, French influence on the construction of phrases and sometimes of sentences. In recent years doubts have been cast on the Chambers thesis: a revival of interest in the links between English and French has led some writers (notably Norman Davis, the editor of the Paston Letters) to suggest that French influence was so pervasive in the late mediaeval period that the concept of continuity is untenable.

But continuity there was, and it rests on a basis broader than Chambers proposed. It does not depend simply on the preservation of Alfredian prose in manuscripts of Middle English homilies. Continuity is the result of the only way in which language is transmitted, by a kind of oral indoctrination. Man learns to speak from man, not from books. His speech habits are formed long before he learns to read. This has meant that the basic structures of English have changed very little, and if a foreign element (introduced from French or elsewhere) is to be viable, it must conform rapidly to English speech habits. The segmented English sentence, stressed in word-groups, each word-group separated from its neighbour by a boundary-marker, the major stress of each group falling on the semantically important word in the group, the groups occurring in a relatively fixed order, the words in each group generally falling in a precisely fixed order—all this, plus the continuity of the original vocabulary and the preservation of the original structural words, has ensured an underlying stability in English speech, and in the prose which is based upon it.

Granted this stability, the English language has been able to take innovation from other languages in its stride. Foreign words, re-sounded with native phonemes and assimilated to the native stress-system, have been easily adopted, and generally retained. Non-native structural patterns ... have not so readily won a place. The late seventeenth century ruthlessly discarded the structural innovations of the renaissance humanists: the French-shaped clausal links of fourteenth- and fifteenth-century prose gained no permanent foothold in the language; most of Chaucer's Gallicisms (like 'al-outerly', patterned on *tout outrement*) were quietly dropped in the century following his death. Prins and Orr have collected many hundreds of "French-based' English phrases from several centuries of English usage. An examination of these suggests that in order to be a candidate for retention (as *tenir sa langue* has been retained in 'hold one's tongue') the foreign phrase must on its introduction be itself structured as if it were already English. The English language has retained numerous extraneous elements, but only—because of the continuous pressure exerted by speech—in terms of its own phonemic, stress, and structural system.

So long as these innovations do not break the mould of English expression, they can be a source of enrichment. But if the exotic influence becomes dominant (particularly if the eye on the printed page rather than the
sensitive ear is the guide), danger is at hand, and a shift towards a speech-
base seems inevitable. Such a reaction occurred at the end of the seventeenth
century, when the 'digressions and swellings' of mid-century were abandoned
by the Royal Society in favour of a 'close, naked, natural way of speaking'.
The revolution of the late seventeenth century is only one, generally the best
documented, of a series of adjustments . . . each of which ensured that English prose did not deviate too far from what it is difficult to call other than a
continuity of the native line.

THE HISTORY OF THE PARAGRAPH

Edwin H. Lewis

It is the object of this chapter, not to state in essay form, woven together
of all the judgments hitherto expressed, a complete view of the history of
the prose paragraph, but to arrange in a somewhat mechanical way the more
important of the theses that I propose.

CHAPTER I

1. ... The modern reference-mark, ¶, (sixth in the printer's list of
reference-marks) is probably descended, not, as held by Mr. Maunde
Thompson, from the original Greek gamma, but from the Latin mark P.

2. ... The modern so-called section-mark, §, is probably derived, not
from the original gamma, as held by Blass, but from the Latin P; surely not
from the combination of two $\int\int$, as taught by certain text-books. The type
of this mark is probably of Italian origin, 1467–1473.

3. ... Indentation is probably not due, as the popular bibliophilic
tradition asserts, to the omission of printed capitals to permit the insertion
of rubricated ones, but to the example of those manuscripts where it is used
without reference to rubrication.

CHAPTER II

4. ... While, for purposes of pedagogy, the writing of single-sentence
paragraphs should largely be discouraged, in view of the natural tendency
of students toward impartial analysis, it is nevertheless not correct to say,

---

From Edwin H. Lewis, *The History of the English Paragraph* (Chicago: University of Chicago
Press, 1894), Ch. 9, "The Prose Paragraph: Summary," pp. 169–177.

with Earle, "that the term paragraph can hardly be applied to anything short of three sentences, though rarely a complete and satisfactory effect is produced by two." For, although there has been a pretty steady decrease, in 300 years, in the use of the paragraphed sentence, most of the eminent writers of English prose have not hesitated to use this device, not merely to mark a transition but to signalize a stadium.

5. ... The only really new phases of rhetorical theory since Bain's "six rules," are Wendell's theory of Mass, and Scott and Denney's theory of Proportion. Wendell's theory of Mass is: "A paragraph whose unity can be demonstrated by summarizing its substance in a sentence whose subject shall be a summary of its opening sentence, and whose predicate shall be a summary of its closing sentence, is theoretically well massed." Scott and Denney's theory of proportion is perhaps sufficiently implied in the following sentence: "Statements which standing alone would properly be independent sentences, are frequently united into one sentence when they become part of a paragraph." The theory implies also the converse of this statement.

6. ... (a) Wendell's theory of Mass is not applicable to any large proportion of existing paragraphs, and is difficult of application except in short paragraphs. Scott and Denney's theory of Proportion is true of those writers who have a conception of the paragraph as an organic whole,—Burke, Macaulay, Arnold, for example. The principle is so strongly operative in the best prose of today that we may probably go so far as to say: in general it is true that in the best modern paragraphs the distance between periods is inversely as the emphasis of each included proposition. (b) It will follow as a corollary from the principle last enunciated, that the tendency (noted by Professor Sherman) of English prose to reduce the sentence to procrustean regularity of length, cannot indefinitely persist.

CHAPTER III

7. ... In the history of English prose there has been, for relatively the same kinds of discourse, no pronounced increase or decrease of the average total number of words per paragraph.

8. ... The paragraph of today contains more than twice as many sentences as did that of Ascham's day. Indeed, if we accept Macaulay's *England* as a present-day norm, the past increase in sentences per paragraph in three hundred years has been far more than one hundred per cent.

9. ... In a list of 73 representative English prosaists, the average word-length of the paragraph falls in the case of each of 52 authors between the limits of 100 words and 300 words. Of these 52 authors, 25 show each an average falling between the limits of 200 words and 300 words; while 27 show each an average falling between the limits of 100 and 200 words. Of these two groups it would be unwarrantable to say that either is superior to the other in paragraph structure. The first includes many authors who are superior in delicacy and variety of proportion—Arnold, Newman, Pater; the second includes many who are superior in terse emphasis—Bolingbroke, Swift, Carlyle, Lamb. But one of the greatest masters of terse emphasis, Macaulay, belongs in the first group, and one of the greatest masters of

delicate and varied proportion, Ruskin, belongs in the second. Most of the writers whose average rises above 300 words are poor paragraphers, De Quincey and Channing being exceptions. Most of those whose average falls below 100 words are writers in whom dialogue predominates, Fuller, Defoe, and Paley being exceptions.

10. ...In a list of 71 representative English prosaists, 5 show an average number of less than 2 sentences to the paragraph; 11 show an average of more than 2 and less than 3 sentences; 11 show an average of more than 3 and less than 4 sentences; 6 show an average of more than 4 and less than 5 sentences; 9 show an average of more than 5 and less than 6 sentences; 10 show an average of more than 6 and less than 7 sentences; 6 show an average of more than 7 and less than 8 sentences; 3 show an average of more than 8 and less than 9; 4 show an average of more than 9 and less than 10; one averages 10+; two average 12+; one averages 14+; one 15+, one 17+. The favorite numbers of sentences are therefore 2+ and 3+, each of which occurs 11 times. Then, in order of frequency, come 6+, 5+, 4+, and 7+, 9+, 8+, 12+, 14+, and 15+ and 17+. Dialogue-writing affects this list but very little. Of the romancers, Irving shows the highest average of sentences, 4.12.

11. ...There has been from the earliest days of our prose a unit of invention much larger than the modern sentence, and always separated, in the mind of the writer, from the sentence-unit, of whatever length. In other words English writers have thought roughly in long stages before they have analyzed such stages into smaller steps.

12. ...The paragraph as we know it comes into something like settled shape in Sir William Temple. It was the product of perhaps five chief influences. First, the tradition, derived from the authors and scribes of the Middle Ages, that the paragraph-mark distinguishes a stadium of thought. Second, the Latin influence, which was rather towards disregarding the paragraph as the sign of anything but emphasis—the emphasis-tradition being also of mediæval origin; the typical writers of the Latin influence are Hooker and Milton. Third, the natural genius of the Anglo-Saxon structure, favorable to the paragraph. Fourth, the beginnings of popular writing—of what may be called the oral style, or consideration for a relatively uncultivated audience. Fifth, the study of French prose, in this respect a late influence, allied in its results with the third and fourth influences. ...

13. ...Throughout the eighteenth and nineteenth centuries, there is, in authors of regular methods, such as Hume and Macaulay, a perceptible but not a strong tendency towards reducing the average length of the paragraph to approximate constancy, in successive large groups of paragraphs. The author in whom the tendency is most pronounced is Macaulay. Here the tendency is so strong as to give a difference of only six words in the average paragraph word-length of the first and second volumes of the *History of England*.

CHAPTER IV

14. ...(*a*) The recent investigations of Professor L. A. Sherman, in the development of the short sentence in English prose, are of much importance

in their bearing upon the history of paragraph structure; but by referring to the short sentence as "analytic," and again, in following the course of the development, by referring to the style of such intuitive (or synthetic) authors as Emerson as "analytic," the writer leads us into temporary confusion. From this it seems best, for the purposes of our discussion, to escape by the invention of certain new terms, as: *segregating*, applied to a style where the sentence of maximum occurrence is short, say, twenty words or less; *aggregating*, to a style where the favorite sentence is long; *redintegrating*, where the method of procedure is psychologically analytic; *intuitive*, where the method is psychologically synthetic—omitting the steps of approach, the intermediate predications. (b) ... The value of Professor Sherman's conclusions regarding the '*oral' style* are slightly impaired for us by the confused terminology mentioned in (12). The consequence of his theory concerning the decrease of predication is the application of the term 'oral" alike to styles redintegrating and intuitive. It seems better to limit the term 'oral style' to one in which the short sentence is employed, but the thought is psychologically redintegrating.

15. (a) The oral style as we now understand it—produced by the expression of redintegrating thought in a segregating sentence—is the style most favorable to the paragraph structure. (b) We may indeed almost define the oral style in terms of the paragraph. Thus: From the moment of the establishment of unity, in the development of the English paragraph, the oral sentence-sense means decreasing the number of predications in the period and increasing the number of propositions in the paragraph, in proportion to the author's conception of his reader's power of interpretation.

16. ... The articulation of clauses without connectives is a help to the coherence of the paragraph in only one of two cases: (a) where the style is impassioned; (b) where the place of connectives is supplied by transitional phrases or clauses. Therefore it is not likely that the decrease in the use of connectives—a decrease explained by Professor Sherman in his *Analytics of Literature*, chapter 26,—will continue indefinitely in prose that expresses proportioned and modulated thought.

CHAPTER V

17. ...Though the paragraph plays no structural part in Anglo-Saxon, it is not rash to say that the paragraphs indicated by the rubricator have, in general, unity of subject, the exceptions being due to causes explained in (18).

18. ... There were four distinct uses of the paragraph-mark, in Anglo-Saxon prose: (a) to mark a logical section; (b) to note any emphatic point; (c) to distinguish formally sacred names; (d) to ornament and distinguish titles, colophons, etc.

19. ...(a) The Anglo-Saxon prose sentence corresponds in length roughly with the sentence of the nineteenth century. (b) The Anglo-Saxon prose sentence increases slowly in length, and when it becomes the Middle-English sentence, reaches, under Latin influence, a length nearly as great as that attained by the latinized sentence of Jacobean times.

20. No English writer before Tyndale has any sense of the paragraph as a subject of internal arrangement.

CHAPTER VI

21. ... In Tyndale we find the earliest writer who can be said to be in any sense a good paragrapher.

22. The most important men after Tyndale in the period from Tyndale to Temple, are Bacon, Hobbes, Browne, and Fuller, in respect of unity; Lord Herbert, Burton, and Bunyan, in distribution of emphasis by variability of sentence-length; Burton in the matter of coherence without formal connectives; Fuller in the establishment of the deductive paragraph order.

CHAPTERS VII–IX

23. The unity of the paragraph becomes nearly unimpeachable in such men as Addison, Shaftesbury, Bolingbroke, Johnson, Hume, Burke. Only the best paragraphers of the nineteenth century, Macaulay, for example, surpass these authors in this respect.

24. Proportion in the paragraph pretty steadily increases from Temple to Arnold, both in the way of assigning due bulk to the amplification of important ideas, and in the way of distributing emphasis by varying sentence-length. The following list will illustrate the latter point, by showing in the first column the percentage of each author in the use of sentences of less than fifteen words, in the second the average sentence-length. In starred authors the percentage[1] of simple sentences, usually one or two points higher than the per cent. of sentences under fifteen words, is substituted in the first column.

	Per cent. of sentences of less than 15 words.	Sentences considered.	Sentence-length.	Sentences considered.
Temple	2	704	53.40	538
*Dryden	6	521	38.44	1300
Locke	8	814	49.80	814
Defoe	8	360	38.68	360
*Swift	13	500	40.00	1171
*Addison	12	500	38.58	898
*Shaftesbury	28	650	26.80	578
*Bolingbroke	14	977	34.86	981
Johnson	9	218	38.15	218
*Hume	12	500	39.81	1200
*Goldsmith	18	500	26.94	868
Burke	29	916	26.09	916
Gibbon	10	1562	31.21	1562
Paley	17	392	37.68	392
Scott	14	1224	32.14	1224
*Coleridge	19	500	37.60	777
Jeffrey	6	545	50.65	545

[1]Mr. Gerwig's figures.

	Per cent. of sentences of less than 15 words.	Sentences considered.	Sentence-length.	Sentences considered.
Lamb	41	529	27.19	529
Landor	22	696	25.43	696
Irving	24	532	26.73	532
*De Quincey	14	500	38.81	815
*Macaulay	34	40,000	23.43	41,579
*Carlyle	18	500	31.56	270
*Newman	16	500	41.44	1228
*Emerson	41	1438	20.58	1179
*Channing	34	2000	25.35	750
*Bartol	44	1500	16.63	805
*Lowell	23	683	31.45	356
*Ruskin	18	718	33.31	814
*Arnold	20	500	34.41	605
*Pater	26	500	38.54	219

25. Coherence by parallel construction of sentences, beginning in crude form in the paragraphs of the sixteenth century Euphuists—Lyly, Nashe, Lodge, and their fellows—is reduced to a flexible and strong principle in Temple, Swift, Shaftesbury, Bolingbroke, Johnson, Hume, Gibbon, and Burke. It is weak in Dryden, Locke, Defoe, Sterne, Goldsmith, Paley. In the next century it continues weak in Scott, Coleridge, Jeffrey, Irving, Emerson, Carlyle; reviving in De Quincey, Macaulay, Arnold. It is neglected by many popular writers of the present day.

26. Coherence secured by so ordering words in the sentence that the mind shall pass from one sentence to another without check, is an art little observed in the sixteenth century. In the seventeenth it is perhaps strongest in Fuller and Burton. In the eighteenth century this principle is tolerably strong in Temple, Defoe, Shaftesbury, Bolingbroke, Fielding, Sterne, Goldsmith. It is very strong in Swift and Burke. It is relatively weak in Johnson, Gibbon. In the nineteenth century the principle is relatively active in Lamb, Macaulay, Newman, and is at its best in Carlyle, for one type, and in Arnold, for another.

27. Coherence secured by the use of connectives is in most active force in the earliest periods of our prose. From the sixteenth century till the opening of the nineteenth it declines, reaching its ebb in the balanced sentences of Gibbon. At the beginning of the nineteenth century the principle became strongly operative in the reactionary prose of Coleridge, but has again declined. Today there are two tendencies, one continuing the decline, the other emphatically but intelligently reacting. The popular prose of the last twenty years tends to drop sentence-connectives. Another stream of writing, represented by the classical prose of Arnold, uses connectives freely but vitally. The present discussion holds that the dropping of inter-sentential connectives cannot successfully be accomplished without danger to one essential prose merit—the merit of reproducing the restrictions and modulations which must characterize good prose of the intellectual type. ...

... Walton uses the highest number of *ands*. Swift, Johnson, Macaulay use no *ands* at all; Gibbon uses but one. Pater curiously exhibits more *ands* than any other man since Walton; but his use of them is not formal merely. Coleridge registers the highest percentage of *buts* since Spenser, while De Quincey practically eschews this word and exhibits about as large a number of interior *howevers* as Coleridge of initial *buts.* Initial *therefore* is little used since Ascham, and interior *therefore* not extensively—Coleridge heading the list with eleven.

28. The favorite type of paragraph in the history of our prose has been the loose type, although certain writers, as Butler in the eighteenth and Macaulay in the nineteenth, have shown some facility in the periodic type.

29. There has been, during the eighteenth and nineteenth centuries, a general tendency to make the topic-sentence of the paragraph short, but not to reduce it to laconic brevity.

30. The better paragraphs of the nineteenth century are far more organic, far more highly organized, than the better ones of the eighteenth.

31. The paragraph structure is, in proportion to the complexity and size of the thought conveyed, more economical of attention than the long periodic sentence; and the rise of the paragraph structure is in no small degree due to this fact.

THE CONTINUITY OF THE PARAGRAPH

Virginia M. Burke

The English paragraph, as a distinct unit, is a Johnny-Come-Lately to prose, to rhetoric, and to pedagogy. Unlike words and sentences, which have been treated extensively by rhetoricians ever since the Renaissance, the paragraph languished unnoticed until the second half of the nineteenth century. George Campbell ignored it in his *Philosophy of Rhetoric* (1776), though his occasional use of the word suggests that he thought the paragraph might exist. Nor is it mentioned by Kames, Blair, or Whately. But Alexander Bain devoted a forty-five page chapter to it in his *Composition and Rhetoric*, published in 1866. Thus Bain was the first rhetorician to recognize the paragraph as a distinct unit.

Texts in rhetoric and composition by American authors were few until English took the lead over the classics in American schools and universities;

From Virginia M. Burke, "The Paragraph: Dancer in Chains," in Robert M. Gorrell, ed., *Rhetoric: Theories for Application* (Champaign, 1968), pp. 37–43, at pp. 37–42. Reprinted with the permission of the National Council of Teachers of English and Virginia M. Burke. Notes have been omitted.

but by the last quarter of the nineteenth century, texts addressed to the lower schools as well as to colleges and universities were increasing rapidly. Among rhetoricians publishing between 1878 and 1891, John F. Genung of Amherst, and A. S. Hill and Barrett Wendell of Harvard took particular pains, and space, to discuss the paragraph. With the publication of Scott and Denney's *Paragraph-Writing* in 1894, the paragraph "arrived" in an entire book devoted to it.

In spite of the concentration on it after 1890, I am not convinced that the paragraph is well defined even now, either in the pages of texts or in the minds of teachers. Let me recall for you Fielding's lines in Chapter I, Book V, of *Tom Jones*, where Fielding guns down critics as "men of shallow capacities," inclined to "mistake mere form for substance," to "adhere to the lifeless letter of the law and reject the spirit." The critic turned legislator and judge, Fielding continues, has established "many rules for good writing ... which have not the least foundation in truth or nature, and which commonly serve for no other purpose than to curb and restrain genius, in the same manner as it would have restrained the dancing master, had the many excellent treatises on that art laid it down as an essential rule that every man must dance in chains." It is my impression that in too many rhetorics and too many classrooms, the paragraph continues to dance in chains.

There is ample evidence that the paragraph was not sharply defined in the minds of many English prosaists, for it was often not distinguished from larger units (chapter and section) or from smaller units (sentences). Some writers frequently produced short paragraphs of fewer than three sentences —Defoe, for example, in his *Essay on Projects* and Johnson in *Rasselas* and the *Rambler*. When this practice was common, it tended to restrain paragraph expansion. Some writers—among them Lyly, Spenser, Defoe, Johnson, and Walton—produced a high number of single sentence paragraphs, in which the single sentences were usually inordinately long. This practice seems to indicate that these writers frequently regarded sentences and paragraphs as identical or, more precisely, equivalent. Some writers averaged such a high number of words per sentence and sentences per paragraph that they appeared to confuse paragraphs with sections or chapters. Hooker's *Ecclesiastical Polity* is an extreme in this direction with averages of forty-one words per sentence and forty-five sentences per paragraph. Taylor and Lowell, though centuries separate them, show high counts in both respects, with Lowell more than occasionally writing paragraphs of over 2,000 words. Milton seems to have had it both ways: frequent single sentence paragraphs and frequent extremely long paragraphs. Apparently, in the minds of seventeenth, eighteenth, and even nineteenth century writers, paragraphs were often confused with both larger and smaller units.

At the heart of this confusion of units was the extremely long sentence, whether periodic or "loose" in structure. The English period, rising in the late sixteenth century on Latin models, reaching extravagance and collapse in the Jacobeans, yet continuing as a highly sophisticated form through the next two centuries, assumed a bulk, complexity, and independence which we associate more with the paragraph than with the sentence today. With its center of gravity at the end, it moved to full semantic circle through an elaborate involutional sequence of hypotactic and balanced elements. While the period dominated the thought and art of many distinguished prosaists, the so-called "loose" sentence was even more in bondage to colon and semicolon so that it, too, assumed unwieldy length and frequently collapsed into disjointed phrase and clause heaps. The fact that for centuries so many writers preferred to bind so many elements into long single sentences delayed dispersion of these elements into the separate sentences required for the paragraph as Bain first described it.

If the paragraph, as we know it, is possible only when internal arrangement is possible, and if internal arrangement is possible only when there are *several* sentences to organize, then the paragraph is a recent phenomenon. This was the conclusion of E. H. Lewis in his study entitled *The History of the English Paragraph*, the single scholarly study of the paragraph that I have been able to discover. Lewis observed that components essential to the paragraph appeared as early as Tyndale, but that these were neither well realized enough nor free enough to synthesize into a clearly differentiated unit until late seventeenth century. And even then, not all components were fully active in the prose of most distinguished writers.

The components Lewis had in mind included the concept of unity of thought and purpose without which paragraphs are mere aggregations. Lewis found this unity at a high level only in eighteenth century writers—Addison, Hume, Johnson, and Burke among them—with Macaulay alone surpassing them in the nineteenth century. Other components include preference for the word order native to English; control and variety in sentence length; and the short sentence, by Lewis's definition a sentence under fifteen words. Lewis concluded that Tyndale was our first "tolerable" paragrapher; that Temple, rather than Dryden, gave the paragraph settled shape; and that Burke, in his oratorical prose, was the "earliest great master" of the paragraph.

Unity of thought and purpose and the presence of *several* sentences seem to be the two minimum essentials for the paragraph. Alexander Bain must have thought so, for all six of his laws assume the presence of several sentences, and five of his laws relate to unity. His first law aims for unity through coherence. Here he exploits semantic and syntactic modes of directing, relating, and dramatizing thought: cumulative, adversative, and subordinating conjunctions; illatives and bridging phrases of all sorts; parataxis; repetition; inversion; and so on. His second law, closely related to the first, calls for semantic and structural parallelism. His third is the germ of the "topic sentence," which should "indicate, unless obviously preparatory, the scope of the paragraph." His fourth law calls directly for unity by implying sustained purpose and forbidding digressions and irrelevancies. His fifth requires consecutiveness, that is, "proximity governed by affinity." And his sixth calls for proportion between principal and subordinate statements so as to reveal their relative importance.

Inadvertently perhaps, Bain created a few confusions which have plagued us ever since. The first confusion arises when we learn that his six laws pertain to all units—sentence, paragraph, section, chapter, and book. Only his third law on the topic sentence has somewhat special application to the paragraph, and then only to one kind of paragraph—the logical-deductive type. Thus it is difficult to conclude that Bain fully defined the paragraph even by contrast. The second confusion arises when he states that between one paragraph and another there is a bigger break in the subject than between one sentence and the next; here, it seems to me, he ignores the "wave" characteristics of the paragraph, characteristics governing its relationships with neighboring paragraphs. Bain's view of the paragraph seems to be a particle view in Pike's sense of the term; and Bain reinforces this particle view by analogizing the paragraph to the sentence. Treatment of the paragraph as particle alone and as analogue to a unit included in it does not seem to be enough to bring the paragraph to full definition.

Barrett Wendell, in his *English Composition* (1891), and Scott and Denney, in *Paragraph-Writing* (1894), necessarily found their guidelines in Bain; but the two books develop along very different lines.

Wendell reduced Bain's six laws to three rules—the familiar Unity, Coherence, and Mass (or Emphasis), which he applied, again following Bain, to all units of writing. He tells us that Unity requires grouping of elements around one single idea. A paragraph has Unity, he says, "when its substance can be stated in a single sentence." Mass, he tells us, requires that the chief parts of a paragraph "should be so placed as readily to catch the eye." Wendell's test for Mass is puzzling indeed: "A paragraph whose unity can be demonstrated by summarizing its substance in a sentence whose subject shall be a summary of its opening sentence and whose predicate shall be a summary of its closing sentence, is theoretically well massed." Some critics believe that Wendell is here describing the paragraph that ought to be. I should dislike to think so, for his concept of Mass freezes the paragraph as particle by excluding its wave characteristics. If paragraphs danced before this legislator got to them, surely they were paralyzed forever after by his overschematization.

Scott and Denney were more able theorists, more serious scholars than Wendell. They were familiar with his Unity, Coherence, and Mass, but they bypassed these in their book to set up five laws for the paragraph. Their law of *Unity* is Bain's concept of oneness in aim and affinity in thought. Their law of *Selection* highlights a sifting process so that not all that might be said will be said; but only that which will best give force and emphasis to the main idea. Their third law of *Proportion* makes more explicit Bain's implication that a unit of thought may need reduction in status and, consequently, in structure, to achieve proportion between major and minor elements. Scott and Denney follow Bain in their fourth law of *Sequence;* but their fifth law of *Variety* stresses diversity insofar as this is consistent with purpose and thought—variety in sentence length and structure; in phraseology and ordering of details; and in paragraph length, as well as in methods of development.

Scott and Denney admit that if the law of unity is clearly understood in its largest sense, it would include their selection, proportion, and sequence. But apparently they suspected it would not be, for they insist that each of their five laws merits study for itself. Thus they keep the field of paragraph study wide instead of narrowing it by overschematization and undue abstractionism.

Wendell's theory of the paragraph was mechanical; Scott and Denney's organic; Wendell analogized from the smaller included unit of the sentence; Scott and Denney avoid flat insistence on this point. Wendell froze the paragraph as particle, ignoring its relationships to larger units, its wave characteristics; Scott and Denney taught that "Whatever peculiarities of function or structure a paragraph possesses must be explainable by its relation to the function and structure of the whole composition." Wendell presented the paragraph in almost tropical terms; Scott and Denney viewed it as an organic part of a larger movement of thought and allowed it reasonable options within this larger movement.

*   *   *   *

It took over twenty-five years for another scholar to challenge Wendell's triad, but Lathrop of Wisconsin did so in 1918, observing that the triad had remained since Wendell's time "unchanged and almost unchallenged as the basis of our instruction in the sentence, the paragraph, and the whole composition." Lathrop considered Wendell's Unity, Coherence, and Emphasis poorly conceived and superficially applied. He characterizes the triad as follows:

> Unity is the unity of details assembled around a principle; coherence mainly closeness of relation between a part and its neighbors; mass or emphasis the relative distinction of parts to the eye. In fine, the whole treatment rests upon the idea of intelligent aggregation.

The problem goes far deeper, Lathrop believes. It arises from Wendell's concept of Unity, Coherence, and Emphasis as *coordinate* principles, a concept which discourages the view of a composition as a "process of development thought of as a whole." Lathrop argues that coherence—orderly sequence—is not coordinate with unity but, rather, an aspect of it. And mass, or emphasis, is coordinate neither with unity nor coherence, but rather, an aspect of coherence; for emphasis is the "realization of the central directing principle of a composition." Paragraphs, then, in Lathrop's view, offer a variety of successive experiences designed to express the primary unity in thought and purpose which conceived them. "There is only one principle, unity," says Lathrop, "of which the other two are manifestations or phases or subsidiary consequences. The principles of structure all rise from the principle of unity."

Like Scott and Denney, Lathrop viewed a composition as process, "a thing fulfilled in time." So he questioned rules and formulas which obscured this view. Unity, Coherence, and Emphasis, taken as coordinate principles, obscure the treatment of a composition as process, as a whole, and are fraught with dangers: the danger of "wooden insistence on a topic sentence"; the danger of overexact marking off of paragraphs; the danger of applying the three principles in mechanical succession; the danger of a mechanical view of structure itself, almost an absolute view. If we follow Lathrop's closely reasoned critique, we see that he calls for a fuller and more flexible definition of the paragraph not only as particle but as wave and as significant segment in a total field of meaning. His critique might be regarded as an effort to release the paragraph from the chains Fielding speaks of.

SUGGESTIONS FOR RESEARCH

1. Sherman (1888, 1892, 1893) found in his studies of sentence length: (1) a gradual decrease in sentence length (measured in number of words) between Thomas More and Macaulay, and (2) a consistency in any single writer's average sentence length. How reliable are Sherman's conclusions? (Examine his statistics and type of sample; for example, Sherman tested only Macaulay's history and essays.) What has happened in sentence length since Macaulay?

2. Gerwig (1894), a student of Sherman's, discovered that modern writers used fewer verbs than did earlier writers, substituting apposition, verbals, and more simple sentences for the earlier larger number of finite verbs. What has been the tendency since 1894?

3. Compare Gordon's (1966, this chapter) understanding of the historical development of the sentence with that of Aurner (1923b), Earle (1891), Jespersen (1894, 1948, 1949), and Kellner (1892).

4. Jespersen (1894) describes growing clearness and regularity in English prose style. Contrast the picture of growing complexity in Scott and Chandler (1932).

5. The paragraph is the most neglected aspect of the history of prose style, perhaps because more sophisticated and precise methods are needed in the description of the paragraph and its history. The essays on the paragraph in *College Composition and Communication* during the past few years —for example, "Symposium on the Paragraph" (1966)—will be helpful. An excellent guide to the historical study of the paragraph is provided by Lewis (1894), whose generalizations, however, need verification.

6. Burke (1968, this chapter) suggests that until recent times paragraphs were often confused with both larger and smaller units. What writers are exceptions in the sixteenth, seventeenth, eighteenth, and nineteenth centuries?

7. Paragraphs function not only internally but as "waves" in relation to neighboring paragraphs, to sequences, and to the whole composition. Compare the way different writers move from paragraph to paragraph and interlock, semantically and syntactically. Here is a large history so far almost totally neglected. See Rodgers (1966).

8. Paragraphs have so seldom been recognized as "little essays" or art forms that we have few terms for describing them. "Gradation" has been suggested to describe how a paragraph moves in its diction, syntax, sentence length, sound, and so on. For example, the opening paragraph of Aldous

Huxley's "Selected Snobberies" artistically progresses from a sentence of six words to the final highly expressive sentence of almost sixty richly balanced and alliterated words. Do writers have a characteristic "gradation"? Here is another neglected history.

9. Lewis (1894, this chapter) believes that Tyndale was our first "tolerable" paragrapher by the criteria set out by Scott and Denney (1894)—unity, selection, proportion, sequence, and variety. Evaluate.

10. Select paragraphs from early writers which seem to be overloaded and could therefore be broken down into several, more unified paragraphs. For example, the passage in Gibbon's *Decline and Fall* beginning "The greatness of Rome (such is the language of the historian)..." and ending "...the profane skeptics who impiously doubt or deny the existence of a celestial power" (anthologized in Miles, 1965) might be divided into nine separate paragraphs.

THE OLD ENGLISH AND MIDDLE ENGLISH PERIODS: FIFTH CENTURY TO 1500

CONTINUITY IN QUESTION: AELFRIC TO ROLLE

R. M. Wilson

In his claims for the continuity of English prose Professor Chambers wrote so interestingly and persuasively that few of his readers have examined as carefully as they might have done the evidence he presented to support his thesis. Though no doubt it badly needed saying at the time, a good deal of the article, strictly speaking, has nothing to do with the main question, being devoted to a demonstration that the alleged decadence of eleventh-century Anglo-Saxon England had no basis in fact. Whether this is true or not is irrelevant. The state of a society is not necessarily reflected in its prose style; and, as Professor Chambers himself showed, excellent vernacular prose was being written under Æthelred II, at a time when state and society were clearly what, in many respects, is usually understood as decadent. It must be admitted that there is something to be said for the view of one of the few critics of the theory, when he points out that in his article Professor Cham-

From R. M. Wilson, "On the Continuity of English Prose," *Mélanges de linguistique et de philologie Fernand Mossé in memoriam* (Paris: Librairie Marcel Didier, 1959), pp. 486–494, at pp. 486–491. Reprinted by permission of R. M. Wilson.

bers, far from demonstrating the continuity of English prose, has merely shown 'that good prose can be written both in Old pre-Conquest English and in the new idiom, and that the same qualities are essential in both cases, namely simplicity, lucidity and clarity'[1].

Certainly, the question is not whether a good prose style had been developed in Anglo-Saxon England, but whether the prose style that was then in use was the ultimate ancestor of the prose of today, and it may be suspected that the problem is a good deal more complicated than has been realized, and is perhaps one which is not susceptible of any clear-cut answer. The fact that Professor Chambers modernizes some of his quotations from Middle English texts helps further to cloud the issue. However slight, the modernization inevitably makes the extract so treated approximate more closely to modern English than would otherwise be the case. It may well be that the modern editorial practice of punctuating and capitalizing Old and Middle English texts on modern English principles also tends to give a false impression of the modernity of the older prose.

It would seem, too, that the different types of prose in early Middle English are not sufficiently distinguished by Professor Chambers. He rightly points out the key position of the *Ancrene Riwle* in any discussion of the problem, but it is doubtful whether that text should be classed together with the pieces comprising the *Katherine Group*, and more particularly with the three saints' lives. In the latter, the regular rhythm and the use of alliteration to bind together clauses and sentences, show a clear influence from the kind of rhythmical prose used by Ælfric in some of his *Lives of the Saints*. The continuity from Old to early Middle English of this kind of prose has been demonstrated clearly enough[2], but equally clearly it has no connexion with the development of the modern prose. Such alliterative prose is found only rarely and under special circumstances in Rolle or in the later writers supposed to be in the direct line of descent. In Rolle, and in the other mystical prose of the fourteenth and fifteenth centuries, the heightened prose style seems to owe its effects to the Latin rhetoricians of the twelfth and thirteenth centuries rather than to Ælfric. This is also the case with the prose of some of the works loosely connected with the *Katherine Group*, such as the *Ureisun of God Almihti*, the *Wohunge of Ure Lauerd*, and *A Lofsong of ure Louerde*[3]. And even within the group itself there are differences. *Sawles Warde* has reminiscences of the four-stress line of the saints' lives, but the rhythm is not nearly so regular, while in *Hali Meiðhad* there is practically nothing at all of the poetic prose. In it, alliteration is not used regularly to give emphasis to a rhythm consistently maintained, and when it does occur it adds nothing to the poetic qualities of the prose.

---

[1] A. A. PRINS, *French Influence on English Phrasing* (Leiden 1952), p. 18.

[2] See D. BETHURUM, "The Connection of the *Katherine Group* with Old English Prose" (*Journal of English and Germanic Philology*, xxxiv, 553–64).

[3] On this, see Margery M. MORGAN, "*A Talking of the Love of God* and the Continuity of Stylistic Tradition in Middle English Prose Meditations" (*Review of English Studies*, (*NS*), iii, 97–116), and R. M. WILSON, "Three Middle English Mystics" (*Essays and Studies*, 1956, pp. 87–112).

On the whole, then, in any consideration of the continuity of English prose from Old to Modern English, the *Katherine Group* must be ignored. Continuity from Old to early Middle English certainly appears there, but this kind of rhythmical alliterative prose seems to have no influence on, or continuity with, the later homiletic prose claimed as the inspiration of the *Authorized Version.* On the other hand, it may well be that the *Ancrene Riwle* remains as the key to the whole problem. A general reading of it gives the impression of a prose very different in kind from that of the saints' lives of the *Katherine Group.* It has a more simple and direct movement, and although the exalted passages often have a well-defined rhythm, it is not nearly so invariable as that in the saints' lives. The regular use of alliteration that we find in them is missing; the immediate debt is clearly to the rhetorical systems of the time, and it is on the whole independent of the ornate prose of the late Old English period[4]. The prose of the *Ancrene Riwle* may well have a much closer affinity with the modern prose, though this remains to be proved. In any case, it does not follow that it also shows continuity between the simpler type of Old English prose and the usual homiletic prose of the Middle English period. It may or may not do so, but so far no proof one way or the other has been offered. In particular, no detailed analysis of Old English prose as compared with the prose style of the *Ancrene Riwle* has been made, either by Professor Chambers or by anyone else. General impressions, such as those of the present writer recorded above, are not adequate as evidence; it is only by a close analysis of the prose that continuity or the reverse can be demonstrated.

In fact all the evidence that we are offered is a succession of extracts from the various works, with only very general statements about them:

The syntax of Rolle is that of today.

The spelling is strange, and there are many Northern words and phrases—but, apart from these things, what is there in this passage (i.e. one from Rolle) which is not modern English?

And whilst Rolle writes modern English, the first Wicliffite version, written thirty-five years after Rolle's death, is almost incredibly crude.[5]

The syntax of Rolle is by no means always that of today, and in the given passage there is a good deal that is not modern English. Nor do the passages quoted from Wiclif bear out too well the claims for the superiority of Rolle or Hilton. It is, in any case, apparently assumed that general impressions, gathered from a simple reading of the quotations, are all the evidence necessary, and that no other proof is needed.

But if Professor Chambers provides little real evidence of continuity, his critics are usually equally vague, and similarly substitute subjective statements for evidence. For example:

---

[4] See Agnes M. HUMBERT, *Verbal Repetition in the* Ancrene Riwle (Washington 1944).
[5] R. W. CHAMBERS, *On the Continuity of English Prose* (London 1932), pp. cii, ciii.

There is no denying that the language of Chaucer and Gower, the ancestors of modern English, is fundamentally different from what we know as Anglo-Saxon, or Old English. The complicated declensions of Old English have disappeared, the conjugations are deeply undermined, the whole word-order is changed and ceases in the main to be that of German and runs parallel to that of French. It is, essentially, a new language[6].

The point, of course, *has* been denied, nor does it seem profitable to compare the language of poetry with that of prose. In Chaucer and Gower the exigencies of rhyme may well lead to a different kind of word-order from that which is normally found in prose, and it may be that in some ways this is nearer to that of French. But even if that be the case, it would have no relevance to the question of the continuity of English prose unless it were first shown that there is no difference between the language of poetry in Chaucer and Gower and the language of contemporary prose. Moreover, even if the conclusion that this English 'is essentially a new language' be accepted, this in itself is not necessarily proof of any lack of continuity. That would demand not only a demonstration that the new is different from the old, but also that the one is not to be derived from the other in any of its essentials, and no attempt has been made to show that this is the case. Similarly, in his valuable work on English phraseonomy, A. A. Prins appears to misinterpret the meaning of the term *continuity*. It may be, as he argues, that Chambers in his use of the word was only trying 'to establish the fact that what is good and valuable in Modern English prose, goes back to Old English (or rather Anglo-Saxon) and that the latinizing and gallicizing—to which he objects— are due to a foreign influence which did not contribute to the development of a good English prose style'[7], but this seems an undue simplification. No one would maintain that modern English prose is the same as Old English, and most would agree with Prins that it has changed greatly, partly perhaps by reason of French and Latin influence on phraseonomy, sentence structure and vocabulary. No doubt, by the end of the Middle Ages, 'it is a new language that emerges'[8], but the real point is whether, at any one time, these or other influences were so great as to cause a complete break in the prose style, or whether old characteristics persisted side by side with the gradual infiltration of new influences, so that in no one period could there be said to be a break between what went before and what came after. If we are to demonstrate the continuity of English prose it is essentially the structure of the individual sentence at the different periods that must be examined, and until this has been done we can hardly say definitely whether continuity exists or whether there was in fact a complete break at one period or another.

---

[6]J. ORR, "The Impact of French upon English," in *Words and Sounds in English and French* (Oxford 1953), p. 38.

[7]PRINS, *op. cit.*, p. 13.

[8]PRINS, *op. cit.*, p. 20. But to say that this new language is «essentially in harmony with the character of its people: a happy compromise showing little sense of that hard, clear, logical quality of French or the gracelessness of the pure Teutonic strain», reveals a romantic attitude towards language that one hoped had long since disappeared from scholarship.

So far as they go, the arguments of Prins are merely the reverse of those of Chambers. They are equally subjective, and in the main consist in printing various extracts, and denying that they show any continuity:

> There certainly is no continuity between Old and Modern English either in vocabulary or word-formation or in the relation between the various parts of speech ... And it can hardly be denied that these points greatly affect the style of both prose and poetry.

> Who will maintain that the presence of so many Romance words does not affect the language and style of this writer (i.e. Rolle), especially if it comes to groups like *suffer penance, have delight in* ... etc.

> Though the proportion of Romance words is fairly low here (i.e. in Hilton's *Epistle on Mixed Life*), yet they come in syntactic units like *pity and compassion, cry mercy* and *precious ointment*, which again shows how they cannot but have affected the author's style[9].

These are merely subjective impressions, and no attempt is made to show whether the new elements have in fact affected the style of the author, and if so in what way. Certainly, the investigation on phraseonomy by Prins, useful as it is, does not in itself afford definite proof against continuity. His evidence for some of the periods is necessarily scanty, but it still shows that French phrases passed gradually into the language from perhaps the middle of the eleventh up to the twentieth century. And, moreover, the picture is blurred by the absence of all indication of the extent to which native phrases continue side by side with the French, and he ignores the fact that some of the French phrases had only a short life in the language. To say that the presence of such French phrases in any given writer 'cannot but have affected (his) style' is useless, unless the writer is prepared to show exactly what changes have resulted.

In fact little definite proof either for or against continuity has so far been given, nor is it possible in the space available to deal with the question in the necessary detail. All that can be done is to attempt an indication of the kind of evidence that must be sought, and although this is limited here to the transition from Old to early Middle English, similar investigations for other periods will be necessary before the case can be definitely decided one way or the other.

What in fact are the ways in which modern English prose differs from the prose of the Old English period, and how far can the changes which have taken place be traced as coming in gradually and without any single and definite break? Some obvious differences are:

1. In vocabulary.
2. The loss of inflexional endings, with a consequent
   a) Increase in the importance of word-order, and
   b) Increased use of prepositions.
3. Differences in word-order.

---

[9]PRINS, *op. cit.*, pp. 13, 14, 15.

4. Differences in sentence structure, cf., for example, the Old English fondness for clauses linked by *and*, where modern English has conjunctions showing the relationship between them.
5. Development of the compound tenses of the verb.
6. The loss of many impersonal verbs.
7. The loss of the subjunctive.
8. The loss of grammatical gender.
9. The development of different syntactical constructions.
10. The development of different methods of punctuation.

Many of these points have been dealt with in some detail by various scholars, but usually in isolation. Others, and particularly the syntax and the differences in word order, have hardly been touched at all. Some of the changes may have had no influence on the prose style; others may have had much. But it is not enough to say of any one of them that it *must* have had such an effect. It is necessary to show whether in fact it did, and if so in exactly what way. Until this has been done, and the various changes have been traced in detail, nothing useful can be said about the continuity or otherwise of English prose. The obvious beginning is to concentrate on the differences between late Old English and early Middle English, though with the warning that even if continuity can be proved here, it would still remain to be demonstrated during the later periods. . . .

THE INFLUENCE OF FRENCH
AND CONVERSATION

Norman Davis

As everyone knows, it was not until the late fourteenth century that English came to be largely accepted again, instead of French, as the normal medium of written prose communication in government and education. It had never ceased to be used in homilies and in devotional writings such as those of Richard Rolle; and it can never have ceased to be used in the ordinary business of daily life at its humbler levels. Awareness of *prose* as a

From Norman Davis, "Styles in English Prose of the Late Middle and Early Modern Period," *Langue et Littérature* (Paris, 1961), Vol. 161, F.I.L.L.M. Langue et Littérature de la collection Bibliothèque de la Faculté de Philosophie et Lettres de l'Université de Liège, pp. 165–181, at pp. 168–181. Reprinted by permission of the Bibliothèque de la Faculté de Philosophie et Lettres and Norman Davis. All but one of the notes have been omitted.

distinct literary medium also first finds expression in English in the fourteenth century, in Robert Manning's verse *Chronicle*, finished in 1338.

* * * *

It is from this time over the next century that experiments in writing
English secular prose are of critical importance in leading on to an accepted
view of how English prose might suitably be written. By the end of the
fifteenth century, as we can now recognize after the event, standards of prose
writing had been attained which are essentially those that suit the qualities
of modern English. These standards were never lost, but they were often
ignored or wilfully departed from in the sixteenth and seventeenth centuries
by writers intent more on display than communication. There was plenty of
this in the fifteenth century also; but Caxton's famous dilemma, put into
print in 1490, shows how much careful thought he and his associates gave to
the choice of a kind of English that would be generally approved for its ready
intelligibility: 'And thus bytwene playn, rude, and curyous I stande
abasshed. But in my iudgemente the comyn termes that be dayli vsed ben
lyghter to be vnderstonde than the olde and auncyent Englysshe'.
Some of the most distinguished prose-writers of the fifteenth century—
Pecock, Skelton, Malory, and often Caxton himself—wrote in styles so individual that critics have long felt them to lie outside the main stream of
English prose. Thus Pecock, with intricate sentence-construction and eccentric word-order:

For to wite cleerly what is doon pryncipaly in this book folewing and in the
oþere bookis to hym perteynyng, and for what eende and purpos þei were maad, it is
to wite þat foure þingis ben necessarie to ech mannys good lyvyng, which iiij not
oonly ben necessarie and mowe not be lackid of vs for oure good living to be had,
but also þei ben at þe ful sufficient as for al þat is necessarie to oure good living to
be had.

And Skelton with his extraordinary 'aureation':

[Our former predecessours of olde] whiche alle in nombre be acquyted of their
moche vertuous and notable guydynge with historyous monumentis of remem-
braunce intermynable; whos famous names inscrybed be, wyth laureate lettres
inviolably euermore to endure, emonge the celestial senatours entronanysed and
crowned with the contynuel enverdured laureate leues of victoryous tryumphe in
the gloryous cyte of fame.

Malory, with much simpler words and constructions than either of these,
is unmatched in his exploitation of rhythm—'the unexpounded miracle of
style,' as Professor Vinaver has called it.
So when Chambers's *Continuity* appeared it was received with something like the sense of relief that comes from the solution of an old teasing
problem. Chambers argued, with eloquence and conviction, that the true
monuments of typical English prose in the fourteenth and fifteenth centuries
were devotional writings like those of Walter Hilton and Nicholas Love,
which were distinguished by a lucid and noble simplicity, and by an elegant

rhythm; qualities which could be traced back to the *Ancrene Riwle* at the beginning of the thirteenth century and beyond it to the prose of the Anglo-Saxons, especially of Ælfric. He held that this was the tradition of prose style that More followed, and consequently that it was from this source that the central current of modern prose directly flowed:

> It is strange to reflect how our English prose has been handed down to Tudor times, from the days of King Alfred and Abbot Ælfric, not by clerks working in the royal chancelleries, but through books originally written to be read in lonely anchor-holds or quiet nunneries.
> ... the anonymous author of the *Ancren Riwle*, Richard Rolle, Walter Hilton, and Sir Thomas More are main piers of the bridge which connects Tudor prose with the prose of Ælfric and of Alfred.

Chambers wrote so attractively, and selected his illustrations so skilfully that his thesis has come to be accepted by many scholars and teachers as established truth. But in recent years there have been several expressions of reserve or dissent, on various grounds[1]; and the time has certainly come to examine these opinions again with reference to a wider background than Chambers chose to consider.

Most readers would agree that the prose of Hilton or of Love, at its best (as in the examples selected by Chambers), is clear in expression, beautiful in movement, and admirably in harmony with the capabilities of English at the time. What Chambers meant when he described it as the direct descendant of Old English prose like Ælfric's, or indeed of Middle English like the *Ancrene Riwle*, he never made sufficiently clear. One would suppose that he meant that in spite of the far-reaching changes in the content and operation of the *language*—in vocabulary, inflexion, syntax, and rhythm —the essential qualities of *style*, whatever they might be in isolation from these elements, persisted. Professor Prins has objected that even in the *Ancrene Riwle*, and much more in Love, there are so many Latin and French words, phrases, and constructions that 'they cannot but have affected the author's style'. I believe this to be entirely true, if we understand 'style' with any precision, as I take it we do in this company. It is nevertheless apparent that the *Ancrene Riwle* and Love are 'affected' to very different degrees, and the question when quantity transforms quality is a difficult one. Any selection may be accused of being tendentious, so let us take without prejudice the opening lines of the *Ancrene Riwle* and of Love's *Mirror:*

> *Ancrene Riwle:* 'Louerd', seið Godes spuse to hire deorewurðe spus, 'þeo þe riht lvuieð þe, þet beoð riht þeo þet libbeð efter riwle; and ӡe, mine leoue sustren, habbeð moni dai iremd on me efter riwle. Moni cunne riwle beoð, auh two beoð among alle þet ich chulle speken of þuruh ower bone, mid Godes helpe. Þe on riwleð þe heorte, þe makeð hire efne and smeðe ....'.

---

[1]See for example H. S. BENNETT, 'Fifteenth Century Secular Prose', *R. E. S.*, XXI (1945), 257–63; A. A. PRINS, *French Influence in English Phrasing* (Leiden, 1952), pp. 10–20; C. L. WRENN, 'English Literature. Earliest Times to Chaucer' in *Encyclopædia Britannica* (1955); R. M. WILSON, 'On the Continuity of English Prose', in *Mélanges de linguistique et de philologie Fernand Mossé in memoriam* (Paris, 1959), pp. 486–94.

Love: Quecumque scripta sunt, ad nostram doctrinam scripta sunt ... These ben the wordes of the grete doctour and holy apostil Paul. Considerynge that the goostly lyuynge of all trewe cristen creatures in this world stant specialy in hope of the blisse and the lyf that is to come in another world; and for also moche as tweyne thinges principally norisshen and strengthen this hope in man (that is pacience in herte and ensaumple of vertues and good lyuynge of holy men writen in bookes) and souereynly the wordes and the dedes written of oure lord Jesu Crist, veray God and man, for the tyme of his bodily lyuynge here in erthe; therefore to strengthe vs and comforte vs in this hope spekith the apostil the wordes aforseide. . . .

Even Love is not very heavily coloured, in this passage, with romance *vocabulary*, but the structure of the sentence is altogether foreign to the Old English tradition. In the passage I have quoted from the *Ancrene Riwle*, on the other hand, the presence of a few simple French words like *spus* and *riwle* seems insufficient to destroy the Englishness of the whole. Chambers, I am sure, would not have admitted that foreign words, or even phrases, in themselves were enough to disqualify an author from a place in the 'English' tradition. He did not concern himself with this more technical aspect of style at all, and seems to have had in mind something quite vague and ill-defined —'a certain tone of self possession' (p. cxv) which he associated first with 'the English of the *Ancren Riwle* and its group' and then with Rolle, Hilton, *The Cloud of Unknowing*, and Love, and found 'by no means so often' in the revived English secular prose. Other terms he applied to the 'English' tradition were 'noble in its simple lucidity' (p. cxv) and 'this « plain and open » style' (p. cxx). There is no doubt such a thing as a tone of self-possession in prose, and it can no doubt be observed in some of the work of these authors. But the description is not nearly precise enough to serve as a measure of continuity of style. Certainly Chambers admitted far too much to his approbation of 'simple lucidity'. 'The English of the *Ancren Riwle* and its group', he wrote; but the English of the *Ancrene Riwle* and its group is far from being a stylistic unity. In some of the manuscripts it has a unity of spelling, grammar, some characteristic words, some characteristic imagery; but the highly alliterated rhythmical manner of *St. Juliana* and *St. Margaret* is utterly different from the style of the simpler parts of the *Ancrene Riwle* such as I have quoted. The *Ancrene Riwle* itself uses many styles. We need only compare with that simple opening such bold imagery as this: 'ʒif þu wult ðet te holie rode stef beo þi scheld, and tet Godes stronge passiun falsie þes deofles wepnen, ne drauh þu hit nout efter ðe, auh hef hit on heih, abuuen þin heorte heaued iþine breoste eien'. 'Thy heart head' and 'thy breast eyes' are astonishingly condensed 'conceits' in a passage that begins plainly enough.

Many of the most characteristic elements in the composition and style of the *Ancrene Riwle* are certainly drawn not from the Old English tradition of Ælfric, but from much later manuals of preaching method; and on this ground in particular the *Ancrene Riwle* is ill fitted to bear the weight of 'the bridge' between Old English and later prose. The associated saints' lives of the 'Katherine Group' owe much more to the alliterative tradition of Old English; but this highly patterned writing is important only in the history of devotional treatises, not to the future of English prose at large.

Nevertheless, consideration of rhythmical writing of this special kind reminds us that rhythm is a vital part of prose and that any attempt to link the prose of the fifteenth century with that of Old English must take account of it. One of Chambers's quotations from Love is this: 'And whoso coveiteþ to knowe þe fruyte of vertuouse silence, ȝif he have affeccioun and wille to trewe contemplatyf lyvynge, wiþouten doute he schal be bettre tauȝte by experience þan by writynge or techynge of man'. The Englishness of this is not very marked in vocabulary or syntax—*whoso coveiteþ to knowe þe fruyte of vertuouse silence*, for instance, is peculiarly English only in the placing of *vertuouse* before its noun. Is it, then, like Old English rhythm? Surely not. Without venturing to dogmatize on how Ælfric himself might have turned this sentence, we may be confident that he would not have produced the movement of *the fruyte of vertuouse silence* or *have affeccioun and wille to trewe contemplatyf lyvynge*, or even the group of purely English words, *by writynge or techynge of man*. A lesser contemporary of Ælfric, perhaps, might have said something like this: 'Se ðe gewilnað þone wæstm arfæstre stilnesse understandan, gif he soðre sceawunge lif lufie and gesece, witodlice þurh drohtnunge geleornað he bet þonne þurh manna gewrit oððe lare'.

The difference lies partly in the loss of so many of the Old English inflexions, and the concords required by gender, partly in the new kind of rhythm of words like *contemplative* and *experience*. The rhythm of the English of Ælfric could not be reproduced in the English of Love except in occasional passages of simple structure such as 'O my dere sustres, where is now my son? Sothly he is gone away fro us, he that was al oure ioye and oure comforte and the liȝt of oure eiȝen'. Even here the rhythm of *my dere sustres* is not precisely that of *mine leofan sweostor*, but it is not different enough to invalidate the comparison. So far as it is possible to generalize from impression, the tendency in prose rhythm in late Old English was mainly falling, and that in late Middle English much more variable when falling and much more commonly rising than it had been in Old English. So Ælfric in a typical passage:

Þær beoð fela tacna æteowode, and untrume gehælde and fram eallum frecednyssum alysede þurh ðæs apostoles ðingunge. Þæs him getiðað Drihten Crist, þam is wuldor and wurðmynt mid Fæder and Halgum Gaste a buton ende.

And Love in a typical passage, of mainly English vocabulary:

for it is semely to hym that is in hiȝe degre to do grete thinges and worthy; and to hym that is a manful man to suffre hard thinges; for tho thinges that ben harde and payneful schal sone passe, and thoo thinges that ben ioyful and gloriouse schal come after.

When all this is considered, more than 'a certain tone of self-possession' is needed to link the two periods. And even if it were a more satisfying criterion than it is, can 'a tone of self-possession' be accepted as a peculiarly English characteristic?

Once secular prose begins to appear late in the fourteenth century it flourishes exceedingly, not only in works that may broadly be called 'literary', such as romances and chronicles, but also in public and private documents and letters. In competence, naturally, it varies greatly, for it was written by a large number of people of very different attainments for a host of purposes. Its most striking feature is precisely this variety and range—a heterogeneity far too great, surely, for it to have been modelled exclusively on the religious prose of a limited number of texts, however popular and however well written these may have been. The business men of the fifteenth century would not seek models for their letters in devotional writers like Love any more than they would form their grammatical usage on a court poet like Chaucer. Most of the ordinary prose of the fifteenth century makes no attempt at rhythmical patterns of the kind much favoured by some of the writers of devotional texts, such as *A Talkyng of the Love of God*. Some of it shows great familiarity with the technicalities of the law—far too great familiarity for its grace or even clarity; some of it is so exclusively practical in intent that it cares nothing for form of any kind. Yet for a new field of writing the average level of lucidity is high, and the concern for some kind of shapeliness is a good deal stronger than might have been expected.

This cannot be the writing of newly literate people who have simply picked up their language with their pens. The writers must somewhere have acquired the rudiments of composition, some doubtless taught to translate Latin into English by schoolmasters in the tradition of that great educational innovator John of Cornwall, who in 1347–8 was a teacher of grammar to the kin of the founder of Merton College in Oxford. But their wider understanding of how to write many of them must have acquired, or at least improved, from French example. Trevisa said that because of John of Cornwall's innovation in teaching 'children of grammar school know no more French than their left heel'. This is doubtless the kind of exaggerated disapproval with which scholars and teachers in any century judge the deficiencies in learning of their juniors. The number of translations from French throughout the fifteenth century, while it no doubt shows that there was a market among those who could not read the originals, shows also that there were many translators who could. And we must remember that England held Calais, and Caxton began his printing in Bruges. In the development of a practical secular prose French was nearly two centuries in advance of English. Simple and lucid narrative, of the kind so praised by Chambers in England, was fully achieved by Villehardouin in the early thirteenth century, and apparently scarcely later by the authors of *Perlesvaus* and the *Prose Lancelot*—and the style of *Perlesvaus* has lately been judged 'almost modern when compared with that of historical writers like Villehardouin or Joinville'.

In the fourteenth and fifteenth centuries it was not particularly difficult to adapt the general movement and structure of French sentences to English. It will be appropriate here to remember how easily and closely *Mandeville's Travels*, which was evidently written in French in this city of Liège about 1360 (whatever the real name of the author and the exact part played by Jean d'Outremeuse), was rendered into a plain but mainly competent English by about 1400. To take a brief passage from the Prologue:

Qar nous sumes appellez Cristiens de Crist, qest nostre piere; et, si nous sumes droitz filz de Dieu, nous deuons leritage qe notre piere nous ad lesse chalenger et houster de mayns des estranges. Mes au iour de huy orgoil, couetise et enuye ont ensi les coers de seignurs terriens enflaumez qils entendent pluis a autry desheriter quils ne font chalanger et a conquere leur droit et propre heritage desuisdit.

In the English version of MS. Cotton Titus C xvi this becomes:

> For wee ben clept cristene men after crist oure fader. And ʒif wee be right children of crist we oughte for to chalenge the heritage þat oure fader lafte vs, and do it out of hethene mennes hondes. But now pryde, couetyse, and envye han so enflawmed the hertes of lordes of the world þat þei are more besy for to disherite here neyghbores more þan for to chalenge or to conquere here right heritage before seyd.

The English of this is more 'advanced' than the French in that it places the objects of two of the sentences in the modern order—'we oughte for to chalenge the heritage' instead of 'nous deuons leritage . . . chalenger'. But otherwise it is very close. Translators generally knew enough to modify French word-order to suit English idiom, but gained from having firmly-constructed sentences before them. Nor was it only a matter of direct translation; example must have been still more influential. It is true that the example was not, especially in the fifteenth century, uniformly good; the pretentious diction that so disfigures many of Caxton's translations is largely imitated from the French originals. But the long tradition of competent writing was far more significant than this passing fashion. Certainly the volume and importance of French vocabulary and phrasing in English prose of this time proves that French was much in the minds of many English writers. There is nothing surprising or new about this, except that it is insufficiently emphasized in the literary histories. It is not credible that the infant English secular prose of the fifteenth century should have made its halting steps without a helping hand from the already self-assured French which was so well known. That English poetry drew enormously upon French everyone has always seen. We must recognize that in prose style also, as in so many other things, English owes much to France.

I do not suggest that secular prose came into being only because of the example of France, or that it learnt nothing from the earlier English religious prose; only that English religious tradition by itself is not enough to account for the comparative proficiency that so many and various writers so early attained.

Prose of some literary pretension cannot be entirely divorced from more workaday writing directed to merely practical ends of administration or business. From the late fourteenth century onwards there is a great body of writing in English of this utilitarian kind which cannot have been directly modelled on foreign example—any more than on devotional treatises. The richest record of such writing is in the great collections of letters. Here, for instance, is John Shillingford, mayor of Exeter, reporting his mission to London in 1447:

> The Saterdey next ther after the mayer came to Westminster sone apon ix. atte belle, and ther mette wᵗ my lorde Chaunceller atte brode dore a litell fro the stcire

fote comyne fro the Sterre chamber, y yn the courte and by the dore knellyng and salutyng hym yn the moste godely wyse that y cowde and recommended yn to his gode and gracious lordship my feloship and all the comminalte, his awne peeple and bedmen of the Cite of Exceter. He seyde to the mayer ij. tymes « Well come, » and the iij^de. tyme» Right well come Mayer, » and helde the mayer a grete while faste by the honde, and so went forth to his barge and w^t hym grete presse, lordis and other, &c. and yn especiall the tresorer of the kynges housholde, w^t wham he was at right grete pryvy communicacion. And therfor y, mayer, drowe me apart, and mette w^t hym at his goyng yn to his barge, and ther toke my leve of hym, seyyng these wordis,
My lord, y wolle awayte apon youre gode lordship and youre better leyser at another tyme ».

And here is Edmund Clere, a minor member of the household of King Henry VI, reporting in 1455 the King's recovery from a period of insanity:

And on the Moneday after noon the Queen came to him, and brought my Lord Prynce with her. And then he askid what the Princes name was, and the Queen told him Edward; and than he hild up his handes and thankid God therof. And he seid he never knew him til that tyme nor wist not what was seid to him, nor wist not where he had be whils he hath be seke til now. And he askid who was god-faderes, and the Queen told him, and he was wel apaid. . . And my Lord of Wynchestre and my Lord of Seint Jones were with him on the morow after Twelftheday, and he spake to hem as well as ever he did; and when thei come out, thei wept for ioye.

This letter, unpolished as it is, as it were echoes in advance some of the most potent rhythms of later English: Malory's "Than was there wepynge and wryngyng of handes, and the grettest dole they made that ever made men'; the Book of Ruth, 'for whither thou goest, I will go; and where thou lodgest, I will lodge'; Bunyan's 'I laid me down in that place to sleep; and as I slept, I dreamed a dream'.

This very "plain' style is extraordinarily well managed in all the collections of letters of the fifteenth century, especially by some of the women. Thus Margaret Paston as a young wife, writing to her husband in 1441: 'Ye have lefte me sweche a rememraunse that makyth me to thynke uppe on yow bothe day and nyth wanne I wold sclepe'. Jane Stonor, writing to her husband about 1470: 'Now farewelle, goode syr, and Gode ʒeve yow goode nyghte and brynge yow welle home and in schorte tyme'. And Margery Paston, to her husband in 1481: 'Ser, I prey you if ye tary longe at London that it wil plese [you] to sende for me, for I thynke longe sen I lay in your armes.'

None of the women at this date can, alas, have had the benefit of a university education. Their management of language cannot be the result of any training in grammar, still less rhetoric. Doubtless they picked up something from their family chaplains and village priests, as the common use of pious formulas of commendation or greeting shows; they may have been helped by their clerks, for they seldom wrote their own letters; but mostly they had to depend on the speech they heard about them. We are obliged to admit that such unvarnished and naive compositions of people of small education are distinguished only in quantity and variety from much that is accepted as literature. Their range is limited, and there are shapeless wastes surrounding the 'anthology pieces'; but the heart of the matter is there.

This informal language is an essential source of rhythms and constructions for writers of more literary prose. It is in this element of the language, I think, that the link between the best of the devotional prose and the best of the secular prose in fact consists. When Hilton writes, for example, 'And if he come for to telle his desese and ben confortid of þi speche, here hym gladli and suffre hym seye what he wyle for ese of his oune herte', he is drawing on the same fund of language as John Paston III a hundred years later, in a very different mood, when he writes to his wife Margery, 'He is the man that brought yow and me togedyrs, and I had lever then XL *li.* ye koud with your playster depart hym and hys peyne.'

It has been objected that when the plain language of speech is 'raised from the common to the literary level' what we hear is 'no longer the rhythms of secular prose, but the unmistakable cadences of the devotional treatises'. This is sometimes so, as I have said, in appropriate places such as Agnes Paston's 'This worlde is but a thorughfare, and ful of woo; and whan we departe therfro, righth noughght bere wyth us but oure good dedys and ylle'. But it is surely not at all true of John Paston III's manner in the letter I have quoted, or of much else that shows a marked ability to shape and balance a sentence to emphasize its point; thus John Paston II on his brother's marriage negotiations:

> Yowre mater is ferre spoken off and blowyn wyde, and iff it preve noo better I wolde that it had never be spoken off. Also, that mater noysyth me that I am so onkynde that I lette alle togedre. I thynke notte a mater happy, nore weell handelyd, nore poletykly dalte wyth, when it can never be fynysshyd wythowte an inconvenyence, and to any suche bargayne I kepe never to be condescentyng nere off cowncell. Iffe I weere att the begynnyng off suche a mater, I wolde have hopyd to have made a better conclusyon, iff they mokke yow notte. Thys mater is drevyn thus ferforthe wythowte my cowncell; I praye yow make an ende wythowte my cowncell. Iffe it be weell, I wolde be glad; iff it be oderwyse, it is pite. I praye yow troble me no moore in thys mater.

The relation between this kind of writing and the religious prose is not one of derivation or descent. It depends upon the common use of the resources of common speech.

I have not, of course, said anything that has not been said before. What I have tried to do is to lay the emphasis in a way which is not, I think, at present usual. In the formation of what seems to us today to be the most successful English prose of the early modern period I would give much more weight than is commonly allowed to the two factors of French example and conversational use. If pressed, I should hold that conversational use was the more important in providing the essential rhythms, and French example in ordering the construction of sentences. When in the latter half of the seventeenth century English prose came in large measure to be refashioned, Dryden held that its new clarity was due to the practice of cultivated conversation — 'the best and greatest advantage of our writing . . . proceeds from conversation'; that in turn owed much to the Court, and so to French example. The circumstances at the end of the Middle Ages were by no means the same, but the comparison is nevertheless suggestive. The French prose tradition itself was evidently, in its earlier stages, built upon conversational use. Professor von Wartburg goes so far as to claim that 'La prose artistique n'existait presque pas avant Rabelais. Les chroniqueurs du 13ᵉ et du 14ᵉ s., les nouvellistes du 15ᵉ s. écrivaient à peu près comme ils auraient parlé, sans se mettre en frais au point de vue du style'.

We are therefore brought back in both English and French to the fundamental importance of the spoken word in the creation and development of clear, serviceable prose, and to the need for writers to keep their writing in touch with their speech. It was deviation from the path of this time-honoured truth, in pursuit of pomp and circumstance, that spoilt too much of English prose for a century and a half after it had so hopefully established itself in secular use in the course of the fifteenth century.

THE INCREASE IN LOGICAL CONSTRUCTION

Samuel K. Workman

Until 1460 or 1470, the Middle English prose writers appear to have lacked the habit of associating pattern of thought with pattern of expression or form. Whether or not they perceived the full pattern of thought from its beginning, their attention to the form did not embrace the whole but was habitually concentrated only upon the part immediately under expression. In respect to form, their basic unit for composition in prose was the single statement, approximately the single construction or sentence member.

The part of this habit in illogical combinations of constructions may be seen in the use of the pleonastic pronoun, not as figure of speech but redundant after an inserted sentence-member:

but the erle forasmoche as he was made by auctoryte of the parlement, *he* wolde not obey the pryue scale.

This is a small ineptitude, with slight if any effect upon the sense or the structure. Its interest lies in the reflection it gives of the writer's psychology of form. After inserting even so short a sentence-member he forgot the

---

From Samuel K. Workman, *Fifteenth Century Translation as an Influence on English Prose* (Princeton: Princeton University Press, 1940), Ch. 2, "The Original Prose of the Transition," pp. 33–58, at pp. 35–41, 57–58. Reprinted by permission of Princeton University Press. Notes have been omitted.

nature of his original construction. 'The erle' was retained as a thought, as the use of a pronoun shows. But the form of the final statement was conceived only in terms of itself; and the writer, feeling obliged to provide a subject for his verb, did so with a redundancy that was not at all conscious.

Another frequent usage of the time, the synthetic verb—ellipsis of the subject—though exactly the opposite of pleonasm, was often the result of inattention to the form of the whole sequence of thought. Examples may be found at random in the earliest original English chronicles:

And in the vj yere . . . went the Erle of Salusbury, with a grete retenewe of men of armys and archeris, by comaundement of the Kynge and of alle the Counseile of Engelonde, *&* *made* hym the Leftenaunt or alle the partyes of Fraunce . . . forto distroye the Kynges enemyes . . . And so he departid . . . .

And from thens she was brought to Westmynstre, and þere was hir terement holden and doon rially; *and* þere *buryed* in the chapell of oure Lady.

And in this same yere . . . a seruant þat was with a man of Hakney, ij myle from London, come with his mayster to London, *and bought* vitayle and must for dignte, forto sende hoom to his wife, for she was grete with childe, And the fals creature, when he come hoom slewe þe wife . . . .

In the first of these the Earl did not make himself lieutenant, any more than in the other two it was the 'interrment' which was buried or the servant who bought the food. The synthetic verb is in part a relic of the time when an inflectional ending made the subject clear. But verbal inflections never had the power to identify the subject from among two or more nouns when person and number were the same. In each case quoted, the ambiguity has come because the writers composed the form of their sentences by short units. The subjects of the statements about buying or burying or making— that is, the thought-relationships of the statements—were, of course, clear in the writers' minds. But at the moment of constructing the statement, there was no regard to the form of any outside part of the sentence.

Asymmetrical coordination has a more important effect upon the form of prose. In his study of this Middle English usage, Mr. Urban Ohlander gives a psychological explanation of it which implies the habit of composing by short units: 'In ME., which was more unhampered by grammatical and stylistic inhibitions, asymmetrical coordination has a wider scope. . . . Whereas a reasonably careful modern writer avoids disturbing asymmetries either by choosing symmetrical expressions from the beginning or by revising what he has written, a ME. writer was seemingly not so scrupulous in that respect, the latter's language reflecting rather the spoken language of his times. Thus it may happen that when the writer gets to the second member, he is forced to give this an asymmetrical form because there is no other symmetrical expression available, unless, of course, he revises the first member to bring it into conformity with the second. In other cases the second member's assuming an asymmetrical shape may be due to the writer's confusing mentally the actual form of the first member with a synonymous expression which determines the form of the second member (blending, 'contamination').'

In the following excerpt from an English sermon of about 1400, the basic structure is a sequence of coordinations. Aside from the adjective clauses there are only three verbal constructions of subordinating type. Yet two of these are used asymmetrically.

For he [the great nobleman] wold be callid manly and worchypfull; and also in holdyng of grete festes, feding riche men. And the pore man stondythe at the gate with an empti wombe. He may rather have a knoc then a crust of brede. And so these riche men will feede them that hathe no nede; and he that hathe nede schall go with-owte. Then commythe mynstrells and cowrtyers, and thei schall have grete yftes. And there gothe ther expences a-wey, be-cawse thei wold be magnyfyed, and to bere theire name a-bowte of grete worchype.

The writer of this appears to have had a pattern present in his mind, a pattern of short equal blocks of thought. But lacking a consciousness of the grammatical cast of the blocks, he simply added any thought he wanted in the most convenient construction at hand. Thus to him 'becawse' did not introduce a new clausal form, but was simply a connective between thoughts, and 'to bere' represented only the same connection repeated; his pattern had nothing to do with mechanics of expression.

Here again the disruption is more in form than in clarity of meaning. But when a writer with the same psychology used a greater variety of constructions, the sense itself must sometimes have been seriously obscured at least to a reader if not to a listener, usage notwithstanding. A good instance may be had, this time from secular literature, in the very opening page of Lydgate's *The Serpent of Division.*

Whilome, as olde bookis maken mencion, when tholde noble famous citie of Rome was most shyning in his felicitie and flowring in his glory, liche as it is remembered in bookis of olde antiquyte—the prime temps of his fundacion, whenne the wallis were reised on heithe bi the manly & prudent diligence of Remvs and Romvlus; fro þe which tyme þe citie stood vnder governaunce of kyngis, tyl at the tyme Tarquyne soone of Tarquyne the prowde, for his outragious offence doone vnto Lucresse wife to þe worþy Senatour Callatyne . . . pvnysshing of whiche trespace by the manly pursuite of Collatyns kynrede and ful assente of all the Senate the name of kyngis ceased in the citie of Rome for evur more, and all the Roial stokke of þe forsaide Tarquyne was proscripte & put in exile.

Here it is hard to trace even any pattern of thought. Before he has gone very far Lydgate himself seems to have forgotten what he started out to say. Certainly he paid no attention to how he started to say it. Still, the basic procedure of composition here can be seen to be the same as in the sermon just quoted. The only difference is that Lydgate has cast his successive blocks of thought in subordinating rather than coordinating constructions. Some of these may have been considered demonstrative rather than relative ('froþe which tyme'; 'in pvnysshing of whiche trespace'). But it is plain from the uncompleted constructions at the opening that Lydgate had very little awareness of the connection between syntactical form and logic of thought.

Anacoluthon, sometimes obscuring the sense, sometimes only the form, is frequent in Middle English prose. It is found more often in complex or hypotactic structure than in paratactic, the reason no doubt being that there was less chance for misfitting when the constructions were all the same. Any writer using a variety of constructions was likely to overlook the requirements of logic. This was true not only of secular writers who pretended to no especial education in rhetoric, men like Edward of York at the beginning of the century or Caxton toward the end. Anacoluthic sentences are to be found in the usually careful prose of Reginald Pecock, one of whose literary ambitions was that his works be translated into Latin. Two examples appear within three pages of *The Book of Faith*.

and the iie is this, setting not bi forto folowe the determynaciouns and the holdingis of the chirche in mater of feith; and that for as myche as thei presupposen as what may be sufficiently provid and wherto thei alleggen witnessing of Seynt Austyn in his book of Baptym aȝens Donatists, that the chirche may erre in determynyng articlis for feith; wherfore foloweth that the labour . . . shulde be the profitablist labour . . . *etc.*

. . . It is not ynouȝ that the seid bokis be writen . . . and that the bokis schulde opene to hem that thei erren; but tho bokis musten be distributed and delid abrood to manye, where that nede is trowid that thei be delid: and that the seid erryng persoonys take longe leiser, forto sadli and oft overrede tho bokis, unto tyme thei schulen be wel aqueyntid with tho bokis, and with the skilis and motivis therynne writen, and not forto have in oon tyme or ii tymes a liȝt superficial overreding or hering oonly. Forwhi. . . oold custom . . . wole make . . . *etc.*

*   *   *   *

Sentences thus illogically composed continue to appear well after the end of the fifteenth century. By that time, however, and for at least twenty years before 1500, the tendency appears to have greatly lessened. Thirty-four pages from John Fisher's *Treatise concernynge the Seuen Penytencyal Psalmes*, published in 1509, show no instances of anacoluthon whatever, and only three of asymmetrical coordination. Fisher often used the synthetic verb, but only twice in the pages is the subject ambiguous. In about six thousand words from the latter pages of Robert Fabyan's *Chronicles*, published in 1516 but written by 1504, there are only two instances of anacoluthon, two of asymmetrical coordination, and three of the ambiguous synthetic verb. More significant, a London chronicle written about 1485 shows, in about the same length, only one instance of anacoluthon, three of asymmetrical coordination, and none of the ambiguous synthetic verb. The London chronicle is a significant example not only because of its early date but because of its obscurity; it is found only in manuscript and is likely to have been the work of an average writer of the time.

The prevailing 'correctness' or logical consistency in the sentence structure of early sixteenth century prose has been often remarked, and the explanation given for it has been the revival of learning. It is true that the function—and the importance—of logic in English syntax might be learned by the study of Latin. Pecock probably, and very likely Fortescue, isolated cases in the fifteenth century, achieved the prevailing correctness of their English sentence structure by placing it in direct analogy with that of Latin. But it has been observed above that logical inconsistency was apparently connected with the habit of composition by short units of thought. The tendency of syntactical usage toward correctness may therefore have resulted not so much from an analytical understanding of the science of grammar as from a broadened sense of form, a growing habit of planning the expression to fit the whole of a sequence of thought. That such a growth was taking place may be seen from other changes in fifteenth century prose which do not involve the correctness of the structure.

*   *   *   *

There are, then, two respects in which the late fifteenth century chroniclers indicate the broadening of the unit of composition. First of all, the very change from a simple and uniform to a complex and varied structure reflects a tendency to combine and inter-relate. Since the natural tendency of narrative is the other way, it is likely that those who made this first change had decided for the importance of form, both as an end in itself and as a means of expressing the variety which had always existed among the different parts of a thought-relationship. Complex structure had been used before—and was at first used by the chroniclers —without a realization of the accord needed between thought and form. Thus the second and more important change was toward accuracy in this accord. Inconsistencies of logic became practically eliminated. Sentence-members were seldom constructed without reference to their fitness and proportion in the period as a whole.

Rare before the third quarter of the fifteenth century, these traits are well established in the prose of the early sixteenth. They are characteristic in the work of outstanding figures like Fisher, More, Tyndale, or Lupset, and likewise in that of writers who were anonymous or relatively obscure, the 'Translator of Livius', the author of *A Manifest Detection*, or John Bourchier and Simon Fish.

The structural qualities of the prose of this period have been described by Mr. J. A. Gee and, less analytically, by Professor J. P. Krapp; there is no need to take up each writer again. Between Tyndale and More or between the Translator of Livius and Simon Fish, there are, of course, a great many differences of style. But for the present study the important comparison is between their prose and that in corresponding *genres* of fifty or more years before. It is not only the religious prose that suggests such a comparison; *The Life of Henry V* or *A Manifest Detection* can be compared to the early chronicles; Bourchier's prefaces to Caxton's; or Fish's attacks on prelates to the attacks on manners in the early sermons.

Naturally there appear a great many semblances in the writers' interests, in the acuteness or confusion of their observations, in the naturalness or pomposity of their tone, and even in the devices which they used for disposition. But in one quality there is a constant difference. In structural form the earlier prose appears naive, the later is plainly matured.

SUGGESTIONS FOR RESEARCH

1. Study the arguments pro and con concerning "native" English. Williamson (1951) and Prins (1952) assume Latin influence existed from earliest times. According to Prins, "Alfred, apart from the original prefaces and insertions, is too closely bound to his Latin originals to be considered either a good example for later times or a good specimen of 'native' English prose." Gordon (1966), on the other hand, declares that Alfred adapted the Latin independently: "He is unaffected by Latin word-order, rendering unerringly into the natural word-order of English." See also Toor (1966).

2. Examine Andrew's (1940) argument that the supposed paratactic structure of Old English has been overemphasized. What is the consensus today?

3. Examine the arguments over the influence of French on the formation of English sentence structure. Gordon (1966) supported R. W. Chambers' (1932) belief in the continuity of English prose from Alfred to the present. Prins (1952), arguing for the crucial importance of French, believes that "there certainly is no continuity between Old and Modern English either in vocabulary or word-formation or in the relation between the various parts of speech." N. Davis (1961, this chapter) backs up Prins: "If pressed, I should hold that conversational use was the more important in providing the essential rhythms [of Middle English], and French example in ordering the construction of sentences." Search out the strengths and weaknesses in their reasoning and proofs. Who seems particularly persuasive?

4. Study the plain and ornate styles of Old English and Middle English. Compare, for example, Aelfric with Wulfstan and both with Alfred. Then compare the *Ancrene Riwle* with Wycliffe's style. Assess the scholarship dealing with plain-ornate, seeking to determine the reliability of methods and the validity of conclusions in each book or essay.

5. Recently the euphuistic style has been traced to the beginnings of English prose. All commentators assume that the style which Croll (1929) labels "baroque" and Williamson (1951) "pointed" did not appear in English until the late sixteenth century. Can you find traces of the Senecan "curt" style prior to the sixteenth century?

6. Lewis (1894) argues: "No English writer before Tyndale has any sense of the paragraph as a subject of internal arrangement." Is he correct?

7. Examine Caxton's Prologue to *Eneydos* in the original. Explain his punctuation, taking account of the full stop, colon, diagonal stroke, capital letters, and paragraph sign. What do you find strange about Caxton's vocabulary, and how do you explain it? Translate Caxton into modern English, and explain the differences between your version and his. Caxton admired French and Latin models. Can you find evidences of this admiration in his style? Follow this procedure with other early writers.

CHAPTER III

THE RENAISSANCE PERIOD: 1500–1660

CHARACTERS OF STYLE:
SIDNEY, LYLY, GREENE, AND NASHE

Walter F. Staton, Jr.

"Before we come to the precepts of garnishing an oracion, we thinke good, bryeffly to shewe you of the three kyndes of stile or endyghting, in the whych all the eloquucion of an oratoure is occupied. For that there be three sundry kyndes, called of the Grekes characters, of us figures, I trowe there is no man, though he be meanlye learned, but he knoweth, namely when we se so manye wryters of sciences, bothe Greke and latine, whych haue ben before tyme, to haue folowed for the mooste parte sundrye sortes of wrytyng, the one ynlyke to the other. And there hath bene marked inespecially thre kyndes of endightynge: The greate, the smal; the meane." So Richard Sherry prefaced his discussion of the characters of style in 1550. Similar discussions appear in Wilson's *Arte of Rhetorique*, Puttenham's *Arte of Poesie*, and Ben Jonson's *Discoveries*. Yet as William G. Crane has observed, sixteenth-century writers on style, though they occasionally

From Walter F. Staton, Jr., "The Characters of Style in Elizabethan Prose," *Journal of English and Germanic Philology*, LVII, No. 2 (April, 1958), pp. 197–207, at pp. 197–198, 200–207. Reprinted by permission of the University of Illinois Press. Notes have been omitted.

mention the three characters, universally concern themselves only with the embellished and elaborate style. There are no treatises on the art of plain talk; apparently, and possibly with some reason, these men felt that plain talk came naturally to Elizabethan Englishmen.

The doctrine of the three characters of style did, however, have a definite effect on the literary practice of Elizabethan prose writers. Sherry is undoubtedly right that there were few men so "meanlye learned" that they did not know of it; the writers frequently mention it and clearly attempt to follow it in their writings. It is important that we recognize the pervasiveness of this doctrine if we wish to have a clear understanding of the evolution of Elizabethan literary taste. For the modern reader is tempted to see a reaction against the elevated style in the contrast between *Euphues* and *Arcadia* on the one hand and the social pamphlets of Greene and Nashe on the other, and to conclude with G. P. Krapp that "the natural tendency towards the end of the sixteenth and in the seventeenth century was to react in favor of a simpler style." A reaction against Euphuism there certainly was around 1590, but it was a reaction against the particular kind of ornateness that Euphuism featured, rather than against ornateness in general. Ornamental prose continued to be in fashion to the end of the sixteenth century and beyond; the plain writing of the 1590's is to be explained by the doctrine of the characters of style rather than by a major change in literary taste.

*   *   *   *

Sir Philip Sidney is like Ascham in using as his normal literary mode the elegant and ornate middle style and in varying style with subject. Kenneth Myrick has traced in some detail the variations of style in *The Defense of Poesie* and concludes that "the style varies almost exactly as Quintilian would have approved." Unlike the style of *The Defense*, however, that of the *Arcadia* rises frequently to the level of the lofty style. When Sidney prefaces an emotional scene, "Truely Sir, a very good Orator might haue a fayre field to use eloquence in, if he did but onely repeate the lamentable and truely affectionated speeches," we can imagine the writer shifting his stylistic gears. A good example of such a high-flown passage is Gynecia's lament at the beginning of Book Two:

... having a great while throwne her countenaunce ghastly about her (as if she had called all the powers of the worlde to witnesse of her wretched estate) at length casting up her watrie eyes to heaven, O Sunne (said she) whose unspotted light directs the steps of mortall mankind, art thou not ashamed to impart the clearnesse of thy presence to such a dust-creeping worme as I am? O you heavens (which continually keepe the course allotted unto you) can none of your influences prevaile so much upon the miserable *Gynecia*, as to make her preserve a course so long embraced by her? O deserts, deserts, how fit a guest am I for you, since my hart can people you with wild ravenous beastes, which in you are wanting? O Vertue, where doost thou hide thy selfe? or what hideous thing is this which doth eclips thee? or is it true that thou weart never but a vaine name, and no essentiall thing, which hast thus left thy professed servant, when she had most need of thy lovely presence? O imperfect proportion of reason, which can too much forsee, & too little prevent. Alas, alas (said she) if there were but one hope for all my paines, or but one excuse for all my faultinesse. But wretch that I am, my torment is beyond all succour, & my evill deserving doth exceed my evill fortune. For nothing els did my husband take this straunge resolution to live so solitarily: for nothing els have the winds delivered this straunge guest to my country: for nothing els have the destinies reserved my life to this time, but that only I (most wretched I) should become a plague to my selfe, and a shame to womankind. Yet if my desire (how unjust so ever it be) might take effect, though a thousand deaths folowed it, and every death were followed with a thousand shames; yet should not my sepulcher receive me without some contentment. But alas, though sure I am, that *Zelmane* is such as can answere my love; yet as sure I am, that this disguising must needs come for some foretaken conceipt. And then, wretched *Gynecia*, where canst thou find any smal ground-plot for hope to dwel upon? No, no, it is *Philoclea* his hart is set upon: it is my daughter I have borne to supplant me. But if it be so, the life I have given thee (ungratefull *Philoclea*) I will sooner with these handes bereave thee of, then my birth shall glory, she hath bereaved me of my desires. In shame there is no comfort, but to be beyond all bounds of shame.

This passage contains most of the ornaments which are characteristic of Sidney's middle style: compound words, metaphor, hyperbole, antithesis, parallelism, paronomasia. In the case of paronomasia ("prevaile ... preserve," "hide ... hideous," "to live ... delivered ... my life"), Sidney is, if anything, more restrained than in passages where he is trying to charm and delight. In addition to these ornaments, however, the passage contains a number of devices which are more or less typical of the lofty style. The facts that Gynecia's torment is presented in a feigned speech or prosopopoeia and that in this speech she apostrophizes the sun, heavens, etc., are certainly indications of the impassioned style; *The Defense of Poesie*, which contains all the ornaments listed above, in profusion, has only two apostrophes. The gestures and facial expression ascribed to Gynecia are those of the tragic orator. While the various kinds of word repetition are ubiquitous in Sidney's writings, they are somewhat more conspicuous in high-flown passages, and we may infer from his praise of Cicero's famous "thunderbolt of eloquence" in *The Defense* that he regarded "O deserts, deserts" as particularly moving. Such writing can, of course, easily become bombastic and sensational, but we may observe that Sidney is not here merely multiplying words, that there is a thought structure in the passage.

Sidney could, of course, write unadorned English, as his letters show; he simply found no literary use for such a mode. John Lyly, who achieved his principal fame with his elegant middle style, did, however, find one literary use for the low style—that of answering Martin Marprelate. We can study the evolution of Lyly's normal style from 1578 to around 1590 or, if we include his two letters to Queen Elizabeth, to 1598. The proper conclusion of such a study is that Lyly joined in the general reaction against the style of *Euphues*, a reaction in the direction, not of plain English, but of more diversified ornamentation. If he wrote in the low style in *Pap with a Hatchet* (1589), it was through necessity not choice; in his apologetic epistle "To the Indifferent Reader," which is itself certainly elegant enough, he explains, "I seldome vse to write, and yet neuer writ anie thing, that in speech might seeme vndecent, or in sense vnhonest; if here I haue vsed bad tearmes, it is

because they are not to be answered with good tearmes." For Lyly, as for
Ascham and Sidney, the decent middle style was proper on most occasions.
In essaying the low style in *Pap with a Hatchet*, he relied largely on what he
conceived to be low diction; he can rail, he says, "if *Martin* haue not barreled
vp all rakehell words." The low words in *Pap* include slang, interjections,
and nonsense phrases apparently associated with Elizabethan raillery. Lyly
also carefully avoids the graces of the ornate style. Once he deviates into
elegance: "They studie to pull downe Bishopps, and set vp Superintendents,
which is nothing else, but to raze out good *Greeke*, & enterline bad *Latine*.
A fine period; but I cannot continue this stile, let me fal into my olde vaine."
Evidently a fine period for Lyly in 1589 contained little paronomasia, but
careful antithesis, isocolon, and rhythm. On the other hand, while it is not
what we today would call a good plain style, Lyly's "olde vaine," i.e., the
low style, is more than mere carelessness. The author of *Euphues* surely had
to take some pains to write such stuff as: "Tush, (what care I) is my poisie;
if hee meddle with mee, Ile make his braines so hot, they shall crumble and
rattle in his warpt scull, like pepper in a dride bladder." Probably the
principal element in this style is the use of words with unromantic connota-
tions—instead of precious stones and exotic animals, pepper and dried
bladders, or Nashe's mustard pots and brewers' aprons.

In 1589, the year of *Pap with a Hatchet*, Robert Greene's *Menaphon*
announced its author's rejection, after nearly ten years of discipleship, of
Lyly's famous style. The style Greene strove toward in *Menaphon*, however,
was Arcadianism. Neither here nor in his later writings does he reject
ornamentation as the mark of good prose; throughout his so-called "social
pamphlets" of 1591–92 there are passages in the elegant style whenever the
subject—an address to the gentle reader or an idyllic description—demands
it. In *Greene's Vision*, published in 1592 but written around the time of
Menaphon, he presents, like Lyly in the preface to *Euphues*, the apparent
contradiction of writing against stylistic graces while practising them:

Such schollers deserue much blame, as out of that pretious fountaine of learning
will fetch a pernitious water of vanitie: the trees that grow in *Indea* haue rough
barks, but they yeeld pretious gummes: and the stones in *Sicillia* haue a duskie
couller, but being cut they are as orient as the sunne: so the outward phrase is not
to be measured by pleasing the eare, but the inward matter by profiting the minde:
the puffing glorie of the loftie stile shadowing wanton conceipts is like to the skin
of a serpent that contriues impoysoned flesh, or to a panther that hath a beautiful
hide but a beastly paunch.

Greene is here, of course, inveighing principally against immoral writing,
but there is a strong implication that he felt his own style to have "rough
bark" and "duskie couller" and that the lofty style, whether "shadowing
wanton conceipts" or not, has a "puffing glorie." The apparent contradiction is explained by the concept of the florid middle style, which is what
Greene must have felt his own ornamented manner to be. The "puffing
glorie of the loftie stile" Greene found probably in the works of the tragic
dramatists of his day.

But while Greene's style did not evolve from ornamentation to plain English, Greene did find more literary uses for the low style than did his predecessors. In *The Second Part of Cony-Catching* (1592) he gave his reason for writing in this vein: "But heere by the way, giue me leaue to answere an obiection, that some inferred against me, which was, that I shewed no eloquent phrases, nor fine figuratiue conueiance in my first booke [of cony-catching] as I had done in other of my workes: to which I reply that το πρεπον, a certaine decorum is to bee kept in euerie thing, and not to applie a high stile in a base subiect." C. S. Lewis remarks of this explanation, "The passage suggests that Greene felt himself not to be essaying a new kind of excellence but to be absolved from caring how he wrote, and the pamphlet itself confirms this." It is true that Greene's works, the "Cony-Catching" pamphlets included, are full of careless pages, and it is highly probable that Greene, like his contemporaries and indeed like Cicero, viewed the low style with dogmatic scorn. Nevertheless Greene displays at times a manner of writing that is both plain and vivid and that can scarcely have been achieved without a degree of art. The Chauccrian fabliau in *Greene's Vision* has some good examples of this manner of writing:

A bonnie Lassie she was, verye well tuckt vp in a Russet Petticoate, with a bare hemme, and no Fringe, yet had shee a Red lace, and a Stomacher of Tuft Mockado, and a Partlet cast ouer with a prittie whippe, and drest she was in a Kerchiffe of Holland, for her Father was a Farmer: her girdle was greene, and at that hung a large Leather Purse with faire threaden Tassels, & a new paire of yellow gloues, tufted with redde rawe Silke verie richly: and forsooth this Maides name was Kate.

Of interest here are the specific details and the use of inversion, both of which were later to be typical of Nashe. The avoidance of the figures of sound and thought is obvious, but to appreciate the choice of diction we should, perhaps, compare the passage with one in Greene's elevated manner:

This *Lewsippa*, was so perfect in the complection of her bodie, and so pure in the constitution of her minde, so adorned with outward beautie, and endued with inward bountie, so pollished with rare vertues and exquisite qualities, as she seemed a seemely *Venus*, for her beautie, and a second *Vesta*, for her virginitie: yea, Nature and the Gods hadde so bountifully bestowed their giftes upon her, as Fame her selfe was doubtfull whether she should make greater report of her excellent vertue, or exquisite beautie.

Surely after years of "adorning" princesses, Greene could not relax his vigilance and find himself "tucking up bonnie lassies"! But the Elizabethan writer who most fully exploited the low style was Thomas Nashe, whose first published piece was a rather contentious preface to Greene's *Menaphon* (1589). In this preface Nashe contrasts several groups of extravagant and unlearned writers, principally the tragic dramatists, who write "that *sublime dicendi genus*, which walks abroade for wast paper in each serving-mans pocket" with Greene's "*Arcadian Menaphon*, whose attire (though not so stately, yet comely) doth intitle thee aboue all other to that *temperatum dicendi genus* which *Tully* in his Orator termeth true eloquence."

It is not important to our present purpose that Cicero nowhere makes such a statement as is here attributed to him; what is important is that Nashe specifically describes *Menaphon*, and possibly *Arcadia* also, as being couched in the middle style. Nashe's antipathy for the lofty style, expressed here, was not an enduring attitude; for he was not entirely in jest when he wrote in *Nashes Lenten Stuffe* (1597): "Know it is my true vaine to be *tragicus Orator* ... not caring for this demure soft *mediocre genus*, that is like water and wine mixt togither; but giue me pure wine of it self, & that begets good bloud, and heates the brain thorowly." Examples of Nashe's tragic oratory abound in the more emotional sections of *Christs Teares ouer Ierusalem* (1593) and *The Unfortunate Traveller* (1593). From the former, for instance, Miriam's prosopopoeia before eating her child:

Though *Dauid* sung of mercy and iudgement together, yet cannot I sing of cruelty and compassion together; remember I am a Mother, and play the murdresse, both at once. O, therfore in my words doe I striue to be tyrannous, that I may bee the better able to enact with my hands. Sildome or neuer is there any that doth ill, but speakes ill first. The tongue is the encouraging Captaine, that (with daunger-glorifying persuasion) animates al the other corporeall parts to be ventrous. He is the Iudge that doomes & determines; the rest of our faculties and powers are but the secular executioners of his sentence. Be prest, myne hands, (as Iaylegarding officers) to see executed whatsoeuer your superior tong-slaying Iudge shall decree. Embrawne your soft-skind enclosure with Adamantine dust, that it may drawe nothing but steele vnto it. Arme your selues against my sonne, not as my sonne, but my bedde-intercepting Bastard, begotten of some strumpet. My hart shall receiue an iniunction imaginarily to disinherite him. No relenting thought of mine shall retraite you with repentant affectionate humors.

In such a passage we find the ornamentation typical of the later Elizabethan middle style: antithesis, paronomasia (though not so much of these as one would have found in the heyday of Euphuism), metaphor, compound words, periphrasis, as well as the prosopopoeia and apostrophe of the lofty style.

The evolution of Nashe's middle or normal style illustrates well the shift in taste of his day. He began writing in the shadow of Lyly, and thus in *The Anatomie of Absurditie* (written in 1587) he attacked modern women Euphuistically:

Maides and Matrons now adaies be more charie of their store, so that they will be sure they will not spend too much spittle with spynning, yea theyr needles are nettles, for they lay them aside as needlesse, for feare of pricking their fingers when they are painting theyr faces ... Shee had rather view her face a whole morning in a looking Glasse then worke by the howre Glasse, shee is more sparing of her Spanish needle then her Spanish gloues, occupies oftner her setting sticke then sheeres, and ioyes more in her Iewels, then in her Iesus.

Nashe relies here, it will be observed, entirely upon antithesis, parallelism, and paronomasia, the Euphuistic devices. His later denunciations of Euphuism and of "running on the letter" do not mean that he had renounced these figures, any more than do Sidney's similar denunciations. Nashe's later writing no longer relies solely on these figures, but on metaphor, word repetition, and artificial diction as well. Thus, when in 1593 he again condemned women, it was in the following vein:

Ever since *Evah* was tempted, and the Serpent preuailed with her, weomen haue tooke vpon them both the person of the tempted and the tempter. They tempt to be tempted, and not one of them, except she be tempted, but thinkes herself contemptible. Vnto the greatnesse of theyr great Grandmother *Evah*, they seeke to aspire, in being tempted and tempting. If not to tempt and be thought worthy to be tempted, why dye they & diet they theyr faces with so many drugges as they doe, as it were to correct Gods workmanship, and reprooue him as a bungler, and one that is not his crafts Maister? Why ensparkle they theyr eyes with spiritualiz'd distillations? Why tippe they theyr tongues with *Aurum potabile*? Why fill they vp ages frets with fresh colours? ... Theyr heads, with theyr top and top gallant Lawne babycaps, and Snow-resembled siluer curlings, they make a playne Puppet stage of. Theyr breasts they embuske vp on hie, and theyr round Roseate buds immodestly lay foorth, to shew at theyr handes there is fruite to be hoped. In theyr curious Antick-woven garments, they imitate and mocke the Wormes and Adders that must eate them. They shew the swellings of their mind, in the swellings and plumpings out of theyr apparrayle.

These passages, it is fair to say, illustrate not only the evolution of Nashe's middle style, but also the deficiencies thereof. He was more successful with the low style, by contemporary as well as modern standards, judging from the sales of his various pamphlets. Here, eschewing ornamentation, he relies on concrete details, slang, and interjections and gains a vividness and vigor rare in Elizabethan prose. Thus in *Pierce Penilesse* (1592) he censures bourgeois women in the low style:

In an other corner, Mistris Minx, a Marchants wife, that will eate no Cherries, forsooth, but when they are at twenty shillings a pound, that lookes as simperingly as if she were besmeard, and iets it as gingerly as if she were dancing the canaries: she is so finicall in her speach, as though she spake nothing but what shee had first sewd ouer before in her Samplers, and the puling accent of her voyce is like a fained treble, or ones voyce that interprets to the puppets.

But to say that Nashe was successful in the low style is not to say that he preferred it. Like Lyly and Greene, he used it when his subject required it, but he continued to write ornamented prose also and probably felt that the greatest literary achievements were to be made there. His praise of "mellifluous Playfere" and dispraise of the unsophisticated Thomas Deloney seem to indicate such a preference. And if it were true that the Elizabethan who was most successful in the low style regarded it as fit only for low subjects, it would not be strange. For the theory of the characters of style was a school doctrine, and Elizabethan literary taste was to a great extent formed in the schools.

CICERONIANISM
AND ANTI-CICERONIANISM

Gilbert Highet

There were two different schools of prose style in the baroque age. Both turned to classical models for inspiration and to classical theories for authority. Both were continued in the prose of the nineteenth and twentieth centuries; and both were actually re-creations of rival schools of prose-writing which had flourished in Athens, in the empire of Alexander, in Rome, and in the early Christian church. The history of European prose demonstrates perhaps more clearly than that of any other branch of literary art that contemporary literature can be neither understood nor practised unless it is seen as part of a continuous and permanently vital tradition.

One of these styles was of course founded on the work of the greatest master of prose who ever wrote: the Roman Cicero (106–43 B.C.). He himself had a number of styles—colloquialism in his private letters, half-formal dialogue in his philosophical and critical treatises, and a tremendous variety of modes of oratory in his speeches. But the style in which he is most powerful and most fully himself is a full, ornate, magnificent utterance in which emotion constantly swells up and is constantly ordered and disciplined by superb intellectual control.

Even while Cicero was reigning as the greatest orator in Rome, his style was attacked by his friends and critics. They pointed out that it was a development of the manner of the Athenian orator Isocrates, which in its careful symmetry is often painfully affected; and that the tricks of Isocrates had been taken over and elaborated and pumped full of even more artificial emotionalism by the Greek orators and rhetorical schools of Asia Minor. They called it 'Asiatic', and set up against it their standard of 'Attic' brevity, simplicity, sincerity.[1]

---

[1] In this section I am much indebted to the brilliant essays of Professor M. W. Croll. See in particular his ' "Attic Prose" in the Seventeenth Century', in *Studies in Philology*, 18 (1921), 2. 79–128; 'Muret and the History of "Attic" Prose', in *PMLA*, 39 (1924), 254–309; and 'The Baroque Style in Prose', in *Studies in English Philology . . . in honour of Frederick Klaeber* (Minneapolis, 1929), 427–56. Professor Croll prefers to use the phrase 'baroque style' for only one of the two rival schools of prose which flourished in the late sixteenth, the seventeenth, and the eighteenth centuries: the 'anti-Ciceronian' school. That is, of course, his right; but I cannot help thinking that baroque architecture and music, highly decorated, full of complex symmetries and counterbalancing variations on a fundamentally simple design, have more in common with the elaborations of Ciceronianism, and that either a style like Johnson's should be called pure baroque or the term should be extended to cover both styles.

Abridged from Gilbert Highet, *The Classical Tradition: Greek and Roman Influences on Western Literature* (New York: Oxford University Press, 1949), Ch. 18, "Baroque Prose," at pp. 322–335. Copyright 1949 by Oxford University Press, Inc. Used by permission. Some of the notes have been omitted, and the remainder renumbered to run in sequence. By "baroque," Highet means the sixteenth and seventeenth centuries.

After Cicero's death the writers and orators of Rome, realizing that they could go no farther in elaborating his characteristic style of balanced orotundity, turned towards the ideals of Atticism. Sentences now became brief. Clauses were curt, often jolty in rhythm. Connectives were dropped, balance avoided; the thought-content became denser; where Cicero built up his paragraphs to a crescendo of crashing sound, the writers of the early empire ignored harmony, cultivating epigrammatic brilliance and preferring paradox to climax. This was not pure Atticism. There was little or nothing like it in the work of the Athenian orators and prosateurs. But in its short sentences, its simple vocabulary, its apparent informality, it was quite Attic: its less likeable exaggerations were force-grown in the hot competition of the rhetorical schools and the literary salons of the empire. Its greatest master was Seneca (c. 4 B.C.–A.D. 65); and something of it can be seen in the poetry of his nephew Lucan, who turned away from Vergil's mellifluous harmonies as Seneca had turned away from Cicero's organ-tones. A generation later the historian Tacitus (c. A.D. 55–c. 120) worked out an even stranger style, within the same school, based on the calculated surprises of asymmetry. And in the writings of the early church fathers the same contrasting schools appeared—one sonorous and complex, symmetrical and smooth and richly nourished, the other brief, vigorous, thought-loaded, often eccentric, sometimes obscure. St. Augustine was the Christian Cicero, and the other school was headed by the brilliant Tertullian.

With the beginning of the Renaissance, the amazing strength and flexibility of Cicero's style was recognized once more. It was copied by writers of Latin prose on almost every subject. For centuries the diplomacy of the European chanceries was carried on not only in the language, but in the precise vocabulary, and word-order, and cadences of Cicero's speeches. There was a long and fierce dispute between scholars who held that Cicero was an unchallengeable 'authority' and that no modern writer could use Latin words or constructions not found in his works, and those, more liberal, who pointed out that Latin was still a living language which modern authors could expand and alter to their own needs. Since this was a dispute about the use of the Latin language, it does not come within the scope of our book. But it was closely connected with another dispute which does.

Many writers in the vernacular languages felt that the 'big bow-wow' style of speaking and writing was bogus. All style is artificial, no doubt; but they held that prose should at least give the appearance of being natural. They therefore turned away from Cicero and most of the devices he had developed, and, as models for modern prose, picked Seneca and Tacitus. Some of them went farther back, to Demosthenes and Plato. The aim of them all was to be personal, to avoid formalism. On the models of Seneca's moral essays and Tacitus' histories—and, to a much smaller extent, Demosthenes' plainer speeches and Plato's quieter dialogues—they created the prose of most modern essays and character-sketches, the prose in which some great modern sermons have been written.

Of this second style the chief masters were:

Francis Bacon (1561–1626)
Sir Thomas Browne (1605–82)

Robert Burton, author of *The Anatomy of Melancholy* (1577–1640)
Jean de La Bruyère (1645–96)
John Milton (1608–74)
Michel de Montaigne (1533–92)
Blaise Pascal (1623–62).

The prose of this school has again been subdivided into two types—
the loose manner, in which short clauses are built up into larger sentences
and paragraphs by light and informal connexions, with little symmetry; and
the curt manner, where there are no connexions whatever, and thought after
thought is dropped from the writer's mind as it is formed.[2]   The reader
supplies the links.

Here is a beautiful example of the loose manner, from Burton's *Anatomy
of Melancholy*. Burton is talking about the dangers and delights of building
castles in the air, and how the habit grows on those who indulge in it:

'So delightsome these toys are at first, they could spend whole days and nights
without sleep, even whole years alone in such contemplations, and fantastical meditations, which are like unto dreams, and they will hardly be drawn from them, or
willingly interrupt, so pleasant their vain conceits are, that they hinder their ordinary
tasks and necessary business, they cannot address themselves to them, or almost to
any study or employment, these fantastical and bewitching thoughts so covertly, so
feelingly, so urgently, so continually set upon, creep in, insinuate, possess, overcome,
distract, and detain them, they cannot, I say, go about their more necessary business,
stave off or extricate themselves, but are ever musing, melancholizing, and carried
along, as he (they say) that is led round about a heath with a Puck in the night,
they run earnestly on in this labyrinth of anxious and solicitous melancholy meditations, and cannot well or willingly refrain, or easily leave off, winding and un-
winding themselves, as so many clocks, and still pleasing their humours, until at
last the scene is turned upon a sudden, by some bad object, and they being now
habituated to such vain meditations and solitary places, can endure no company, can
ruminate of nothing but harsh and distasteful subjects.'

It is a style, not for speaking, but for reading and lonely brooding: it
gives the impression of overhearing Burton's—or the melancholiac's—actual
thoughts as they ramble on and grow out of one another and become ever
more intricately involved in a world of their own.   Its modern descendant
is the profoundly meditative, luxuriantly evocative style of Marcel Proust.

The curt manner is more pithy, more drastic:

'In the great Ant-hill of the whole world, I am an Ant; I have my part in the
Creation, I am a Creature; But there are ignoble Creatures.   God comes nearer; In
the great field of clay, of red earth, that man was made of, and mankind, I am a clod;

---

[2]The distinction is made by Professor M. W. Croll, 'The Baroque Style in Prose'
(cited in n. 1), 431 f.   It is important to grasp the difference in the origins of the two styles.
The *période coupé*, the 'curt manner', was consciously modelled on Seneca.   The 'loose
manner' was not really modelled closely on any classical author, but was built up from the
double wish (*a*) not to be formal like Cicero, and (*b*) to reflect the flexibility and the
occasional inconsequence and vagueness of the processes of thought.

I am a man, I have my part in the Humanity; But Man was worse than annihilated again.'[3]

However, most of the anti-Ciceronian authors passed fairly freely from one of these manners to the other, according to their subject-matter, and some were not averse to an occasional flight of Ciceronian rhetoric, provided they could return to firm ground after it.

This style, in its two developments, 'loose' and 'curt', was not only a method of arranging words. It was a way of thinking. It carried with it some potent moral and political implications. Since Ciceronian style was that of the church, of the universities, of the Jesuits, of the foreign offices, and of orthodoxy generally, this Senecan and Tacitean manner was associated with unorthodoxy and even libertinism. It was the voice of Seneca the Stoic, boldly independent and subject to God's will alone, the philosopher who was driven to death by a tyrant. It was the voice of Tacitus, the bitter historian who denounced tyranny by describing it, whose books were often made a cloak for the exposition of Machiavellian political theory. Pascal's brilliant letters against the Jesuits were partially modelled on the Stoic discourses of Epictetus, in which thought appears, like an athlete, stripped and ready for the contest. Seventeen centuries earlier a pupil of the Stoics had upheld simplicity of style against Cicero, and the rights of the citizen against Caesar: he was Brutus, the champion of the republic.

This was the style used by most of the great seventeenth-century prose writers. With the eighteenth century its eccentricities were planed down, and its wilful asymmetries discouraged: it began to assume the tone of polite semi-formal conversation; in time, it merged into the unassuming, straightforward, graceful simplicity of light eighteenth-century prose.

Meanwhile another style had been building up, a perfect echo of Cicero in vernacular prose. Varying from one language to another, varying also between authors and between subjects, it still was so fundamentally Ciceronian that it is often easier to detect the Roman cadences in a page of it than to tell which of the baroque stylists wrote the page. The greatest names in this field are:

Joseph Addison (1672–1719)
Jean-Louis Guez de Balzac (1597–1654)
Jacques-Bénigne Bossuet (1627–1704)
Louis Bourdaloue (1632–1704)
Edmund Burke (1729–97)
François de Salignac de La Mothe-Fénelon (1651–1715)
Edward Gibbon (1737–94)
Samuel Johnson (1709–84)
Jonathan Swift (1667–1745).

They were all highly educated men. As Johnson said of Greek, 'Learning is like lace: every man gets as much of it as he can.' Some of them

---

[3] Donne, Sermon 34 (St. Paul's, Whitsunday 1623).

hated the institution to which they went—like Gibbon; or the people who
taught them—like Voltaire; some, like Addison, loved the university; some
did badly at it through bad discipline, like Burke and Swift; but all did a
great deal of quiet solitary thinking and reading in large libraries (poor
Johnson in his father's bookshop), usually enough to form their minds
before they were twenty years of age.

The most obvious benefit derived from their classical reading is shared
by both schools of baroque writers, Ciceronians and anti-Ciceronians alike.
This is a rich variety of imaginative and intellectual material derived from
Greco-Roman literature. All the works of all of them are full of it. They
could not keep it out. They would not keep it out: any more than a well-
educated man nowadays would choose to suppress his knowledge of art and
music. It makes a bond between them all, whether they are separated by
time, like Browne and Burke, or by country and religion, like Bossuet and
Gibbon. They seem to belong to a single society of cultured men. Sometimes their membership in the society appears to exclude those of us who
know no Greek and Latin. That may be one reason for the comparative
neglect of these authors nowadays, when we would rather read a biography
of Gibbon than his history. Yet it gave their writings much beauty, a fund
of noble and powerful allusions, memories, and comparisons for which no
satisfactory modern substitute has been found, a richness of imagination
which offsets their cool rational style, and an impersonality which, by
taking them out of their immediate present, helps to make them immortal.

*   *   *   *

It is scarcely necessary to point out how all these writers were stimulated
by contact with the great minds of Rome and Greece. Even when they did
not quote the classics directly, they grew greater by their consciousness of
eternity. Before writing his finest sermons Bossuet used to read the best of
classical poetry, in order to raise his thoughts to the highest attainable pitch
of nobility; and, preparing himself to compose the funeral sermon on Queen
Marie-Thérèse, he shut himslef up alone, and for many hours read nothing
but Homer.

Besides this, the Ciceronian writers all used, in very various degrees, a
number of stylistic devices derived from Latin and Greek prose, which
through their work have now become naturalized in most modern languages.
Their aim was to produce an impression of *controlled power*. They chose to
do this by making their prose sonorous; rich; and, most important, symmetrical.

To achieve sonority they used long words derived directly from Latin,
rather than short ones derived from Anglo-Saxon or smoothed down by
passage through Old French. Bossuet, for instance, speaks of the Virgin
as *chair angélisée* (a phrase taken straight out of Tertullian); he is the first
to use the word *appréhensif*, and one of the first to write *régime*, *sapience*,
locution. Samuel Johnson's predilection for ponderous Latin nouns, adjectives, and verbs is well known: bipartition, equiponderant, vertiginous,
expunge, concatenation, irascibility, and his favourite, procrastination.
Boswell observed that he actually thought in simple Saxon terms, and then
translated into Latin, or rather into Johnsonese. *'The Rehearsal'*, he said,

'has not wit enough to keep it sweet'; and then, after a pause, 'it has not vitality enough to preserve it from putrefaction.'[4] This was what Goldsmith laughed at when he said that if Johnson were to write a fable about little fishes he would make them talk like whales. It should be remembered, however, that few of the baroque prose-writers introduced many new words from Latin. On the contrary, they cut many out which had been tentatively brought in by the men of the Renaissance. What they really did was to apply their taste to those already introduced as experiments, and to select and naturalize those which we now use. Johnson's mistake was to use so many words of Latin derivation and heavy intellectual content closely together without relief to the ear or the mind.

This mistake was not made by the French prosateurs. Balzac, chief of the founders of French baroque style, set his face sternly against every kind of word that kept French from being clear and harmonious: provincial expressions, archaisms, neologisms, and latinisms—not *all* words of Latin derivation, but those which, to a sensitive ear, sounded strange, heavy, pedantic, incompletely naturalized.[5] By such careful discernment he and others forged the fine, sharp, glittering steel of French prose, one of the best tools of thought ever created by man.

Yet prose is not only a tool. It can also be an instrument of music. The most skilful, least monotonous, and subtlest of the baroque musicians in words was Browne, who produced his finest effects by blending simple Anglo-Saxonisms with organ-toned words from Rome:

'We whose generations are ordained in this setting part of time, are providentially taken off from such imaginations; and, being necessitated to eye the remaining particle of futurity, are naturally constituted unto thoughts of the next world, and cannot excusably decline the consideration of that duration, which maketh pyramids pillars of snow, and all that's past a moment. . . . Gravestones tell truth scarce forty years. Generations pass while some trees stand, and old families last not three oaks.'[6]

For the sake of richness the baroque prose-writers chiefly cultivated repetition—either the use of synonyms, which is repetition of meaning, or the use of homophones, which is repetition of sound. Of this style, synonyms in twos and threes are a sure mark and unmistakable characteristic:

'supporting, assisting, and defending';[7]

---

[4]Boswell, *Life of Johnson* (Oxford ed., 1924), 2. 569.
[5]See G. Guillaumie, *J. L. Guez de Balzac et la prose française* (Paris, 1927), 132 f. Balzac attacked the use of such words as *onguent* and *auspices* ('c'est parler latin en français'), and reproached even Richelieu for calling someone a *pétulant exagérateur*. He himself, nevertheless, used words like *vécordie*, *helluon*, and *remore* (= *retard*): which shows, not that his standards were uneven, but that the plague of pedantic latinisms was very widespread. His real name, by the way, was Guez; Balzac was the name of a property in his mother's dowry, and he added it in order to appear noble.
[6]Browne, *Urn Burial*, c. 5.
[7]Johnson, *Life of Savage*.

'deliberate and creeping progress unto the grave';[8]

'la vertu du monde; vertu trompeuse et falsifiée; qui n'a que la mine et l'apparence';[9]

'the bonds and ligaments of the commonwealth, the pillars and the sustainers of every written statute';[10]

'de donner (aux maux) un grand cours, et de leur faire une ouverture large et spacieuse';[11]

'read not to contradict and confute; nor to believe and take for granted; nor to find talk and discourse; but to weigh and consider'.[12]

Homophones are more difficult to manage, but often very powerful:

'we are weighed down, we are swallowed up, irreparably, irrevocably, irre-coverably, irremediably';[13]

'prose admits of the two excellences you most admire, diction and fiction';[14]

and a famous modern example:

'government of the people, by the people, for the people'.[15]

An effective variation of this device, practised by none more magnificently than by Cicero, and learnt from him by most modern orators, is anaphora— repetition of the same word or phrase in the same position in successive clauses, hammering the idea home. Thus:

'Ce n'est là que le fond de notre misère, mais prenez garde,
    en voici le comble
    en voici l'excès
    en voici le prodige
    en voici l'abus
    en voici la malignité
    en voici l'abomination
        et, si ce terme ne suffit pas,
en voici, pour m'exprimer avec le prophète, l'abomination de la désolation.'[16]

---

[8]Browne, *Letter to a Friend.*
[9]Bossuet, *Sur l'honneur du monde*, 2.
[10]Milton, *Areopagitica.*
[11]Bossuet, *Sur la justice*, 3.
[12]Bacon, *Of Studies.*
[13]Donne, Sermon 66 (29 Jan. 1625/6).
[14]Pope, *Letter to a Noble Lord.*
[15]Lincoln, *Gettysburg Address.*
[16]Bourdaloue, *La Misère de notre condition.* (He went on, after this heaping up of separate terms, to work out each separately. See F. Brunetière, 'L'Éloquence de Bourdaloue', in *Études critiques sur l'histoire de la littérature française*, huitième série (Paris, 1907), 151 f.)

The noblest achievement of the baroque writers of prose is symmetry. Symmetry does not necessarily mean 1 = 1 balance, although it can mean that. A baroque cathedral, with a single great dome in the centre of its structure, is symmetrical. In prose as elsewhere, symmetry means a balanced proportion of parts corresponding to their importance in the general structure. Cicero was such a master of this art that he could extend it all through a long speech, balancing clauses in a sentence, sentences in a paragraph, paragraphs in a section, and sections one against another throughout the entire oration. This is not an external trick. The essence of it is logic; and it was during the baroque age, from the study of Cicero's oratory, that the leading speakers became fully familiar with the necessity for dividing each subject into large, easily distinguished, easily correlated aspects, and then subdividing those aspects into smaller topics to be handled separately. Bad speeches by uneducated men usually fail in this. Adolf Hitler, for example, had very little idea of it, and never wrote a good speech except when he happened to hit on a good idea for a framework before beginning; but emotional as they were, most of his speeches (public and private) were rambling and ill digested. Jesuit orators, on the other hand, are particularly skilful in the art of division, or logical analysis, which is emphasized in their training. A good instance is the second retreat sermon in Joyce's *A Portrait of the Artist as a Young Man*, but any Jesuit sermon will show it. In his sermon *On the Kingdom of God* Bourdaloue says the kingdom of God is

1 like a treasure, hidden away;
2 like a victory, to be fought for;
3 like a reward, kept in store;

and then subdivides each of these divisions—for instance, in 2 the victory must be won, first over the flesh, then over the Devil, then over the world.

On a smaller scale, the commonest methods of achieving symmetry in sentences and paragraphs are antithesis and climax. Both are familiar to us; we use them constantly; but it was the writers of the Renaissance and the baroque age who learnt them from the Greco-Roman prose authors, and developed them for us.

Antithesis can range all the way from the opposition of single words to the opposition of clauses, sentences, and paragraphs.[17]

---

[17]'Trouvez-moi, je vous en défie, dans quelque poète et dans quelque livre qu'il vous plaira, une belle chose qui ne soit pas une image ou une antithèse'. (Voltaire, quoted by Guillaumie (cited in n. 5), 444.) Antithesis ran mad in a comparatively early elaboration of English prose style—Euphuism. The precise origin of this curious set of mannerisms has not yet been determined. However, in an article called 'The Immediate Source of Euphuism' (*PMLA*, 53 (1938), 3. 678–86), W. Ringler gives reason for believing that Lyly and the others got it from the brilliant and celebrated Latin lectures of John Rainolds, of Corpus Christi College, Oxford, whose effects they set out to reproduce in English. The next question is, if this is true, where did Rainolds get it? Mr Ringler thinks he modelled his style on 'St. Augustine and Gregory Nazianzen'—which seems rather hard to believe—and on the teaching of the anti-Ciceronian humanist Vives. Now Vives himself was at Corpus from 1523 to 1525, and gave two remarkable courses of lectures (Sandys, *A History of Classical Scholarship*, Cambridge, 1908, 2. 214–15): he was a friend of Erasmus, another opponent of the imitation of Cicero, and was a superb teacher. If we consider that Euphuism is (*a*) highly formal

'No man is an island, entire of itself; every man is a piece of the continent, a part of the main';[18]

*   *   *   *

(The plan of having doctors to attend all legislators would) 'open a few mouths which are now closed, and close many more which are now open; curb the petulancy of the young, and correct the positiveness of the old, rouse the stupid, and damp the pert'.[19]

Of course the baroque poets, both dramatic and satiric, are full of it:

> Damn with faint praise, assent with civil leer,
> And, without sneering, teach the rest to sneer.[20]

Climax, which means 'ladder', is the enlargement and elevation of one thought through a graded description of its various aspects, in balanced words, phrases, sentences, or paragraphs rising to a powerful termination. Thus—

'But, my Lords, who is the man that, in addition to these disgraces and mischiefs of our army, has dared
> to authorize and associate to our arms the tomahawk and scalping-knife of the savage?
> to call into civilized alliance the wild and inhuman savage of the woods?
> to delegate to the merciless Indian the defence of disputed rights?
> and to wage the horrors of his barbarous war against our brethren?'[21]

And here is an overwhelming address to the atheist, by Dr. Donne:[22]

'I respite thee not till the day of judgement, when I may see thee upon thy knees, upon thy face, begging of the hills that they would fall down and cover thee from the fierce wrath of God, to ask thee then, Is there a God now? I respite thee not till the day of thine own death, when thou shalt have evidence enough that there is a God, though no other evidence but to find a Devil, and evidence enough that there is a heaven, though no other evidence but to feel hell; to ask thee then, Is there a God now? I respite thee but a few hours, but six hours, but till midnight. Wake then; and then, dark, and alone, hear God ask thee then, remember that I asked thee now, Is there a God? and if thou darest, say No.'

---

and artificial, (*b*) carefully symmetrical, (*c*) highly alliterative, (*d*) excessively learned and (*e*) not Ciceronian, we might conjecture that it was an English reflection of a newly created type of Latin style, worked out by a humanist like Vives who wished to achieve as much intricacy and artistry as Cicero without using Cicero's own patterns. (The speeches of Isocrates, whom Vives would no doubt know, combine alliteration and assonance and antithesis rather like Euphuism, although more moderately.)

[18] Donne, *Devotions*, 17.
[19] Swift, *A Voyage to Laputa*, c. 6.
[20] Pope, *Epistle to Dr. Arbuthnot*, 201–2.
[21] Pitt on the war with the American colonies (*On the Motion for an Address to the Throne*, 18 Nov. 1777).
[22] Donne, Sermon 48 (25 Jan. 1628/9).

Within climax there is one symmetrical device which is so natural and adaptable that it can be used on almost every level of speech without seeming artificial. And yet it was invented by Greek teachers of rhetoric; not all the Romans adopted it or managed it with confidence; but Cicero above all others made it his own; and, although it is not native to the modern European languages, it has now, without leaving the realm of artistic prose, entered the ordinary speech of western nations. This is the tricolon. Tricolon means a unit made up of three parts. The third part in a tricolon used in oratory is usually more emphatic and conclusive than the others. This is the chief device used in Lincoln's Gettysburg Address, and is doubled at its conclusion:

'But, in a larger sense, we cannot dedicate—we cannot consecrate—we cannot hallow this ground.'
'We here highly resolve that these dead shall not have died in vain—that this nation, under God, shall have a new birth of freedom—and that government of the people, by the people, for the people, shall not perish from the earth.'

Although Lincoln himself knew no Cicero, he had learnt this and other beauties of Ciceronian style from studying the prose of the baroque age, when it was perfected in English, in French, and in other tongues.

'Mummy is become merchandise, Mizraim cures wounds, and Pharaoh is sold for balsams.'[23]

'La gloire! Qu'y a-t-il pour le chrétien de plus pernicieux et de plus mortel? quel appât plus dangereux? quelle fumée plus capable de faire tourner les meilleures têtes?'[24]

'The notice which you have been pleased to take of my labours, had it been early, had been kind; but it has been delayed till I am indifferent, and cannot enjoy it; till I am solitary, and cannot impart it; till I am known, and do not want it.'[25]

Such devices (as is evident from the examples quoted) were not used separately but in combination. And there were many more of them. The art lay in combining them aptly. A piece of good baroque prose was planned as carefully and engineered as elaborately, with as many interlocking stresses, as bold a design, and as strong a foundation as a baroque palace or a Bach Mass. And although modern prose is seldom constructed so systematically, these devices are now among its natural instruments. The best writers and speakers use them freely. Audiences remember them. Every American recalls the tricolon in which Roosevelt stated the country's need of broader social assistance:

---

[23] Browne, *Urn Burial*, c. 5.
[24] Bossuet, *Oraison funèbre d'Henriette d'Angleterre*.
[25] Johnson, *Letter to Lord Chesterfield*. From a later age there is a famous and beautiful tricolon in Landor's *Aesop and Rhodope*:

'Laodameia died; Helen died; Leda, the beloved of Jupiter, went before.'

'one-third of a nation, ill-housed, ill-clad, ill-nourished'.

And, acting by instinct, the popular memory of both Britain and America
has condensed Churchill's most famous phrase from its original shape into
another immortal tricolon:

'blood, sweat, and tears'.

The debt of English to the King James version of the Bible, and through it
to Hebrew literature, is very great; but such phrases as these show that the
debt of English and the other western European languages to the classical
critics, historians, and orators is much greater. The best modern prose has
the suppleness of the Greeks, the weight of Rome.

CURT AND LOOSE PROSE:
JONSON, SHAKESPEARE, AND BACON

Jonas A. Barish

1

Since Jonson's stylistic habits differ so radically from Shakespeare's, a rapid
comparison of representative passages may serve here as a convenient point
of departure. First, the opening prose speech from the first part of *Henry IV:*

> *Falstaff.* Now *Hal*, what time of day is it Lad?
> *Prince Hal.* Thou art so fat-witted with drinking of olde Sacke, and vnbutton-
> ing thee after Supper, and sleeping vpon Benches in the afternoone, that thou hast
> forgotten to demand that truely, which thou wouldest truly know. What a diuell
> hast thou to do with the time of the day? vnlesse houres were cups of Sacke, and
> minutes Capons, and clockes the tongues of Bawdes, and dialls the signes of
> Leaping-houses, and the blessed Sunne himselfe a faire hot Wench in Flame-coloured
> Taffata; I see no reason, why thou shouldest bee so superfluous, to demaund the
> time of the day. (L. 369; *IHIV* I.ii.1–13)

Then, two opening speeches from *Every Man out of his Humour* and
Poetaster:

Reprinted by permission of the publishers from Jonas A. Barish, *Ben Jonson and the Language
of Prose Comedy*, Ch. 2, "Prose as Prose," at pp. 45–51, 54–66. Cambridge, Mass.: Harvard
University Press, Copyright, 1960, by the President and Fellows of Harvard College. Some
of the notes have been omitted, and the remainder renumbered to run in sequence.

Come, come, leaue these fustian protestations: away, come, I cannot abide these gray-headed ceremonies. Boy, fetch me a glasse, quickly, I may bid these gentlemen welcome; giue 'hem a health here: I mar'le whose wit 'twas to put a prologue in yond' sackbuts mouth: they might well thinke hee'd be out of tune, and yet you'ld play vpon him too. (*EMO* Ind. 319–325)

Young master, master OVID, doe you heare? gods a mee! away with your *songs*, and *sonnets*; and on with your gowne and cappe, quickly: here, here, your father will be a man of this roome presently. Come, nay, nay, nay, nay, be briefe. These verses too, a poyson on 'hem, I cannot abide 'hem, they make mee readie to cast, by the bankes of *helicon*. Nay looke, what a rascally vntoward thing this *poetrie* is: I could teare 'hem now. (*Poet.* I.i.4–11)

The first thing we notice is that the rhythm of the Shakespearean passage is slower, fuller, more oratorical, that of the Jonsonian passages more abrupt, staccato, and sharp. And these differences can be quickly traced to the fact that Shakespeare is using not only longer phrases, but a more oratorical, more symmetrical syntax than Jonson. In

> Thou art so fat-witted
> with drinking of olde Sacke,
> and vnbuttoning thee after Supper,
> and sleeping vpon Benches in the afternoone,

we find not only the parisonic exactness of "drinking," "vnbuttoning," and "sleeping," but the fact that the three phrases are arranged in climactic order: each succeeding one represents a more advanced stage in Falstaff's surrender to sloth, and each is longer than its predecessor; with "sleeping vpon Benches in the afternoone" we reach the fullest phrase and Falstaff's final collapse into indolence. But this sequence itself forms only a suspension, the first, or causal, half of the "so...that" pattern..., and leads into a resolution, the assertion of an effect, which itself turns a somewhat intricate little antithesis on the object of "demand." The question that follows serves as a pause, and also to reengage the logical machinery of the argument. After which the Prince embarks on another periodic sentence, more elaborate than the first, with a much more strongly marked climax—

> vnlesse
> houres were cups of Sacke,
> and minutes Capons,
> and clockes the tongues of Bawdes,
> and dialls the signes of Leaping-houses,
> and the blessed Sunne himselfe a faire hot Wench in
> Flame-coloured Taffata

—and consequently a more incisive resolution, which forms a cadence not only to the sentence itself but to the whole speech, and crowns the argument of it at the same time. The speech has thus a beginning, a middle, and an end —an introductory flourish, a development, and a full close—and its internal parts are constructed with similar solidity.

By contrast, the speeches of Carlo Buffone and Luscus simulate live language much more closely, or seem to, and the reason is that they reject the figures of balance, parallel, and climax used by Shakespeare. They are heavily punctuated with monosyllabic expletives like "Come, come," "gods a mee," "Nay looke," which introduce a nervous stutter into the rhythm and prevent it from achieving any full curve. Occasional symmetrical details, such as the "fustian protestations" and "gray-headed ceremonies" of Carlo, jab at each other instead of acting as rhythmic pairs, or else, as in "away with your *songs*, and *sonnets*; and on with your gowne and cappe," they suggest self-conscious cuteness on the part of the speaker. Logical connectives are scarce. In "fetch me a glasse, quickly, I may bid these gentlemen welcome; giue 'hem a health here," the expected "that" or its equivalent between the first two clauses and the "and" that might have linked the second two have both been suppressed, so that Carlo seems to be pouncing convulsively from one idea to another. "Giue 'hem a health here," stitched on its apposition, has the air of a sudden afterthought. Then the malicious remarks about the boy, who has gone off-stage to fetch a glass, consist of three clauses glaringly unlike. Like Prince Hal in his final sentence, Carlo pursues a single metaphor through his, but the inequality among the members sets them tensely at odds with each other instead of engaging them in a cooperative enterprise, and the rhythm, as a result, is jagged and discontinuous instead of round and sonorous.

At such moments, Jonson reproduces the accent of living speech so convincingly that he seems to have abandoned rhetorical artifice. We are indebted to Morris Croll for showing that this kind of language, which moves in streaks and flashes rather than with a steady pulsation, springs itself from a highly articulate rhetorical theory, that of anti-Ciceronianism, that it has its roots in certain philosophical attitudes, chiefly Stoic and libertine, and that it has its own preferred masters of style in Seneca and Tacitus.

The writers whom Croll calls "baroque"—a term that will be adopted here for its convenience without any insistence on its exactness[1]—shared a distrust of the Ciceronian mode of sentence formation. This is not to say that they despised Cicero, the Vitruvius of Renaissance prose, or were uninfluenced by him, but only that they reacted against his oratorical manner. Jonson's admiration of Cicero is writ large (too large) in *Catiline*, and elsewhere, but Jonson was one of the least Ciceronian of writers. Ciceronian style was marked above all by the periodic sentence, as in the passage from

---

[1] The struggles to convert this concept from art history into a meaningful term for literary history have not been entirely happy. The further attempt to differentiate, as the art historians do, between "baroque" and "mannerist" in literature has only compounded confusion and darkened counsel. René Wellek's caveat against the promiscuous use of "baroque" ("The Concept of Baroque in Literary Scholarship," pp. 77–109) has not prevented the appearance of more speculation concerning the baroque *Zeitgeist*, more freewheeling analogies between the arts, more attempts to define "baroque" in narrowly stylistic terms, as well as a generous quota of rebukes from the cautious. The present study will use the term "baroque" because Croll used it, because there is no satisfactory substitute, and because—for all its uncertainties —it still seems a useful way of suggesting stylistic procedures that may, in the last analysis, transcend the bounds of a single art and relate to a whole cultural conformation.

Henry IV above,[2] where the syntax remains incomplete up to some well-defined turning point, with phrases and clauses tending to mass themselves in parallel formation on both sides of the turning point. The characteristic effects of this style were achieved by advance planning: one knew from the outset of a period where it was going and how it was going to get there. When it reached its destination, it afforded the gratification of a design finally complete, every piece falling into its place in the whole. Baroque style, on the other hand, aimed to give the impression, at least, of spontaneity, and hence its first concern was to break the stranglehold of the suspended sentence, to keep its syntax unencumbered and uncommitted, so as to be free to improvise in any way at any moment.

Now it may be objected with perfect justice at this point that Hal's speech *does* give the impression of spontaneity, that far from seeming artfully composed, it sounds as casually offhand as the speeches of Carlo or Luscus. Improvisation needs ground rules, and Hal's construction of a certain syntactic frame gives him freedom: he does not have to worry about what to do with his clauses, or where to put them. Having erected a rapid scaffolding that presupposes some degree of balance and likeness, he can proceed to forget it and concentrate on the details; he can extemporize, as he does, with lordly abandon. The suspended sentence, for him, is no stranglehold, but a set of strong struts. Shakespeare may be planning his effects with the utmost care, but Hal, at least, seems to be talking with perfect naturalness. One wonders, then, whether baroque writers were not misled, partly by abuses of Ciceronian style, partly by its origin in formal oratory, into thinking that it contained some intrinsic barrier to uninhibited thought; whether, tilting against the reader's expectations, they did not find themselves conducting campaigns of sabotage that involved more premeditation than the premeditated style they were warring against; whether, as a result, their own rhetoric is not parasitic in a peculiar way, unthinkable without the background of "normal" Renaissance practice.

In any event, baroque writers regarded Ciceronianism as an invitation to glibness and insincerity, and their first aim was to replace its logical schemes with various nonlogical maneuvers of their own, which Croll has grouped into the two categories of the "curt style" and the "loose style."

The curt style, illustrated above in the passage from *Every Man out of his Humour*, owes its name, and its other names of *stile coupé* and *stile serré*, to its abruptness and choppiness in contrast to Ciceronian "roundness"; its characteristic device is the so-called "exploded" period, formed of independent members not linked by conjunctions but set apart by a vocal pattern of stress, pitch, and juncture rendered typographically by a colon or a semicolon, sometimes a comma. The members of the exploded period tend to brevity, also to inequality of length, variation in form, and unpredict-

---

[2]Of course the Shakespearean passage is not really Ciceronian, but only relatively or approximately so in contrast with Jonson. "The Ciceronian style," as Croll has pointed out, "cannot be reproduced in English, or indeed in any modern language. The ligatures of its comprehensive period are not found in the syntax of an uninflected tongue; and the artifices necessary to supply their function must produce either fantastic distortion or insufferable bombast." ("Attic Prose," *Schelling Anniversary Papers*, p. 134.)

ability of order; hence they are likely to suggest the effect of live thinking rather than of logical premeditation. The "mere fact" or main idea of the period is apt to be exhausted in the first member; subsequent members explore the same idea imaginatively, through metaphor or aphorism or example, but not through ordered analysis.

Natures that are hardned to *evill*, you shall sooner breake, then make straight; they are like poles that are crooked, and dry: there is no attempting them.[3] (*Disc.* 36–38)

They are, what they are on the sudden; they shew presently, like *Graine*, that, scatter'd on the top of the ground, shoots up, but takes no root; has a yellow blade, but the eare empty. (*Disc.* 685–688)

The great theeves of a State are lightly the officers of the Crowne; they hang the lesse still; play the Pikes in the Pond; eate whom they list. (*Disc.* 1306–08)

In each of these instances, the initial member encompasses the central idea at a single stroke; the members that follow illuminate or particularize with metaphor. In the last example, Jonson exchanges one metaphor for another: the officers of the crown start as thieves of the state and end as great pikes in a pond. And if one were to quote the period that follows, one would discover the same officers turning into fowlers who spread nets for harmless birds but allow the hawks and buzzards to escape. The progress of such a period, then, is typically not a logical sequence but "a series of imaginative moments occurring in a logical pause or suspension,"[4] in which ideas develop out of each other associatively rather than according to any predetermined scheme. That the curt style cannot dispense with logic altogether is perhaps too obvious to need saying. What it can do is to excise logical ligatures, to play haphazardly and capriciously with its elements so as to minimize the sense of logical straitness.

Because of the freedom of its internal elements, the curt period lends itself to the expression of quick shifts in feeling, afterthoughts, self-corrections, unexpected interpolations or dislocations of attention, and since in so doing it simulates so convincingly the processes of live thought, it becomes an ideal instrument for certain kinds of theatrical prose. Jonson uses it in a variety of ways. One characteristic way is to turn it into a vehicle for wit, allowing each successive clause, as it springs from its predecessor, to exploit the latent potentialities of a metaphor:

Ne're trust me, CVPID, but you are turn'd a most acute gallant of late, the edge of my wit is cleere taken off with the fine and subtile stroke of your thin-ground tongue, you fight with too poinant a phrase, for me to deale with. (*CR* I.i.77–81)

---

[3]Citations from Jonson throughout are to the edition of C. H. Herford and Percy and Evelyn Simpson, 11 vols. (Oxford 1925–1952). The following abbreviations are used . . . :

> *Disc.: Timber, or Discoveries*
> *CR: Cynthia's Revels*
> *EMO: Every Man Out of his Humour*
> *Poet.: Poetaster*
> *SW: Epicene, or The Silent Woman* . . . .

[4]Croll, "Baroque Style". . . .

Here the epithet "acute" used by Mercury in the first clause prompts its own figurative extension into the "thin-ground tongue" of the second, after which the pointed tongue becomes the sword with which Cupid "fights" his combats of wit. . . .

*　　*　　*　　*

It should perhaps be emphasized that the speeches of such characters as Wasp, Tucca, and Carlo Buffone do not represent a mere tic of punctuation on the one hand or a mere slavish transcription of heard language on the other, but a distinct style; their barking phrases translate into stage idiom the staccato effects of *stile coupé*. It is true enough that people often speak so, and it is also true that one may find patches of similar language in the popular comedy of the 1590's. But what in earlier writers is a mere incidental twitch Jonson transmutes into a structural principle. He takes the sprawling, ramshackle popular language and disengages from it the strain congenial to his own rhetorical bent, thus effecting a kind of merger between colloquial speech and his own Stoic models. The result is a stage prose that combines the vitality of live language with the authority and expressive potency of a formed rhetoric.

The highly impressionable Shakespeare was not likely to be immune to influence from this rhetorical current, and it may be suggested that along with the primary voice . . . , Shakespeare has a subsidiary voice that sounds much like a modified version of the curt style. One might, however, prefer to call the Shakespearean variant something like "plain statement," since it tends to consist of a procession of simple declarative or imperative clauses with little of the "explosiveness" peculiar to curt style:

I haue dogg'd him like his murtherer. He does obey euery point of the Letter that I dropt, to betray him: He does smile his face into more lynes, then is in the new Mappe, with the augmentation of the Indies: you haue not seene such a thing as tis: I can hardly forbeare hurling things at him, I know my Ladie will strike him: if shee doe, hee'l smile, and take't for a great fauour. (L.284; *TN* III.ii.81–89)

I would the Duke we talke of were return'd againe. this vngenitur'd Agent will vn-people the Prouince with Continencie. Sparrowes must not build in his house-eeues, because they are lecherous: The Duke yet would haue darke deeds darkelie answered, hee would neuer bring them to light: would hee were return'd. (L.92; *MM* III.ii.183–190)

Looke, th'vnfolding Starre calles vp the Shepheard; put not your selfe into amazement, how these things should be; all difficulties are but easie vvhen they are knowne. Call your executioner; and off with *Barnardines* head: I will giue him a present shrift, and aduise him for a better place (L.95: *MM* IV.ii.219–227)

*　　*　　*　　*

Such speeches show certain traits of the *stile coupé*: its discontinuousness, its avoidance of logical particles, its shifts in grammatical form, perhaps above all its apparent innocence of rhetorical cunning. They differ from their Jonsonian counterparts in that the members tend to be more equal in length, and also longer, so that the rhythm is slower and gentler. Characteristically Shakespeare will insert into the middle of an otherwise highly wrought discourse one or two such clauses, which have the effect of tranquilizing the rhythm, of affording a moment's breathing-space for the actor and a pause in the forward march of the argument.

What the Shakespearean passages do not have is the bristling asymmetry of the Jonsonian speeches. George Williamson has objected to Croll's emphasis on this trait, and suggested that Croll, having commited himself to the analogy with baroque, was led to discover asymmetry in places where, in fact, symmetry predominates.[5] Williamson, by way of rejoinder, illustrates from Bacon, and with this correction, insofar as it applies to Bacon, one can only gladly agree: asymmetry, where it occurs in Bacon, remains tangential. But Jonson is another matter. "Asymmetrical" seems to define the shape of Jonson's prose so exactly that one is tempted to use it to describe the topography of his mind. Jonson delights in bending the logical axis of syntax a few degrees one way or another in order to interrupt a symmetrical pattern, to sprawl suddenly or compress unexpectedly in a way that pulls the reader up short. One may get at the difference between Bacon's style and Jonson's by comparing a passage from *The Advancement of Learning* with Jonson's adaptation of it in the *Discoveries*.

This grew speedily to an excess; for men began to hunt more after words than matter; more after the choiceness of the phrase, and the round and clean composition of the sentence, and the sweet falling of the clauses, and the varying and illustration of their works with tropes and figures, than after the weight of matter, worth of subject, soundness of argument, life of invention or depth of judgment.[6]

The thing that impresses itself on one immediately here is the careful regularity of the sentence. The exact antithesis "more after words than matter" undergoes artful expansion in the member that follows, first into four aspects of the hunt after words:

the choiceness of the phrase,
the round and clean composition of the sentence,
the sweet falling of the clauses,
the varying and illustration of their works with tropes and figures.

The four phrases fall neatly into two sets of two each. In each set the second phrase is longer than the first, and each of the phrases of the second set is longer than its counterpart in the first. One result of this strict geometrical plotting is to produce an effect of climax, to bring us to a rhythmic plateau on the phrase "with tropes and figures," after which the second half of the antithesis elaborates itself serenely into a series of five component phrases that observe exact correspondence of parts. If one were to continue quoting at this point, one would discover Bacon launching into a new sequence of parallel statements extending through five sentences: "Then grew the flowing

---

[5] *The Senecan Amble*, p. 145, p. 156, n. 1.
[6] *The Advancement of Learning*, Everyman ed., p. 24.

and watery vein of Osorius the Portuguese bishop, to be in price. Then did
Sturmius ... Then did Car of Cambridge ... Then did Erasmus ... Then grew
... In sum ..." As for the sentence preceding the quoted extract, it leads up
to the antithesis between words and matter by enumerating four reasons why
"eloquence and variety of discourse" came to be preferred to solidity of
thought. The extract from Bacon, then, not only displays a high degree of
formal clarity in itself: it forms part of a sequence that is highly articulated
logically, that unfolds in parallel and antithetic statements and that preserves
parisonic correspondence in many of its inner parts in order to emphasize its
logical divisions.

When we turn to Jonson's paraphrase, the first thing we notice is that the
period in question is no longer a complete grammatical unit. It is fused to
what precedes it, by virtue of the fact that its first verb, "make," simply
forms the last in a series of subordinate verbs dependent on "Wee must" in
the prior sentence. The prior sentence itself issues a plea for patience in the
study of style that flickers restlessly back and forth between positive and
negative counsel. The plea concludes, then, with the paraphrase from Bacon:

Then make exact animadversion where style hath degenerated, where flourish'd, and
thriv'd in choisenesse of Phrase, round and cleane composition of sentence, sweet
falling of the clause, varying an illustration by tropes and figures, weight of Matter,
worth of Subject, soundnesse of Argument, life of Invention, and depth of Judgement.
This is *Monte potiri*, to get the hill. For no perfect Discovery can bee made upon
a flat or a levell. (*Disc.* 2116–24)

Jonson has eliminated Bacon's dichotomy between rhetorical curiosity and
solidity of thought, and lumped together the phrases from both sides of
Bacon's antithesis in a single top-heavy series. Further, he has cut away
most of the articles and all the connectives, so that the period now produces
an unexpected effect of abruptness. Finally, he has embedded the passage in
what is itself, so to speak, an asymmetrical context, commencing with the
freely zigzagging period that precedes the quoted excerpt, and ending with
the two brusque periods that close the section like two hammer blows. He
ends, hence, with a gnarled and knotted texture only remotely akin to the
clearspun weave of the Baconian original.

One does find occasional stretches of exact or nearly exact symmetry in
Jonson, but these tend to have a sledge-hammer brevity that transmits first
of all a sense of power, and only secondarily the feeling of balance: "Some
wits are swelling, and high; others low and still: Some hot and fiery; others
cold and dull: One must have a bridle, the other a spurre" (*Disc.* 678–680).
And when Jonson uses exact symmetry in his plays, he is almost always
ridiculing it as an affectation on the part of the speaker. But in fact symmetrical repetition in Jonson infrequently extends—as it does here—beyond
the bounds of a single clause. For the most part it is phrasal rather than
clausal symmetry, which means that it appears in unpredictable clumps; and
so instead of shaping the outlines of the syntax as a whole, and providing
clear signposts from one unit of utterance to the next, it merely intensifies the
prevailing irregularity.

There shall the Spectator see some, insulting with Joy; others, fretting with Melancholy; raging with Anger; mad with Love; boiling with Avarice; undone with Riot; tortur'd with expectation; consum'd with feare: no perturbation in common life, but the Orator findes an example of it in the Scene. (*Disc.* 2537–43)

The violent verbal adjectives, the absence of linking terms, the heavy pointing, place a greater and greater weight on each member of the series, especially since nothing signals to us when the series will end. The series erupts, flings itself at us with steadily increasing pressure, and then gathers and collapses into the summary that follows the colon. The sentence travels through fields of force rather than through preordained paths of logic.

The fact is that although Bacon pioneered in anti-Ciceronianism, his own style remains conservative in another way. As George Williamson has shown, Baconian prose has close affinities with Euphuism,[7] and Euphuism imposes constraints of its own. If the suspensions of a Ciceronian period demand grammatical resolution, the symmetrical configurations of Euphuistic prose demand psychological resolution—the more so the more the logicality of the design becomes evident, the more the reader comes to expect for each turn a counterturn. In a context of precise antitheses, the first half of an antithesis, no matter how self-contained grammatically, cries out for its matching other half. "The unicorn is white; the hippogriff is black. The unicorn is graceful; the hippogriff is clumsy. The unicorn is caught by maidens;..." One might speak of such a suspension as paratactic, occurring after a grammatically closed unit, in the manner of a coordinate clause, in contrast to the hypotactic suspension of Ciceronian style, where the grammar remains "open" until the suspension is resolved. But whatever term one applies to it, one must recognize that such a technique sets up expectations as exigent as those of the more familiar Ciceronian variety. Bacon's style, on the whole, commits itself to satisfying such expectations. The baroque writers properly speaking are those who eschew both sorts of suspension, the hypotactic and the paratactic, or—even more important—who initiate periodic or symmetrical motions only to frustrate them.

This is precisely Jonson's procedure. Where he arouses expectations of symmetry, it is usually for the purpose of violating it. When an implicitly symmetrical pattern is perpetually being disturbed and thwarted by small changes in form, we have the phenomenon of symmetry clashing with asymmetry that is at the heart of baroque stylistic practice.[8] The following passage, encompassing several periods, adheres as closely as Jonson ordinarily ever does to a strict oratorical pattern:

And an intelligent woman, if shee know by her selfe the least defect, will bee most curious, to hide it: and it becomes her. If shee be short, let her sit much, lest when shee stands, shee be thought to sit. If shee haue an ill foot, let her weare her gowne the longer, and her shoo the thinner. If a fat hand, and scald nailes, let her carue the lesse, and act in gloues. If a sowre breath, let her neuer discourse fasting: and

---

[7] *The Senecan Amble*, pp. 89, 115, 118, 120, 184, and *passim*.
[8] Croll, "Baroque Style"....

alwaies talke at her distance. If shee haue black and rugged teeth, let her offer the lesse at laughter, especially if shee laugh wide, and open. (*SW* IV.i.37–46)

The anaphoral "If shee" and "let her" establish a repeated figure on which Jonson plays constant and surprising variations. The short first member of each period undergoes its own vicissitudes: "If shee *be* short," "If shee *haue* an *ill foot*," "If a fat hand, and scald nailes" (the verb vanishes, and its object unexpectedly doubles), "If a sowre breath" (the object becomes single again), "If shee haue black and rugged teeth" (the verb re-enters with a new configuration of one noun and two modifiers as object). The parallel apodoses shift form even more fluidly, maintaining an air of exact symmetry and yet escaping from it at every moment. The result is not symmetry but asymmetry, perpetual displacements and dislocations of detail within a rhythmically symmetrical framework. This, moreover, from the play of Jonson's which more than any other simulates effects of balance in its dialogue.

2

The loose style, Croll's other subcategory of the baroque, differs from the curt style in that it prefers to multiply connectives rather than to suppress them. It tends also to longer members and longer periods, but its character is determined by its habit of heaping up conjunctions and by the kind of conjunctions it chooses: simple coordinates such as "and" and "or," which involve the least possible syntactic commitment to what has gone before, and, even more typically, the stricter relative and subordinating conjunctions used as though they were mere coordinates. And all this, as Croll urges, in order to free the period from formal restraints, to enable it to move with the utmost license from point to point, to follow nothing but the involutions of the thinking mind. For the enchaining suspensions of the Ciceronian period the loose style substitutes its own devices, the parenthesis and the absolute construction. The usefulness of the latter especially to a writer working in a resolved style is, as Croll has explained, that of all constructions it is "the one that commits itself least and lends itself best to the solution of difficulties that arise in the course of a spontaneous and unpremeditated progress." It gives a writer carte blanche, enabling him to interrupt himself at will so as to travel in any cross-direction he pleases without dictating any alteration of the original syntax. It may be thrust in almost anywhere, and by its very nature—absolute, independent—forces most of the burden of logical connection upon the reader. Both the parenthesis and the absolute construction are favorites with Jonson, and sometimes he uses the two together in the same sentence.

... and presently goe, and redeeme him; for, being her brother, and his credit so amply engag'd as now it is, when she shal heare (as hee cannot him selfe, but hee must out of extremitie report it) that you came, and offered your selfe so kindly, and with that respect of his reputation, why, the benefit cannot but make her dote, and grow madde of your affections. (*EMO* V.viii.14–20)

Jonson has here made the absolute construction elliptical, by withholding the subject, "he," while the parenthesis intrudes with the utmost casualness and tenuousness of reference into the middle of a subordinate clause.

The most massive instance of Jonson's use of the absolute construction may be quoted as a curiosity of the loose style:

Mary, your friends doe wonder, sir, the *Thames* being so neere, wherein you may drowne so handsomely; or *London*-bridge, at a low fall, with a fine leape, to hurry you downe the streame; or, such a delicate steeple, i' the towne, as *Bow*, to vault from; or, a brauer height, as *Pauls*; or, if you affected to doe it neerer home, and a shorter way, an excellent garret windore, into the street; or, a beame, in the said garret, with this halter; which they haue sent, and desire, that you would sooner commit your graue head to this knot, then to the wed-lock nooze; or, take a little sublimate, and goe out of the world, like a rat; or a flie (as one said) with a straw i' your arse: any way, rather, then to follow this goblin *matrimony*. (*SW* II.ii.20-32)

In this quintessentially Jonsonian loose period, we are confronted immediately either with a drastic ellipsis, which must be filled in with some phrase ("Mary, your friends doe wonder, sir, *why you do not make away with yourself at once*") in order to complete the sense, or else with a huge series of absolute constructions that seems to behave as a suspension and yet never leads to a resolution. Seems to behave so, at least, to a reader. A reader is likely to demand the completion of syntactic patterns much more stringently than a listener, who is accustomed, in talk, to hearing such patterns form, dissolve, and drift off into others without ever fulfilling themselves. The reader awaits with a certain tension the decisive return that will close the orbit; a listener may be perfectly content to let the syntax turn into a wandering fire. And since Jonson was in this case writing for the stage, he may simply have pushed to an extreme the tendency of the baroque period to deal brusquely with its own syntactic commitments.

The absolute constructions here, it may be noticed, are in themselves, after the first, somewhat elliptical, requiring the reinstatement of the verbal phrase "being so neere" in each case. Then the extreme irregularity of the parallel members should be observed; each has its own unique configuration of subordinate clauses or modifying phrases or epithets, so that gradually the sense of parallel form all but evaporates, and we are left with a series of defiantly dissimilar constructions hooked together with "or's" and "and's," spinning freely in grammatical space and almost uncontrolled by any center of gravity. The effect of climax proceeds partly from the simple agglomeration of details and partly from the rhythmic speedup toward the end that leads into the recapitulary formula, "any way, rather, then to follow this goblin *matrimony*."

A further trait of loose style illustrated in this passage is what Croll has called the "linked" or "trailing" period, occurring "when a member depends, not upon the general idea, or the main word, of the preceding member, but upon its final word or phrase alone." The effect of such tactics is, as usual, to reduce to its minimum the interdependence of the successive members, to give the period, at any moment, a thrust forward into new areas. Truewit enumerates several of the high places from which Morose may fling himself before leading up to the mention and then to the proffering of a noose. At this point a shift to the relative "which," dependent as it is solely on the word "halter," deflects the absolute constructions from their course and leaves them stranded, at the same time catapulting the period into new grammatical territory. The period now follows a trajectory determined by the verb "desire," and lands finally a great distance from its starting point. This technique of pushing a period forward into fresh syntactic domain with scarcely a backward glance at the ground already traveled is one way in which anti-Ciceronian writers avoided the oratorical or "circular" Ciceronian period with its necessary return to some initial syntactic postulate. And it was this disregard of what he considered self-evident principles of grammatical law and order that led Coleridge to describe Senecan style as a series of thoughts "strung together like beads, without any causation or progression," and caused Saintsbury to complain of the abuse of conjunctions among seventeenth-century writers, who tended "apparently out of mere wantonness, to prefer a single sentence jointed and rejointed, parenthesised and postscripted, till it does the duty of a paragraph, to a succession of orderly sentences each containing the expression of a simple or moderately complex thought"[9]—a stricture from which he unaccountably exempted Jonson.

But the writers in question intended to be wanton as the mind is wanton, to transcribe the process of thought onto the page instead of stifling it, as they thought, within prescribed logical schemes. "Je ne peints pas l'estre. Je peints le passage: non un passage d'aage en autre, ou, comme dict le peuple, de sept en sept ans, mais de jour en jour, de minute en minute."[10] Whether in fact a process of thought has any verifiable reality apart from the words that incarnate it, and whether, if so, the irregular modes of syntax preferred by most of the anti-Ciceronians are necessarily any truer to thought, any more "natural," than the suspensions of the Ciceronians or the perfected antitheses of Euphuism, are questions that Renaissance authors did not raise. They assumed that regularity was artful, irregularity natural and spontaneous, and they wrote accordingly. In the case of Jonson, a mild paradox emerges: despite his fervent belief in the hard labor of composition, for which he was both admired and ridiculed by his contemporaries, he adopted a rhetorical mode associated with improvisation. Probably— despite his own protestations to the contrary (*Disc.* 695–700)—he worked as hard to roughen and irregularize his prose as others did to polish and regularize. As George Williamson has demonstrated, imitation of Seneca could lead to something very close to Euphuism. In Jonson's case it did not. He copied in Seneca only the vein of curtness and asymmetry for which he had a temperamental affinity, and in so doing produced a style more Senecan than Seneca's, insofar as Senecanism implied rebellion against rhetorical constraint.

---

[9] "English Prose Style," in *Miscellaneous Essays* (London, 1892), p. 7.
[10] Montaigne, "Du repentir," *Essais*, ed. Albert Thibaudet, Bibliothèque de la Pléiade (Paris, 1958), p. 899.

THE PURITAN
ANTI-RHETORICAL STYLE

Harold Fisch

I

The change which overcame English prose in the seventeenth century, has
been well described by numerous literary historians on both sides of the
Atlantic during the last seventy years or so. An important landmark was a
paper by R. F. Jones in 1930, in which he pointed out, among other things,
the striking differences in style between Glanvill's *Vanity of Dogmatizing*
(1661) and the same material revised some time afterwards to form the fifth
of his *Essays on Several Important Subjects* (1676). On such grounds,
scholars came to take the years immediately following the Restoration as the
period in which the new style was born. A special significance was attached
to the date of the incorporation of the Royal Society, 1662, for the new
writers were all more or less closely associated with the Society and were
influenced not only by the empirical and rationalist character of its philosophical teaching but also by its linguistic policy as formulated, for instance,
by its first historian, Thomas Sprat, in his *History of the Royal Society*
(1667). Of more recent years, Professor L. C. Knights in an essay entitled,
'Bacon and the Seventeenth Century Dissociation of Sensibility,' has stressed
the significant place of Francis Bacon, both as a theorist and a practical innovator, in the movement for a 'mathematical plainness' of expression. This
enabled one to date the movement, in its early beginnings, from about 1605,
the year of the publication of Bacon's *Advancement of Learning*.

   The object of this article is to indicate the efforts of a quite different
group of people, namely the Puritans, from an even earlier date, to limit the
use of rhetoric and assure the predominance of a plain and severe style. The
Puritans were primarily concerned, of course, with a fit prose for sermons
and works of devotion, but in an age when religious standards occupied a
central place in men's thoughts and actions, a rhetorical ideal of this kind
was bound to have the most widespread consequences in other fields.

   The Puritan contribution has not passed entirely unnoticed by scholars.
W. Fraser Mitchell, in his study of the seventeenth century sermon, gives
some attention to it, laying particular stress on the work of Perkins and
Baxter. His conclusion is as follows:

When the politicians called home the king the plain style triumphed; but while to the
Royal Society must be given the honour of definitely hall-marking the new style, to
the more temperate among the Puritan preachers belongs the praise of having demonstrated to large masses of the nation, learned and unlearned, the possibilities of a

From Harold Fisch, "The Puritans and the Reform of Prose-Style," *Journal of English
Literary History*, XIX (Dec., 1952), 229–248, at pp. 229–234, 245–247. © The Johns Hopkins
Press. Reprinted by permission of the Johns Hopkins Press. Notes have been omitted.

simple, straightforward, unencumbered prose. Unattractive as it often was in itself, the Puritan sermon became a dam from which might be led the smooth but powerful current that was to set in motion English prose of a slightly later time.

F. P. Wilson and D. Bush show themselves aware of the plain Puritan sermon as a definite genre in the seventeenth century. The fullest treatment, however, is to be found in Perry Miller's *The New England Mind* (New York, 1939), where a chapter is devoted to the plain style of the Puritans. Professor Miller shows, with particular reference to the New England Puritans, how the object of preaching was reduced to three main headings: doctrine, reason and use. The Puritan sermon was constructed according to a bald system of logical exposition; the imaginative element being reduced to a minimum. The difference between the Puritans and their Anglican contemporaries, in this respect, was very marked. Professor Miller points out that

the Anglican sermon is much more an oration, much closer to classical and patristic eloquence, while the Puritan work is mechanically and rigidly divided into sections and subheads, and appears on the printed page more like a lawyer's brief than a work of art.

In all, the character of the Puritan sermon has been fairly well described. There is room for further clarification, however, especially with regard to (a) the earlier beginnings in England of this rhetorical, or rather, anti-rhetorical, ideal, (b) its doctrinal warrant and basis and (c) its connections with other linguistic fashions of the century which were tending to bring about the plain style of the Restoration period.

II

The earliest full expression of the Puritan view which I have so far come across, is by Lawrence Chaderton, preaching at Paul's Cross in 1578. It is worth noting that Chaderton later became the first Master of the Puritan foundation in Cambridge, Emmanuel College, when it was established in 1584. A whole generation of 'left-wing' Churchmen and others of great influence in the national life, were to pass under his influence. He begins his sermon by declaring:

I purpose to speake particularly, not in the excellencie of wordes, or in the inticyng speach of mans wisedome, but in plaine euidence and demonstration of the trueth.

And having thus laid down his own policy, he goes on to criticize those who follow a different one:

But alas, who preacheth thus? nay who doth not judge this kinde of preaching to be voyde of learning, discretion and wisdome? Wherfore many doe stuffe their sermons with newe deuised words, and affected speaches of vanitie.... Many with un-necessary sentences, prouerbes, similitudes, and stories collected out of the wrytings of prophane men: many with curious affected figures, with Latine, Greeke, and Hebrue sentences, without any just occasion offered by their texte.

The standard which Chaderton lays down for a true pulpit-style, it will be noted, is based upon a literal evocation of a chapter of Paul's first Epistle to the Corinthians:

And I, brethren, when I came to you, came not with excellency of speech or of wisdom, declaring unto you the testimony of God... And my speech and my preaching was not with enticing words of man's wisdom, but in demonstration of the Spirit and of power. (2: 1, 4)

The same doctrine is reiterated in the second Epistle, 'Seeing that we have such hope, we use great plainness of speech' (3: 12), where it is taken as the starting point for a comparison between the Law and the Gospel. Now, it is generally recognized that Calvin and his followers approached the Scriptures as a whole (including the Old Testament) through the medium of Paul's epistles. For this reason, it is not surprising that a great deal of stress was laid upon these texts and that, as a result, a literary self-denying ordinance came to be taught, in line with the whole Puritan warfare against the World, the Flesh and the Devil. It was thought that the whole weight of Scripture lay behind this injunction and a resistance to the allurements of the imagination came to be regarded as an essential part of the defensive armament of the true Christian warrior.

These same texts became the cornerstone of the Puritan argument for Chaderton's successors too....

*   *   *   *

...it must be evident, that a style of preaching based upon the anti-rhetorical principles of Chaderton was already in vogue among the Puritan clergy at a relatively early date. As to the evidence provided by the Puritan sermon itself little can be said since as a rule the 'prophets' spoke extemporarily and informally without committing their words to writing, much less to print. What survives is the printed sermon material of the more literary-minded Puritans such as Chaderton and John Rainolds. These would obviously be less harsh in quality than the normal effusions of the Puritan pulpit. Rainolds, in particular, valued both learning and eloquence and was not averse from quoting Pagan authorities: but even with him, I think, a certain austerity is visible, a tendency to make his points briefly with a minimum of metaphor and to manage his arguments with summaries where possible. There can also be no doubt that he fully identified himself with the arguments of Chaderton against the excessive use of wit and learning. In the following passage, taken from one of his Elizabethan *Sermons on Haggai*, he is dealing with the use of foreign languages in the pulpit but there is an undertone of criticism directed against the over-abundant use of rhetoric and ornament:

'To preach or prophesy, therefore, is not to speak strange language, if we will ever have the people edified; but we must prophesy as the prophets and apostles did, in plain evidence of spirit and speech, rather to profit than to please either ourselves or those whom we speak unto; which, if either we would follow the apostle's judgment, or did mind so much the people's profit as he did, we would be much more willing to do so ourselves also. For though he 'could speak as many and more languages

than any of them all, yet had he rather (said he) speak five words plainly and profit-
ably to instruct others, than ten thousand in a strange tongue,' 1 Cor. xiv. 19. And it
is well worth the observing that which the apostle hath noted already, that when
God spake in a strange language, he did it because of the people's infidelity, 1 Cor.
xiv. 22; and it was no mercy but a judgment that the Lord would speak with other
tongues to that people, Isa. xxviii. 11. 'For all that will they not hear me, saith the
Lord.'

[The conclusion of Part II and all of Part III have been omitted.]

IV

One cannot, I think, avoid the conclusion that the Puritans through their
stylistic habits, helped to shape the type of plain prose which became increasingly the standard after the Restoration. The fact that their political
power came to an end at this period should not lead us to think that their
influence on the national life had ceased. Quite on the contrary, the development of the great Puritan Middle Class was only beginning at this period and
the indirect influence of Calvinist teaching in the economic and social sphere
was to be felt to an increasing extent in the two hundred years that followed.
In a sense, the great age of Whiggery and Middle Class Dissent dates from
the Glorious Revolution of 1688, rather than from the parliamentary rising
of 1642.

The men of the new age to whom the credit (or blame) for introducing
the new style is usually ascribed by historians of literature were all, if not
actually Calvinist in belief, at any rate strongly influenced by Calvinism.
Thus Tillotson, to whom Dryden acknowledged so large a debt in connection
with the formation of his own prose-style, had begun his ecclesiastical career
in the Puritan camp and had only later adopted a moderate position under
the influence of the natural religion of Chillingworth. His style, with its
logical subdivisions, its austerity, and its tone of rational self-possession,
is undeniably of the new age, but it is also undeniably of Puritan extraction.
The following, from a sermon, would be a good example:

This question, "whether the world was created and had a beginning, or not?" is a
question concerning an ancient matter of fact, which can only be decided these two
ways; by testimony, and by probabilities of reason. Testimony, is the principal
argument in a matter of this nature, and if fair probabilities of reason concur with
it this argument hath all the strangth it can have: now both these are clearly on the
affirmative side of the question, viz. that the world was created, and had a beginning.
1. Testimony; of which there be two kinds, divine and human. . . . Human testimonies
are of two sorts; universal tradition, and written history.

This passage clearly owes something to the influence of the Royal Society
(especially in its stress on rational proof) but in its subdivisions and di-
chotomies, it is no less clearly in the methodical, logical tradition of the
Puritans.

*   *   *   *

The group which cannot of course be overlooked in this connection is
that centered on the Royal Society itself. The part played by the Society in

the standardization of the language (—it went to the length, just before the death of Cowley, of setting up a sub-committee to consider linguistic reforms—) is too well-known to require further treatment here. The Society's intimate historical connection with the Puritan movement, however, is not always fully appreciated. That it owed its original inspiration in a large measure to the pansophic schemes of Comenius is no accident. With him a Calvinistic other-worldliness had been combined with an energetic utilitarianism in worldly matters. It is hard to say whether Comenius was first and foremost a Baconian or a Puritan. The two ideals could apparently co-exist very happily. Thus, to take another example, John Wilkins, the first Secretary of the Royal Society, was a good Calvinist, and a brother-in-law of Cromwell. He wrote a manual on plain preaching in 1646 which is of some importance as an *ars concionandi* in the tradition of Chaderton and Perkins, only more moderate. Later on, he also wrote a tract on language problems for the Royal Society. This was his *Essay towards a Real Character and a Philosophical Language* (1668). There he elaborated a project, first designed by Bacon, for a system of signs and hieroglyphs to be used for the communication of scientific information. The Puritan attempts early in the century at pulpit-reform may be said to have had an indirect influence upon the linguistic ideals of the Royal Society and the Society again, through the clergy who were connected with it, rediffused these policies throughout the established church in the Restoration era.

SCIENCE AND THE PLAIN STYLE

Joan Bennett

In the sixty odd years between Francis Bacon's trumpet call to progress in *The Advancement of Learning* and the triumphant, self-confident reply of the Royal Society, English prose transformed itself. Pulpit orators, political theorists, or virtuosi shaped their style in accordance with a current doctrine. Out of a new way of looking at the world was born a new way of writing, and the prevalent change in practice was accompanied by a clearly articulated change in theory. The new prose was shaped to accord with the new tasks imposed upon the writer. The men who used it were often in radical opposition to one another; but the time spirit united them none the less, as we can see when we survey them from our distance in time.... Less and

From Joan Bennett, "An Aspect of the Evolution of Seventeenth-Century Prose," *Review of English Studies*, XVII, No. 67 (July 1941), 281–297, at pp. 281–282, 284–289, 292–294, 296–297. Reprinted by permission of the Clarendon Press, Oxford. Most of the notes have been omitted.

less were men content to 'understand a mystery without a rigid definition, in an easie Platonick description'. Sir Thomas Browne's 'visible world that is but a picture of the invisible, wherein as in a pourtract, things are not truely, but in equivocall shapes; and as they counterfeit some more reall substance in that invisible fabrick', gradually ceased to be thought the 'proper study of Mankind'. With few exceptions men ceased to be interested in the perceived world as an adumbration of the eternal; they were interested in it because it could be known, and managed to man's advantage. As attention confined itself more and more to the fact that can be verified by experience, whether material fact or moral fact, so certain qualities of prose which were once its glory, became an impediment. When the eagle decides to walk, its wings are an encumbrance.

The prose writer's new purpose was to deal with matters of fact, that could be verified. The approach to a problem that was discovered to be proper for a natural philosopher, was widely applied to all the affairs of men, to the saving of souls or the ordering of society, no less than to the inquiry into the possibility of constructing a clinical thermometer. Consequently the meaning of words should, it was thought, be defined with the same precision for any discourse, as for the description of an experiment. Bacon writes:[1]

Yet certaine it is that wordes, as a Tartars Bowe, doe shoote backe uppon the understanding of the wisest, and mightily entangle, and pervert the Judgment. So as it is almost necessary in all controversies and disputations, to imitate the wisedome of the Mathematicians, in setting downe in the verie beginning, the definitions of our wordes and termes, that others may knowe howe wee accept and understand them, and whether they concurre with us or no.

Hobbes insists again and again on the troublesome confusions that arise from ill-defined words, 'for neither error, nor non-sense, can without a perfect understanding of words, be detected'.[2] Like Bacon, he turns to the mathematicians as exemplars of the proper way to use language; they at least, cannot go wrong in their reasoning through ignorance of the meaning of the words they use.

* * * *

Bacon, Hobbes, and Locke are directly concerned with 'discourses that pretend to inform and instruct'. Knowledge was their object, and knowledge as it was then understood, matters of fact and of the relation between facts, and knowledge about social and political utility. But it is not only such men as these who sound a retreat from the arts of rhetoric; it is sounded as frequently in the advice to preachers, which abounds in the years following the Restoration. From the pulpit, too, men were to look principally for clear information about the world we live in, and therefore—

Amongst the first things that seem to be useless, may be reckon'd the high-tossing and swaggering Preaching; either mountingly Eloquent or profoundly Learned.

---

[1] *Advancement of Learning*, Bk. 11.
[2] *Leviathan*, 1651, Pt. 1, c. 11.

It may be noted in passing that those undeveloped metaphors 'high-tossing and swaggering' (as though the preacher were a too spirited horse, requiring the curb) are entirely characteristic of Eachard's own lively style. But the persistent distrust of metaphor was eventually to have its effect in draining the life blood from English prose; and John Eachard, gifted writer though he was, must bear his share of the responsibility. He particularly disliked the far-sought comparisons common in the 'metaphysical' preaching of the first half of the century. He contrasts their overlavish use of metaphor with the economy of those 'Masters of Eloquence' Tully, and Cæsar, in whose writings, he says:

if you do light upon one or so, it shall not make your hair stand right up, or put you into a fit of Convulsion; but it shall be so soft, significant, and familiar, as if 'twere made for the very purpose. But as for the common sort of People that are addicted to this way of expression in their discourses; away presently to both the Indies, rake Heaven and Earth, down to the bottom of the Sea, then tumble over all Arts and Sciences, ransack all Shops and Ware-houses, spare neither Camp nor City, but they will have them. So fond are such deceived ones of these same gay words, that they count all discourses empty, dull, and cloudy, unless besparkl'd with these Glitterings.

The sermons of John Donne will yield examples of all the types of imagery Eachard refers to here, and even of the abrupt transitions from image to image, although Donne more often exhausts one before he passes on to another.

Here, for instance, is a passage from Sermon XXXIII, *LXXX Sermons*, on the text: *While Peter yet spake these words, the Holy Ghost fell on all them which heard the word.*

Here the Holy Ghost is said to have fallen, which denotes a more earnest communicating of himselfe, a throwing, a pouring out of himselfe, upon those, upon whom he falls: he falls as a fall of waters, that covers that it falls upon; as a Hawk upon a prey, it desires and it will possesse that it falls upon; as an Army into a Country, it Conquers, and it Governs where it fals. The Holy Ghost fals, but far otherwise, upon the ungodly. *Whosoever shall fall upon this stone, shall be broken, but upon whomsoever this stone shall fall, it will grind him to powder.* Indeed, he fals upon him so, as haile fals upon him; he fals upon him so, as he fals from him, and leaves him in an obduration, and impenitiblenesse, and in an irrecoverable ruine of him, that hath formerly despised and despighted the Holy Ghost. But when the Holy Ghost fals not thus in the nature of a stone, but puts on the nature of a Dove, and a Dove with an Olive-branch, and that in the Ark, that is, testimonies of our peace, and reconciliation to God, in his Church, he fals as that kinde of lightning, which melts swords, and hurts not scabbards; the Holy Ghost shall melt thy soule, and not hurt thy body. . . .

Donne's images define and bring home to the senses or the imagination of his hearers, the various ways in which they are to understand the meaning of a phrase in the text. They are not arguments but illustrations. For instance, whether or no there really is 'a kind of lightning, which melts swords, and hurts not scabbards', is irrelevant. It is enough that men have at some time believed there could be, or even, merely, that they can conceive such a thing as possible when the image is offered to them. But Eachard clearly thinks of similitude as some sort of sham argument offering for a truth something which may be a mere deception . . . .

* * * *

Behind all this lies an assumption about the nature and purpose of metaphor. Eachard is not concerned solely with the way in which a metaphor affects the reader's consciousness of the thing it represents (which Dr. I. A. Richards calls the 'tenour' as distinguished from the 'vehicle'); he is expecting something from the image (or 'vehicle') itself. And what he is expecting is accurate information. John Hoskins in his *Directions for Speech and Style* (1600) made a statement which might, if separated from the examples he gives, be thought to carry the same implication: 'Besides', he writes, 'a metaphor is pleasant because it enricheth our knowledge with two things at once, with the truth and with a similitude . . .' John Smith repeats this word for word in his *Mysterie of Rhetorick Unveiled*, 1657 (a work largely composed of such unacknowledged quotations) and Hobbes makes the point in other words and more explicitly:

> *Metaphors* please; for they beget in us, by the *Genus*, or by some *common* thing to that with another, a kind of *Science*: as when an *Old Man* is called *Stubble*, a man suddainly learns that he grows up, flourisheth, and withers like Grass, being put in mind of it by the qualities common to *Stubble* and *old men*.

Hobbes' example (taken from Homer via Aristotle) is described by him in such a way as to draw attention to facts common to grass and men, the facts of growth and decay; he ignores the emotional effect of the image and presents it as offering us 'a kind of Science'. The examples Hoskins chooses, and his comments on them, suggest that he meant something rather different by his words: 'enrich our knowledge with two things at once'. Here are two of his examples, both taken from his usual source, Sidney's *Arcadia*:

> *heads disinherited of their natural seigneuries* whereby we understand both beheading and the government of the head over the body as the heir hath over the lordship which he inheriteth. Of the same matter in another place: *to divorce the fair marriage of the head and the body*, where besides the cutting off the head we understand the conjunction of head and body to resemble marriage.

It is clear that these peculiar metaphors do not convey any *facts* beyond their 'tenour' (that is, an execution). What appears to please Hoskins in them is that they may suggest that the relation between the parts of the body represents or symbolizes political and social relations in the body politic. To value metaphor because it suggests relations between things 'apparently unlike' is not the same as to value it because it conveys knowledge. The particular kind of truth, or accurate correspondence with fact, which Eachard demands from metaphor would exclude all illustrations drawn from myth or fable (whereas Hoskins approves of these). In short, the road along which the later critics of prose style are pointing is the one that leads to Dr. Johnson's strictures on the mythology of *Lycidas*, and, ultimately, to Wordsworth's vain effort to be rid of his whole heritage of poetic language.

It is a profound mistrust of the art of rhetoric that we see developing in the latter half of the seventeenth century.

Increasingly that once admired art is thought of as a cunning device, an art of deception. In the *Leviathan* Hobbes describes rhetoricians as egotistical deceivers who

have in their speeches, a regard to the common Passions, and opinions of men, in deducing their reasons; and make use of Similitudes, Metaphors, Examples and other tools of Oratory, to persuade their Hearers of the Utility, Honour, or Justice of following their advise.

His view is that no honest Counsellor ought to use

metaphoricall Speeches, tending to the Stirring up of Passion, (because such reasoning, and such expressions, are usefull only to deceive, or to lead him we Counsell towards other ends than his own).

With perfect consistency, we find him in *The Art of Rhetoric* advocating all the known tricks as a profitable study for lawyers and politicians, since, as he there tells us,

Rhetorick, is that Faculty, by which we understand what will serve our turn concerning any Subject to win belief in the hearer.

There is a sharp contrast, implied by Hobbes throughout his treatment of the subject, between eloquence and all its tools on the one hand, and statements of facts and reasoned deductions from them on the other. In other words, rhetoric is contrasted with truth as he and his contemporaries understood it. The ideal set forth in Sprat's *History of the Royal Society*, of a use of language which would enable men to deliver 'so many things in so many words', dominated the age in its attempts to formulate a theory of prose style. Closely connected with this belief in a possible exact correspondence between words and things, was the value set in theory (though seldom in practice) upon brevity. Supposing truth to be simple and easily apprehended by man's reason, (if only reason can be disembarrassed from feeling), it will follow that the more shortly and barely facts and reasons are uttered, the better.

Robert South's view of 'brevity', expressed in a sermon advocating short prayers, is precisely that of Hobbes, whom he describes in the same sermon as 'the impious author of *Leviathan*'. South writes:

In Brevity of Speech a Man does not speak so much Words, as Things; Things in their precise and naked Truth; and stripped of their Rhetorical Mask, and their Fallacious Gloss: and therefore, in Athens they circumscribed the Pleadings of their Orators by a strict Law, cutting off Prologues and Epilogues, and Commanding them to an immediate Representation of the Case, by an impartial and succinct Declaration of meer Matter of Fact. And this was indeed to speak Things fit for a Judge to hear, because it argued the Pleader also a Judge of what was fit for him to speak.

The metaphor of the 'naked' truth occurs again in Baxter's *Gildas Silvianus* or *The Reformed Pastor*:

> Truth loves the Light, and is most beautiful when most naked. It is a sign of an envious enemy to hide the truth; and it is sign of an Hypocrite to do this under the pretence of revealing it: and therefore painted obscure Sermons (like painted Glass in the windows that keep out the light) are too oft the marks of painted Hypocrites. If you would not Teach men, what do you in the Pulpit? If you would, why do you not speak so as to be understood?

The advice to preachers, offered by so many divines at this time, either in books or treatises devoted to that purpose, or in their own sermons, is consciously directed against the survival of old practices. These men believe, as firmly as Dryden does, that they are living in a new and better time, in which new and better ways of expressing oneself are available. This is not, of course, the whole story. They also believe—as when have men not believed?—that they are living in particularly wicked and degenerate times. They cry out against the profligacy and atheism of Restoration England and agree in ascribing the evil very largely to 'the ingeneous author of a very bad book, I mean the *Leviathan*'. Sometimes, those of them who are not members of the Royal Society will hint a distrust also of the new reliance on experimental proof: South links the profligates with the experimenters in a sermon entitled (characteristically) *The Practice of Religion Enforced by Reason*.

*   *   *   *

All this new doctrine about style is closely connected with a new purpose which governs the practice of the preacher no less than of the natural philosopher. Men are to preach religion and morals (the two are scarcely distinguished) as they are to explore the secrets of nature, in order to be of use. The object of natural philosophy is less and less to unveil the final cause; it is more and more to apply knowledge to the control of the material world. Sir Thomas Browne wrote:

> Every Essence, created or uncreated hath its final cause, and some positive end, both of its Essence and Operation. This is the cause I grope after in the works of Nature; on this hangs the Providence of God.

But when he writes like this, he shows himself as still belonging to the old world of thought, the world of the Scholastic Philosophers. Bacon, in *The Advancement of Learning*, pointed out another road:

> For the handling of *finall causes* mixed with the rest of *Philosophicall enquiries*, hath intercepted the severe and diligent enquirie of all *reall and physicall causes*, and given men occasion, to stay upon these *satisfactorie and specious causes*, to the great arrest and prejudice of furder discoverie.

The road he pointed out led, as he knew it would, to the discovery of the behaviour of nature in order that she might be harnessed to man's needs:

For it is no more, but by following, and as it were, hounding Nature in her wanderings, to bee able to leade her afterwardes to the same place againe.

Just as the aim of the natural philosopher was to discover facts that could be tested and made use of (although of course the disinterested love of truth was also operative in the researches of many of them), so the preacher too, confined himself more and more to such moral truths as could be verified by experience and made use of in social life.   Joseph Glanvill, in *Concerning Preaching*, defines the aims of preaching and handles its rules accordingly: 'The end of Preaching must be acknowledged to be the Instruction of the hearers in Faith and Good Life, in order to the Glory of God, and their present and future happiness.... I shall handle the rules of Preaching under these four heads.   It ought to be plain, practical, methodical and affectionate'.   He warns the preacher against becoming involved in expounding such doctrines as are 'speculative and nice': these he may let alone, 'but those that guide and incourage us in Virtue and Goodness, must be often explained and enforced'.

Locke, in *The Reasonableness of Christianity as Delivered in Scripture*, clearly implies that the truth or otherwise of the Christian revelation (truth, in the sense of correspondence with fact) is relatively unimportant.   The importance of religion lies in its utility as a guide to morals.

*   *   *   *

Religion is here seen as a substitute for moral philosophy.   The 'knowledge of morality by meer natural light' is hard to reach, and most men have not the intelligence or the education to arrive at it.   Revealed religion is recommended as a short cut, but Locke has no doubt that the same moral truths can, by those who have the time and the ability, be discovered by 'natural reason' as are inculcated by religion.   This belief is shared by the preachers:

A Thing or Action is said to be morally Good or Evil, as it is agreeable or disagreeable to right Reason, or to a rational nature.

Tillotson's sermons afford the clearest example of the general tendency of the pulpit orator to address himself to the good sense of his hearers.   The mere titles of his sermons are an indication of his attitude: *The Wisdom of being Religious*; *The Folly of Scoffing at Religion*; *The Advantages of Religion to Societies*; *The Precepts of Christianity not Grievous*.

*   *   *   *

The close relation between the new thought and the new style can be illustrated by juxtaposing passages from Donne and from Tillotson in which the subject matter is similar.   Here, for instance, is a passage from each on the subject of atheism: Tillotson's is cool and reasoned, it is addressed to the judgment, whilst the patterned rhythmical passage from Donne is addressed to the imagination.   Tillotson argues:

that the principles of Religion, the *belief of a God* and *another life*, by obliging men to be virtuous, do really promote their temporal happiness.   And all the privilege that atheism pretends to, is to let men loose to vice, which is naturally attended with temporal inconveniences. And if this be true, then the atheist cannot pretend this Reason, (which is the only one I can think of) to dispute against Religion, much less to rally upon it viz. charity to mankind. For it is plain that it would be no kindness to any man, to be undeceived in these principles of Religion, supposing they were false. Because the principles of Religion are so far from hindring, that they promote a man's happiness even in this world; and as to the other world, there can be no inconvenience in the mistake: For when a man is not, it will be no trouble to him, that he was once deceived about these matters.

Thus Tillotson reasons, without images, without any marked rhythmical pattern, appealing to the common sense of his hearers. Donne on the other hand cries out against the atheist, using his characteristic incremental repetitions and all the devices of his rhetoric to terrify any member of his congregation who may be that way inclined:

> Poore intricated soule! Riddling, perplexed, labyrinthicall soule! Thou couldest not say, that thou beleevest not in God, if there were no God; Thou couldest not beleeve in God, if there were no God; If there were no God, thou couldest not speake, thou couldest not thinke, not a word, not a thought, no not against God; thou couldest not blaspheme the Name of God, thou couldest not sweare, if there were no God: For, all thy faculties, how ever depraved, and perverted by thee, are from him; and except thou canst seriously beleeve, that thou art nothing, thou canst not beleeve that there is no God. If I should ask thee at a Tragedy, where thou shouldest see him that has drawn blood, lie weltring, and surrounded in his owne blood, Is there a God now? If thou couldst answer me, No, These are but Inventions, and Representations of men, and I believe a God never the more for this; If I should ask thee at a Sermon, where thou shouldest heare the Judgements of God formerly denounced, and executed, and redenounced, and applied to present occasions, Is there a God now? If thou couldest answer me, No, These are but Inventions of State, to souple and regulate Congregations, and keep people in order, and I beleeve God never the more for this; Bee as confident as thou canst, in company; for company is the Atheists Sanctuary; I respit thee not till the day of Judgement, when I may see thee upon thy knees, upon thy face, begging of the hills, that they would fall downe and cover thee from the fierce wrath of God, to aske thee then, Is there a God now? I respit thee not till the day of thine own death, when thou shalt have evidence enough, that there is a God, though no other evidence but to finde a Devill, and evidence enough, that there is a Heaven, though no other evidence, but to feele Hell; To aske thee then, Is there a God now? I respit thee but a few houres, but six houres, but till midnight. Wake then; and then darke, and alone, Heare God aske thee then, remember that I asked thee now, Is there a God? and if thou darest, say No.

In the latter half of the seventeenth century prose tended to move away from poetry; and so for a time did verse, if by the word 'poetry' we understand the language of intuition and imagination, rather than of sense-perception and judgment. 'What the imagination seizes as Beauty must be Truth', Keats was to write. But, for a hundred years at least, it was thought that truth could only be discovered by the judgment, arranging and comparing the data offered to the senses. The utmost that the imagination had to do in the business was to decorate the findings of the judgment, so as to make them available to the weaker understanding of the common man.

REAFFIRMATION OF THE
PLAIN-STYLE TRADITION

Hugh MacDonald

Broadly speaking, much literary English prose underwent development, or at any rate changes, though slowly, between 1600 and 1660. These changes lay mostly in getting rid of excessive tropes, figures, and antitheses, and dropping part of the Elizabethan vocabulary. Writing tended, on the whole, to become more lucid. Soon after 1660 the rhetorical, and often heavily latinized, prose was discarded rather suddenly, except by an occasional writer who had survived from the past generation.

These dates are, of course, only approximate points in the stages of the evolution of prose style. In fact such general statements must, from their nature, be somewhat nebulous; and when attention is called to the change which our prose underwent after the Restoration, there is an important side to the matter which it is as well to remember. There was, I think, less a change in prose, though a change there undoubtedly was, than an almost universal disappearance of a certain kind of prose. For there had existed throughout the first half of the century, as there had existed from the days of Chaucer, or for that matter King Alfred, a straightforward prose in which it was quite easy to say plain things plainly.

*   *   *   *

The prose of the first fifty years of the seventeenth century was not homogeneous; for Donne, Sir Thomas Browne, and Jeremy Taylor, who are often classed together as characteristic writers of the period, had not, in fact, much in common, except that they are unlike the authors who succeeded them.

Taylor was only eighteen when Donne died in 1631. His style is easier and more harmonious than Donne's. Though they are both rhetorical they both use a good deal of simple language. Neither is like Browne, whose rhetoric is the effect of a heavier and more latinized language and of sentences written with a skill which ensures that the words shall produce an almost direct physical sensation in the reader. None of them bases the construction of his sentences on Latin as Milton often does. The prose of all three and of many others of their time may however be conveniently classified as rhetorical. No doubt the artificialities which were often part of this prose were to a considerable extent the result of fashion, and had had a counterpart in *Euphues*, which had established a mode of writing in the 1580's. Of course the rhetorical prose of the seventeenth century was, at its best, far more successful than pure euphuism had been, but both were apart from traditional English prose. Each style was used in its day by only a

From Hugh MacDonald, "Another Aspect of Seventeenth-Century Prose," *Review of English Studies*, XIX, No. 73 (Jan. 1943), 33–43, at pp. 34–40. Reprinted by permission of the Clarendon Press, Oxford. Notes have been omitted.

limited number of authors, and not always by those authors themselves. Shakespeare, after all, did not write like Lyly, nor did Sir Thomas Browne write his private letters, his recipe for roasting mutton, or even his description of a thunderstorm, in the manner of the fifth chapter of *Urn Burial*. Many intelligent men were fully aware of the different ways in which it was possible to preach or write. Abraham Wright, a Fellow of St. John's College, Oxford, in 1656 published a volume called: *Five Sermons in Five Several Styles or Waies of Preaching. First in Bp. Andrew's Way, Second in Bp. Hall's Way, Third Dr. Maine's and Mr. Cartwright's Way, Fourth in the Presbyterian Way, Fifth in the Independents' Way.* The late Professor R. W. Chambers has pointed out that in Malory's time Malory's idiom was not the normal idiom of the period. Anthologies, which tend to be made up of ornate passages, have rather distorted our view; and it is possible also that too much has been made of Sprat's famous directions on 'the proper method of discourse' in his *History of the Royal Society*, 1667.

The use of hard words and strange metaphors had certainly been common with many writers for a long time before 1660. There were indeed books available for those who had not a ready turn for thinking of substitutes for normal English nouns and expressions. Henry Cockeram's *English Dictionarie*, 1623, for instance, suggested the use of 'concessation' for 'loitering', 'facinorous' for 'very wicked', 'incogitancy' for 'rashness', 'fumiditie' for 'smoke', and so on. Thomas Blount in his *Glossographia* (1656) says that he has 'shun'd the old Saxon words, finding them grown more obsolete than others.' Glanvill's treatment of *The Vanity of Dogmatizing* (1661) is an excellent illustration of the change which took place. In a revision of the book, published four years later as *Scepsis Scientifica*, he tells us that he is now 'more gratified with manly sense flowing in a natural and unaffected eloquence than in the musick and curiosity of fine metaphors and dancing periods'. Where he used the same material, he often made small changes. In a sentence which occurs in *The Vanity of Dogmatizing*—'the Disease of our Intellectuals is too great not to be its own Diagnostick'—the word 'Diagnostick' became 'evidence' in 1665. He wrote again 'against confidence in Philosophy' in *Essays on Several Important Subjects* (1676), and this time he used a less grandiloquent language, as the title of the book indicates. The difference between Cowley's early and late essays is, as is well known, fairly well marked. But of much greater importance than this is the fact that the splendour of the great rhetorical writers disappeared, and the more lucid but thinner and less emotive language of Tillotson and Dryden took its place. Rhetorical writing, in fact, especially when highly charged with metaphor, became, as Mrs. Bennett suggests, suspect and even repellent to the new generation, for it was held that it made the statement of facts difficult (which of course it often did); though Dryden himself, whose business was with literature and not with science, was conscious that language had become poorer as it had become more 'correct'. He hints at this in prologues written before and after his *Apology for Heroic Poetry and Poetic License* (1677), to which Mrs. Bennett alludes.

What Mrs. Bennett calls a new way of looking at the world, or 'the concrete nature of experimental philosophy', as it has been defined, of necessity helped to modify the language. Sir Thomas Browne's poetical musings on his dying patient in *A Letter to a Friend* are very different from the exact clinical pictures of Sydenham, and the language of one would have been quite inappropriate to the other. I mention Sydenham because he presents a curious contrast to Browne, and the two men serve as a warning against attempting strict chronology in a history of style. Sydenham's description of the gout is still used in medical textbooks: a modern writer on medicine would hardly be likely to speak, as Browne does, of the Spring as the 'time of the year when the leaves of the fig-tree resemble a daw's claw'. Yet *A Letter to a Friend* was not written till after two of Sydenham's books had been published.

There was also a general tidying-up of prose which is shown in Dryden's *Essay of Dramatic Poesie*. In the second edition, published in 1684, he was more careful about the relative pronoun and about syntax generally than he had been in the first edition of 1668. He re-wrote several of the sentences so that prepositions might not be left at the end of them.

Sir William Craigie tells me that the meaning of words tended to become crystallized, and to be less dependent on their context, about 1675.

But when all this has been granted we must not, as I have said, forget that along with prose which acted or was intended to act directly on the emotions, or was merely eccentric, there was produced plenty of simple work-a-day prose which was close to spoken English. Dean Milman's statement in *The Annals of St. Paul's* (2nd ed. 1869) 'that there was as complete anarchy in the prose as in the religion of the land' cannot be sustained.

Mrs. Bennett quotes passages from Hobbes and Eachard urging the necessity of perspicuous language or warning against extravagant metaphors. This was really an old topic, for, to take two instances at random, Roger Ascham had complained in *The Scholemaster* (1570) of the 'strange and inkhorne terms' in Hall's *Chronicles*; and Ben Jonson in his *Discoveries* had said that 'the chief virtue of style is perspicuity'. No doubt Hobbes and Eachard had good reasons for what they wrote, but the inference to be drawn from their remarks, as from Sprat's directions, should, I think, be limited. Though Hobbes was speaking of language generally, he probably had in mind the necessity for extreme precision of language when writing on subjects such as psychology, political theory and so on, in which he was specially interested. Eachard's attack was directed against the clergy, who have always been liable to use florid language in the pulpit. A famous Oxford preacher, who became Headmaster of Rugby, used about 1840 such sentences as 'Let the scintillations of your wit be like the coruscations of summer lightning, lambent but innocuous'; and only the other day, before the eight-o'clock news, people were told 'to sterilize their minds with the antiseptic of truth'.

I cannot do more in a short article than remind readers of a very few of the authors of the first half of the seventeenth century whose style was simple in construction, and free from conceits, recondite words and far-fetched metaphors. The syntax was less stabilized and the sentences were often somewhat stiffer than they became after Dryden's influence had made itself felt, but if one allows for this and for the personal idiosyncrasy of each writer, it is probable that as much simple prose was written between

1600 and 1660 as prose which was elaborate or pedantic. I am not so much concerned with the value of the simple prose of this period, as with its existence.

In Elizabethan times Deloney, whose stories must have been representative of a good deal of popular fiction, and were themselves widely read by the middle classes, wrote simply enough, as almost any passage from *Jack of Newbury* will show:

> At length the guests being come, the widow bade them all heartily welcome. The Priest and the Tanner seeing the Taylor, mused what he made there: the Taylor on the other side, marvelled as much at their presence. Thus looking strangely one at another, at length the widow came out of the kitchen in a fair train gown stuck full of silver pins, a fine white cap on her head, with cuts of curious needle work under the same and an apron before her as white as the driven snow: then very modestly making curtsey to them all she requested them to sit down.

Many of the dramatists, in their prose passages, use ordinary English idiom. Apart from the clue given by an occasional word it would frequently be difficult to assign a date to them. Middleton perhaps, in particular, exemplifies this. Bacon himself is an outstanding example of the variety of English which a single author might have at his command. He is aphoristic, though of course lucid, in his *Essays*. He is lucid, even if his language is somewhat latinized, in *The Advancement of Learning*; and in *The New Atlantis* he is simplicity itself:

> We sailed from Peru (where we had continued by the space of one whole year), for China and Japan, by the South Sea; taking with us victuals for twelve months; and had good winds from the east, though soft and weak, for five months space and more. But then the wind came about, and settled in the west for many days, so we could make little or no way, and were sometimes in purpose to turn back. But then again there arose strong and great winds from the south with a point east, which carried us up (for all that we could do) towards the north; by which time our victuals failed us, though we had made good spare of them.... And it came to pass that the next day about evening, we saw within a kenning before us, towards the north, as it were thick clouds, which did put us in some hope of land; knowing how that part of the South Sea was utterly unknown; and might have islands or continents, that hitherto, were not come to light.

It might be supposed that public speeches would contain an abnormal amount of rhetoric at this time, but a glance through the collection of *British Orations* will show that the speeches of Sir John Eliot in 1628, Strafford in 1641, and Charles I in 1642, are not more ornate than those delivered in the eighteenth and nineteenth centuries. Here is a short passage from Eliot.

> For the next undertaking, at Rhé, I will not trouble you much; only this in short. Was not that whole action carried against the judgment and opinion of those that were of the council? Was not the first, was not the last, was not all in the landing— in the intrenching—in the continuance there—in the assault—in the retreat—without their assent? Did any advice take place of such as were of the council?

Howell in his *Familiar Letters* (except for an occasional pedantic word), Ludlow in his *Memoirs*, and Shaftesbury in his character of Henry Hastings, use direct and plain language which is free from extravagant expressions. Bunyan's language was in part the language of the Bible, but, as Sir Charles Firth says, he 'also used the everyday language of the seventeenth-century workman or shopkeeper, which was a much more homely and less dignified dialect than the language of the Bible'. His style was inherent in him, as anyone can see if he will turn to his first book, *Some Gospel Truths Opened* (1656).

Izaak Walton is perhaps too obvious to need mention. His vocabulary is modern and his style lucid; in fact his prose is so limpid and easy that he is perhaps sometimes overlooked, because of the difficulty of saying much about him. But individual as his style is, he is not unique, and *The Complete Angler* (1653) and his *Lives* of Donne (1640) and Wotton (1651) are as much part of English literature as the prose of Milton and Donne. What Sir Herbert Grierson long ago called 'the unconventional purity and naturalness' of the metaphysical poets and 'a diction equally appropriate to prose and verse' could not possibly have been absent from the prose written when the metaphysical poets flourished. It is to be found in George Herbert's *Country Parson* written soon after 1630 as well as in Walton's writings. Hobbes, unlike Eachard writing twenty years later, followed his own precepts. His sentences are pre-Dryden, but his language is bare and is as clear as language can be. His eloquence, when he is eloquent, arises, I suppose, in part from his extraordinary directness, as in the famous passage in *Leviathan* (1651) on a state of war.

In such condition there is no place for Industry, because the fruit thereof is uncertain: and consequently no culture of the Earth: no Navigation, nor use of the commodities that may be imported by sea; no commodious Building; no Instruments of moving and removing such things as require much force; no knowledge of the face of the Earth; no account of Time; no Arts; no Letters; no Society; and which is worst of all, continual fear and danger of violent death; and the life of man, solitary, poor, nasty, brutish, and short.

It would be tedious to continue with examples. I will only suggest that a great deal of our prose, whether it is what is called literary or not, has at all times corresponded closely to the spoken language. No one can suggest want of directness and lucidity in the reported talk of Ben Jonson and Selden. It is doubtless the conversational element in style which has kept a great part of our written language substantially unchanged, whatever diction some authors of outstanding powers may have chosen to adopt.

It would be interesting to enquire how far the rhetorical style was directly due to the kind of teaching given in schools and Universities. Much of the language of the clergy to which Eachard takes exception was probably the pulpit language of ex-Fellows of Colleges who had taken livings. Donne, Milton, and Jeremy Taylor were learned men in a way which Dryden, though a King's Scholar at Westminster and a Trinity man, was not. Euphuism and irrelevant learning were common in the writings of the Elizabethans who had been to the Universities. An enlargement of the curriculum took place, at any rate at Oxford, between 1600 and 1650, though this was only part of the growing interest in science.

SUGGESTIONS FOR RESEARCH

1. Much has been written about the Anti-Ciceronian style, but amazingly little about the Ciceronian style in English prose. What was Cicero's style? What features are distinctive? Which English writers imitated or resembled him? Are there varieties of the style?

2. Explain the relationship between the figures of classical rhetoric (tropes and schemes) and the Ciceronian, schematic, and pointed styles.

3. How do Croll and Williamson differ in their explanations of "baroque" prose style? Particularly compare Croll (1929, "The Baroque Style in Prose") with Williamson (1951, "The Rhetorical Forms of Style"). Then contrast Adolph's (1968) point of view.

4. Apply a modern system of grammatical description to a piece of pointed or schematic prose. What difference in conclusions do you discover?

5. Read samples of sixteenth- and seventeenth-century criticism in the original. Compare their punctuation, spelling, and syntax with other writers of the times.

6. Employ one of the modern methods of discourse analysis to examine the coherence of a prose passage. See Gleason (1968).

7. Almost no studies have been made of the purposeful use of sentence length to enforce meaning in paragraphs. Select a few paragraphs that appear to have significant sentence variety, count the words in each sentence (and measure the lengths of the sentences with a ruler), and then in the context of the paragraph and surrounding argument or narrative, suggest why the sentences were given the lengths they have.

8. Study the development and change in the style of one writer. See R. Clark (1969).

9. W. N. King (1955) has persuasively challenged past belief that Lyly's style had no logical or organic relationship to situation and character. Confront other apparently mechanical prose to discover relationships between style and speaker, narrator, or dramatic situation.

10. Is Jonson's prose true to his stylistic theories in *Timber*?

11. Examine Vickers' (1968b) description of Bacon's style, which is contrary to Croll's (1923) and Williamson's (1951) descriptions. Extend Vickers' methodology to other Renaissance stylists. Compare his approach in this book to that in his book on Shakespeare (1968a).

12. Read Umbach (1945) on Donne's "metaphysical" style. Notice that no syntactical characteristic is suggested. In the essays labeled "metaphysical" by Umbach, is there a typical syntax which should be considered part of the style?

13. Select a passage for levels-categories analysis. See Hasan's 1964) use of Halliday's (1962) system to analyze William Golding's *Free Fall* and Angus Wilson's *Anglo-Saxon Attitudes*.

14. Make a list of the characteristics of the so-called plain style and a list of "plain" stylists. Test the characteristics by the practice.

SELECTIONS FOR ANALYSIS

THOMAS WILSON (c. 1525–1581)
From The Art of Rhetoric

Plainness What It Is

Among all other lessons, this should first be learned, that we never affect any strange inkhorn terms, but so speak as is commonly received: neither seeking to be overfine, nor yet living overcareless, using our speech as most men do, and ordering our wits, as the fewest have done. Some seek so far for outlandish English, that they forget altogether their mothers' language. And I dare swear this, if some of their mothers were alive, they were not able to tell, what they say, and yet these fine English clerks, will say they speak in their mother tongue, if a man should charge them for counterfeiting the king's English. Some far-journeyed gentlemen at their return home, like as they love to go in foreign apparel, so they will powder their talk with oversea language. He that cometh lately out of France, will talk French English, and never blush at the matter. Another chops in with Angleso Italiano [Italianate English]: the Lawyer will store his stomach with the prating of peddlers.... The fine Courtier will talk nothing but Chaucer. The mystical wise men, and poetical clerks, will speak nothing but quaint proverbs, and blind allegories, delighting much in their own darkness, especially, when none can tell what they do say. The unlearned or foolish fantastical, that smells but of learning (such fellows as have been learned men in their days) will so Latin their tongues, that the simple cannot but wonder at their talk, and think surely they speak by some Revelation. I know them that think Rhetoric, to stand wholly upon dark words, and he that can catch an inkhorn term by the tail, him they count to be a fine English man, and a good Rhetorician.

From Thomas Wilson, *The Arte of Rhetorique* (*1553*), a facsimile reproduction with an introduction by Robert Hood Bowers (Gainesville, Fla.: Scholars' Facsimiles and Reprints, 1962), pp. 183–184. Reproduced by permission of Scholars' Facsimiles and Reprints. The orthography has been modernized.

ROGER ASCHAM (1515–1568)
From The Scholemaster

Imitatio

Ye know not, what hurt ye do to learning, that care not for wordes, but for matter, and so make a deuorse betwixt the tong and the hart. For marke all aiges: looke vpon the whole course of both the Greeke and Latin tonge, and ye shall surelie finde, that, whan apte and good wordes began to be neglected, and properties of those two tonges to be confounded, than also began, ill deedes to spring: strange maners to oppresse good orders, newe and fond opinions to striue with olde and trewe doctrine, first in Philosophie: and after in Religion: right iudgement of all thinges to be peruerted, and so vertue with learning is contemned, and studie left of: of ill thoughtes cummeth peruerse iudgement: of ill deedes springeth lewde taulke. Which fower misorders, as they mar mans life, so destroy they good learning withall.

From William Aldis Wright, ed., "The Second Booke: The Ready Way to the Latin Tong," *English Works 'Toxophilus'*, *'Report of the Affaires and State of Germany'*, *'The Scholemaster'* (Cambridge: Cambridge University Press, 1904), pp. 265–266.

RICHARD MULCASTER (1530?–1611)
From The First Part of the Elementarie

That the English tung hath in it self sufficient matter to work her own artificiall direction, for the right writing thereof

It must nedes be that our English tung hath matter enough in hir own writing, which maie direct her own right, if it be reduced to certain percept, and rule of Art, tho it haue not as yet bene thoroughlie perceaued.

The causes why it hath not as yet bene thoroughlie perceaued, ar, the hope & despare of such, as haue either thought vpon it, and not dealt in it, or that haue delt in it, but not rightlie thought vpon it.

For som considering the great difficultie, which theie found to be in the writing thereof, euerie letter almost being deputed to manie, and seuerall, naie to manie and wellnigh contrarie sounds and vses, euerie word almost either wanting letters, for his necessarie sound, or hauing some more than necessitie requireth, began to despare in the midst of such a confusiō, euer to find out anie sure direction, whereon to ground Art, and to set it certain. And what if either theie did not seke, or did not know how to seke, in right

From E. T. Campagnac, ed., *Mulcaster's Elementarie* (Oxford: Clarendon Press, 1925), pp. 85–87. Reprinted by permission of the Clarendon Press, Oxford. Marginal gloss has been omitted.

form of Art, and the composing method? But whether difficultie in the thing, or infirmitie in the searchers, gaue cause thereunto, the parties them selues gaue ouer the thing, as in a desperat case, and by not medling thorough despare, theie helped not the right.

Again som others bearing a good affection to their naturall tung, and resolued to burst thorough the midst of all these difficulties, which offered such resistēce, as theie misliked the confusion, wherewith the other were afraid, so theie deuised a new mean, wherein theie laid their hope, to bring the thing about. Wherevpon som of them being of great place and good learning, set furth in print particular treatises of that argument, with these their new conceaued means, how we ought to write, and so to write right. But their good hope by reason of their strange mean, had the same euent, that the others despare had, by their either misconceauing the thing at first, or their diffidence at the last. Wherein the parties them selues no dout deserue some praise, and thanks to, of vs and our cuntrie in both these extremities of hope and despare, tho theie helped not the thing, which theie went about, but in common apparence, did somwhat hinder it rather. For both he, that despared in the end, took great pains, before diffidence caused him giue ouer to despare: and he that did hope by his own deuise to supply the generall wāt, was not verie idle both in brain, to deuise, and in hand to deliuer the thing, which he deuised. Which their trauell in the thing, and desire to do good, deserue great thanks, tho that waie which theie took, did not take effect.

SIR PHILIP SIDNEY (1554-1586)
From The Defence of Poesie

Since then *Poetrie* is of al humane learnings the most ancient, and of most fatherly antiquitie, as from whence other learnings have taken their beginnings; Since it is so universall, that no learned nation doth despise it, nor barbarous nation is without it; Since both *Romane* & *Greeke* gave such divine names unto it, the one of prophesying, the other of making; and that indeed that name of making is fit for him, considering, that where all other Arts retain themselves within their subject, and receive as it were their being from it. The *Poet* onely, onely bringeth his own stuffe, and doth not learn a Conceit out of a matter, but maketh matter for a Conceit. Since neither his description, nor end, containing any evill, the thing described cannot be evil; since his effects be so good as to teach goodnes, and delight the learners of it; since therein (namely in morall doctrine the chiefe of all knowledges) hee doth not onely farre passe the *Historian*, but for instructing is well nigh comparable to the *Philosopher*, for moving, leaveth him behind him. Since the holy scripture (wherein there is no uncleannesse) hath whole parts in it Poeticall, and that even our Savior Christ vouchsafed

From Albert Feuillerat, ed., *"The Defence of Poesie," Political Discourses, Correspondence, Translations*, Vol. 3 of *The Complete Works of Sir Philip Sidney* (Cambridge: Cambridge University Press, 1923), pp. 25–26. Reprinted by permission of Cambridge University Press.

to use the flowers of it: since all his kindes are not onely in their united formes, but in their severed dissections fully commendable, I thinke, (and thinke I thinke rightly) the Lawrell Crowne appointed for tryumphant Captaines, doth worthily of all other learnings, honour the *Poets* triumph. But bicause we have eares aswell as toongs, and that the lightest reasons that may be, will seeme to waigh greatly, if nothing be put in the counterballance, let us heare, and as well as we can, ponder what objections be made against this Art, which may be woorthie either of yeelding, or answering.

WILLIAM CAMDEN (1551-1623)
From **Remaines Concerning Britain**

Languages
Whereas our tongue is mixed, it is no disgrace, when as all the tongues of *Europe* do participate interchangeably the one of the other, and in the learned tongues, there hath been like borrowing one from another. As the present *French* is composed of *Latin, German,* and the old *Gallique,* the *Italian* of *Latin* and *German-Gotish,* and the *Spanish* of *Latine, Gotish-German,* and *Arabique,* or *Morisquo.* Yet it is false which *Gesner* affirmeth, that our tongue is the most mixt and corrupt of all other. For if it may please any to compare but the Lords Prayer in other languages, he shall find as few *Latine* and borrowed forrain words in ours, as in any other whatsoever. Notwithstanding the diversitie of Nations, which have swarmed hither, and the practise of the Normans, who as a monument of their Conquest, would have yoaked the English under their tongue, as they did under their command, by compelling them to teach their children in Schools nothing but French, by setting down their laws in the Norman-French and enforcing them most rigorously to pleade and to be impleaded in that tongue onely for the space of three hundred years, untill King *Edward* the third enlarged them first from that bondage. Since which time, our language hath risen by little, and the proverb proved untrue, which so long had been used, *Jack would be a gentleman, if he could speak any French.*

From William Camden, *Remaines Concerning Britain* (6th impression, printed by Thomas Warren for Isabella Waterson, 1657), pp. 29-30. The modern "s" has been used.

SIR FRANCIS BACON (1561-1626)
From **Of the Advancement of Learning**

The Second Book
6. Another diversity of method, whereof the consequence is great, is the delivery of knowledge in aphorisms, or in methods; wherein we may observe

From William Aldis Wright, ed., *The Advancement of Learning* (5th ed.; Oxford: Clarendon Press, 1900), pp. 172-173.

that it hath been too much taken into custom, out of a few axioms or observations upon any subject, to make a solemn and formal art, filling it with some discourses, and illustrating it with examples, and digesting it into a sensible method. But the writing in aphorisms hath many excellent virtues, whereto the writing in method doth not approach.

7. For first, it trieth the writer, whether he be superficial or solid: for aphorisms, except they should be ridiculous, cannot be made but of the pith and heart of sciences; for discourse of illustration is cut off; recitals of examples are cut off; discourse of connexion and order is cut off; descriptions of practice are cut off. So there remaineth nothing to fill the aphorisms but some good quantity of observation: and therefore no man can suffice, nor in reason will attempt, to write aphorisms, but he that is sound and grounded. But in methods,

Tantum series juncturaque pollet,
Tantum de medio sumptis accedit honoris,

as a man shall make a great show of an art, which, if it were disjointed, would come to little. Secondly, methods are more fit to win consent or belief, but less fit to point to action; for they carry a kind of demonstration in orb or circle, one part illuminating another, and therefore satisfy. But particulars being dispersed do best agree with dispersed directions. And lastly, aphorisms, representing a knowledge broken, do invite men to inquire further; whereas methods, carrying the show of a total, do secure men, as if they were at furthest.

ROBERT BURTON (1577–1640)
From The Anatomy of Melancholy

Democritus to the Reader

I have no such authority, no such benefactors, as that noble Ambrosius was to Origen, allowing him six or seven amanuenses to write out his dictates; I must for that cause do my business myself, and was therefore enforced, as a bear doth her whelps, to bring forth this confused lump; I had not time to lick it into form, as she doth her young ones, but even so to publish it as it was first written, *quicquid in buccam venit* [whatever came uppermost], in an extemporean style, as I do commonly all other exercises, *effudi quicquid dictavit genius meus* [I poured out whatever came into my mind], out of a confused company of notes, and writ with as small deliberation as I do ordinarily speak, without all affectation of big words, fustian phrases, jingling terms, tropes, strong lines, that like Acestes' arrows caught fire as they flew, strains of wit, brave heats, elogies, hyperbolical exornations,

From the book *The Anatomy of Melancholy* by Robert Burton. Vol. One. Pp. 31–32. Edited by Holbrook Jackson. Everyman's Library Edition, 1932. Published by E. P. Dutton & Co., Inc. and used with their permission. Notes have been omitted.

elegancies, etc., which many so much affect. I am *aquæ potor* [a water-drinker], drink no wine at all, which so much improves our modern wits, a loose, plain, rude writer, *ficum voco ficum et ligonem ligonem* [I call a fig a fig and a spade a spade], and as free, as loose, *idem calamo quod in mente* [what my mind thinks my pen writes], I call a spade a spade, *animis hæc scribo, non auribus* [I write for the mind, not the ear], I respect matter, not words; remembering that of Cardan, *verba propter res, non res propter verba* [words should minister to matter, not vice versa], and seeking with Seneca, *quid scribam, non quemadmodum*, rather what than how to write.... So that as a river runs sometimes precipitate and swift, then dull and slow; now direct, then *per ambages* [winding]; now deep, then shallow; now muddy, then clear; now broad, then narrow; doth my style flow: now serious, then light; now comical, then satirical; now more elaborate, then remiss, as the present subject required, or as at that time I was affected. And if thou vouchsafe to read this treatise, it shall seem no otherwise to thee than the way to an ordinary traveller, sometimes fair, sometimes foul; here champaign, there enclosed; barren in one place, better soil in another: by woods, groves, hills, dales, plains, etc. I shall lead thee *per ardua montium, et lubrica vallium, et roscida cespitum, et glebosa camporum* [over steep mountains, slippery glades, wet grass, and sticky fields], through variety of objects, that which thou shalt like and surely dislike.

BEN JONSON (1572–1637)
From Timber, or Discoveries

Reading, Speaking and Writing Well
Custom is the most certain mistress of language, as the public stamp makes the current money. But we must not be too frequent with the mint, every day coining; nor fetch words from the extreme and utmost ages, since the chief virtue of style is perspicuity and nothing so vicious in it as to need an interpreter. Words borrowed of antiquity do lend a kind of majesty to style and are not without their delight sometimes, for they have the authority of years and out of their intermission do win to themselves a kind of grace like newness; but the eldest of the present and newest of the past language is the best. For what was the ancient language, which some men so dote upon, but the ancient custom? Yet when I name custom, I understand not the vulgar custom, for that were a precept no less dangerous to language than life if we should speak or live after the manners of the vulgar; but that I call custom of speech which is the consent of the learned, as custom of life, which is the consent of the good. Virgil was most loving of antiquity, yet how rarely doth he insert *aquai* and *pictai*! Lucretius is scabrous and rough in these; he seeks them as some do Chaucerisms with us, which were better expunged and banished. Some words are to be culled out for ornament

From Ralph W. Walker, ed., *Ben Jonson's "Timber" or "Discoveries"* (Syracuse: Syracuse University Press, 1953), pp. 42–43. Reprinted by permission of Syracuse University Press. Notes have been omitted.

and colour, as we gather flowers to strew houses or make garlands; but they are better when they grow to our style, as in a meadow where, though the mere grass and greenness delights, yet the variety of flowers doth heighten and beautify. Marry, we must not play or riot too much with them, as in *paronomasies*; nor use too swelling or illsounding words, *quae per salebras, altaque saxa cadunt*. It is true there is no sound but shall find some lovers, as the bitterest confections are grateful to some palates.

THOMAS HOBBES (1588–1679)
From Leviathan

Of Man
But the use of words in registring our thoughts, is in nothing so evident as in Numbring. A naturall foole that could never learn by heart the order of numerall words, as *one*, *two*, and *three*, may observe every stroak of the Clock, and nod to it, or say one, one, one; but can never know what houre it strikes. And it seems, there was a time when those names of number were not in use; and men were fayn to apply their fingers of one or both hands, to those things they desired to keep account of; and that thence it proceeded, that now our numerall words are but ten, in any Nation, and in some but five, and then they begin again. And he that can tell ten, if he recite them out of order, will lose himselfe, and not know when he has done: Much lesse will he be able to adde, and substract, and performe all other operations of Arithmetique. So that without words there is no possibility of reckoning of Numbers; much lesse of Magnitudes, of Swiftnesse, of Force, and other things, the reckonings whereof are necessary to the being, or well-being of man-kind.

When two Names are joyned together into a Consequence, or Affirmation; as thus, *A man is a living creature*; or thus, *if he be a man, he is a living creature*, If the later name *Living creature*, signifie all that the former name *Man* signifieth, then the affirmation, or consequence is *true*; otherwise *false*. For *True* and *False* are attributes of Speech, not of Things. And where Speech is not, there is neither *Truth* nor *Falshood*. *Errour* there may be, as when wee expect that which shall not be; or suspect what has not been: but in neither case can a man be charged with Untruth.

Seeing then that *truth* consisteth in the right ordering of names in our affirmations, a man that seeketh precise *truth*, had need to remember what every name he uses stands for; and to place it accordingly; or else he will find himselfe entangled in words, as a bird in lime-twiggs; the more he struggles, the more belimed. And therefore in Geometry, (which is the onely Science that it hath pleased God hitherto to bestow on mankind,) men begin at settling the significations of their words; which settling of significations, they call *Definitions*; and place them in the beginning of their reckoning.

From A. R. Waller, ed., *Leviathan, or the Matter, Forme & Power of a Commonwealth, Ecclesiasticall and Civill* (Cambridge: Cambridge University Press, 1904), pp. 16 18.

By this it appears how necessary it is for any man that aspires to true Knowledge, to examine the Definitions of former Authors; and either to correct them, where they are negligently set down; or to make them himselfe. For the errours of Definitions multiply themselves, according as the reckoning proceeds; and lead men into absurdities, which at last they see, but cannot avoyd, without reckoning anew from the beginning; in which lyes the foundation of their errours. From whence it happens, that they which trust to books, do as they that cast up many little summs into a greater, without considering whether those little summes were rightly cast up or not; and at last finding the errour visible, and not mistrusting their first grounds, know not which way to cleere themselves; but spend time in fluttering over their bookes; as birds that entring by the chimney, and finding themselves inclosed in a chamber, flutter at the false light of a glasse window, for want of wit to consider which way they came in. So that in the right Definition of Names, lyes the first use of Speech; which is the Acquisition of Science: And in wrong, or no Definitions, lyes the first abuse; from which proceed all false and senslesse Tenets; which make those men that take their instruction from the authority of books, and not from their own meditation, to be as much below the condition of ignorant men, as men endued with true Science are above it. For between true Science, and erroneous Doctrines, Ignorance is in the middle. Naturall sense and imagination, are not subject to absurdity. Nature it selfe cannot erre: and as men abound in copiousnesse of language; so they become more wise, or more mad than ordinary. Nor is it possible without Letters for any man to become either excellently wise, or (unless his memory be hurt by disease, or ill constitution of organs) excellently foolish. For words are wise mens counters, they do but reckon by them: but they are the mony of fooles, that value them by the authority of an *Aristotle*, a *Cicero*, or a *Thomas*, or any other Doctor whatsoever, if but a man.

THE RESTORATION PERIOD AND THE EIGHTEENTH CENTURY: 1660–1798

UTILITARIAN PROSE: HOLLAND *versus* LANCASTER

Robert Adolph

Throughout this book I have been bravely meddling. I have held that Restoration prose represents the general neglect of the "qualitatively unique" ... in favor of some more quantitative and useful end. Especially as it came under the influence of the spirit (if not often the method) of Bacon, "Science" in the latter part of the seventeenth century—or at least, that part of "Science" which affected prose style—is but one aspect of this "obscure prior movement." The same neglect ... is taking place in all other areas as well, including those indifferent or hostile to science. I can see no reason to single out the New Philosophy or any impossibly broad definition of "Science" as the influence on everything else. The escape from subjectivity is universal.

My intention ... is to go beyond the scholarly controversies ... to isolate the specific linguistic elements which distinguish the new styles from the old. I make no claim to cover the topic completely. For this we need a more syste-

---

Reprinted from *The Rise of Modern Prose Style*, Ch. 6, "The New Prose of Utility," pp. 244–256, by Robert Adolph by permission of The M.I.T. Press, Cambridge, Massachusetts. Copyright © 1968 by The Massachusetts Institute of Technology. Notes have been omitted.

matic way of comparing styles than any we now have. Here our best hope seems to be the recent efforts to unite traditional stylistic criticism with linguistics. Until this effort has proceeded much further than it now has, I find myself restricted to what I concede at the outset is a sketchy survey.

From the Restoration on, normal literary prose is, to use McLuhan's terms, a "linear" product of the "print culture." The chief aim of such prose is useful public communication. Therefore it is made to seem "rational" or "precise" or "neoclassic," terms of which the Restoration would have approved but which are not inclusive or accurate enough to describe the prose itself.

Of course performance is never as exclusive as theory. In the various kinds of imaginative literature, and especially in as oral and relatively private a medium as the comedies of King Charles's court, the prose is less impersonally utilitarian and more intimate. Even so, the language of prose comedy in *The Man of Mode* is unlike that of *Much Ado About Nothing*. For much the same reasons, Bunyan's and Defoe's austere narratives are worlds apart stylistically from Elizabethan fiction, as are the lean Burnet and the rotund Clarendon from the earlier biographers and character-writers.

PROSE IN GENERAL

Let us begin by comparing two translations of an identical passage in Plutarch. The first is Philemon Holland's (1603) and the second P. Lancaster's (1684):

> It seemeth at the first sight, that there is no difference betweene envie and hatred, but they be both one. For vice (to speake in generall) having (as it were) many hookes or crotchets, by means thereof as it stirreth to and fro, it yeeldeth unto those passions which hang thereto many occasions and opportunities to catch holde one of another, and so to be knit and enterlaced one within the other; and the same verily (like unto diseases of the body) have a sympathie and fellow-feeling one of anothers distemperature and inflammation: for thus it commeth to passe, that a malicious and spightful man is as much grieved and offended at the prosperitie of another, as the envious person: and so we holde, that benevolence and good-will is opposite unto them both, for that it is an affection of a man, wishing good unto his neighbour: and envie in this respect resembleth hatred, for that they have both a will and intention quite contrary unto love: but forasmuch as no things like to the same, and the resemblances betweene them be not so effectuall as to make them all one, as the differences to distinguish them asunder; let us search and examine the said differences, beginning at the very source and original of these passions.

> Envy and Hatred are passions so like each other, that they are often taken for the same; and generally all the vices are so confusedly twisted and entangled, that they are not easily to be distinguished: for, as differing diseases of the Body agree in many the like causes and effects; so do the disturbances of the Mind. He who is in Prosperity, is equally an occasion of grief both to the Envious, and Malicious Man: therefore we look upon Benevolence, which is a Willing our Neighbours good, as an opposite to both Envy and Hatred; and fancy these two to be the same, because they have a contrary purpose to that of Love. But their Resemblances make them not so much One, as their Unlikeness, distinct: therefore we endeavour to describe each of them apart, beginning at the Original of either Passion.

Mild and straightforward, Philemon Holland is no racy and eccentric "Elizabethan" like Greene or Dekker. Nevertheless he is writing in another world from Lancaster's. Why do we read Holland one way and Lancaster another when they are both "saying the same thing?" I think we can answer this question by comparing the vocabulary, figurative language, and syntax of the two texts.

Vocabulary. Linguists distinguish "nominal" from "verbal" styles. Nominal style is more impersonal, more esoteric or technical, and has fewer clauses and complex sentences and less variety of sentence patterns. I think it is clear that Holland's style is more verbal than Lancaster's. This is not because Holland has more verbs. A statistical comparison would be meaningless. What is decisive for style is what the verbs and nouns are doing. In a nominal style the verbs are chiefly operative, mere markers to indicate distinctions and logical processes to the reader. They are the pale, well-behaved verbs whose meaning is not affected by their subject or context. In their invariability they have the virtues of well-defined nouns. In the verbal style, on the other hand, verbs are descriptive or, more rarely, evaluative, imperative, or interjections. They are affected by their contexts. For example, we can compare Holland's "it *stirreth* to and fro, it *yeeldeth* unto those passions which *hang* thereto many occasions and opportunities to *catch holde* one of another, and so to be *knit* and *enterlaced* one within the other" with Lancaster's "all the vices *are* so confusedly *twisted* and *entangled*, that they are not easily to be *distinguished*." Holland's verbs are more descriptive both of the subject matter and Holland's attitude to it than Lancaster's.

Let us name one vocabulary "verbal descriptive" and the other "nominal operative." Where the former records the observations and attitudes of the speaker, the latter merely indicates the processes of abstract logic. The verbal descriptive style will contain more complex sentences and subordinate qualifying elements expressing the point of view of the speaker. Thus Holland has more syntactic variety than Lancaster's series of ratios.

Nouns and adjectives, as well as verbs, are operative in the Restoration, descriptive in the earlier prose. In the Restoration nouns are very important, frequently doing the jobs that verbs or verbal constructions performed previously. The Restoration habit of capitalizing nouns is significant. Adjectives, which frequently merely fill out a description in the early prose, more often point out a distinction in the Restoration. For example, in Holland's "for it commeth to passe, that malicious and spightfull man is as much grieved and offended at the prosperitie of another, as the envious person," "malicious and spightfull" and "grieved and offended" are in part merely rhetorical doublets. In Lancaster's "he who is in Prosperity, is equally an occasion of grief both to the Envious, and Malicious Man" there is no such padding. A substantive, "occasion of grief," has replaced Holland's verbal construction, while the adjectives ("Envious, and Malicious") now only point out a logical distinction.

In nominal operative prose, nouns appear to have unique, invariable meanings unaffected by their contexts. "We look upon Benevolence," writes Lancaster, "which is a Willing our Neighbours good, as an opposite to both Envy and Hatred," making "Benevolence" operate as a token or counter neatly parallel to Envy and Hatred in a sort of definition.

This neatness—"precision," the Restoration would have called it—is not present in Holland's tangle of subordinate clauses. One has the feeling in reading Restoration prose that ordinary nouns such as Envy, Benevolence, and Hatred actually stand for fixed, technical concepts, of which everyone has a clear and distinct idea, and which have already been defined. The nominal operative style is, in other words, an expression of the nominalistic philosophy of the age—and of *our* age—with its distrust of "ordinary language." Nouns and adjectives in the verbal descriptive style, on the other hand, have the characteristics of verbs in that style. Often they seem brought in on the spur of the moment and therefore not clearly defined. They may reveal what the author felt at a given moment about the subject matter, but the function of language in the Restoration was to argue or explain purposefully. If Lancaster read Holland's translation he would not have regarded "hookes" and "crotchets" as suitable for serious discourse. They are too idiosyncratic, not impersonal enough. They describe, but they do not advance the Argument.

There is a more dramatic contrast between the old and new vocabulary in a comparison of the versions of Montaigne by that robust Elizabethan John Florio (1603) and Charles Cotton (1686):

& au lieu de m'esguiser l'appetit par ces preparatoires & avant-ieux, on me le lasse & affadit.

And whereas with these preparatives and flourishes, or preambles, they think to sharpen my taste, or stirre my stomacke, they cloy and make it wallowish.

Instead of whetting my Appetite by these Preparatives, they tire, and pall it.

The Elizabethan adds synonyms ("preparatives and flourishes, or preambles") and extra phrases ("sharpen my taste, or stirre my stomacke") not to define the application of the first word or phrase but to make everything more rhetorically or dramatically emphatic. He is more interested in giving us his own feelings about the text than in translating with "accuracy." He is delighted with language for its own sake. A juicy, homey word like "wallowish" is not to be found in Cotton, who would keep the diction on the impersonal level of objective argumentation. Florio's boisterous inaccuracy and his promiscuous heaping-up of words from all sorts of experience goes against Decorum and would have been offensive to Cotton. In fact, Cotton goes in exactly the opposite direction by eliminating Montaigne's "avant-ieux."

Translations of another passage from the *Essais* illustrate the transition from descriptive to operative language:

Ce sont les pieds de paon, qui abbatent son orgeuil. . . .

It is the fouleness of the peacocks feete, which doth abate his pride, and stoope his gloating-eyed tayle. (Florio . . .)

They are the Peacocks Feet that abate his pride. (Cotton . . .)

An expression like Florio's sudden "gloating-eyed" is too casual, too unexpected, and too whimsical to serve in the Argument for Cotton and, indeed, Montaigne himself. In this splendid image Florio adds to Montaigne
the sensuous "fouleness" and, what is the most outstanding visual feature
of the peacock, his tail. Montaigne's simple "orgeuil" is too abstract for
Florio, who must provide a visual equivalent for everything. He must get
across the exact appearance of the peacock's tail, with its little circular
whorls like gloating eyes; but Cotton is concerned only with the Sense of the
Argument.

In general then the earlier prose, though quite lively, is static, but intimate and descriptive, while in the Restoration prose always seems to be
moving toward a goal or indicating a causal process. Lancaster writes, "As
differing diseases of the Body agree in many the like causes and effects; so
do the disturbances of the Mind," while Holland knows not "causes and
effects" but has "and the same verily (like unto diseases of the body) have a
sympathie and fellow-feeling one of anothers distemperature and inflammation." In effect we have a metaphorical and padded description for
Lancaster's progression of causal relations and distinctions.

Figurative language. ...[D]espite its manifestos the Restoration did use
figurative language. It is a special kind, however, one in which the relation
of "figure" to "sense" is clearly spelled out. Each figure is long, linking together a chain of causal relationships. Where the Elizabethan figure is
casual, as in the Florio extracts above, startling, and suggestive, the later
ones are more formal and restrictive. Where the earlier prose has clusters of
similes or metaphors with referents drawn from areas remote from the subject at hand, the Restoration prefers isolated metaphors with vehicle and
tenor closely related to each other and to the discourse.

We can compare the treatments of Plutarch's disease simile. In Holland
the simile ("like unto diseases of the body") is tossed off casually in a parenthesis. Holland gives much more attention to the figure itself, with its two
doublets ("sympathie and fellow-feeling one of anothers distemperature and
inflammation"). The primary meaning is: Certain vices are like certain
diseases in that they are hard to distinguish. But there are at least two sub-
merged metaphors in Holland: first, vice is morbid, like a disease; second,
vices and diseases are like two friends drawn together by common suffering.
Like so many Elizabethan figures, this conglomeration is "mixed." Friends
are not the same kind of thing as diseases. But we are not conscious of this
in the fairly dense metaphorical texture of Holland's prose.

With Lancaster, on the other hand, all the relationships are spelled out
formally, in a sort of ratio: certain diseases are similar in their causes and
effects, just as certain vices are. There is never any witty attempt to say that
vices are like diseases themselves. Lancaster says only that vices have the
same relation to each other that diseases have. Unlike things—vices and
diseases—are kept in separate compartments. The figure is not "mixed."
The elements of the comparison are hauled out not, as is chiefly the case with
Holland, for their intrinsic interest, but for whatever contribution they make
to useful argumentation. Where Holland's figures fuse disparate concepts
together, Lancaster analyzes them apart into causal relations. Therefore
Holland's figures turn on verbs ("stirreth," "yeeldeth," "hang," "catch

holde")—the most suggestive, fusing element of language—and Lancaster's on nouns, sharply set off and balanced. Where Holland has interlocking clusters of figures Lancaster has hardly any at all. Lancaster's vices "tangled and entwined" has almost no metaphorical value. As metaphors these words are completely played out or "adequated." They are therefore safe to use since their meanings are invariable and they express no individual quirk of an author comparing unlike things. They have the virtues of well-defined nouns.

Holland wants us to experience his own "direct sensuous apprehension" of thought. So he gives us several quick metaphors: vices are like things with hooks and crotchets which wiggle about, catching up neighboring passions, which are then somehow knit together. It is more an impressionistic blur, the way we understand things when emotional or relaxed, than a sharply focused isolated image. Essentially Holland's translation, like so much early prose, is a series of alternative ways of describing one thing. Gustav Stern has described metaphor as a "verbal shorthand" saving periphrasis. "It gives the emotion directly, instead of talking about it; it does not describe, but makes us experience." His account only holds for the earlier metaphor not the Restoration variety. Restoration metaphor does not save periphrasis, it is periphrasis. It does not make us experience but assists in the argument or is merely ornamental.

Syntax. ...We should note...that while Lancaster's syntax is almost a set of mathematical ratios, these are not balanced rigidly or even antithetically. Where balance in much Elizabethan prose and in the asymmetrical "Anti-Ciceronianism" is obtrusive and often obviously antithetical, in the Restoration it is quieter. This is because it is subsumed under the progress of The Argument. In Holland, as in "Anti-Ciceronianism," parenthetical elements (for example, "like unto diseases of the body") remain parenthetical; in Lancaster they are incorporated into The Argument —even when not necessary for it—and of course into the balanced syntax.

Before going on to the various prose genres, I would like to mention a concept in linguistics which may provide us with a way of ordering these observations on the inseparable concerns of vocabulary, figurative language, and syntax. In "Patterns and Ranges" Angus MacIntosh says, "The meanings a given word has (however we may define meaning) are in some direct way associated with our experience of that word in a variety of contexts, our association of that word with other words which have, in our experience, a somewhat similar range, and our association of the word with other words of similar shape, but not always etymologically related." There are a limited number of words with which any given word may cohabit. Words, as MacIntosh puts it, "have only a certain potential of collocability".... When confronted with an unusual collocation—"molten feather" is MacIntosh's example—we can write it off as meaningless, search about for some unexperienced meaning (for example, a new, little-known meaning for "feather"), or "seek to read into one or the other of the words some plausible extension of a familiar meaning" by "postulating an extension of range for which we can find reasonably close parallels".... Much of the time when we read Elizabethan prose we are performing this last task; we almost never are when we read Restoration prose. Florio's "stoope his gloating-eyed tayle" is certainly an unusual collocation for which we must imagine "some plausible extension of a familiar meaning." This means, first of all, more work for the reader, and, as we have seen, more work for the reader means less "precision" or "clarity," in the Restoration sense. Now, Truth for the Restoration is always Clear and Distinct. Therefore prose such as Florio's must be banished utterly. Since the serious purpose of prose is the presentation of The Argument, Cotton has only "They are the Peacocks Feet that abate his pride." One metaphor is still there, but the other, with its unusual collocation, has disappeared.

For the Restoration, metaphor in general is suspect since all metaphors are, in a sense, unusual collocations. In the Restoration metaphor, however, the collocation is made less unusual because the reader's work is done for him. The extension of the meaning is "unfolded" chiefly by the balanced syntax with its implicit ratios. The dominant and contrasted position of the substantives ("they," "Feet," "pride") gives the effect of a ratio. The reader's work is made easier because, as in a well-constructed mathematical problem, the solution for the unknown X follows logically from what has gone before. Cotton (as well as Montaigne) has given us the answer a few ratios earlier: "Nature has ordered the most troubles of Actions to be the most common, by that to make us equal, and to parallel Fools and wise Men, Beasts and us. Even the most contemplative and prudent man, when I imagine him in this posture, I hold him an impudent Fellow to pretend to be prudent and contemplative. They are the Peacocks Feet that abate his pride." X equals Troublesome Actions. But what does Florio's "gloating-eyed tayle" equal? This expression is from another "range" (in MacIntosh's terminology) altogether. The Restoration would have said the figure was not "proper." We come upon it utterly unprepared. It is not part of a logical progression but seems struck off in the first heat of composition. The intention of a style like Florio's seems to be the articulation of the mind of the writer or "speaker" himself in contrast to the impersonal, "precise" Restoration vein.

Just as Restoration syntax and figurative language offer few surprises compared to the Elizabethan, so the later vocabulary has fewer unusual collocations. Following MacIntosh...we may classify style into four categories:

1. Normal collocations, normal grammar,
2. Unusual collocations, normal grammar,
3. Normal collocations, unusual grammar,
4. Unusual collocations, unusual grammar.

Elizabethan prose tends to head down toward number four, Restoration prose up to number one. If all prose were in style number one there would be no difference between language as a system of fixed norms and language in actual practice. All language would be "correct."

What we have come upon here is a facet of the famous—and vexed— distinction in linguistics between language and speech, *langue* and *parole*. *Langue* is the way the linguistic code "ought" to be used by everybody;

parole is the way it actually is used by different people. Saussure's point, of course, was that, although *langue* underlies *parole*, no one ever does use *langue* pure and simple. The Restoration, with its passion for a universal, impersonal, "proper," and "correct" language, sought to abolish the distinction between *langue* and *parole*. Only in this way could prose be understood by all, and thereby become able to fulfill its main function of utilitarian communication.

THE ROYAL SOCIETY AND GLANVILL

Richard F. Jones

... It is a stroke of good fortune for our purposes that in 1676 Glanvill published a third abbreviated version of the *Vanity of Dogmatizing*, as the first of seven essays combined to form a volume with the title, *Essays on Several Important Subjects in Philosophy and Religion*. A comparison of this essay with the first version affords nothing short of a revelation. Under the influence of the Royal Society the author's changed stylistic standards had established complete control over his writing, and had caused him to revise with a ruthless hand work written under the inspiration of the great prose writers of the Commonwealth. Furthermore, though in the second edition he had contented himself with an apology, leaving the style little changed, he would not permit the treatise to go forth again until it had become "quite changed in the way of writing." It is hardly necessary to do more than display parallel passages to show what science was doing to prose.

That all bodies both *Animal*, *Vegetable*, and *Inanimate*, are form'd out of such particles of matter, which by reason of their figures, will not cohaere or lie together, but in such an order as is necessary to such a specifical formation, and that therein they naturally of themselves concurre, and reside, is a pretty conceit, and there are *experi-*

Reprinted by permission of the Modern Language Association from Richard F. Jones, "Science and English Prose Style in the Third Quarter of the Seventeenth Century," *PMLA*, XLV (1930), 977–1009, at pp. 992–996. Notes have been omitted.

ments that credit it. If after a decoction of *hearbs* in a Winter-night, we expose the liquor to the frigid air; we may observe in the morning under a crust of ice, the perfect appearance both in *figure*, and *colour*, of the *Plants* that were taken from it. But if we break the *aqueous Crystal*, those pretty *images* dis-appear and are present dissolved.

Now these *airy Vegetables* are presumed to have been made, by the reliques of these *plantal emissions* whose avolation was prevented by the *condensed inclosure*. And therefore playing up and down for a while within their liquid prison, they at last settle together in their natural order, and the *Atomes* of each part finding out their methodical Situation till by breaking the Ice they are disturbed, and those counterfeit *compositions* are scatter'd into their first *Indivisibles*.   *Vanity*, p. 46.

And there is an experiment.... That after a decoction of Herbs in a frosty Night, the shape of the Plants will appear under the Ice in the Morning: which Images are supposed to be made by the congregated *Effluvia* of the Plants themselves, which loosly wandring up and down in the Water, at last settle in their natural place and order, and so make up an appearance of the Herbs from whence they were emitted. *Essays*, p. 11.

Gone is the Brownesque "swelling" sentence at the beginning of the first passage, and the touch of beauty that adorned the account of the experiment has vanished; while the "vicious abundance of phrase" and "volubility of tongue" that characterize the remainder of the quotation have given way to the "plain and familiar words" and the "close, naked, natural way of speaking" of the later version.

But this is so largely prosecuted by that wonder of men, the Great *Des-Cartes*, and is a Truth that shines so clear in the Eyes of all considering men; that to goe about industriously to prove it, were to light a candle to seek the Sun. *Vanity*, p. 28.

Upon which position all the Philosophy of Des-Cartes stands: And it is so clear, and so acknowledg'd a Truth, among all considering Men, that I need not stay to prove it. *Essays*, p. 5.

For body cannot act on anything but by motion; motion cannot be received but by quantitative dimensions; the soul is a stranger to such gross substantiality, and hath nothing of quantity, but what it is cloathed with by our deceived phancies; and therefore how can we conceive under a passive subjection to material impressions. *Vanity*, p. 29.

For Body cannot act on anything, but by *Motion*; *Motion* cannot be received but by *Matter*, the Soul is altogether immaterial; and therefore, how shall we appreciate it to be subject to *such* Impressions. *Essays*, p. 6.

If we will take the literal evidence of our Eyes; the *Æthereal Coal* moves no

To *Sense* the *Sun stands still* also; *and no Eye* can perceive its Actual motion.

more than this *Inferior clod* doth. *Vanity*, p. 78.	*Essays*, p. 20.

And thus, while every age is but another shew of the former, 'tis no wonder that Science hath not outgrown the dwarfishness of its *pristine stature*, and that the *Intellectual world* is such a *Microcosm. Vanity*, p. 138.	And thus while every Age is but another *shew* of the *former*, 'tis no wonder that human science is *no more* advanced above its *ancient Stature. Essays*, p. 10.

In these passages there is an obvious change from "specious tropes" and "vicious abundance of phrase" to a "primitive purity and shortness," in which "positive expressions" and "native easiness" are manifest. The reduction of these "wide fetches and circumferences of speech" to a direct and "natural way of speaking" brings out in vivid relief not only the way in which the scientific spirit was destroying the sheer joy in language, but also how the definite linguistic stand taken by the Royal Society was producing results.

Nor is the composition of our bodies the only wonder; we are as much nonplust by the most contemptible *Worm* and *Plant*, we tread on. How is a drop of Dew organiz'd into an Insect, or a lump of Clay into animal Perfections? How are the Glories of the Field spun, and by what Pencil are they limn'd in their unaffected bravery? By whose direction is the nutriment so regularly distributed into the respective parts, and how are they kept to their specifick uniformities? If we attempt Mechanical solutions, we shall never give an account, why the Wood-cock doth not sometimes borrow colours of the Mag-pye, why the Lilly doth not exchange with the Daysie, or why it is not sometime painted with a blush of the Rose? Can *unguided matter* keep it self to such exact conformities, as not in the least spot to vary from the *species*. That divers Limners at a distance without either copy, or designe, should draw the same *Picture* to an undistinguishable exactness, both in form, colour, and features; this is more conceivable, then that *matter*, which is so diversified both in quantity, quality, motion, site, and infinite other circumstances, should frame it self so absolutely according to the Idea of it and its kind. And though the fury of *Appelles*, who threw his Pencil in a desperate rage	*Blind Matter* may produce an *elegant* effect for once, by a great Chance; as the Painter accidentally gave the Grace to his Picture, by throwing his Pencil in rage, and disorder upon it; But then *constant* Uniformities, and Determinations to a *kind*, can be no *Results* of *unguided Motions. Essays*, p. 11.

upon the Picture he had essayed to
draw, once casually effected those lively
representations, which his Art could
not describe; yet 'tis not likely, that one
of a thousand such praecipitancies
should be crowned with so an unexpected an issue. For though *blind
matter* might reach some elegancies in
individual effects; yet specifick con-
formities can be no *unadvised* productions, but in greatest likely hood, are
regulated by the immediate efficiency of
some *knowing agent. Vanity*, pp. 44 ff.

Here, indeed, is merciless pruning. The "amplification of style" found in the
extended illustrations, touched with beauty, of the composition of bodies,
has been unhesitatingly cut away, for Glanvill's changed standard reveals in
it only a "trick of flaunting metaphor," "specious tropes and figures," and
he now feels that the discussion has been rendered "tedious by wide fetches
and circumferences of speech." Certainly condensation could go no further
than is manifested in the later version. How completely has vanished the
feeling for beauty in language, as well as a spirit of enthusiasm and imaginative activity.

NEO-CLASSICISM: ADDISON

Jan Lannering

If Samuel Johnson stands for the culmination of Neo-classical prose style,
Addison represents its first stage of maturity. In the opinions of the leading
eighteenth-century critics Addison was the chief pattern for plain, easy, and
perspicuous writing. Johnson asserted for once and all that Addison's prose
was »the model of the middle style», and that »Whoever wishes to attain an
English style, familiar but not coarse, and elegant but not ostentatious, must
give his days and nights to the volumes of Addison». The great authority

From Jan Lannering, *Studies in the Prose Style of Joseph Addison* (S. B. Liljegren, ed., Essays
and Studies on English Language and Literature; Uppsala, Sweden: University of Uppsala,
1951), Ch. 2, "Sentence Structure," at pp. 82–96, 123–126. Reprinted by permission of Jan
Lannering. Notes have been omitted. Quotations are from *The Spectator*, ed. Henry Morley,
London, 1888.

on rhetoric, Hugh Blair, considered Addison's style »the highest, most correct, and ornamented degree of the simple manner», and »the safest model for imitation». It is true Addison shared this position with Swift, but the highly individual style of the latter could be admired only; it was beyond imitation. Addison, on the other hand, possessed a style »always equable, and always easy, without glowing words or pointed sentences». His prose seems to have been regarded as the epitome of the Neo-classical striving after order and balance.

*　　*　　*　　*

The loose style as it appears in Browne, and before him in Montaigne, Bacon, and Donne among others, may thus be said to consist of a) the elements of the curt Senecan style: short terse main clauses, often not connected syntactically and often with variation of subject; and b) the end-linking form with dangling qualifications, often a kind of sorites reasoning. The curt style was the dominating element in the prose of the Anti-Ciceronians up to the Restoration. In the latter half of the century the end-linking form became more and more common, but the curt element was still conspicuous. This is the style of the Restoration essayists, Dryden, Cowley, Halifax, and Temple among others, and with this generation the Senecan tradition of style had its last representatives. Those men put down their thoughts more or less as they occurred to them and did not care much about where to end the periods or the distinctions between main statements and qualifying matter. They had recourse above all to precise and racy diction, pointed antitheses, similes, and metaphors.

Still there was, during the latter half of the century, a growing need of perfection of form, of a just proportion between the units of language, and of grace and ease of expression. The demand for measured and balanced prose began to make itself felt as early as about the middle of the century. Grace and ease of literary expression implied order and coherence of the parts of the period. The loose period had to be recast into real units of thought with subordinated matter clearly distinguished from and firmly connected with the main statement(s). By this means a just distribution of emphasis on the different parts of the sentence would be possible; in other words, the sentence would be harmonious and balanced.

The man who did more than anybody else to satisfy this demand was Joseph Addison. In the following analysis of the characteristic patterns of sentence in his prose I shall try to demonstrate, partly with the help of comparisons with Dryden and Swift, the technique Addison employed in his building of sentences, and to what extent his usage signified a break with that of the previous generation.

ADDISON'S USAGE

When we try more closely to estimate the specific qualities that go to make up the easy fluency of Addison's prose, we are faced with great, almost insurmountable difficulties. His style is elusive, like that of most Augustan essayists: only still more so because the personal element in it is so much less obvious than in the prose of, say, Dryden, Steele, or Swift. As a journalist he had to vary his subjects and the way in which to treat them, and accordingly we find him employing all kinds of composition, often in one and the same paper. That is one reason why it is so difficult to compare Addison's style with, for example, that of Dryden in terms of adequate criticism; Dryden's prefatory essays are all of a rather specialized discursive kind.

Still it should be possible to detect some fundamental principles for the texture of Addison's prose style. We have already made some observations to this effect in the chapter on parallelism. That study was limited to the highly organized discursive essay for the simple reason that this is where parallelism belongs in the first place. Now coherence, too, is quite obviously a matter of organization. It is in fact the essential end of organization, while parallelism sometimes is an essential means to coherence. In consequence, to study coherence in Addison we should begin with and concentrate upon the discursive essay. There is a further very important reason for so doing, namely the comparison of Addison's prose texture with that of previous generations. This is one of the fundamental purposes of the whole study. And the only suitable material for a historical study of prose structure is discursive prose.

Another difficulty occurs as we try to define our method and its application to the language. The usual and natural way is to study the unit of language, the sentence, in its different forms: single, compound, and complex.

The snag is that up to the end of the seventeenth century there have been frequent discrepancies between the unities of thought and language. Thus the unit of language called the period was more or less standardized by Cicero to contain not more than four clauses representing a main thought with immediately relevant modifications. This limitation of the period was required for reasons of oral performance; not more should be contained in it than what could be uttered in one breath. In a synthetic language such as Latin this could be done without any very great difficulties, but not so in the analytic English. What was expressed in Latin by one word might require a complete clause in English; »senem» is translated by »when he was an old man,» and so on. This is one reason—and probably the most important— why the English period, especially up to the Restoration, could be seen to assume large, sometimes enormous proportions. The second sentence of Milton's pamphlet *Of Reformation* has about 400 words, and there are several sentences of around 200 words, for instance, in *Areopagitica*. Clarendon is another notable example. Thus the sentence was made to carry far more than it was meant for, and the function of the full stop as the marking of one complete thought was taken over by the colon and the semicolon. The *cola* became the units of thought corresponding to the classical standard. A consequence of this was that the significance of the full stop was largely reduced. The decision whether a full stop or a colon or semicolon should be used was often left to the discretion of the printer.

From about the last quarter of the seventeenth century, however, the habits of punctuation, like those of expression in general, began to settle down to certain standards established by the complexity of factors which promoted the Neo-classical principles of style. Addison's punctuation is fairly definite; there are no material differences in this respect either between the MS and the newspaper edition of the *Spectator*, or between the latter and the edition in four volumes revised by the author. In later editions, however, there are frequent alterations, though of small significance.

We may, then, be reasonably safe in regarding the sentence as a convenient unit of language for the purpose of studying coherence in Addison's prose, but we cannot use the sentence as a basis for comparison with earlier masters of prose without important modifications. Purely statistical evidence on average length of sentence and clauses per sentence of different authors, which has been presented from time to time by various scholars, must therefore not be taken at its face value, particularly not if we compare pre-Restoration authors with post-Restoration ones. Still, with these modifications, statistical computation clearly illustrates a marked tendency toward shortening the sentence during the Restoration. From an average of 60 words per sentence in Bacon (*Advancement of Learning*) and 50 in Milton (*Areopagitica*) the sentence narrows down to 38–40 in Dryden, Addison, and Swift. These three represent the general tendency. There is, however, at least one notable exception or rather deviation from this general trend. Browne belonged to the generation following Bacon and was a contemporary of Milton, yet his average of words per sentence is 33 only. Figures do not tell us anything about the qualities that are the most important in a study of style, namely the factors that go to the making of what we somewhat vaguely call tone and movement. The latter, which more directly concerns us now, is a quality of coherence; it has to do with transition and connection within the sentence and between sentences and paragraphs. The average length of sentence for Browne suggests a resemblance of style with the Augustans, while in fact he differs widely from them.

»Among our classic prose writers,» says Minto, »Addison is the standing example of a loose style. He is ostentatiously easy and flowing, making no effort to be periodic, but rather studiously avoiding the periodic structure. In his expository papers, when he is not expressly aiming at point, he takes the utmost freedom in adding clauses of explanation and amplification after he has made a full statement.»

Minto's definition of »loose style» evidently differs from the one suggested in the preceding chapter, which signifies the frail, end-linking connection between sometimes vast sets of clauses characteristic of Montaigne and Browne. Otherwise Minto's observation is on the whole correct.

To show Addison's technique of composition I have selected some examples from discursive papers in the *Spectator*. In so far as he differs from his great contemporaries, chiefly Dryden and Swift, this will as far as possible be illustrated.

1. Complex Sentences with One Main Clause
Addison usually begins a sentence with a statement in the form of a main clause followed by modifications:

The two great Ornaments of Virtue, which shew her in the most advantageous Views, and make her altogether lovely, are Chearfulness and Good-Nature. These generally go together, as a Man cannot be agreeable to others who is not easy within himself. They are both very requisite in a virtuous Mind, to keep out Melancholy

from the many serious Thoughts it is engaged in, and to hinder its natural Hatred of
Vice from souring into Severity and Censoriousness. (*Sp.* 243: 9)

This passage consists of three sentences of varying form but all having
the natural order of commonly accepted prose style.   In the first sentence the
main clause is inverted with subject and predicate severed by dependent
clauses.   Inversion serves emphasis, and as we have observed, Addison
handles emphatic devices with the utmost care.   He has recourse to inversion
only in cases where inversion would be natural, for instance in sentences
where the subject balances the predicate.   The effect of emphasis here is
further reduced through the insertion of the redundant relative clauses.   The
three sentences all begin with the main statement, whole or part of it; they
represent the vast majority of sentences of Addison as well as of most prose
writers since the Restoration.

He takes great liberties in separating the subject of the main clause from
its predicate, particularly when the subject is a person.   We find several
examples of this in his essays on Milton's Paradise Lost:

Milton, tho' his own natural Strength of Genius was capable of furnishing out
a perfect Work, has doubtless very much raised and ennobled his Conceptions, by
such an Imitation as that which *Longinus* has recommended. (*Sp.* 339: 3)

This principle leads him away from conversational order into periodicity; the only form of periodicity found in Addison.

Milton, to keep up an agreeable Variety in his Visions, after having raised in the
Mind of his Reader the several Ideas of Terror which are conformable to the Descrip-
tion of War, passes on to those softer Images of Triumphs and Festivals, in that
Vision of Lewdness and Luxury which ushers in the Flood. (*Sp.* 363: 18)

Sometimes Addison crowds whole systems of modificatory clauses and
phrases belonging to the subject between it and the verb; the procedure is
quite the reverse of his habitual order.   The use of this type is restricted to
judgment of a complex of things; hence it is exclusively critical in Addison's
hands.   One more example from the Milton essays:

Adam's Distress upon losing sight of this beautiful Phantom, with his Exclamations of Joy and Gratitude at the discovery of a real Creature, who resembled the
Apparition which had been presented to him in his Dream; the Approaches he makes
to her, and his Manner of Courtship; are all laid together in a most exquisite
Propriety of Sentiments. (*Sp.* 345: 14)

This form, a mannerism in his critical papers, is, however, periodical
only in a technical sense.   There is nothing here of the tone and movement
which belongs to the sixteenth- and seventeenth-century period, nothing of
the elevation of style that is the most essential part of its meaning.   Compare
this sentence from Milton:

For although a poet, soaring in the high reason of his fancies, with his garland
and singing robes about him, might, without apology, speak more of himself than I

mean to do; yet for me sitting here below in the cool element of prose, a mortal thing among many readers of no empyreal conceit, to venture and divulge unusual things of myself, I shall petition to the gentler sort, it may not be envy to me. (*The Reason of Church Government.*)

This manner was altogether foreign to Addison's nature, his cultural outlook and his aim. It soared far above the »middle» style that was Addison's, the style of »polite learning.» Moral philosophy for coffee-houses required a linguistic medium identical with that of well-bred conversation, not with the emotive grandeur of thought reflected in Milton's vaulted sentences. Addison's intellectual powers were limited to the province of the familiar essay, and of this limitation he made a supreme virtue. His philosophical speculations, even on intricate matters, never leave the reader in the dark, his ordering of thoughts is easy to follow at a glance. The periodic form just described is only a convenient means of comprehending a diversity of things or qualities under one head.

The form of sentence that Addison primarily employs and which we have described at the outset of this analysis may for want of a better term be called »sequence.» The term needs definition, as it may imply high organization of clauses as well as loose order, hypotaxis as well as parataxis. The common meaning of the term is perhaps one of clauses syntactically end-linked to each other with the thought moving forward by each clause as in the following example:

At the same time Sir Roger rode forward, and alighting, took up the Hare in his Arms; which he soon delivered up to one of his Servants with an Order, if she could be kept alive, to let her go in his great Orchard; where it seems he has several of these Prisoners of War, who live together in a very comfortable Captivity. (*Sp.* 116: 7)

This form of sequence belongs primarily to narrative or semi-narrative prose, coherence depending on a course of events. But the term may also be used, though perhaps inadequately, of any series of modifying clauses and phrases following upon a main statement. Not infrequently Addison spins out a sentence to considerable length by applying clauses and phrases which elucidate a thought or fact without bringing in altogether new aspects or turns of event. We have already studied one way in which he practices this, namely clausal and phrasal parallelism. And, as we shall see, parallelism plays a predominant, though not always conspicuous, part in Addison's sequence.

In the following two examples the rôle of parallelism as a means of coherence is evident enough:

For we may further observe, that Men of the greatest Abilities are most fired with Ambition: And that on the contrary, mean and narrow Minds are the least actuated by it: whether it be that a Man's Sense of his own Incapacities makes him despair of coming at Fame, or that he has not enough range of Thought to look out for any Good which does not more immediately relate to his Interest or Convenience, or that Providence, in the very Frame of his Soul, would not subject him to such a Passion as would be useless to the World, and a Torment to himself. (*Sp.* 255: 2)

Thus is Fame a thing difficult to be obtained by all, but particularly by those who thirst after it, since most Men have so much either of Ill-nature, or of Wariness, as not to gratify or sooth the Vanity of the Ambitious Man, and since this very Thirst after Fame naturally betrays him into such Indecencies as are a lessening to his Reputation, and is it self looked upon as a Weakness in the greatest Characters. (*Ibid.*: 10)

Those are characteristic examples of a common type of complex sentence in Addison. The striking feature about them is that neither of them contains more than one main clause. It is placed at the beginning of the sentence and is followed by sequences of dependent clauses of eight in the former and five in the latter period. Yet the reasoning is perfectly clear in both cases and is comprehended at a glance. What makes these sentences so lucid is partly the careful choice of words, partly—and perhaps to a higher degree—the organization of the clauses into clearly defined patterns. In the above cases the patterns are those of parallelism. In the first sentence the parallel is indicated by »whether it be that ... or that ... or that ... ;» in the second we have the parallel of »since ... and since ... ;» the latter being subdivided into two predicate members; »and since this very Thirst ... betrays him into ... ; and is it self looked upon ... » But the forms of parallelism here differ on one important point from those of which we have made a special study above; they differ from the latter in that they are parallels of distinction and thus necessary, being conditioned by the nature of the discourse in hand, while the other kind, as we have observed, are largely of a pleonastic character.

The parallel construction here has the important function of serving as a skeleton of the reasoning by furnishing a system of dependent and sub-dependent clauses, or what is termed hypotaxis. The hypotactic system is in fact the chief virtue of Addison's sentence structure; it ensures coherence, however great the complexity of his matter, and it is the main reason why his prose is at once flowing and perspicuous. Like most features of good prose it is not noticed, except when absent. The regularity of such sentences with their recurring pattern of clauses may seem, if anything, tedious and insipid to the modern reader, but was surely a source of delight to the reading public of the eighteenth century.

Sometimes, however, his sense of proportion failed, and he took too much into the sentence. Even an ardent admirer of his style like Blair could not approve of this period:

I must therefore desire him to remember, that by the Pleasures of the Imagination, I mean only such Pleasures as arise originally from Sight, and that I divide these Pleasures into two Kinds: My Design being first of all to Discourse of those Primary Pleasures of the Imagination, which entirely proceed from such Objects as are before our Eyes, and in the next place to speak of those Secondary Pleasures of the Imagination which flow from the Ideas of visible Objects, when the Objects are not actually before the Eye, but are called up into our Memories, or formed into agreeable Visions of Things that are either Absent or Fictitious. (*Sp.* 411: 3)

There are many examples of this kind in the series of essays on the Pleasures of the Imagination, from the first essay of which the example above is taken. Blair and Minto among others have remarked on this mis-placement of clauses in Addison. Minto finds that »It is chiefly in the papers on the Pleasures of the Imagination that the inconvenience of this loose style is felt, and then chiefly because it goes along with a vague and rambling train of thought.» And Blair in his sentence-by-sentence criticism on part of this series of essays (Nos. 411–414) says about this sentence that» It is a great rule in laying down the division of a subject, to study neatness and brevity as much as possible. The divisions are then more distinctly apprehended and more easily remembered. This sentence is not perfectly happy in that respect. It is somewhat clogged by a tedious phraseology. 'My design being first of all to discourse—in the next place to speak of—such objects as are before our eyes—things that are either absent or fictitious.' Several words might have been spared here; and the Style made more neat and compact.»

All the examples of sentence structure in Addison hitherto quoted have had two things in common: only one main clause, placed in an initial position, and a more or less highly organized system of hypotaxis resting on a framework of parallel clauses. As to the first of these two features, it is observed by Blair that Addison always kept the natural order of speech and never had recourse to the inversions so widely employed by authors who endeavoured to imitate the Latin. Blair finds that» For the most part, with us, the important words are placed in the beginning of the Sentence ... And this, indeed, seems the most plain and natural order, to place that in the front which is the chief object of the proposition we are laying down. Sometimes, however, when we intend to give weight to a Sentence, it is of advantage to suspend the meaning for a little, and then bring it out full at the close.» —As examples of the ambitions of authors to imitate the Latin inversions in English Blair mentions Milton, Gordon—who in his translation of Tacitus has the expression »Into this hole, thrust themselves three Roman senators»—and, among Addison's great contemporaries, Pope and Shaftesbury. In contrast to Shaftesbury Addison is seen to be always »following the most natural and obvious order of the Language; and if, by this means, he has less pomp and majesty than Shaftesbury, he has, in return, more nature, more ease and simplicity; which are beauties of a higher order.»

Blair, with Hurd and, of course, Johnson, had most to do with forming the traditional opinion on Addison's style. They all applied themselves to the task with the attitude of critical evaluation founded on the doctrine of correctness. Blair praises Addison's natural order of speech, by which he means the method of starting with the main proposition. At the same time he finds that he wastes words: the style could have been more neat and compact. Minto points out the freedom with which he adds clauses of explanation and amplification to a full statement. Neither of them goes further than that; they do not try to explain how Addison could attain clearness and perspicuity at all with this way of writing.

[Sections 2–6 have been omitted.]

7. Addison's Rôle in the Making of the Modern English Sentence Structure

Dryden's prose style may be said to be the sum total of the achievements of English prose during the seventeenth century. With Addison a new phase in the history of prose style begins. It is not only that Addison perfected the instrument forged by Dryden, as is often said; there are, as we have seen, fundamental differences between them in most of the factors that determine literary communication. And these differences are clearly observable as we compare their styles, although the development of English as a vehicle for expository reasoning towards a standardized essay style was practically finished by Dryden and left little to be improved upon. Swift, again, is contemporary with Addison, but his prose style shows a strong kinship with the freedom of expression of the past generations. In so far as Swift can be paired with anybody in matters of style it would be with South, who himself was rather old-fashioned compared with his contemporaries Tillotson, Temple, and Dryden.

Where Addison most clearly differs from Dryden—and also from Swift —is in the nature and, one might say, the supply of matter; hence in the nature of its treatment: in vocabulary and in clausal and periodic structure, in imagery. Dryden is all the time talking shop, he is always discussing problems and facts about which he has the most thorough knowledge and experience of his time. Therefore he has an enormous wealth of matter, of arguments, relevant and irrelevant circumstances, associations:—»thoughts, such as they are, come crowding in so fast upon me that my only difficulty is to choose or to reject, to run them into verse, or to give them the other harmony of prose.» For Addison the nature and supply of matter presented quite different problems. Addison was to all intents and purposes a lay-preacher. His ambition was »to enliven morality with wit and to temper wit with morality,» and his topics were consequently to a large degree of an abstract and general nature. To this come other important circumstances: he had to observe the limit of space in his paper, and see that he did not give his readers more than they could chew. All this contributed to limit the scope of matter to a considerable degree.

Now it is natural that—even apart from psychological factors—wealth of factual matter has a tendency to reduce the problem of form to relative insignificance, as is the case with Dryden, and on the contrary, a limited supply of matter—especially abstract matter—would depend greatly on form. There is much in what de Quincey has to say on a similar question that applies to the Dryden-Addison situation. A man who has absolute facts to communicate from some branch of study external to himself,» says de Quincey, »... is careless of style; or at least he may be so because he is independent of style, for what he has to communicate neither readily admits, nor much needs, any graces in the mode of communication; the matter transcends and oppresses the manner. The matter tells without any manner at all. But he who has to treat a vague question, such as Cicero calls a *questio infinita*, where everything is to be finished out of his own peculiar feelings, or his own way of viewing things (in contradiction to a *questio finita* where determined *data* from without already furnish the main materials) soon finds that the manner of treating it not only transcends the matter, but very often, and in a very great proportion, is the matter.»

In comparing the essential features of sentence structure of Addison with those of Dryden and Swift my aim has been to point out the new cast of the period that sets Addison apart from his famous contemporaries. It appeared that both Dryden—who also stands for many other Restoration writers—and Swift took liberties in the joining of clauses that Addison would never allow himself. This is, however, not clearly evident from a purely syntactical analysis. If we construct diagrams of sentences for instance with M = main clause, D = dependent clause, d = sub-dependent clause, d^1 = »sub-sub-dependent» clause, s = clauses »saved» by the absolute participle construction; and apply the system on, say, the second sentence of the first paragraph of Swift's Political Lying: »We are told the devil is the father of lies, . . .» we get the following diagram: MDD; DdDss. Dd^1d; $sddd^1$. The example of Dryden quoted above would yield a similar pattern. Addison does not go to these extremes, but according to syntactical diagrams he does not stop far short of them. The third sentence of the third paragraph of the *Sp.* 411. »I must therefore desire him to remember . . .» has this diagram: MDD; sdd^1; $dd^1d^2d^2d^2d^3$. The difference seems to be slight. But if we turn from structural relation to thought relation, the difference is enormous. For Swift and Dryden every new clause brings in a new stage of reasoning, each clause being loosely related to the one before it. Dryden and most of the writers of the late seventeenth century have a tendency to use dependent clauses as vehicles for immediate continuity of reasoning; Swift also has definite leanings in this direction. Addison, on the other hand, uses dependent clauses as subordinated delegates for the meaning he does not express through the main clauses. What Addison introduced was simply a method of obtaining coherence which for its efficacy depends partly on close relations of meaning between the parts of the sentence, and partly on the widest possible spreading of natural sense-content emphasis.

So far as sentence structure goes this means, I think, a decisive turning-point towards modern English prose. It would be wrong to say that Addison alone stood for the new order—we must include the collaborators of the *Tatler* and the *Spectator* and the *Guardian* such as Steele and Hughes—but in this respect Addison certainly set the tone.

PARALLELISM: JOHNSON

W. K. Wimsatt, Jr.

Among the qualities of Samuel Johnson's style most often noticed by critics has been something which they called "balance" or "parallelism." There has been no doubt what things these terms referred to, what clauses or phrases,

From W. K. Wimsatt, Jr., *The Prose Style of Samuel Johnson* (New Haven: Yale University Press, 1941), Ch. 1, "Parallelism," pp. 15–37, at pp. 15–20, 22–32. Copyright © 1941 by Yale University Press. Reprinted by permission of Yale University Press. Notes have been omitted.

or at least what were the most conspicuous examples. On the other hand there is a distinction, suggested even in the two terms "parallelism" and "balance," which has been either overlooked or, if noticed, pursued with disregard for the relation between the two qualities distinguished. These two qualities are parallelism of meaning and parallelism of sound. Perhaps it is the first that a critic has been more aware of when he used the term "parallelism," and perhaps the second, when he used "balance." And it is the second by which he is carried off when he dallies with the terms "cadence" and "rhythm." We may begin to form an opinion of Johnson's parallelism when we consider that of sound as auxiliary to, and made significant by, that of meaning. Parallel meaning, or multiplied similar meaning—that is one of the basic notions to be explored for Johnson's style, and those who have used terms like "repetition" and "amplification" have been nearer the truth than those who have talked most of "balance."

Any series of connected meanings is in some degree a parallel series. The least degree of parallelism is that the sentences (or clauses, or phrases, or words) are all parts of the same discourse—with reference to the whole meaning each has the status of member. The highest degree is some kind of immediate equality with reference to a third element, and this supported by some equality of form. Suppose three clauses, the first of which tells the cause of an act, the second the act, and the third its consequence. These three meanings are parallel if the sequence is taken as a whole and if as a whole it is referred to a fourth meaning. Yet they are nonparallel if considered in their reciprocal relations. Further, if the first and second be considered as the cause of the third, they assume a special parallel relation of their own; and if the second and third be considered as the result of the first, they too assume their own parallel. Not that in a single passage all these parallel meanings will occur simultaneously, or with equal emphasis. It is the function of syntax and other forms of meaning to show the intended relations of such members to one another and to a whole or another member of a whole in which they occur.

An opposite but equally basic element of all discourse is that of difference. If two clauses are parallel, say as illustrations of a third statement, they must yet differ between themselves in some degree however slight, or both would not be used. If the first and second members of the example used above express a cause of which the meaning of the third member is the effect, the first and second are so far parallel, yet they are different too inasmuch as they express a cause and effect relation between themselves. If beets and carrots are referred to only as examples of vegetables, they are yet different, for beets are not carrots.

*   *   *   *

There are in general three explicit ways of binding groups of words, of indicating parallel: by the use of conjunctive or disjunctive words; by the syntax of words, that is, the relation of one word to two or more others; and by the repetition of identical words. These ways, especially the first two, have an affinity and frequently appear in combination. ... Repetition of an initial word, especially of some more emphatic or special word, is called by the rhetoricians "anaphora." These three explicit ways of parallel are the inevitable expressions of any writer who dwells upon, elaborates, or emphasizes any point, even for a moment.

We move nearer to the characteristically Johnsonian parallel with the next degree, that of implicitly expressive forms. I say "forms," not "form," and mean a relation between A and B and one between X and Y, as opposed to a relation of A to both X and Y which makes X and Y parallel. Thus: a subject ... makes both its predicated verbs parallel. This is explicitly expressive. But if a subject is followed by its predicate in one clause, and another subject is followed by its predicate in a second clause, the parallel exists only by the occurrence of these two like forms side by side and is expressive only implicitly. If the clauses are joined by a conjunction, this adds explicit reference to the parallel, yet the parallel continues to exist independently and is greater or less in accordance with the resemblance in form of the clauses.

All like syntactic constructions create, of course, insofar as they are like, an implicitly expressive formal parallel. Such a parallel, however, of such unavoidable occurrence, is not what I wish to class as a parallel of implicit expression. This parallel begins only when like syntactic positions are filled by words of like substance and like weight or emphasis.

and as this practice is a commodious subject of raillery to the gay, and of declamation to the serious, it has been ridiculed, with all the pleasantry of wit, and exaggerated with all the amplifications of rhetorick

Here we have not two sentences, but two predicates each of three emphatic elements, each of these elements in the one exactly paralleled in syntax, and closely paralleled in substance, by each in the other, and two of them closely paralleled in weight of sound. Further, the two halves of the predicate are matched by two halves in the introductory dependent clause, these halves themselves each consisting of two elements closely matched. So the whole construction is a quintuple parallel, broken, so that the arrangement is: a,b;v,w: :c,d,c;x,y,z. This is formal parallel, implicitly expressive. For the sake of brevity, let us hereafter call it "implicit parallel."

Having begun with an elaborate example, we must now return to the germ of the matter. The simplest form which implicit parallel can assume is that where the emphatic elements in parallel positions consist of a single word each and are the whole of the members—that is, in simple pairings of words, whether with or without conjunctive or disjunctive words or elements of identity.

> faults and follies
> labour or hazard
> so smooth and so flowery
> to enlarge or embellish
> against warning, against experience

It seems to me that the parts of speech involved are of no consequence to our classification.

In simple pairs of words a writer may be said to employ an unavoidable measure of implicit parallel, but it is plain that in the next degree of implicit parallel, where there are two elements in each member, he has sought something that might easily have been avoided. Two nouns, for example, each modified by an adjective in the same position, make a conspicuous parallel, especially if the adjectives are of about the same weight. A good many alternatives are obvious: that either or both of the nouns lack the adjective, or that either or both be modified in some other way. The parallel has considerable value as implicit expression. Again, what parts of speech constitute the double elements is a matter of no concern. There are a good many possibilities:

> retrenching exuberances and correcting inaccuracies
> integrity of understanding and nicety of discernment
> unnatural thoughts and rugged numbers
> shaven by the scythe, and levelled by the roller
> judgment is cold, and knowledge is inert

So a writer may continue to multiply parallel elements, relating the elements within the members by any kind of syntax. For instance, three elements:

> examples of national calamities,
> and scenes of extensive misery

Four elements:

> the various forms of connubial infelicity,
> the unexpected causes of lasting discord

Or he may reach five elements, as in the example with which this series was begun.

We have classed multiplications according to the degrees of parallelism which they exhibit—that is, the elements of parallel in each member. Another classification is possible, according to the number of members. All the examples of implicit parallelism given so far have been of two members. The example of multiplication (with parallelism only of substance) taken from Hazlitt had three members. But any degree of parallelism may appear in two, three, or more members. One element in three members:

> reproach, hatred, and opposition

Two elements in three members:

> her physick of the mind,
> her catharticks of vice,
> or lenitives of passion

The greater the number of elements, or the greater the number of members, the rarer the phenomenon, the more space it takes in its context, and the more significant it is of the style of the author.

*   *   *   *

Every pairing of words, as we have seen, affirms (or denies) two notions which are alike insofar as they are paired (have the same immediate relation to a third notion) and which are different insofar as one adds anything to the other. In some, in "constituent and fundamental principle," the emphasis is so far on the harmony of these notions that little if any difference, or range, is adverted to. In others, in "Critick and Philosopher," there is stress on the equal relation of these two notions to a third, "Aristotle," and with this a clear advertence to the distinction between the two. It is but carrying this tendency to its limit to assert the equal relation of two opposites in a scale to a third notion:

> that vehemence of desire which presses through
> right and wrong to its gratification

Right and wrong are antithetical, yet here, where both are affirmed in the same respect, their expressive value is that of a pair placed at extremes of a range and so emphasizing its length. Rasselas and Imlac press over crags and brambles. Vehemence of desire presses through right and wrong.

> to find, and to keep
> names for day and night
> none of them would either steal or buy

There is little point in arguing whether each of these involves an antithesis or only a distinction.

Antithetic parallel is of course limited to two members. But, like the other forms of multiplication, it admits multiple elements of implicit parallel and sometimes through these shows itself more clearly as antithesis. It may have two elements:

> a state too high for contempt
> and too low for envy

Or three:

> partiality, by which some vices have hitherto
> escaped censure, and some virtues wanted recommendation

And so on, though perfect examples are very scarce.

Antithesis of this sort I should like to call antithesis I, to distinguish it from the truer antithesis ..., which we may call antithesis II. While antithesis I in pointing out opposite notions either affirms or denies both in the same respect, antithesis II makes a distinction in order to affirm one part and deny the other. Antithesis I, inasmuch as it is an antithesis, is often on the verge of becoming antithesis II. If we affirm both A and its opposite B, our affirmation frequently takes the form: Not only A but B, in which case we see more easily that what we mean implies: Not A alone but both A and B, and this is antithesis II. . . .

*   *   *   *

In the course of analyzing Johnson's parallelism I have, as a matter of fact, done a good deal of counting both in selected passages of Johnson and in passages of Addison and Hazlitt taken by way of contrast. But in the comparative description which follows I have assumed that general statement, illustrated, is more intelligible than statistical scrupulosity and equally entitled to credence.

Three passages from Johnson have been set against three from Addison and three from Hazlitt, but not with any intention of illustrating the history of English prose. The chronological positions of Addison and Hazlitt might be reversed. The two have simply been chosen as points recognized to be at some distance from Johnson in the field of prose style.

From Johnson I have chosen *Rambler* No. 2, *Idler* No. 10, and a section of the *Life of Pope*. For the degree to which they exemplify his whole tendency, one may consult a later chapter, where the consistency of his style is considered. But a study of style ought not to be primarily a study of average style; it is too likely to lead to no conclusion. The same recognition of meaning that leads us to choose certain characteristics for attention leads us to choose the places where they may be found. If it is plain that Johnson's *Idlers* are on the whole of a lighter, less philosophic cast than the *Ramblers*, and that the narrative portions of the *Lives* are less discursive than the discursive portions (for it is just as plain as that), and if we look on Johnson as most different from other writers when he is being philosophic or discursive, there is no reason why we should average the characteristics of all his ways of writing in order to see what is distinctive of the Johnsonian style. I have chosen these three passages because they display a consistent texture of the characteristics which critics for a century and a half have called Johnsonian. *Rambler* No. 2, "The necessity and danger of looking into futurity," is a fair example of Johnson's abstract, moral, or philosophic essay; *Idler* No. 10, "Political credulity," of his treating a didactic theme more concretely; the section from the *Life of Pope*, of his later discursive style.

From Addison I have chosen a part of *Spectator* No. 177, "Good-nature as a moral virtue" (which shows us Addison writing on something like a Johnsonian topic); all of *Spectator* No. 106, "Sir Roger de Coverley's country seat" (which treats a more typically Addisonian, seminarrative subject); and a part of *Spectator* No. 267, "Criticism on Paradise Lost." From Hazlitt I have chosen part of the essay "On the Love of the Country," part of "My First Acquaintance with Poets," and part of the lecture "On Dryden and Pope."

One of the first things that may be learned from a comparison of these nine passages is that we cannot assign to the simple quality of multiplication any effect distinctive of Johnson's prose. Numerically: if one counts all the multiplications of all classes (all coordinate words, phrases, and clauses, of all degrees of explicit and implicit parallel) in each passage, it is found that Johnson far outweighs Addison, but that Johnson himself is outweighed by Hazlitt. We may say of Johnson and Hazlitt that in contrast to Addison their style is marked by the tendency to multiplication. But Johnson is distinguishable from Hazlitt and, more strikingly than by mere multiplication, from Addison in those two tendencies which we have seen are founded in multiplication—that toward emphasis rather than range, and that toward parallelism of forms. I resume first the discussion of parallelism.

In multiplications having only explicit parallel—syntax, conjunctions, identical words—Johnson, Addison, and Hazlitt are again about equal if their usages are merely counted. But if examples are compared (i.e., if our definitions are refined), then even in these common prose elements Johnson's inclination to parallel may be seen. In general Johnson tends to greater use of identical elements, to nearly identical constructions of almost equal length and weight—things which become particularly noticeable in multiplications of three or more members. Consider a long multiplication from Hazlitt:

No doubt, the sky is beautiful; the clouds sail majestically along its bosom; the sun is cheering; there is something exquisitely graceful in the manner in which a plant or tree puts forth its branches; the motion with which they bend and tremble in the evening breeze is soft and lovely; there is music in the babbling of a brook; the view from the top of a mountain is full of grandeur; nor can we behold the ocean with indifference.

There is a momentary inclination to implicit parallelism here: "the clouds sail...the sun is." The identical element "there is" appears twice. But on the whole, for the shortness of the members and the similarity of the material, there is marked variation. Beside this see one from Addison:

You would take his Valet de Chambre for his Brother, his Butler is grey-headed, his Groom is one of the gravest men that I have ever seen, and his Coachman has the Looks of a Privy-Counsellor.

"His" is a rather unobtrusive identical element in each member, and "is" appears as the main verb of two consecutive members. The four nouns, "Valet de Chambre," "Butler," "Groom," and "Coachman" tend to be elements of implicit parallel. But the first is a compound of three words and is the object of a verb, while the other three are all subjects and single words. The general variety in constructions and positions of emphasis through the fourth members is plain. Beside these two multiplications see one from Johnson:

He has known those who saw the bed into which the pretender was conveyed in a warming-pan. He often rejoices that the nation was not enslaved by the *Irish*. He believes that king *William* never lost a battle, and that if he had lived one year longer he would have conquered *France*. He holds that *Charles* the first was a papist. He allows there were some good men in the reign of queen *Anne*, but the peace of *Utrecht* brought a blast upon the nation, and has been the cause of all the evil that we have suffered to the present hour. He believes that the scheme of the *South Sea* was well intended, but that it miscarried by the influence of *France*. He considers a standing army as the bulwark of liberty, thinks us secured from corruption by septennial parliaments, relates how we are enriched and strengthened by the electoral dominions, and declares that the publick debt is a blessing to the nation.

Here we have seven sentences, each beginning with the element of identity "he" followed by the main verb, which in each case is a verb of mental action. "He has known," "rejoices," "believes," "holds," "allows," "believes," "considers." Four of these verbs are followed by the conjunction "that." In the third sentence "that" is repeated, so that the sentence makes a pair of members, each about equal in weight to the sentences which have preceded. The fifth sentence is divided antithetically, with two parts following "but," and each about equal to the introductory stem, and all three not much different in length and weight from the simpler sentences. The sixth sentence has two antithetical parts, the second reënforced with a "that." And in conclusion comes a quadruplet laid out on the four main verbs "considers," "thinks," "relates," "declares," to all of which the subject is the first word, "he." In the eleven words of saying and thinking which govern the constructions of this long multiplication, there is a weighty element of parallel and one which is manifestly designed.

*   *   *   *

We may proceed to multiplications with implicit parallel. The number of those with one element only (doublets, triplets, or quadruplets of single words) is actually less for Johnson than for Hazlitt, an effect which may be considered only complementary of Johnson's opportunism in the elaboration of parallels of two or more elements. It is in such more complicated parallels that the Johnsonian tendency is manifest beyond question. Here both statistics and comparison of examples speak eloquently. This is preeminently the Johnsonian province.

Even in the simpler of these constructions Hazlitt is much inclined to irregularities. He will have one member longer by a prepositional phrase: "in its simple majesty, in its immediate appeal to the senses." He will separate the members by a phrase which explicitly modifies one and is understood of the other: "a strange wildness in his aspect, a dusky obscurity." Or he will add another adjective to one member: "the sequestered copse and wide extended heath." Johnson more regularly follows the models: "excitements of fear, and allurements of desire," "fluctuating in measures, or immersed in business."

Neither Hazlitt nor Addison ever reaches Johnson's extremes. When Hazlitt writes:

the utmost grandeur to our conceptions of nature, or the utmost force to the passions of the heart

it is for him an excessively heavy parallel. And so for Addison when he writes:

from some new Supply of Spirits or a more kindly Circulation of the Blood

Johnson does not begin to be unusual until he writes something like a doublet of five elements, cut in half and alternated, such as that we have already quoted from *Rambler* No. 2, or, if we may go afield to *Rasselas*, a triplet of doublets, the first doublet having four elements, the second, two, and the third, seven:

the various forms of connubial infelicity, the unexpected causes of lasting discord, the diversities of temper, the oppositions of opinion, the rude collisions of contrary desire where both are urged by violent impulses, the obstinate contests of disagree-able virtues, where both are supported by consciousness of good intention

Or, if we go to *Rambler* No. 129, an antithesis of four elements, chopped and alternated, so that instead of the commoner A,A,A,A: B,B,B,B, we have A,A:B,B; A:B,A:B.

according to the inclinations of nature, or the impressions of precept, the daring and the cautious may move in different directions without touching upon rashness or cowardice

Such constructions, though they occur but rarely, yet fill a large space and are conspicuous among the emphatic effects of the whole writing.

We have seen that any member of a writing stands in a relation of equality and in one of difference to the members adjacent to it. A writer may insist, by explicit or implicit means, on the equality or on the opposite, the difference of the members within their frame of equality or parallel. He may exploit one kind of meaning or the other. And if he does one or the other consistently, his writing must assume a surface or texture of meaning directly relatable to this. If he recurrently gives to his multiplied phrases or clauses a turn toward equality, then the relations of member to member, of premise to premise and to conclusion, will be strengthened and plain; the whole sequence of meaning will have a high degree of coherence and regularity—but this will be at the expense of modulation, of individuality of premise, of variety. In a given multiplication in a given writing there must always be a specific demand for a degree of parallel and for an inverse degree of variety. Either a greater parallel or a greater variety will be the detail of meaning that better completes the whole intended meaning of the composi-tion, fills it out to the greater relevancy and satisfaction. When Hazlitt says of Johnson, "All his periods are cast in the same mould, are of the same size and shape, and consequently have little fitness to the variety of things he professes to treat of," he accuses Johnson of preferring the meaning of parallel to a more relevant meaning of variety.

SENECAN LOOSE STYLE: STERNE

J. M. Stedmond

Morris W. Croll distinguishes two main types of anti-Ciceronian style: the "curt" and the "loose," with the aphoristic *style coupé* forming the core of

From J. M. Stedmond, "Style and *Tristram Shandy*," *Modern Language Quarterly*, XX (1959), 243–251, at pp. 245–246. Reprinted by permission of *Modern Language Quarterly* and J. M. Stedmond. A note has been omitted.

the "baroque" reaction against the overelaborate Ciceronian periods so common among Renaissance prose stylists. Among the most notable features of the curt period are the lack of syntactic connections between main clauses and the fact that the idea of the whole period is contained in the first clause—the advance thus being not logical, but rather in a series of new expressions of the concept first stated. The description, early in Volume I of *Tristram Shandy*, of Parson Yorick's journey through his parish astride his horse, is an excellent example of the curt period:

> Labour stood still as he pass'd,—the bucket hung suspended in the middle of the well,—the spinning-wheel forgot its round,—even chuck-farthing and shuffle-cap themselves stood gaping till he had got out of sight. . . .

But this is only part of a longer, looser construction. More typically Sternean is the following version of what Croll refers to as the "loose" period:

> But I was begot and born to misfortunes;—for my poor mother, whether it was wind or water;—or a compound of both,—or neither;—or whether it was simply the mere swell of imagination and fancy in her;—or how far a strong wish and desire to have it so, might mislead her judgment;—in short, whether she was deceived or deceiving in this matter, it no way becomes me to decide. . . .

Syntactic links are provided, but they connect no lucid and coherent train of logic. The narrator seems intent to give the impression that he is jotting down his thoughts just as they come into his mind, together with any parenthetical asides which they suggest. The loose period expresses even better than the *style coupé* the anti-Ciceronian prejudice against formality of procedure and the rhetoric of the schools. It obtains its characteristic effects by using syntactic links, such as relative pronouns and subordinating conjunctions, which are, logically, strict and binding, to advance the idea, and yet, at the same time, it relaxes at will the tight construction which they seem to impose.

Tristram's "good-humoured, Shandean style," written, he claims, "one half *full*,—and t'other *fasting*," often seems almost a parody of the baroque period. Here is a passage from Volume VI, for example, in which the loose style is unmistakably caricatured:

> I told the Christian reader—I say *Christian*—hoping he is one—and if he is not, I am sorry for it—and only beg he will consider the matter with himself, and not lay the blame entirely upon this book,—
> I told him, Sir—for in good truth, when a man is telling a story in the strange way I do mine, he is obliged continually to be going backwards and forwards to keep all tight together in the reader's fancy—which, for my own part, if I did not take heed to do more than at first, there is so much unfixed and equivocal matter starting up, with so many breaks and gaps in it,—and so little service do the stars afford, which, nevertheless, I hang up in some of the darkest passages, knowing that the world is apt to lose its way, with all the lights the sun itself at noon day can give it— and now, you see, I am lost myself! . . .

All the tendencies inherent in the loosely linked, "trailing" period are here carried to the extreme, with the inevitable result—utter confusion.

SUGGESTIONS FOR RESEARCH

1. The eighteenth century is generally described as the age of perspicuity and intelligibility in prose style. As E. Morgan (1951) states it, "after 1660 there was a broadening tendency for matter to outweigh expressiveness." Search for evidence which would contradict that easy generalization. Who else, besides Swift (*A Tale of a Tub*) and Sterne, are highly expressive writers?

2. According to Lewis (1894), "Proportion in the paragraph pretty steadily increases from Temple to Arnold, both in the way of assigning due bulk to the amplification of important ideas, and in the way of distributing emphasis by varying sentence-length." Test these assertions by examining selected texts from the history of prose. What is the state of the paragraph prior to Temple? Who in the eighteenth century is most outstanding in the due proportion of his paragraphs; who least? What criteria do you employ to measure proportion?

3. See the definition of "gothic" style in the Glossary. Examine a passage in a so-called gothic novel to determine exactly what stylistic traits are actually characteristic of such a novel.

4. Adolph (1968) concludes that "normal prose after the age of Glanvill remains a means of useful communication rather than self-expression or overt artifice." In contrast, Dobrée (1934) perceives the development of a "profound division" between the spoken and the written language in the seventeenth century: "The stylists of the eighteenth century seem to have taken their writing farther and farther away from their speech." Which argument is better supported? What does Adolph mean by a prose of "useful communication"? What does Dobrée mean by "speech"?

5. Kraus (1968) dramatizes the variety of Ben Franklin's styles, which he attributes to Franklin's responsiveness to different occasions, purposes, and audiences. What other Restoration and eighteenth-century writers composed in a variety of styles? Select various brief passages by one writer which seem stylistically diverse and by a close analysis define the causes of the diversity.

6. Combine the methods of Adolph (1968, pp. 26–44 and 246–256) with those of Craddock (1968) for the analysis of other texts.

7. Survey the various descriptions of plain style. Which one is the best? Construct a better description from the best approaches, and examine selected passages by your criteria. See Milic (1967a).

8. Compare the various analyses of one author—for example, Craddock (1965) and Hayes (1965) on Gibbon. Evaluate the relative quality of the studies.

SELECTIONS FOR ANALYSIS

JOHN BUNYAN (1628–1688)
From Preface to Grace Abounding to the Chief of Sinners

I could have enlarged much in this my discourse, of my temptations and troubles for sin; as also of the merciful kindness and working of GOD with my soul: I could also have stepped into a style much higher than this, in which I have here discoursed, and could have adorned all things more than here I have seemed to do, but I dare not: GOD did not play in tempting of me; neither did I play, when I sunk as into a bottomless Pit, when *the pangs of Hell caught hold upon me*; wherefore I may not play in my relating of them, but be plain and simple, and lay down the thing as it was. He that liketh it, let him receive it; and he that doth not, let him produce a better. *Farewell.*

From S. C. Freer, ed., *Grace Abounding to the Chief of Sinners; or a Brief and Faithful Relation of the Exceeding Mercy of God in Christ to His Poor Servant John Bunyan* (London: Methuen, 1903), pp. 5–6. A footnote has been omitted.

THOMAS SPRAT (1635–1713)
From The History of the Royal Society

Their Manner of Discourse
Thus they have directed, judg'd, conjectur'd upon, and improved *Experiments.* But lastly, in these, and all other businesses, they have come under their care; there is one thing more, about which the *Society* has been most sollicitous; and that is, the manner of their *Discourse*: which, unless they had been very watchful to keep in due temper, the whole spirit and vigour of their *Design*, had been soon eaten out, by the luxury and redundance of *speech.* The ill effects of this superfluity of talking, have already overwhelm'd most other *Arts* and *Professions*; insomuch, that when I consider the means of *happy living*, and the causes of their corruption, I can hardly forbear recanting what I said before; and concluding, that *eloquence* ought to be

---

From Jackson I. Cope and Harold Whitmore Jones, eds., *The History of the Royal Society* (St. Louis: Washington University Studies, 1958), pp. 111–113. Reprinted by permission of Washington University Press. The modern "s" has been used.

banish'd out of all *civil Societies*, as a thing fatal to Peace and good Manners. To this opinion I should wholly incline; if I did not find, that it is a Weapon, which may be as easily procur'd by *bad* men, as *good*: and that, if these should onely cast it away, and those retain it; the *naked Innocence* of vertue, would be upon all occasions expos'd to the *armed Malice* of the wicked. This is the chief reason, that should now keep up the Ornaments of speaking, in any request: since they are so much degenerated from their original usefulness. They were at first, no doubt, an admirable Instrument in the hands of *Wise Men*: when they were onely employ'd to describe *Goodness, Honesty, Obedience*; in larger, fairer, and more moving Images: to represent *Truth*, cloth'd with Bodies; and to bring *Knowledg* back again to our very senses, from whence it was at first deriv'd to our understandings. But now they are generally chang'd to worse uses: They make the *Fancy* disgust the best things, if they come found, and unadorn'd: they are in open defiance against *Reason*; professing, not to hold much correspondence with that; but with its Slaves, *the Passions*: they give the mind a motion too changeable, and bewitching, to consist with *right practice*. Who can behold, without indignation, how many mists and uncertainties, these specious *Tropes* and *Figures* have brought on our Knowledg? How many rewards, which are due to more profitable, and difficult *Arts*, have been still snatch'd away by the easie vanity of *fine speaking*? For now I am warm'd with this just Anger, I cannot withhold my self, from betraying the shallowness of all these seeming Mysteries; upon which, *we Writers*, and *Speakers*, look so bigg. And, in few words, I dare say; that of all the Studies of men, nothing may be sooner obtain'd, than this vicious abundance of *Phrase*, this trick of *Metaphors*, this volubility of *Tongue*, which makes so great a noise in the World. But I spend words in vain; for the evil is now so inveterate, that it is hard to know whom to *blame*, or where to begin to *reform*. We all value one another so much, upon this beautiful deceipt; and labour so long after it, in the years of our education: that we cannot but ever after think kinder of it, than it deserves. And indeed, in most other parts of Learning, I look on it to be a thing almost utterly desperate in its cure: and I think, it may be plac'd amongst those *general mischiefs*; such, as the *dissention* of Christian Princes, the *want of practice* in Religion, and the like; which have been so long spoken against, that men are become insensible about them; every one shifting off the fault from himself to others; and so they are only made bare common places of complaint. It will suffice my present purpose, to point out, what has been done by the *Royal Society*, towards the correcting of its excesses in *Natural Philosophy*; to which it is, of all others, a most profest enemy.

They have therefore been most rigorous in putting in execution, the only Remedy, that can be found for this *extravagance*: and that has been, a constant Resolution, to reject all the amplifications, digressions, and swellings of style: to return back to the primitive purity, and shortness, when men deliver'd so many *things*, almost in an equal number of *words*. They have exacted from all their members, a close, naked, natural way of speaking; positive expressions; clearsenses; a native easiness; bringing all things as near the Mathematical plainness, as they can: and preferring the language of Artizans, Countrymen, and Merchants, before that, of Wits, or Scholars.

JOHN DRYDEN (1631–1700)
From Defence of the Epilogue

In the first place, therefore, it will be necessary to state, in general, what this refinement is, of which we treat; and that, I think, will not be defined amiss: *An improvement of our Wit, Language, and Conversation; or, an alteration in them for the better.*

To begin with Language. That an alteration is lately made in ours, or since the writers of the last age (in which I comprehend Shakespeare, Fletcher, and Jonson), is manifest. Any man who reads those excellent poets, and compares their language with what is now written, will see it almost in every line; but that this is an improvement of the language, or an alteration for the better, will not so easily be granted. For many are of a contrary opinion, that the English tongue was then in the height of its perfection; that from Jonson's time to ours it has been in a continual declination, like that of the Romans from the age of Virgil to Statius, and so downward to Claudian; of which, not only Petronius, but Quintilian himself so much complains, under the person of Secundus, in his famous dialogue *de Causis corruptae Eloquentiae.*

But, to show that our language is improved, and that those people have not a just value for the age in which they live, let us consider in what the refinement of a language principally consists: that is, *either in rejecting such old words, or phrases, which are ill sounding, or improper; or in admitting new, which are more proper, more sounding, and more significant.*

The reader will easily take notice, that when I speak of rejecting improper words and phrases, I mention not such as are antiquated by custom only, and, as I may say, without any fault of theirs. For in this case the refinement can be but accidental; that is, when the words and phrases, which are rejected, happen to be improper. Neither would I be understood, when I speak of impropriety of language, either wholly to accuse the last age, or to excuse the present, and least of all myself; for all writers have their imperfections and failings: but I may safely conclude in the general, that our improprieties are less frequent, and less gross than theirs. One testimony of this is undeniable, that we are the first who have observed them; and, certainly, to observe errors is a great step to the correcting of them. But, malice and partiality set apart, let any man, who understands English, read diligently the works of Shakespeare and Fletcher, and I dare undertake, that he will find in every page either some solecism of speech, or some notorious flaw in sense; and yet these men are reverenced, when we are not forgiven. That their wit is great, and many times their expressions noble, envy itself cannot deny:

> *Neque ego illis detrahere ausim*
> *Haerentem capiti multâ cum laude coronam.*

From "Defence of the Epilogue; or an Essay on the Dramatic Poetry of the Last Age" in W. P. Ker, ed., *Essays of John Dryden* (Vol. 1; Oxford: Clarendon Press, 1900), pp. 164–167.

But the times were ignorant in which they lived. Poetry was then, if not in its infancy among us, at least not arrived to its vigour and maturity: witness the lameness of their plots; many of which, especially those which they writ first (for even that age refined itself in some measure), were made up of some ridiculous incoherent story, which in one play many times took up the business of an age. I suppose I need not name *Pericles, Prince of Tyre*, nor the historical plays of Shakespeare: besides many of the rest, as the *Winter's Tale, Love's Labour Lost, Measure for Measure*, which were either grounded on impossibilities, or at least so meanly written, that the comedy neither caused your mirth, nor the serious part your concernment. If I would expatiate on this subject, I could easily demonstrate, that our admired Fletcher, who writ after him, neither understood correct plotting, nor that which they call *the decorum of the stage*. I would not search in his worst plays for examples: he who will consider his *Philaster*, his *Humorous Lieutenant*, his *Faithful Shepherdess*, and many others which I could name, will find them much below the applause which is now given them. He will see Philaster wounding his mistress, and afterwards his boy, to save himself; not to mention the Clown, who enters immediately, and not only has the advantage of the combat against the hero, but diverts you from your serious concernment, with his ridiculous and absurd raillery. In his *Humorous Lieutenant*, you find his Demetrius and Leontius staying in the midst of a routed army, to hear the cold mirth of the Lieutenant; and Demetrius afterwards appearing with a pistol in his hand, in the next age to Alexander the Great. And for his Shepherd, he falls twice into the former indecency of wounding women. But these absurdities, which those poets committed, may more properly be called the age's fault than theirs: for, besides the want of education and learning (which was their particular unhappiness), they wanted the benefit of converse: but of that I shall speak hereafter, in a place more proper for it. Their audiences knew no better; and therefore were satisfied with what they brought. Those, who call theirs *the Golden Age of Poetry*, have only this reason for it, that they were then content with acorns before they knew the use of bread, or that ἅλις δρυὸς was become a proverb. They had many who admired them, and few who blamed them; and certainly a severe critic is the greatest help to a good wit: he does the office of a friend, while he designs that of an enemy; and his malice keeps a poet within those bounds, which the luxuriancy of his fancy would tempt him to overleap.

But it is not their plots which I meant principally to tax; I was speaking of their sense and language; and I dare almost challenge any man to show me a page together which is correct in both. As for Ben Jonson, I am loath to name him, because he is a most judicious writer; yet he very often falls into these errors: and I once more beg the reader's pardon for accusing him of them. Only let him consider, that I live in an age where my least faults are severely censured; and that I have no way left to extenuate my failings, but by showing as great in those whom we admire[.]

From A Parallel of Poetry and Painting

To imitate Nature well in whatsoever subject, is the perfection of both arts; and that picture, and that poem, which comes nearest to the resemblance of Nature, is the best. But it follows not, that what pleases most in either kind is therefore good, but what ought to please. Our depraved appetites, and ignorance of the arts, mislead our judgments, and cause us often to take that for true imitation of Nature which has no resemblance of Nature in it. To inform our judgments, and to reform our tastes, rules were invented, that by them we might discern when Nature was imitated, and how nearly. I have been forced to recapitulate these things, because mankind is not more liable to deceit, than it is willing to continue in a pleasing error, strengthened by a long habitude. The imitation of Nature is therefore justly constituted as the general, and indeed the only, rule of pleasing, both in Poetry and Painting. Aristotle tells us, that imitation pleases, because it affords matter for a reasoner to inquire into the truth or falsehood of imitation, by comparing its likeness, or unlikeness, with the original; but by this rule every speculation in nature, whose truth falls under the inquiry of a philosopher, must produce the same delight; which is not true. I should rather assign another reason. Truth is the object of our understanding, as good is of our will; and the understanding can no more be delighted with a lie, than the will can choose an apparent evil. As truth is the end of all our speculations, so the discovery of it is the pleasure of them; and since a true knowledge of Nature gives us pleasure, a lively imitation of it, either in Poetry or Painting, must of necessity produce a much greater: for both these arts, as I said before, are not only true imitations of Nature, but of the best Nature, of that which is wrought up to a nobler pitch. They present us with images more perfect than the life in any individual; and we have the pleasure to see all the scattered beauties of Nature united by a happy chemistry, without its deformities or faults. They are imitations of the passions, which always move, and therefore consequently please; for without motion there can be no delight, which cannot be considered but as an active passion. When we view these elevated ideas of nature, the result of that view is admiration, which is always the cause of pleasure.

From "A Parallel of Poetry and Painting, Prefixed to the Version of Du Fresnoy *De Arte Graphica*" in W. P. Ker, ed., *Essays of John Dryden* (Vol. 2; Oxford: Clarendon Press, 1900), pp. 136–137.

JOSEPH ADDISON (1672–1719)
From The Spectator

No. 476, Friday, September 5, 1712

—Lucidus ordo.—Hor. . . .
Method gives light.

Among my daily papers which I bestow on the public, there are some which are written with regularity and method, and others that run out into the wildness of those compositions which go by the name of essays. As for the first, I have the whole scheme of the discourse in my mind before I set my pen to paper. In the other kind of writing, it is sufficient that I have several thoughts on a subject, without troubling myself to range them in such order, that they may seem to grow out of one another, and be disposed under the proper heads. Seneca and Montaigne are patterns for writing in this last kind, as Tully and Aristotle excel in the other. When I read an author of genius who writes without method, I fancy myself in a wood that abounds with a great many noble objects, rising among one another in the greatest confusion and disorder. When I read a methodical discourse, I am in a regular plantation, and can place myself in its several centers, so as to take a view of all the lines and walks that are struck from them. You may ramble in the one a whole day together, and every moment discover something or other that is new to you; but when you have done, you will have a confused imperfect notion of the place: in the other your eye commands the whole prospect, and gives you such an idea of it as is not easily worn out of the memory.

From *The Spectator: A New Edition with Biographical Notices of the Contributors* (Cincinnati: Applegate, 1857), p. 568.

From The Spectator

No. 135, Saturday, August 4, 1711

Est brevitate opus, ut currat sententia—Hor. . . .
Let brevity dispatch the rapid thought.

I have somewhere read of an eminent person, who used in his private offices of devotion to give thanks to Heaven that he was born a Frenchman: for my own part, I look upon it as a peculiar blessing that I was born an Englishman. Among many other reasons, I think myself very happy in my country, as the language of it is wonderfully adapted to a man who is sparing of his words, and an enemy to loquacity.

As I have frequently reflected on my good fortune in this particular, I

From *The Spectator: A New Edition with Biographical Notices of the Contributors* (Cincinnati: Applegate, 1857), p. 184.

shall communicate to the public my speculations on the English tongue, not doubting but they will be acceptable to all my curious readers.

The English delight in silence more than any other European nation, if the remarks which are made on us by foreigners are true. Our discourse is not kept up in conversation, but falls into more pauses and intervals than in our neighboring countries; as it is observed, that the matter of our writings is thrown much closer together, and lies in a narrower compass than is usual in the works of foreign authors; for, to favor our natural taciturnity, when we are obliged to utter our thoughts, we do it in the shortest way we are able, and give as quick a birth to our conceptions as possible.

This humor shows itself in several remarks that we may make upon the English language. As first of all by its abounding in monosyllables, which gives us an opportunity of delivering our thoughts in few sounds. This indeed takes off from the elegance of our tongue, but at the same time expresses our ideas in the readiest manner, and consequently answers the first design of speech better than the multitude of Syllables, which makes the words of other languages more tunable and sonorous. The sounds of our English words are commonly like those of string-music, short and transient, which rise and perish upon a single touch; those of other languages are like the notes of wind-instruments, sweet and swelling, and lengthened out into a variety of modulation.

In the next place we may observe, that where the words are not monosyllables, we often make them so, so much as lies in our power, by our rapidity of pronunciation; as it generally happens in most of our long words which are derived from the Latin, where we contract the length of the syllables that gives them a grave and solemn air in their own language; to make them more proper for dispatch, and more conformable to the genius of our tongue. This we may find in a multitude of words, as "liberty, conspiracy, theater, orator," etc.

The same natural aversion to loquacity has of late years made a very considerable alteration in our language, by closing in one syllable the termination of our preterperfect tense, as in these words, "drown'd, walk'd, arriv'd," for "drowned, walked, arrived," which has very much disfigured the tongue, and turned a tenth part of our smoothest words into so many clusters of consonants.

JONATHAN SWIFT (1667–1745)
From A Proposal for Correcting, Improving and Ascertaining the English Tongue

To the Most Honourable Robert *Earl of Oxford, &c.*
My Lord,

What I had the Honour of mentioning to your Lordship some Time ago in Conversation, was not a new Thought, just then started by Accident or

From Herbert Davis with Louis Landa, eds., *A Proposal for Correcting the English Tongue in Polite Conversation* (Oxford: Basil Blackwell, 1957), pp. 5–6. Reprinted by permission of Basil Blackwell, Publisher.

Occasion, but the Result of long Reflection; and I have been confirmed in my Sentiments by the Opinion of some very judicious Persons, with whom I consulted. They all agreed, That nothing would be of greater Use towards the Improvement of Knowledge and Politeness, than some effectual Method for *Correcting*, *Enlarging*, and *Ascertaining* our Language; and they think it a Work very possible to be compassed, under the Protection of a Prince, the Countenance and Encouragement of a Ministry, and the Care of proper Persons, chosen for such an Undertaking. I was glad to find your Lordship's Answer in so different a Style, from what hath been commonly made use of on such like Occasions, for some Years past; *That all such Thoughts must be deferred to a Time of Peace:* A Topick which some have carried so far, that they would not have us by any Means think of preserving our Civil or Religious Constitution, because we are engaged in a War abroad. It will be among the distinguishing Marks of your Ministry, My Lord, that you had a Genius above all such Regards; and that no reasonable Proposal for the Honour, the Advantage, or the Ornament of your Country, however foreign to your more immediate Office, was ever neglected by you. I confess, the Merit of this Candour and Condescension is very much lessened; because your Lordship hardly leaves us Room to offer our good Wishes; removing all our Difficulties, and supplying our Wants, faster than the most visionary Projector can adjust his Schemes. And therefore, my Lord, the Design of this Paper is not so much to offer you *Ways and Means*, as to complain of a *Grievance*, the Redressing of which is to be your own Work, as much as that of paying the *Nation's Debts*, or opening a Trade into the *South-Sea*; and although not of such immediate Benefit, as either of these, or any other of your glorious Actions, yet perhaps in future Ages not less to your Honour.

My Lord, I do here, in the Name of all the learned and polite Persons of the Nation, complain to your Lordship as *First Minister*, that our Language is extremely imperfect; that its daily Improvements are by no Means in Proportion to its daily Corruptions; that the Pretenders to polish and refine it, have chiefly multiplied Abuses and Absurdities; and, that in many Instances, it offends against every Part of Grammar....

LORD CHESTERFIELD (1694–1773)
From Letter to His Son

No. 1672, 24 November O.S. 1749
Style is the dress of thoughts; and let them be ever so just, if your style is homely, coarse, and vulgar, they will appear to as much disadvantage, and be as ill received as your person, though ever so well proportioned, would, if dressed in rags, dirt, and tatters. It is not every understanding that can judge of matter, but every ear can and does judge, more or less, of style; and

From Bonamy Dobrée, ed., *Letters: 1748–1751*, Vol. 4 of *The Letters of Philip Dormer Stanhope, 4th Earl of Chesterfield* (London: Eyre and Spottiswoode, 1932), pp. 1442–1443. Reprinted by permission of Eyre and Spottiswoode (Publishers) Ltd.

were I either to speak or write to the public, I should prefer moderate matter, adorned with all the beauties and elegances of style, to the strongest matter in the world, ill-worded and ill-delivered. Your business is negotiation abroad, and oratory in the House of Commons at home. What figure can you make in either case, if your style be inelegant, I do not say bad? Imagine yourself writing an office-letter to a Secretary of State, which letter is to be read by the whole Cabinet Council, and very possibly afterwards laid before Parliament; any one barbarism, solecism, or vulgarism in it would, in a very few days, circulate through the whole kingdom, to your disgrace and ridicule.

SAMUEL JOHNSON (1709–1784)
From The Rambler

No. 60, Saturday, 13 October 1750

I have often thought that there has rarely passed a life of which a judicious and faithful narrative would not be useful. For, not only every man has, in the mighty mass of the world, great numbers in the same condition with himself, to whom his mistakes and miscarriages, escapes and expedients, would be of immediate and apparent use; but there is such an uniformity in the state of man, considered apart from adventitious and separable decorations and disguises, that there is scarce any possibility of good or ill, but is common to human kind. A great part of the time of those who are placed at the greatest distance by fortune, or by temper, must unavoidably pass in the same manner; and though, when the claims of nature are satisfied, caprice, and vanity, and accident, begin to produce discriminations and peculiarities, yet the eye is not very heedful, or quick, which cannot discover the same causes still terminating their influence in the same effects, though sometimes accelerated, sometimes retarded, or perplexed by multiplied combinations. We are all prompted by the same motives, all deceived by the same fallacies, all animated by hope, obstructed by danger, entangled by desire, and seduced by pleasure.

From W. J. Bate and Albrecht B. Strauss, eds., *Samuel Johnson "The Rambler"* (Vol. 1; New Haven: Yale University Press, 1969), p. 320. Reprinted by permission of Yale University Press. Notes have been omitted.

From Preface to A Dictionary of the English Language

It is the fate of those who toil at the lower employments of life, to be rather driven by the fear of evil, than attracted by the prospect of good; to be exposed to censure, without hope of praise; to be disgraced by miscarriage,

---

From E. L. McAdam, Jr., and George Milne, eds., *Johnson's Dictionary: A Modern Selection* (New York: Pantheon Books, a Division of Random House, Inc., 1963), pp. 3–4. © Copyright, 1963, by E. L. McAdam, Jr. Reprinted by permission of Random House, Inc.

or punished for neglect, where success would have been without applause, and diligence without reward.

Among these unhappy mortals is the writer of dictionaries; whom mankind have considered, not as the pupil, but the slave of science, the pionier of literature, doomed only to remove rubbish and clear obstructions from the paths of Learning and Genius, who press forward to conquest and glory, without bestowing a smile on the humble drudge that facilitates their progress. Every other authour may aspire to praise; the lexicographer can only hope to escape reproach, and even this negative recompense has been yet granted to very few.

I have, notwithstanding this discouragement, attempted a dictionary of the English language, which, while it was employed in the cultivation of every species of literature, has itself been hitherto neglected, suffered to spread, under the direction of chance, into wild exuberance, resigned to the tyranny of time and fashion, and exposed to the corruptions of ignorance, and caprices of innovation.

When I took the first survey of my undertaking, I found our speech copious without order, and energetick without rules: wherever I turned my view, there was perplexity to be disentangled, and confusion to be regulated; choice was to be made out of boundless variety, without any established principle of selection; adulterations were to be detected, without a settled test of purity; and modes of expression to be rejected or received, without the suffrages of any writers of classical reputation or acknowledged authority.

Having therefore no assistance but from general grammar, I applied myself to the perusal of our writers; and noting whatever might be of use to ascertain or illustrate any word or phrase, accumulated in time the materials of a dictionary, which, by degrees, I reduced to method, establishing to myself, in the progress of the work, such rules as experience and analogy suggested to me; experience, which practice and observation were continually increasing; and analogy, which, though in some words obscure, was evident in others.

In adjusting the *orthography*, which has been to this time unsettled and fortuitous, I found it necessary to distinguish those irregularities that are inherent in our tongue, and perhaps coeval with it, from others which the ignorance or negligence of later writers has produced. Every language has its anomalies, which, though inconvenient, and in themselves once unnecessary, must be tolerated among the imperfections of human things, and which require only to be registred, that they may not be increased, and ascertained, that they may not be confounded: but every language has likewise its improprieties and absurdities, which it is the duty of the lexicographer to correct or proscribe.

DAVID HUME (1711–1776)
From Of Tragedy

It seems an unaccountable pleasure, which the spectators of a well-written tragedy receive from sorrow, terror, anxiety, and other passions that are in themselves disagreeable and uneasy. The more they are touched and affected, the more are they delighted with the spectacle; and as soon as the uneasy passions cease to operate, the piece is at an end. One scene of full joy and contentment and security, is the utmost that any composition of this kind can bear; and it is sure always to be the concluding one. If in the texture of the piece, there be interwoven any scenes of satisfaction, they afford only faint gleams of pleasure, which are thrown in by way of variety, and in order to plunge the actors into deeper distress by means of that contrast and disappointment. The whole art of the poet is employed, in rousing and supporting the compassion and indignation, the anxiety and resentment, of his audience. They are pleased in proportion as they are afflicted, and never are so happy as when they employ tears, sobs, and cries, to give vent to their sorrow, and relieve their heart, swollen with the tenderest sympathy and compassion.

From *Essays: Literary, Moral, and Political* by David Hume, Esq., The Historian (London: Ward, Lock, n.d.), pp. 127–128.

CHAPTER V

THE NINETEENTH AND TWENTIETH CENTURIES: 1798–

FROM EDWARDS TO TWAIN

Josephine Miles

We seem to have come a traceable way in prose, though not to a predictable future; a way that has led from one sort of strong predication through many substantival ramifications to a new sort of strong predication supported by qualities rather than by connections—another level deeper, or higher, as we may choose to see it.

To test this view of a progression in styles, we may look more briefly at a parallel series, separated spatially by an ocean and temperamentally by a revolution, but joined in common language. We speak of an American prose style—that active, rationalistic structure that seems to be characteristic of our best known prose writers and related closely to its English sources in the Renaissance. Its form is patent in its famous early preacher, Jonathan Edwards. His first of twenty sermons is dated September, 1740, and proceeds after the statement of text, doctrine, and some comment on the first proposition, as follows:

From *Style and Proportion: The Language of Prose and Poetry* by Josephine Miles (Boston: Little, Brown, 1967), Ch. 3, "Styles in American Prose," pp. 62–78, at pp. 62–70, 77–78. Copyright © 1967, by Little, Brown and Company (Inc.). Reprinted by permission of the author and publisher. Notes have been omitted, and the extra space between phrase units in quotations has not been reproduced.

Noah's undertaking was of great difficulty, as it exposed him to the continual reproaches of all his neighbors, for that whole hundred and twenty years. None of them believed that he told them of a flood, which was about to drown the world. For a man to undertake such a vast piece of work, under a notion that it should be the means of saving him, when the world should be destroyed, it made him the continual laughing-stock of the world. When he was about to hire workmen, doubtless all laughed at him, and we may suppose, that though the workmen consented to work for wages, yet they laughed at the folly of him who employed them. When the ark was begun, we may suppose that every one that passed by and saw such a huge hulk stand there, laughed at it, calling it *Noah's folly*.

Here we have the familiar Renaissance structure, strong in verbs and connectives. We see the simple subject-predicate combination loaded with following phrases within following clauses. The peroration is vividly active, much like Emerson's, but characteristically more negative:

You have been once more warned to-day, while the door of the ark yet stands open. You have, as it were, once again heard the knocks of the hammer and axe in the building of the ark, to put you in mind that a flood is approaching. Take heed therefore that you do not still stop your ears, treat these warnings with a regardless heart, and still neglect the great work which you have to do, lest the flood of wrath suddenly come upon you, sweep you away, and there be no remedy.

Sir Thomas More or John Donne could claim these moving progressions.

Paine's *Common Sense* reflects a familiarly eighteenth-century tradition closer to classical. It begins:

Some writers have so confounded society with government, as to leave little or no distinction between them; whereas they are not only different, but have different origins. Society is produced by our wants and government by our wickedness; the former promotes our happiness *positively* by uniting our affections, the latter *negatively* by restraining our vices. The one encourages intercourse, the other creates distinctions. The first is a patron, the last a punisher.

Along with his vigor, Paine has taken on more nouns, fewer verbs; though still he keeps more verbs than Burke. His balanced structure, here strongly used, is doing the work of the connectives, as in "The first is a patron, the last a punisher."

The next section is ended by the balanced peroration:

In England a king hath little more to do than to make war and give away places; which, in plain terms, is to empoverish the nation and set it together by the ears. A pretty business indeed for a man to be allowed eight hundred thousand sterling a year for, and worshipped into the bargain! Of more worth is one honest man to society; and in the sight of God, than all the crowned ruffians that ever lived.

The balance is set in the modified nouns: *honest man, crowned ruffians*. The American speaks substantially as the Englishman.

Mid-nineteenth-century America provides us, in the work of Emerson, Twain, and Whitman, with the same range of variation we have seen in England: Emerson colloquial as Hazlitt; Twain balanced, in some ways an earlier Shaw; Whitman even beyond Gibbon, beyond Macaulay, in a copious combination of adjectives, nouns, connectives—all but verbs. Note how predicative, crisp, unconnective Emerson sounds in the first short paragraph in *Self-Reliance*:

> Trust thyself: every heart vibrates to that iron string. Accept the place the divine Providence has found for you; the society of your contemporaries, the connexion of events. Great men have always done so, and confided themselves childlike to the genius of their age, betraying their perception that the Eternal was stirring at their heart, working through their hands, predominating in all their being. And we are now men, and must accept in the highest mind the same transcendent destiny; and not pinched in a corner, not cowards fleeing before a revolution, but redeemers and benefactors, pious aspirants to be noble clay plastic under the Almighty effort, let us advance and advance on Chaos and the Dark.

In contrast, the beginning of Whitman's *Democratic Vistas*, with its three adjectives for every verb:

> As the greatest lessons of Nature through the universe are perhaps the lessons of variety and freedom, the same present the greatest lessons also in New World politics and progress. If a man were ask'd, for instance, the distinctive points contrasting modern European, and American political and other life with the old Asiastic cultus, as lingering-bequeath'd yet in China and Turkey, he might find the amount of them in John Stuart Mills's profound essay on Liberty in the future, where he demands two main constituents, or sub-strata, for a truly grand nationality— 1st, a large variety of character—and 2d, full play for human nature to expand itself in numberless and even conflicting directions—(seems to be for general humanity much like the influences that make up, in their limitless field, that perennial health-action of the air we call the weather—an infinite number of currents and forces, and contributions, and temperatures, and cross purposes, whose ceaseless play of counterpart upon counterpart brings constant restoration and vitality.) With this thought— and not for itself alone, but all it necessitates, and draws after it—let me begin my speculations.

After a few paragraphs.

> And now, in the full conception of these facts and points, and all that they infer, pro and con—with yet unshaken faith in the elements of the American masses, the composites, of both sexes, and even consider'd as individuals—and ever recognizing in them the broadest bases of the best literary and esthetic appreciation—I proceed with my speculations, Vistas.

And:

> There is, in sanest hours, a consciousness, a thought that rises, independent, lifted out from all else, calm, like the stars, shining eternal. This is the thought of identity—yours for you, whoever you are, as mine for me.

Compare the fresh objectivity of a third sort of stylist, Mark Twain, in *Life on the Mississippi*:

Imagine the benefits of so admirable a system in a piece of river twelve or thirteen hundred miles long, whose channel was shifting every day! The pilot who had formerly been obliged to put up with seeing a shoal place once or possibly twice a month, had a hundred sharp eyes to watch it for him now, and bushels of intelligent brains to tell him how to run it. His information about it was seldom twenty-four hours old. If the reports in the last box chanced to leave any misgivings on his mind concerning a treacherous crossing, he had his remedy; he blew his steam whistle in a peculiar way as soon as he saw a boat approaching; the signal was answered in a peculiar way if that boat's pilots were association men; and then the two steamers ranged alongside and all uncertainties were swept away by fresh information furnished to the inquirer by word of mouth and in minute detail.

Here are nearly equal adjectives and verbs, and we see that the structure reflects the content: each subject and predicate modified as the sentences go, each sentence direct and complete in its statement, working toward the clear, repeated predications of the last of the paragraph. This is simplicity of structure rather than complexity; it is not interwoven. But though it is simple, it is not bare.

See again a paragraph from "Racing Days":

In the old times, whenever two fast boats started out on a race, with a big crowd of people looking on, it was inspiring to hear the crews sing, especially if the time were nightfall, and the forecastle lit up with the red glare of the torchbaskets. Racing was royal fun. The public always had an idea that racing was dangerous; whereas the opposite was the case—that is, after the laws were passed which restricted each boat to just so many pounds of steam to the square inch. No engineer was ever sleepy or careless when his heart was in a race. He was constantly on the alert, trying gauge-cocks and watching things. The dangerous place was on slow, plodding boats, where the engineers drowsed around and allowed chips to get into the "doctor" and shut off the water-supply from the boilers.

Here is a pattern similar to the first. We see that Twain likes to give us the "color" of the situation—*In the old times*—*if the time was nightfall ... when his heart was in a race*—and the final pile of modification—*where* they drowsed and allowed chips *to get into* and *shut off*. At the same time, the material is not convoluted like Baldwin's, but flatly put: *Racing was royal fun ... the opposite was the case ... no engineer was ever sleepy or careless.* These are Twain's basic tones: the one of downright assertion, the other of enthusiastic qualification by description. They provide, too, when in unexpected combinations, the basis for his humor: "By and by, all the useless, helpless pilots, and a dozen first-class ones, were in the association, and nine-tenths of the best pilots out of it and laughing at it."

Since Twain, discursive American prose has been close to his, close to balance in active progression. Santayana, Eliot, and Baldwin provide examples, in contrast to the stronger colloquial verbs and weaker connectives of a Hemingway or a Lardner. A paragraph from Baldwin's *Notes of a Native Son*, written with—a critic notes—"bitter clarity and uncommon grace" reads ...:

The American student colony in Paris is a social phenomenon so amorphous as to at once demand and defy the generality. One is far from being in the position of finding not enough to say—one finds far too much, and everything one finds is contradictory. What one wants to know at bottom, is what *they* came to find: to which question there are—at least—as many answers as there are faces at the café tables.

The symmetry in repetition is noteworthy and is characteristic of the writing as a whole. Compare, for example, the last, and more elaborate, sentences of the essay:

It is, indeed, this past which has thrust upon us our present, so troubling role. It is the past lived on the American continent, as against that other past, irrecoverable now on the shores of Europe, which must sustain us in the present. The truth about that past is not that it is too brief, or too superficial, but only that we, having turned our faces so resolutely away from it, have never demanded from it what it has to give. It is this demand which the American student in Paris is forced, at length, to make, for he has otherwise no identity, no reason for being here, nothing to sustain him here. From the vantage point of Europe he discovers his own country. And this is a discovery which not only brings to an end the alienation of the American from himself, but which also makes clear to him, for the first time, the extent of his involvement in the life of Europe.

The repeated relative clauses and participles underpin the thought: ... this *past* which ... *the past lived* ... that *other past* ... which, *not* that ... but *only that, having turned* ... having *never demanded* ... this *demand which*, *a discovery which*. Such deliberating prose provides our American counterweight to the colloquial tradition of Emerson, which flourishes now in Hemingway, as in Joyce and Lawrence.

Speaking of stylistic choice, a friend once said of Emerson's: "His noun had to wait for its verb or its adjective until he was ready." These are two of the choices; the third, a connective, was certainly less Emerson's, and he worried about the omission. Because of his lively consciousness of questions of style—in prose as in poetry—and because of his importance in the plain or colloquial British and American traditions, it may be profitable to consider his work more fully in its relations of theory to practice. What are the special traits and traditions of this essayist of ours that set him apart from any other we may know—from Cicero and Seneca on old age, from Montaigne on life and friendship, from the Elizabethan essayists whom he read with such pleasure as a boy, from the sermons he heard, from the eighteenth- and nineteenth-century philosophic and journalistic prose that he read in the English reviews, from Carlyle, whom he admired so directly, from his own American contemporaries, from the wisdom-literature of China, Persia, India, and from his own Bible?

If we read the beginning of his perhaps most famous essay, "Self-Reliance" (which, in the 1840's, followed "History" in introducing his increasingly popular series of "Essays"), we may catch his mode of expression. After presenting three quotations on the theme "Man is his own star," Emerson begins:

I read the other day some verses written by an eminent painter, which were original, and not conventional. The soul always hears an admonition in such lines,

let the subject be what it may. The sentiment they instill is of more value than
any thought they may contain. To believe your own thought, to believe that what is
true for you in your private heart, is true for all men,—that is genius. Speak your
latent conviction, and it shall be the universal sense; for the inmost in due time
becomes the outmost, and our first thought is rendered back to us by the trumpets
of the Last Judgment. Familiar as the voice of the mind is to each, the highest merit
we ascribe to Moses, Plato, and Milton is that they set at naught books and traditions, and spoke not what men, but what *they* thought. A man should learn to detect
and watch that gleam of light which flashes across his mind from within, more than
the lustre of the firmament of bards and sages.

The tone of this beginning is particular and personal: *I read ... your
own*; general and confident: *the soul always hears*; evocative: *the trumpets of
the Last Judgment*; wide-reaching: *Moses, Plato, and Milton*; recommenda-
tory: *speak ... learn*; figurative: *that gleam of light ... more than the lustre
of the firmament*.

In this combination of qualities, Emerson's style is more focused and
condensed than Cicero's, say, or Seneca's, or Montaigne's; it sets its generalities in specific actions and analogies. It is not what we traditionally call
a classic style, either in Latin or in English, because it does not progress as
a full and logical unfolding of thought, but rather moves as if by flashes of
illumination. This is not to say that it is illogical; merely that it does not
give the effect of explicit stress on logical connections. Nor does it stress the
literal qualifications and descriptions with which classical prose is concerned.
So both adjectives and connectives are relatively subordinated to direct
active verbs in the passage. The prose is carried not so much by the contrast,
original and not conventional, though this is a basic contrast; nor by the
adjectives *eminent, true, private, latent, universal, first, last, familiar, highest*;
and not so much by the connectives *by, which, in, than, that, for* and so on;
as it is by the verbs *I read, the soul hears, they instil, may contain, to believe,
what is true, that is genius, speak, it shall be, what they thought, should learn
to detect and watch, light which flashes*.

In abstract terms, this is to say that characteristically Emerson, in this
paragraph, throughout this essay, and again twenty years later in "Illu-
sions," writes a very active, predicative style, one in which the structure is
basically simple statement, to which both modification and connective addition are only minimally necessary, and the sentences relatively short, the
central statements relatively unqualified.

Closest to Emerson are the sermon-makers, like the pre-Elizabethan
Latimer or Tyndale's Epistle of Paul to the Romans, who write in the "low"
style that Walton found noteworthy in the *Complete Angler*; or narrative
writers like the Bunyan of *Pilgrim's Progress* or the Joyce of Molly Bloom's
soliloquy. But these are styles we do not probably think of as Emersonian.
Yet even less so are the classic arguers in the tradition of Hooker, Bacon,
and Locke, or the soaring describers he often loved, like Sir Thomas Browne,
his own contemporaries, like Carlyle, or what he himself called a "mock-
turtle nutriment as in Macaulay."

But in the tradition there is one writer with whom he is so closely allied
that we cannot help but recognize what was, as a youth, his own favorite

reading: Ben Jonson, in his prose *Discoveries*, as in his poetry. Jonson was as singular in his own time as Emerson in his; their sense of the English language as best used in active, concise statements, often making connections by implication, was a sense shared in its extreme by few others, and thus especially lively both in its singularity and in its function as a bond between them. Even their use of specific connectives—the proportion of relative clauses to causal clauses and locational phrases—is striking. Not Plutarch, not Montaigne, nor Bacon, but specifically the aphoristic Jonson of *Timber* is Emerson's direct model. Jonson sounds like this, in "Claritas Patria," from *Timber*:

Greatness of name, in the Father, oft-times helpes not forth, but ore whelmes the Sonne; they stand too neere one another. The shadow kils the growth; so much, that we see the Grand-child come more, and oftener, to be the heire of the *first*, then doth the *second*; He dies betweene; the Possession is the *thirds*.

In contrast is Montaigne's flow of easy subordinates, at least in modern translation, in "To the Reader":

This book was written in good faith, reader. It warns you from the outset that in it I have set myself no goal but a domestic and private one. I have had no thought of serving either you or my own glory. My powers are inadequate for such a purpose. I have dedicated it to the private convenience of my relatives and friends, so that when they have lost me (as soon they must), they may recover here some features of my habits and temperament, and by this means keep the knowledge they have had of me more complete and alive.

Many a discussion of Emerson's style has expressed regret at his effect of abrupt discontinuity and illogicality; and he himself, as he wrestled with his writing, scolded about the sentences that seemed sometimes to repel rather than to attract each other. But the absence of strong explicit connectives does not mean the absence of strong implied connections. See in *Self-Reliance* how Emerson's thought, like Jonson's, specifically moves. He has read some original verses; he generalizes from such originality in such a way that it leads one to trust his own thought as true for all—"inmost" becomes "outmost." As we value great men for what they thought, so we should attend, even more than to what they thought, to what we think. The argument moves between particular and general, and from key word to key word, as *original* leads to *private* to *genius* to *inmost* to *what they thought* to *his mind from within*, using always two sets of contrasts, the *conventional* as too limiting, the *universal* and *outward* as rightly expanding, allowing us to ally our right with that of Moses and Milton.

*　　*　　*　　*

A man who has been called monist, dualist, pantheist, transcendentalist, puritan, optimist, pragmatist, mystic, may well feel dubious about the validity of labels, of adjectives. His style shows us how all of these fit him and how they work together, and over and over he tells us that it is degree he believes in; in degree, the one and the many may work together; God, man, nature may work together; all varieties of difference, from dissimilar to con-

trasting, will share degrees of likeness. His common term *polarity* referred
not to modern positive and negative poles, and not to modern, negative
correlations or annihilations, but to differences or contrasts that are unified
by a common direction, a north star, a magnetic field, a spirit in the laws
and limits of body, a drawing of body along in the directions of spirit—
a golden mean with a lodestar. Rhyme, meter, aphorism, sermon structure
gave stoical feet rather than Aeolian wings to his Aeolian natural world,
and made it go at a workday pace, the early prose most radical in multiple
verbs, the early poetry in minimal connectives, but all ready enough to
state, and then to state again. By thought the transcendentalist could move
from negative to positive, from literal to figurative, "a little beyond." He
could write a smooth pentameter, a rough tetrameter, a smooth and soaring
sermon, a rough and ready aphorism, using essentially the same sentence
structures and vocabularies. It was not that sometimes he had a meter-
making argument but that sometimes his argument was meter-making,
coming to him in association with the old poetry he loved rather than in the
work on a lecture. His relation, in prose as in poetry, was to a great,
simple tradition; to Jonathan Edwards, for example, in American colloquialism. He did not take on the eighteenth- or nineteenth-century structures but
rather adapted their vocabularies to older structures. He therefore prevails
as an artist of *sentence*, in prose as in poetry. American prose, so far as
we have sampled it, supports Emerson in this power. What was native for
England persists in being native for America—predication dominant over
attribution. Without seeing so full a range in American prose, we can yet
see that the moderns exactly parallel the British moderns. Whitman caught
epithetical echoes from overseas. Twain enlarged British classicism by more
energy in adjectives and verbs at once; that is, by a high style carried along
in action. Emerson ... shared with writers as different as Santayana and
Hemingway, as Lardner and Baldwin, the propensity for straight statement-
making, for aphoristic assertion, most characteristic of English prose both
British and American, both Renaissance and modern.

THE PERIODIC TRADITION: DE QUINCEY

William Minto

Although De Quincey complained of the "weariness and repulsion" of the
periodic style, he carried it to excess in his own composition. His sentences
are stately, elaborate, crowded with qualifying clauses and parenthetical
allusions, to a degree unparalleled among modern writers.

From William Minto, *A Manual of English Prose Literature* (Boston: Ginn, 1891), pp. 50–53.

In reviewing Whately's Rhetoric, he naturally objected to the dogma that "elaborate stateliness is always to be regarded as a worse fault than the slovenliness and languor which accompany a very loose style." He maintained, and justly, that "stateliness the most elaborate, in an *absolute* sense, is no fault at all, though it may be so in relation to a given subject, or to any subject under given circumstances." Whether in his own practice he always conforms to circumstances, is a question that must be left to individual taste. There is a certain stateliness in his sentences under almost all circumstances—a stateliness arising from his habitual use of periodic suspensions. To take two examples from his Sketches:—

"Never in any equal number of months had my understanding so much expanded as during this visit to Laxton."

When we throw this out of the elaborately periodic form, we, as it were, relax the tension of the mind, and destroy the stately effect. Thus—

"My understanding expanded more during this visit to Laxton than during any three months of my life."

Again—

"Equally, in fact, as regarded my physics and my metaphysics; in short, upon all lines of advance that interested my ambition, I was going rapidly ahead."

The statement has a very different effect when the periodic arrangement is reversed.

Criticism of single sentences cannot easily be made convincing, and the critic is apt to forget the paramount principle that regard must be had to the context, to the nature of the subject, to the effect intended by the writer. When a single sentence is put upon its trial, there are many casuistical considerations that may legitimately be pleaded by the counsel for the defence. Still, if we try De Quincey by his own rule against "unwieldy comprehensiveness," we must convict him of many violations. In almost every page we find periods that cannot be easily comprehended except by a mind of more than ordinary grasp; and in many cases where, viewed with reference to the average capacity, he cannot be said to overcrowd, he is yet upon the verge of overcrowding. The following sentence may be quoted as one that stands upon the verge. It calls for a considerable effort of attention, and a long succession of such sentences would be exasperating. He is speaking of his youthful habit of scrupulously making sure of the meaning of an order:—

"So far from seeking to 'pettifogulise'—*i.e.*, to find evasions for any purpose in a trickster's minute tortuosities of construction—exactly in the opposite direction, from mere excess of sincerity, most unwillingly I found, in almost everybody's words, an unintentional opening left for double interpretations."

In this case the familiarity and the close connection of the ideas makes the effort of comprehension considerably less. When the subject-matter is so easy, the interspersion of such periods here and there cannot be called a fault.   It is, on the contrary, to most ears an agreeable relief to the monotony of ordinary forms of sentence.   But for the general reader, for the average capacity of easy understanding, such sentence-forms are multiplied to an intolerable degree in De Quincey's writing.   And he does not always escape the besetting fault of long and crowded sentences—intricacy.

As regards the length and elaboration of De Quincey's sentences, it is interesting to compare the first edition of the Opium Confessions with the final revision.   Many alterations consist in filling out the sentences; and, in a good many cases, two sentences are amalgamated into one.   Take the following example, the first few sentences of the section entitled, "The Pleasures of Opium."   In the original edition this stands—

"It is so long since I first took opium, that if it had been a trifling incident in my life, I might have forgotten its date; but cardinal events are not to be forgotten, and from circumstances connected with it, I remember that it must be referred to the autumn of 1804.   During that season I was in London, having come thither for the first time since my entrance at college.   And my introduction to opium arose in the following way.   From an early age I had been accustomed to wash my head in water at least once a-day," &c.

In the revised edition we read—

"It is very long since I first took opium; so long, that if it had been a trifling incident in my life, I might have forgotten its date; but cardinal events are not to be forgotten, and from circumstances connected with it, I remember that this inauguration into the use of opium must be referred to the spring or to the autumn of 1804, during which seasons I was in London, having come thither for the first time since my entrance at Oxford.   And this event arose in the following way: From an early age I had been accustomed," &c.

The four sentences of the original are amalgamated into two, without any condensation of the original bulk.   On the contrary, additions are made, one for the sake of emphasis, another for the sake of a more formal connection.

Unity of Sentence—A casuist would find no difficulty in arguing that De Quincey's sentences are not *over*-crowded.   None of the qualifications or parenthetic allusions could be said to be altogether irrelevant; and the difficulty of grasping the meaning being set on one side, it might be pleaded that, as regards the main purpose of the sentence, and its place among the other sentences of the composition, they are all of them indispensable.

De Quincey, however, often offends beyond the possibility of justification, overloading his sentences in a gossiping kind of way with particulars that have no relevance whatsoever to the main statement.   Of this habit I quote two examples, italicising the irrelevant clauses, and placing one of them in small capitals as being an offence of double magnitude, a second irrelevance foisted in upon the back of the first.   The first sentence relates to the exposure of infants in ancient Greece; the second explains itself.

"And because the ancients had a scruple (no scruple of mercy or of relenting conscience, but of selfish superstition) as to taking life by violence from any creature not condemned under some law, the mode of death must be by exposure on the open hills, where either the night air, or the fangs of a wolf, oftentimes of the great dogs—*still preserved in most parts of Greece (and traced back to the days of Homer as the public nuisances of travellers)*—usually put an end to the unoffending creature's life."

"It is asserted, as a general affection of human nature, that it is impossible to read a book with satisfaction until one has ascertained whether the author of it be tall or short, corpulent or thin; and, as to complexion, whether he be a 'black' man (which, in the 'Spectator's' time, was the absurd expression for a swarthy man), or a fair man, or a sallow man, or perhaps a green man, *which Southey affirmed to be the proper description of many stout artificers in Birmingham too much given to work in metallic fumes;* ON WHICH ACCOUNT THE NAME OF SOUTHEY IS AN ABOMINATION TO THIS DAY IN CERTAIN FURNACES OF WARWICKSHIRE."

The excrescences on the last sentence might be justified on the ground that they are humorous, although in severe exposition the humour would probably be ill-timed; but the parenthetic information in the first is pedantic, and insufferably out of harmony with the rest of the sentence. Still even for this a casuist might find something to say, taking the parenthesis in relation to the subject-matter and De Quincey's pitch of feeling in the treatment of it.

THE POINTED TRADITION: MACAULAY

William Minto

Macaulay's is a style that may truly be called "artificial," from his excessive use of striking artifices of style—balanced sentences, abrupt transitions, and pointed figures of speech.

The peculiarities of the mechanism of his style are expressed in such general terms as "abrupt," "pointed," "oratorical." We shall not attempt to gather together separately all the elements that justify these epithets; but ... the various particulars that go to the making of the "abruptness" and the "point" will be noticed as we proceed.

His sentences have the compact finish produced by the frequent occurrence of the periodic arrangement. He is not uniformly periodic; he often prefers a loose structure, and he very rarely has recourse to the forced inversions that we find occasionally in De Quincey. Yet there is a sufficient interspersion of periodic arrangements to produce an impression of firmness. Taken as a whole, his style is one of the last that we should call loose.

... If we take the word periodic in its restricted sense, we cannot de-

From William Minto, *A Manual of English Prose Literature* (Boston: Ginn, 1891), pp. 87–89.

scribe Macaulay as a composer in the periodic style. The "periodic style," in its narrower sense, implies long and heavy-laden sentences, and Macaulay's tendency is towards the short and light.

Occasionally he uses the long oratorical climactic period, consisting of a number of clauses in the same construction gradually increasing in length so as to form a climax. Thus—

"The energy of Innocent the Third, the zeal of the young orders of Francis and Dominic, and the ferocity of the Crusaders, whom the priesthood let loose on an unwarlike population, crushed the Albigensian Churches."

Again, in a sketch of the Reformation—

"The study of the ancient writers, the rapid development of the powers of the modern languages, the unprecedented activity which was displayed in every department of literature, the political state of Europe, the vices of the Roman Court, the exactions of the Roman Chancery, the jealousy with which the wealth and privileges of the clergy were naturally regarded by laymen, the jealousy with which Italian ascendancy was naturally regarded by men born on our side of the Alps—all these things gave to the teachers of the new theology an advantage which they perfectly understood how to use."

In the last example there are two climaxes in sound.

A large proportion of his sentences contain words and clauses in formal balance; but the effect of this would not be so striking were it not that his composition contains so much antithesis in other modes. The general predominance of antithesis we shall consider in its place under Figures of Speech; here we have to do properly with balanced forms, whether embodying antithesis or not.

He makes considerable use of conventional balanced phrases for amplifying the roll of the sentence. Thus—"After full inquiry, and impartial reflection;" "men who have been tried by equally strong temptations, and about whose lives we possess equally full information;" "no hidden causes to develop, no remote consequences to predict;" "very pleasing images of paternal tenderness and filial duty;" and so forth.

The following is an example of balance without antithesis. It is valuable as an artificial mode of giving separate emphasis to two things involved in the same argument—a preventive against confusion:—

"Now it does not appear to us to be the first object that people should always believe in the established religion, or be attached to the established government. A religion may be false. A government may be oppressive. And whatever support governments give to false religions, or religion to oppressive governments, we consider as a clear evil."

While this mode of statement has undeniably its advantages, it is obviously too startling an artifice to be often employed. The two short sentences, interjected without connectives, are examples of one element of our author's abruptness.

The following passages show balance combined with antithesis:—

"Thus the successors of the old Cavaliers had turned demagogues; the successors of the old Roundheads had turned courtiers. Yet was it long before their mutual animosity began to abate; for it is the nature of parties to retain their original enmities far more firmly than their original principles. During many years, a generation of Whigs, whom Sidney would have spurned as slaves, continued to wage deadly war with a generation of Tories, whom Jeffreys would have hanged for Republicans."

"With such feelings, both parties looked into the chronicles of the middle ages. Both readily found what they sought; and both obstinately refused to see anything but what they sought. The champions of the Stuarts could easily point out instances of oppression exercised on the subject. The defenders of the Roundheads could as easily produce instances of determined and successful resistance offered to the Crown. The Tories quoted from ancient writings expressions almost as servile as were heard from the pulpit of Mainwaring. The Whigs discovered expressions as bold and severe as any that resounded from the judgment-seat of Bradshaw. One set of writers adduced numerous instances in which kings had extorted money without the authority of Parliament. Another set cited cases in which the Parliament had resumed to itself the power of inflicting punishment on kings. Those who saw only one half of the evidence would have concluded that the Plantagenets were as absolute as the Sultans of Turkey; those who saw only the other half would have concluded that the Plantagenets had as little real power as the Doges of Venice; and both conclusions would have been equally remote from the truth."

It is a pretty general opinion among critics that Macaulay overdid this artifice of style. Even his apologist in the 'Edinburgh Review' admitted that his sentences were sometimes "too curiously balanced." As he himself said of Tacitus— "He tells a fine story finely, but he cannot tell a plain story plainly. He stimulates till stimulants lose their power." The worst of it is that exact balance cannot long be kept up, as in the above passage, without a sacrifice of strict truth; both sides are extremely exaggerated to make the antithesis more telling.

TRADITION AND INNOVATION: CARLYLE

Francis X. Roellinger

The style of the essay on Burns is transitional and experimental: Carlyle seems to be striving for an idiom of his own, and in so doing hits upon some

Reprinted by permission of the Modern Language Association from Francis X. Roellinger, "The Early Development of Carlyle's Style," *PMLA*, LXXII (1957), 936–951, at 947–951. Notes have been omitted. References to Carlyle's essays are to *The Works of Thomas Carlyle*, ed. H. D. Traill, Centenary ed. (New York, n.d.). References to *Sartor Resartus* are to the edition by Charles Harrold (New York, 1937).

of the features of the later manner and achieves a recognizable style, but it is uneven and sometimes forced. In the remaining articles written before the first version of *Sartor*, he consolidates this style somewhat short of the reach attempted in the Burns; it is as if he were content with the means in hand until a new end, that of a "Kunstwerk" of his own, declared itself, and new means had to be found.

The recognizable style of the articles written after the Burns is not easy to describe. The occasional characteristic metaphor, apostrophe, rhetorical question, and odd turn of phrase tell only part of the story. These can be found by the diligent searcher, who is inevitably more impressed by their presence than by their absence. In the essay on Heine, for example, he will find this typical figure: "It is curious ... to see with how little of a purely humane interest he looks back to his childhood; how Heine the man has almost grown into a sort of teaching machine, and sees in Heine the boy little else than an incipient Gerundgrinder, and tells us little else but how this wheel after the other was developed in him, and he came at last to grind in complete perfection" (xxvi, 325). Nor will he miss the oratorical interrogation at the bottom of a page of the essay on Voltaire: "What Plough or Printing-press, what Chivalry or Christianity, nay, what Steam-engine, or Quakerism, or Trial by Jury, did these Encyclopedists invent for mankind?" The search for jingling pairs of alliterative words will be even more rewarding: "theogony, theology," "pudding, praise," "vibrations, vibratiuncles," "Dapperism and Dilletantism and rickety Debility." Looking for another hallmark of Carlyle's diction, the pluralizing of proper nouns, he will come up with: "our Knowleses, Maturins, Shiels, and Shees," "Lord Mayor Shows and Guildhall dinners," "Royal and Imperial Societies, the Bibliothèques, Glyphothèques, Technothèques."

But the main current of the style of these essays is seldom recognizable, for despite occasional intrusions of reflective and hortatory passages, the narrative and expository burden is still formidable, and it offers few occasions for stylistic fireworks. The prevailing tone is still that of the polite, impersonal, and anonymous reviewer: "So much, in the province to which he devoted his activity, is Heine allowed to have accomplished. Nevertheless, we must not assert that, in point of understanding and spiritual endowment, he can be called a great, or even, in strict speech, a complete man" (xxvi, 351). What happens to this manner when occasion offers illumination of the apostolic message is well illustrated in the following, on Voltaire's last visit to Paris:

Considered with reference to the world at large, this journey is further remarkable. It is the most splendid triumph of that nature recorded in these ages; the loudest and showiest homage ever paid to what we moderns call literature; to a man that had merely thought, and published his thoughts. Much false tumult, no doubt, there was in it; yet also a certain deeper significance. It is interesting to see how universal and eternal in man is love of wisdom; how the highest and the lowest, how supercilious princes, and rude peasants, and all men must alike show honor to Wisdom, or the appearance of Wisdom; nay, properly speaking, can show honor to nothing else. (xxvi, 437)

If this is one of the earliest, it is also one of the most restrained statements of Carlyle's idea of worship of the hero as man of letters. Departures from conventional expression are slight but recognizable. The first sentence is commonplace, and the second is remarkable only for the use of the semi-colon where conventional practice would suggest the comma. The fuller stop emphasizes each phrase or clause and interrupts the flow of thought. The third sentence shows what is happening to the usual balance and anti-thesis: instead of "there was not only much false tumult but also a certain deeper significance," we have an inversion: "Much false tumult, no doubt, there was in it; yet also a certain deeper significance." The inversion places the balanced elements at opposite ends of the sentence instead of within the conjunctive frame. The last sentence is most prophetic of the later style, not only in its interrupted, staccato parallel phrasing and unusual number of monosyllabic words, but in its use as climax of what Bonamy Dobrée has called the "door-banged" effect: "Nay, properly speaking, can show honor to nothing else."

A comparison of this passage with a brief paragraph on the same subject in *Sartor* shows how far the style of *Sartor* goes beyond the most recognizable manner of the precedent essays. Despite its "door-banged" conclusion, the passage from the Voltaire is almost urbane: Carlyle is as gentle and tolerant as he could be to an unsympathetic subject. Voltaire's journey is admittedly "the most splendid triumph of that nature recorded in these ages," and the qualification, "much false tumult, no doubt," is a mild concession. The writer is above the reader, as he is in most reviews of the day, but his attitude is polite and courteous: if the reader will but look and consider, he will "see how universal and eternal in man is love of wisdom." This attitude to subject and reader reflects in part the truth of Louis Cazamian's observation: "Carlyle's mind was never again so liberal as when he wrote these essays; at this happy period, allied with his rugged independence was a plasticity of mind, a tolerance, that age and fame gravely weakened." The style of the passage from *Sartor* might show the weakening; certainly it shows how the whole form and purpose of that work demanded and received a radical change in style. In it Teufelsdröckh cites Voltaire's last journey to Paris as an instance of hero-worship, which he calls "the corner-stone of living rock, whereon all Polities for the remotest time may stand secure": "Do our readers discern any such corner-stone, or even so much as what Teufelsdröckh is looking at? He exclaims, 'Or hast thou forgotten Paris and Voltaire? How the aged, withered man, though but a Sceptic, Mocker, and millinery Court-poet, yet because he seemed the Wisest, Best, could drag mankind at his chariot-wheels, so that the princes coveted a smile from him, and the loveliest of France would have laid their hair beneath his feet! All Paris was one vast Temple of Hero-worship; though their Divinity, moreover, was of feature too apish.'"

In place of the polite reviewer patiently pointing out the moral to his gentle reader, we have Teufelsdröckh on his inverted tub, scolding and haranguing the multitude. He is introduced by a question from his sup-posititious editor, whose attitude to the reader is hardly distinguishable f: om that of Teufelsdröckh himself, for the implication is that the reader is a dolt because he will *not* "discern any such corner-stone." He will not only fail to see what Teufelsdröckh sees: he will even fail to see a great deal less. This scornful attitude to the reader is, of course, a rhetorical device of deliberate provocation; throughout the work he is frequently addressed as "Fool!" Nevertheless he is apparently expected to know what is alluded to in the question, "Or hast thou forgotten Paris and Voltaire?" No previous mention is made of the incident, nor is the reference self-explanatory; like many other obscure allusions in *Sartor*, it requires a note.

Scorn for the reader is more than matched by contempt for Voltaire, caricatured as "the aged, withered man," called names, "Sceptic, Mocker, and millinery Court-poet," and referred to in the coarse anti-climax of the passage as a "Divinity ... of feature too apish." In the review, by the way, he is the "lean, tottering, lonely old man," to whom "we feel drawn ... by some tie of affection, of kindly sympathy." The scornful exaggeration of the description, including the princes coveting Voltaire's smile, and "the loveliest of France" laying their hair beneath his feet makes something of a paradox of the "vast Temple of Hero-worship." In general, the two passages employ opposed strategies: the strategy of the review is the sympathetic approach; that of *Sartor* might be called the shock treatment.

The truth is that Carlyle mastered at least two styles, the first based on the traditional prose required of the periodical reviewer, the second an unconventional, eccentric idiom designed to meet the requirements of the fiction of Teufelsdröckh and his book on clothes. Perhaps neither was his "natural voice," whatever that may mean; both betray signs of deliberate and painstaking construction. W. C. Brownell has shrewdly suggested that Carlyle's praise of unconsciousness was "a reaction from the discomfort and often the misery with which his extremely conscious composition was attended. No writer ever thought more of *how* he was to do whatever he did. His journal records that he sat three days before the sheet of paper at the top of which the word 'Voltaire' was written before writing a line of his famous essay. Certainly, during that time, he was not thinking what to say."

As a final piece of evidence in favor of Brownell's suggestion and in support of the conclusion of this essay, two more passages might be cited without much comment, for they speak for themselves. The first is from "Characteristics," written after the first version of *Sartor*, and possibly while Carlyle was in the midst of revising and enlarging it. At the time when he had already mastered the idiom of Teufelsdröckh, Carlyle could still, on occasion, write a whole essay in this vein:

If Society, in such ages, had its difficulty, it also had its strength; if sorrowful masses of rubbish so encumbered it, the tough sinews to hurl them aside, with indomitable heart, were not wanting. Society went along without complaint; did not stop to scrutinize itself, to say, How well I perform!, or, Alas, how ill! Men did not yet feel themselves to be "the envy of surrounding nations"; and were enviable on that very account. Society was what we can call *whole*, in both senses of the word. The individual man was in himself a whole, or complete union; and could combine with his fellows as the living member of a greater whole. For all men, through their life, were animated by one great Idea; thus all efforts pointed one way, everywhere there was wholeness. (xxviii, 15)

The second passage, on the same subject, is from *Sartor*:

"Call ye that a Society," cries he again, "where there is no longer any Social Idea extant; not so much as the Idea of a common Home, but only of a common over-crowded Lodging-house? Where each, isolated, regardless of his neighbor, clutches what he can get, and cries 'Mine!' and calls it Peace, because in the cut-purse and cut-throat Scramble, no steel knives, but only a far cunninger sort, can be employed? Where Friendship, Communion, has become an incredible tradition; and your holiest Sacramental Supper is a smoking Tavern Dinner, with Cook for Evangelist? Where your priest has no tongue but for plate-licking? and your high Guides and Governors cannot guide; but on all hands hear it passionately proclaimed: *Laissez faire*: Leave us alone of *your* guidance, such light is darker than darkness; eat your wages, and sleep!" (p.232)

"Characteristics" was not only accepted by Jeffrey's successor, Macvey Napier, and published in the *Edinburgh Review*; it was, according to Froude, "received with the warmest admiration from the increasing circle of young intellectual men who were looking up to [Carlyle] as their teacher, and with wonder and applause from the reading London world" (II, 266). But when *Sartor*, having failed of publication in book form, finally began to appear in *Fraser's Magazine*, which we are told, "had a reputation for audacity, exuberance, and boisterous humor and satire" (*Sartor*, p. 11, n.), no one could tell what to make of it, and Froude informs us that "the writer was considered a literary maniac, and the unlucky editor was dreading the ruin of his magazine" (II, 363). History does not record that any of the "young in-tellectual men" or of the "reading London world" was heard to remark, "I know who wrote the article in the last month's *Fraser's*—Mr. Carlyle. You couldn't mistake his style."

VICTORIAN INDIVIDUALISM

Richard Ohmann

Here is Edmund Burke, responding with feeling to the notion that the state dances when the mob calls the tune:

To avoid, therefore, the evils of inconstancy and versatility, ten thousand times worse than those of obstinacy and the blindest prejudice, we have consecrated the state, that no man should approach to look into its defects or corruptions but with due caution; that he should never dream of beginning its reformation by its subversion;

From Richard Ohmann, "Methods in the Study of Victorian Style," *Victorian Newsletter*, XXVII (Spring, 1965), 1–4. Reprinted by permission of *Victorian Newsletter*. Some of the notes have been omitted, and the remainder renumbered to run in sequence.

that he should approach to the faults of the state as to the wounds of a father, with pious awe and trembling solicitude.[1]

The sentence has enough thickness and weight to contain, not only the core of Burke's political thought, but the core of his style as well. One knows some of the devices from long acquaintance: the periodic opening, with the long infinitive phrase positioned before rather than after the verb it modifies; the neat marshaling of parallel forms: "faults of the state"—"wounds of a father," "evils of inconstancy and versatility"—"those of obstinacy and the blindest prejudice"; the duration of the single syntactic flight (77 words); the generality, and the dependence on abstract nouns like "prejudice" and "subversion." These we consider touchstones of eighteenth-century prose, and of Burke's in particular. Other contours of the sentence are less apparent, though no less typical. Among the abstract nouns, many (e.g., "inconstancy," "solicitude," "obstinacy") derive from adjectives, which is to say that the deep structure of the sentence contains a number of rudimentary structures in the form Noun + Be + Adjective, each of which has undergone a grammatical transformation that couches the adjectival content in nominal form.[2] Again, Burke has a habit of using the possessive mold, so that instead of "reform the state" and "subvert the state" we have "its reformation" and "its subversion," by a series of transformations. More generally, we might mark how coordination works in the interest of compactness, how little repetition there is. We should also note the lack of impedance to syntactic movement: only once does a construction halt midway for another construction to intrude and run its course. Finally, the mood of the sentence is distinctly declarative. To be sure, these observations do not nearly exhaust the makeup of the sentence, much less of Burke's style. But they at least touch the characteristic peaks of expression.

Burke, or some other writer by the same name, *might* have said what he wanted to say in a different manner, for a style implies alternative styles. How can we shift the underpinnings of Burke's sentence to give the same material another shape? By letting constructions interrupt each other. By shaking the phrases out of their tidy parallels. By transplanting the initial phrase to eliminate the periodic element. By expanding some of the constructions that are pared down in coordination. By converting one clause, say, into a rhetorical question. We must also find alternatives to some of the nominalized adjectives, and phrases like "its reformation" will have to assume another form. Taking these editorial liberties, and a few smaller ones, we arrive at a passage, no more than slightly barbarous, that sounds like this:

---

[1] *Reflections on the Revolution in France* . . . .

[2] The linguistic framework that I employ (loosely) throughout this paper is that of generative grammar. The *locus classicus* is Noam Chomsky's *Syntactic Structures* (The Hague, 1957); a convenient place to consult more recent work in the field, by Chomsky and others, is Jerry A. Fodor and Jerrold J. Katz, eds., *The Structure of Language; Readings in the Philosophy of Language* (Prentice-Hall, Englewood Cliffs, N.J., 1964). . . .

To be inconstant, to be versatile, are evils—evils ten thousand times worse than being obstinate or being most blindly prejudiced. Inconstant and versatile! we have consecrated the state to avoid these evils. Although it has defects, therefore, although it is corrupted, no man but a duly cautious one should approach to look into its defects. And should he dream, ever, of beginning to reform the state by subverting it? No, I say, but approach trembling, solicitous, to the faults that it has, and with pious awe, as he would approach to a father's wounds.

Something besides the style has escaped, of which more later; but the stylistic alteration alone takes the passage away from Burke, takes it quite out of the eighteenth century, and in fact, to my ear, places it rather near to this specimen from the 1860's:

Children of God;—it is an immense pretension!—and how are we to justify it? By the works which we do, and the words which we speak. And the work which we collective children of God do, our grand centre of life, our *city* which we have builded for us to dwell in, is London! London, with its unutterable external hideousness, and with its internal canker of *publice egestas, privatim opulentia,*—to use the words which Sallust puts into Cato's mouth about Rome,—unequalled in the world! The word, again, which we children of God speak, the voice which most hits our collective thought, the newspaper with the largest circulation in England, nay, with the largest circulation in the whole world, is the *Daily Telegraph*! I say that when our religious organizations,—which I admit to express the most considerable effort after perfection that our race has yet made,—land us in no better result than this, it is high time to examine carefully their idea of perfection, . . .[3]

This is Arnold, of course, and it is interesting to notice that he writes in a frame of mind not unlike Burke's: both deplore what only Arnold could call "machinery"—external reforms; both are appalled by a rootless vulgarity that the one sees in France and the other in England; both, in fact, are responding to noises made by the mob; both argue for gradualism and tradition; both try to discredit the fanaticism of the hour by imposing a broad historical perspective. So the differences that any reader sees between the two passages cannot be laid to a contrast in allegiance or purpose. And plainly no such contrast can account for the difference between Burke's sentence and my revision, for these have virtually identical content. Style is the discriminator.

I should like to suggest that the contrast between Burke's style and the quasi-Arnoldian style of my revision is a matter of different choices made in expressing the same content, and, if I am right in thinking my revision Arnoldian, that the contrast between Burke and *echt*-Arnold, or between almost any two writers, is of a related kind.[4] To conceive style thus is no more than critics normally and rightly do, except when they pause to *theorize* about style; and the point would hardly be worth making but for the way criticism, in those theoretical interludes, puts on its Sunday best and pro-

---

[3]"Sweetness and Light," *Culture and Anarchy* (New York, 1910), p. 25.
[4]I have argued this point at length in "Generative Grammars and the Concept of Literary Style," . . . in *Word*, December, 1964.

claims that style and content are inseparable.[5] In any case, for the practical critic who is interested in style, the serious questions go well beyond this issue. Of these serious questions, the two main ones are: how can we best describe the choices that make up a style? and, what importance do styles have?

I think that we are on the edge of some better answers to the first question than we have had. Grammatical theory—I refer to generative grammar—has it that there are in any language only a few basic structures, that sentences of these types carry content, and that almost all the sentences of a language that actually occur are built up from the basic sentences by grammatical transformations, and are understood in terms of the content expressed by the basic sentences. Furthermore, the basic sentences that alter and combine, through transformations, to make up a given sentence, may fall into quite different patterns if another set of transformations is applied. For instance, Burke's clause "that he should never dream of beginning its reformation by its subversion" can become "he should never dream of beginning to reform the state by subverting it," or can take any one of numerous other shapes. Content is the same, form different. Now, the stylistic changes I made in Burke's sentence were nearly all of this sort; and every descriptive statement I made about his style can be put as a statement about syntactic transformations. By extension, I would argue that nearly all the major differences between Arnold's style and Burke's have a syntactic foundation, as do stylistic choices in general. Transformational grammar, in short, not only makes possible a coherent theory of style, but facilitates revealing descriptions as well.

An answer to my other question—what importance do styles have?—follows from the hypothesis as to what they *are*. If stylistic choices operate among alternate formulations of propositional content, then a *pattern* of such choices—a style—implies a characteristic way of conceiving, relating, and presenting content. A habit of mind and feeling. A conceptual world. Saying so is easier than proving the point, but since it is perhaps a majority opinion among critics now, I should like to assume it here as an hypothesis.

In any case, it is time to return to Arnold. What are some salient features of his prose that will set him off from, say, Burke and what significance have they? To begin with an obvious one, Arnold favors constructions that have at their grammatical roots the basic pattern, Noun + Be + Predicate Noun. The short passage above includes, for example, "we are children," "it is a pretension," "the work is the city," and six others. Arnold likes labeling and classifying—and *insisting* on his labels—as the tags he has left in our vocabulary will testify: "machinery," "sweetness and light," "Philistines," and so on. He seems convinced that the names we give things have power, and that encircling a concept with labels

---

[5] True, of course, if the sense of the term "content" is attenuated to cover every last evocative flourish and connotative wiggle. But then the dogma becomes a near-truism, and loses interest correspondingly. As important as it once was for critics to stop thinking of style as embellishment it is now perhaps at least as important for us to salvage the narrower and in some ways more helpful sense of "content": i.e., overt, cognitive meaning. Otherwise a distinction is lost, and criticism is the poorer.

or categories advances thought; that if only the right name can be found confusion will dissolve.

Often in Arnold's prose these basic structures are transformed grammatically to emerge as appositives, another mark of his style. And appositives, of course, interrupt the sentence that encases them; hence their prominence is one cause of still another pattern in Arnold's style, the tendency to interpolate, or embed, constructions in one another. When the interpolations do not label or classify, they usually add information, or they qualify, or they supply an additional vantage point from which to see the business at hand, and grasp the manner in which it is maintained: "so I say," or "to use the words which Sallust puts in Cato's mouth." So Arnold's interruptions work toward *definition*, in both senses of that word. His prose strives toward completeness and sharpness, and syntactic forward movement gives quarter when necessary in the service of this aim. Still another stylistic consequence hangs upon these procedures: Arnold's prose has unusual syntactic "depth," for prose in which the clauses are relatively short. By this I mean that one word in the surface structure is likely to play several grammatical roles in the underlying structure.[6] Thus for all Arnold's much noted simplicity and condescension, there is a sense in which his prose is quite complex, though complex *in the interest of* conceptual clarity. Compare Burke: how much less effort he spends in regulating verbal or conceptual traffic, and how much more in saying what happens, or what will happen if. . . .

I have spent some time on this stylistic cluster because it seems to me responsive to a common impulse among Victorian writers: the urge to overcome doubt and confusion in a period when the avenue to truth is far from broad, straight, or public. Many Victorians are concerned, not merely to expose error and speak the plain truth (as is more nearly the case with Burke, Johnson, Shaftesbury, and so on), but to create the very climate of mind within which truth and conviction will become possibilities. Arnold and his contemporaries write in a society where no common framework of feelings and assumptions can be taken for granted, and their prose strains to provide the framework, in addition to the local truths they are arguing. Yet at the same time they believe it not unlikely for conversion to take place, for the culture to redeem its way of life; they prod and insist and jostle the reader with dogged urgency to this end.[7]

---

[6]"Work" and "city" in sentence three have four grammatical roles apiece; "organisations" in the last sentence has five; and so on. The five basic sentences that give the pertinent information about "organisations" are: "we have organisations," "the organisations are religious," "the organisations express an effort," "the organisations land us in a result," and "the organisations have an idea of perfection." The reader must grasp the relations indicated by these sentences or he will not comprehend the sentence Arnold wrote.

[7]These generalities about the Victorian period are not, of course, my own: for views on which I am drawing, see especially Walter Houghton, *The Victorian Frame of Mind; 1830–1870* (New Haven, 1957); William A. Madden, "The Victorian Sensibility," *Victorian Studies*, VII (1963), 67–97; Jerome Hamilton Buckley, *The Victorian Temper; A Study in Literary Culture* (Cambridge, Mass., 1951). The idea of conversion comes from Buckley's chapter, "The Pattern of Conversion," though I am thinking also of Houghton's discussion, "Optimism."

Still other characteristics of Arnold's style answer to these very general beliefs in the decay of intellectual and spiritual community and in the possibility of change. His famous habit of repetition, for instance, is the mark of a writer trying by main force to establish fixed points in the ebbing sea of faith. He cannot, as Burke could, simply draw his central, freighted terms from the public stock of language and count on culture to supply adequate meanings; he must work to lodge both terms and meanings in his audience's sensibility. Again, Arnold's style relies heavily on the constructions that English has for reporting speech and thought: "I say that. . . ," and "our religious organisations, which *I admit to* express. . ." are two examples in the passage at hand. Usually these represent an attempt to put before the reader, not only an idea, but a judgment *on* that idea, or an attitude toward it, or a sense of the precise strength with which it is maintained. Burke and Johnson could count on ideas as a stable medium of exchange; Arnold must always be setting the rates. On the other hand, he distinctly underplays the transformation, so common with Burke, that converts a predicate adjective into a nominal. To speak of "inconstancy" rather than saying that such and such a person is inconstant implies a faith in unchanging and universal qualities that was harder to sustain in 1868 than in 1790. And finally, the questions and imperatives that trouble the discursive flow of Arnold's prose may be partly an acknowledgement that basic accord is a delicate and elusive thing, and partly an attempt to jolt the reader loose from his complacencies.

A caution: the foregoing is a steeply tilted account of Arnold's style. A more level account would naturally include features less easily subsumed in the single current of Arnoldian (and Victorian) thought and feeling which I have italicized. But I have meant to be selective because my subject is neither style nor Arnold's style, but *Victorian* style, and it is convenient to notice that at least some components of Arnold's style and of the conceptual framework it reflects can be understood as deriving from the culture and period he inhabited. The problem I wish to address from now on is: how far can this familiar point be carried?

Given the slant on Victorian style I have proposed, instances from the other great Victorians readily present themselves. Carlyle is a labeler, like Arnold, and out of much the same impulse. He is also lavish with negations, as if called upon personally to deny every received opinion of the age. Newman's style trades heavily on "that" clauses, as Arnold's does, and also has what I have called "syntactic depth." Ruskin leans on questions and imperatives. Pater fills his prose with syntactic interruptions and interpolations, almost to the point of affectation. And his style has another characteristic that fits in the same congeries: he favors a set of transformations that convert verbs into adjectives, in a way that emphasizes process, change, and instability. And so it goes, with one writer after another.

The richest source for any point about rhetoric is John Holloway, *The Victorian Sage: Studies in Argument* (London, 1953); but see also, among others, A. Dwight Culler, "Method in the Study of Victorian Prose," *Victorian Newsletter* (Spring, 1956), pp. 1-4, and Leonard W. Deen, "The Rhetoric of Newman's *Apologia*," ELH, XXIX (1962), 224-38.

But to put the case for a Victorian style in this way is to see immediately that something has gone wrong: in sifting Victorian prose for this or that bit of grammar, one is no longer speaking of styles at all, for a style is a complex and deeply organized working-together of many linguistic patterns, not a handful of isolated devices. And in any case, even the feeblest intuition of style tells us that Arnold's is very different from Newman's, Newman's from Carlyle's, and so on. If we look for a fundamental pattern of syntactic organization shared by all these writers, and not, say, by a corresponding group from the eighteenth century, we will come up empty-handed. There are stylistic *tendencies* that divide Victorians from their eighteenth-century predecessors, but very few clear and pronounced indicators of one century or the other. I have made a preliminary syntactic inventory of prose samples by six major Victorians and six eighteenth-century writers; out of 33 classes of basic sentences and transformations, which constitute the fundamental machinery of English grammar, there are only three on which the two periods contrast significantly: the Victorians use more questions and imperatives; they use the transformation that converts nouns into adjectives less frequently; and—I am unable to account for this—they incorporate more basic sentences with intransitive verbs. Needless to say, these three differences scarcely add up to evidence for a theory of Victorian style. The truth is that in almost every stylistic dimension the Victorians differ nearly as much among themselves as they differ from eighteenth-century writers.

Yet I have argued that style reflects conceptual framework and critics like Houghton have amply shown that there is something worth calling *the* Victorian frame of mind. How can the two points be reconciled? Fairly simply, I think. A man who occupies a given spot in history and culture is urged by his intellectual world to think and feel in certain ways; but the forming power of intellectual culture operates on a mind already formed deeply and intricately, by a thousand sub-cultures, from the nursery on up. Style is responsive to the cut of a writer's mind, and that is only trimmed and decorated by intellectual culture, not created by it.

If this is so, as I imagine it to be, many of us have overestimated the importance of historical periods to the description and understanding of styles.[8] Those of us interested in Victorian prose style will do well to study individual writers intensively, and with the best linguistic theory available, to discover the unique and intriguing shapes that mind and language take among the Victorians. We could take our direction from Newman's excellent comment on style:

while the many use language as they find it, the man of genius uses it indeed, but subjects it withal to his own purposes, and moulds it according to his own peculiarities. The throng and succession of ideas, thoughts, feelings, imaginations, aspirations, which pass within him, the abstractions, the juxtapositions, the comparisons, the discriminations, the conceptions which are so original in him, his views of

---

[8]But at the same time, many critics have emphasized the individuality of Victorian writers—Holloway, for instance, throughout his book, and Houghton, p. 225. See also William E. Buckler's "Introduction" to the Riverside Edition, *Prose of the Victorian Period* (Cambridge, Mass., 1958) and James Sutherland, *On English Prose* (Toronto, 1957), chap. IV.

external things, his judgments upon life, manners, and history, the exercises of his wit, of his humour, of his depth, of his sagacity, all these innumerable and incessant creations, the very pulsation and throbbing of his intellect, does he image forth, to all does he give utterance, in a corresponding language, which is as multiform as this inward mental action itself and analogous to it, the faithful expression of his intense personality, attending on his own inward world of thought as its very shadow, so that we might as well say that one man's shadow is another's as that the style of a really gifted mind can belong to any but himself.[9]

Reliable judgments about the history of style will come after an understanding of styles, and may be quite other than what the textbooks say.

---

[9]"Literature"....

FROM COOPER TO CRANE

Harold C. Martin

That there is a "development" in the style of prose fiction in nineteenth-century American literature no one is likely to dispute. And even a cursory acquaintance with that literature will lead any sensitive reader to conclusions about the development that are generally sound. It is worth while, nonetheless, to look at the evidence and to observe the course over which the noticeable changes have occurred.

Two narrative passages provide a text. The first is the opening paragraph of Stephen Crane's short story "The Open Boat," written in 1898. The other is from the fifth chapter of James Fenimore Cooper's fourth novel, *The Pilot*, written in 1823. This is Crane:

None of them knew the color of the sky. Their eyes glanced level, and were fastened upon the waves that swept toward them. These waves were of the hue of slate, save for the tops, which were of foaming white, and all of the men knew the colors of the sea. The horizon narrowed and widened, and dipped and rose, and at all times its edge was jagged with waves that seemed to thrust up in points like rocks. Many a man ought to have a bath-tub larger than the boat which here rode upon the sea. These waves were most wrongfully and barbarously abrupt and tall, and each froth-top was a problem in small-boat navigation.

And here a somewhat similar scene penned seventy-five years earlier:

From Harold C. Martin, ed., *Style in Prose Fiction* (New York: Columbia University Press, 1959), "The Development of Style in Nineteenth-Century American Fiction," pp. 114–141, at pp. 115–119, 125, 131–133. Reprinted by permission of Columbia University Press. Notes have been omitted.

The rushing sounds of the wind were now, indeed, heard at hand; and the words were hardly past the lips of the young lieutenant, before the vessel bowed down heavily to one side, and then, as she began to move through the water, rose again majestically to her upright position, as if saluting, like a courteous champion, the powerful antagonist with which she was about to contend. Not another minute elapsed, before the ship was throwing the waters aside, with a lively progress, and, obedient to her helm, was brought as near to the desired course as the direction of the wind would allow. The hurry and bustle on the yards gradually subsided, and the men slowly descended to the deck, all straining their eyes to pierce the gloom in which they were enveloped, and some shaking their heads, in melancholy doubt, afraid to express the apprehensions they really entertained. All on board anxiously waited for the fury of the gale; for there were none so ignorant or inexperienced in that gallant frigate, as not to know that as yet they only felt the infant efforts of the wind. Each moment, however, it increased in power, though so gradual was the alteration, that the relieved mariners began to believe that all their gloomy forebodings were not to be realized. During this short interval of uncertainty, no other sounds were heard than the whistling of the breeze, as it passed quickly through the mass of rigging that belonged to the vessel, and the dashing of the spray that began to fly from her bows, like the foam of a cataract.

Now, Cooper's novel—though it is not entirely characteristic of the work with which he is today commonly identified—is in the strongest tradition of the period, that of the historical romance, modeled largely after Scott though influenced also by Fielding and Smollett. *The Pilot* is better than most of the romances published at the time; it is better, even, in some respects, than Cooper's later work; but it is close enough in particulars of style to contemporary works of the kind to provide a proper ground for generalization.

The most striking characteristic of this paragraph—for a modern reader, at least—is its syntax. The sentences are long: the first contains sixty-seven words; the last, fifty; the intermediate four average thirty-eight. All the sentences are complex or compound-complex, to use the grammarian's terms. All of the main clauses but one (the second in the third sentence) are clear of internal complication save for prepositional phrases. That one is the second main clause of a compound-complex sentence; it incorporates, besides an early prepositional phrase, two parallel participial phrases, each of which in turn contains an infinitive phrase and a subordinate relative clause. Moreover, the simplicity of main clauses in the other five sentences is illusory, for the dependent clauses that follow each are as elaborately wrought as the main clause just described. Two have double predicates; all have internal adjectival or adverbial clauses; three have infinitive phrases, active or passive; and the last concludes with a relative clause, an infinitive, and five prepositional phrases, three of them final.

The sentences, we might say, unlike the ship, are heavily ballasted. They surge forward at the outset (only the last one has a phrase before the opening main clause), but they quickly develop complexity, yaw about, lose some of their momentum. That they do not lose more is the result of two things. Seven out of every ten words in the passage are monosyllabic. There are only five words of four syllables and two of five. The preponderance of monosyllables and the frequency of prepositional phrases produce a rising rhythm throughout. Considering the number of monosyllables it is worth noting that accented syllables come together only five times in the whole passage, twice to some semantic effect (*bowed down heavily, all straining*). Given the multiple iambic and anapestic feet and the few collisions of stress, the passage might indeed be unpleasantly undulant throughout if the substantive units, the combination of noun and modifier, did not generally provide emphasized clusters with falling rhythm (*rushing sounds, young lieutenant, upright position, courteous champion*, and so on).

In the felicity of his rhythms, as in the simplicity of opening clauses, Cooper is, in this novel, a better stylist than most of his contemporaries— Irving, of course, excepted. But the general structure of his sentences is also theirs. Even taken apart from vocabulary, this complex style indicates a deliberateness which removes action some distance from direct observation. Its lavish use of phrase and clause produces a syntactical separation of substantive and verb from modifier which reduces immediacy in perception. Its general leisureliness allows it to accommodate exposition and intermittent moralizing as well as narration without change in pace.

*   *   *   *

Though more might be, enough has been said about the paragraph from Cooper's historical romance to give some idea of the vocabulary and syntax that govern the strongest and most serious tradition in the second quarter of the century and to underline the contrast between that tradition and the tradition represented in the opening paragraph from Crane's short story. This paragraph in a story some twelve or thirteen thousand words long contains, like the one from Cooper, six sentences, but those six sentences have fewer than half as many words. Although, in fact, only the first is a simple sentence, the complexity of none is great. There are nine main, or independent, clauses, and only four subordinate ones, and no subordinate clause contains any internal unit other than a prepositional phrase. One of the main clauses, on the other hand, has a double predicate, and another, a quadruple predicate. It is clear that the substance of action, then, is placed in a dominating position. This dominance is reinforced by successive rhythmic stresses at, or near, the opening of main clauses (*eyes glanced level, These waves* [repeated in the sixth sentence], *men knew, all times, each frothtop*). Moreover, the opening sentence is the shortest and sharpest of all: it is of nine words, all but one monosyllabic, and completely simple in syntax.

*   *   *   *

The *language* of Crane's paragraph is as different from that of Cooper's as are their respective patterns of syntax. The number of monosyllables is slightly greater—eight of every ten words instead of seven—and the number of dissyllabic words commensurately smaller; but the passage contains only four longer words, less than a third the proportion in Cooper. What is of greater importance, the number of nouns and verbs increases as the number of adjectives and adverbs declines. The conjunctions, moreover, are overwhelmingly (three to one) coordinates. This dominance of substantives,

verbs, and coordinating conjunctions, coupled with the syntactical characteristics already mentioned, indicates a localizing of action in the agent,
rather than a distribution over the whole surface of the sentence.   Further
scrutiny of the verbs shows that even those cast in the passive voice and the
copulas are here calculated to reinforce action, in this instance action on
rather than by human beings.

The passage begins with a negative—*None of them knew the color of the
sky.* The negative opening is strengthened in the next sentence by the second
predicate: *Their eyes glanced level, and were fastened....* From that point on
the action is not that of the men but of their environment.   The fifth sentence
is generalized: *Many a man ought to have a bath-tub larger than the boat
which here rode upon the sea.* It seems to me a failure, but its intent is surely
to carry even further the annihilation of person begun in the first sentence.

More than half of the verbs themselves are indicative of strong action,
a proportion less exclusive than later decades will require but much more
absorptive than the early part of the century would admit; and, at the center
of the passage, they take complete control: *The horizon narrowed and widened, and dipped and rose....* The nouns, like those in Cooper's paragraph,
are mainly concrete.   Only eight of all the words, however, have roots of
other than Saxon origin.   It is interesting to note that four of these eight
occur in the last sentence, the first two in conjunction with one of the rare
trisyllabic words (*wrongfully and barbarously abrupt*), the other two (*problem, navigation*) in the rather unsuccessful closing predication.   The first two
call for attention because they are part of an effort to wrench words into
new uses, an effort for which Crane was roundly criticized.   The preceding
sentence is of equal interest because of the word *bath-tub.*   To begin with,
the image is unexpected and incongruous; in 1898 it was indecorous as well.
(Is it not the word that one of James's heroes never mentions as the source
of his income?)   Whether or not it is suitable here—I find it uncomfortably
reminiscent of a common nursery rhyme—is for the moment unimportant.
It serves my immediate purpose as an example of mixed diction.

There is, of course, an established tradition of mixed diction in American literature.   Irving, for instance, often uses it for playful mockery:

The villagers gathered in the church-yard to cheer the happy couple as they left the
church; and the musical tailor had marshalled his band, and set up a hideous discord,
as the blushing and smiling bride passed through a lane of honest peasantry to her
carriage.   The children shouted and threw up their hats; the bells rang a merry peal
that set all the crows and rooks flying and cawing about the air, and threatened to
bring down the battlements of the old tower; and there was a continual popping off
of rusty firelocks from every part of the neighborhood. (*Bracebridge Hall*)

And Melville makes a particular virtue of mixture, melting jargon, dialect,
elegant diction and low, apostrophe, rhapsody, and objurgation, in the same
great pot.   Twain and others use it for humor and pathos; the realists, for
irony and sudden contrast.

But the use of *bath-tub* here, like the use of those two adverbs—*wrongfully* and *barbarously*—of a connotation particularly unusual in the context,
is part of Crane's effort, and the effort of a few of his contemporaries, to rely

on intensity of words rather than on variety and volume. In Crane, as in other writers of the period, realistic and romantic, the effort is accompanied by a preference for colloquial vocabulary. The result is a prose in which the possible variety has been deliberately limited, the number of repetitions therefore increased, and in which the use of striking words or images may be disproportionately frequent and, by virtue of the austere economy, particularly noticeable. The function of the author has changed from that of a "teller" to that of an "exciter"; he calculatedly provokes response in his readers by manipulating vocabulary.

FROM HAWTHORNE TO HEMINGWAY

Richard Bridgman

Little has been written about national prose style, for there are legitimate doubts that such an entity exists. A few pioneering explorations of American literature have located important image-rivers flowing through its style. References to gardens, to heroic innocence, and to darkness appear insistently enough in nineteenth-century American writing of all kinds to be regarded as transcending the preoccupations of any single writer. They constitute a part of the general literary response to national experience, that is, they form part of the national stylistic landscape. Beyond these studies of images, however, and short of linguistics, only offhand generalizations have been advanced about an American way of using language. Such generalizations commonly superimpose political assumptions upon the literary medium, finding it, for example, "democratic"—hence, obviously, "direct," "hardy," and "casual." The usefulness of such descriptions, which as Richard Ohmann points out "name without explaining," is easily dismissed; yet, their persistent appearance indicates that readers of American literature feel, even though they cannot substantiate their intuition, that this literature possesses certain distinctive stylistic features. The present study attempts to discover the source of those feelings.

My initial assumption is so broad as hardly to admit dispute: that a change has indeed taken place in American prose style in the last century and a half. Even in the absence of absolute proof (which in stylistic matters is unthinkable) most readers would agree, I should think, that the prose of Erskine Caldwell, John Steinbeck, William Saroyan, and J. P. Marquand

From *The Colloquial Style in America*, "Introduction," pp. 3–14, at pp. 3–13, by Richard Bridgman. Copyright © 1966 by Richard Bridgman. Reprinted by permission of Oxford University Press, Inc. Notes have been omitted.

more closely resembles the prose of Ernest Hemingway than that of Nathaniel Hawthorne. Conversely, the prose of George Lippard, Maria Susanna Cummins, Augusta Evans, Susan Warner, and William Ware has more affinities with Hawthorne than it has with writers in the current century. The very look of Hawthorne's page differs from Hemingway's. Its characteristic form is blocklike with dense and tangled interiors while Hemingway crosses his page with thin lines and chips of language, clean and well-lighted. Can there be any doubt to whom each of the following two sentences belong?

Beyond that darksome verge, the firelight glimmered on the stately trunks and almost black foliage of pines, intermixed with the lighter verdure of sapling oaks, maples, and poplars, while here and there lay the gigantic corpses of dead trees, decaying on the leaf-strewn soil.

We walked on the road between the thick trunks of the old beeches and the sunlight came through the leaves in light patches on the grass.

If we add similar quotations from lesser writers in both centuries, the difficulty of attribution does not appreciably increase:

She bent down on the velvet moss, while the green leaves of the shrubbery encircling her on every side, and the thick branches of trees, meeting overhead in a canopy of verdure, made the place seem like a fairy bower of some olden story.

On one side of the road was forest, healthy-looking pine and elm, dark trunks looking almost black against the pale, milky-green of the new foliage.

Now I would agree that for some purposes style cannot be discussed apart from the context in which it operates. Hawthorne's desire to create a sinister impression for the specific story "Ethan Brand" helped to determine the diction he selected. But style is both initiated by the artist and imposed upon him, so that when Hawthorne chose "darksome verge" and "gigantic corpses" to construct an atmosphere of fatality, he drew upon a vocabulary no longer available to Hemingway. Quite aside from his peculiar training and cast of experience, the writer bears the impress of a communal past and he walks through a shared present, which partially overrides individual volition. This study tries to keep both the social and the personal sources of style in mind, that is, to determine what problems and what solutions were virtually forced upon the writer by his time and to give an account of what the writer deliberately contributed to help bring about this general stylistic change.

If one accepts provisionally the existence of a change in American prose style, then the next pertinent question is, when did it begin? Recently the date 1884 has been advanced from several quarters, most succinctly by Ernest Hemingway: "All modern American literature comes from one book by Mark Twain called *Huckleberry Finn*." As early as 1913 H. L. Mencken was championing Mark Twain: "I believe that he was the true father of our national literature, the first genuinely American artist of the blood royal." Later, William Faulkner agreed, saying: "In my opinion, Mark Twain was the first truly American writer, and all of us since are his heirs, we descended from him."

This critical admiration has not extended to Mark Twain's work as a whole, nor to his literary theories (such as they were), nor to his practical criticisms. One book alone has drawn the praise. Whatever the merits of Mark Twain's other writing, and whatever the weaknesses of *Huckleberry Finn*, everyone—literary hacks, artists, and critics—agrees that the style of this single book has had a major effect on the development of American prose. Herman Wouk, for example, recently proposed that Mark Twain "established at a stroke the colloquial style which has swept American literature, and indeed spilled over into world literature." T. S. Eliot placed Mark Twain with Dryden and Swift as one of those writers "who have discovered a new way of writing, valid not only for themselves, but for others." Lionel Trilling felt that "as for the style of the book, it is not less than definitive in American literature. The prose of *Huckleberry Finn* established for written prose the virtues of American colloquial speech." Most enthusiastic of all has been Bernard DeVoto's assertion: "In a single step it made a literary medium of the American language; the liberating effect on American writing could hardly be overstated."

DeVoto's claim is an attractive one, but does not seem to me historically justified. I believe we have come to accept a false view of the ease with which writers profited by Mark Twain's example. The stylistic possibilities suggested by *Huckleberry Finn* were ignored, misunderstood, cynically exploited, and finally developed (with painful slowness) into durable form. Moreover, one cannot overlook the importance for style of several nationalistic impulses which initiated the idea of a colloquial prose long before Mark Twain's book appeared.

The literary relations of colonial America and the mother country are familiar enough. Seventeenth-century Americans drew sustenance directly from English sources, many of them having been born and educated there. Any differences in the standard styles of the mother country and of the colonies are attributable to the special conditions imposed by the American wilderness and the special preoccupations of the colonists. English examples determined changes in colonial style, as in the eighteenth century when American magazines pirated Augustan poems from their British counterparts and editors encouraged imitations of Waller, Dryden, and Pope. The major American figures maintained the continuity of the English tradition. As Stuart P. Sherman pointed out, "We can distinguish the styles of Franklin, John Adams, and Webster from one another, but not, with any assurance, from that of some British contemporary." Similarly, of early nineteenth-century novelistic style, Leo Marx has commented: "If we ask what is different about German writing, we know very well the first answer to expect: it is written in German. But the language of Cooper is not all that different from that of Scott, and with Cooper's generation the boundary between British and American literature remains uncertain." Only after the achievement of political independence did any significant movement toward the creation of an indigenous literature appear in the United States.

The first surge toward literary independence concentrated more upon content than upon form. Critical battles were joined, for instance, over whether Niagara Falls possessed the intrinsic dignity of Westminster Abbey. Although on some peripheral formal matters, spelling in particular, critics had mixed opinions, the arbiters of taste generally agreed that the crudities of American common speech were to be barred from any decent writer's style. Vulgarity in writing had to be fenced in with quotation marks, or clearly labeled as comic and therefore not to be taken seriously.

Still, a need was felt for a new style in the United States. The theoretical motive for it was to achieve a literary independence commensurate with the political independence already won. So Noah Webster proposed in 1789: "We have ... the fairest opportunity of establishing a national language ... in North America, that ever presented itself to mankind. Now is the time to begin the plan." The literature of the New World was to reflect its republican ideals. Practically, the pressure for a new style came from the already existing components of that new style in popular speech. Americans shared, especially on the frontier, basic experiences that required a vocabulary not precisely equivalent to that considered standard in England. "It is remarkable," said Captain Marryat in 1839, "how very debased the language has become in a short period in America.... They have a dictionary containing many thousands of words which, with us, are either obsolete, or are provincialisms, or are words necessarily invented by the Americans." The sense of regional uniqueness extended far enough in the early 1800's to produce a *Kentucky English Grammar*. It was not altogether a joke for Sam Slick to comment, "I never seed an Englishman yet that spoke good English."

The linguistic situation in the United States was historically unique. Romantic, nationalistic, and practical pressures impelled American writers to evolve a new means of expression out of the casual discourse of the nation. There, if anywhere, "American" was to be heard. Not that the American language was a new language, distinct from English. Compared to the gross differences which existed between French when it was first being adapted for serious literary use and the Latin from which it was derived, the distinctions between American informal speech and standard literary English were subtle. There was a spoken language in the United States with a natural way of using it (American), and there was a literary language with an accepted way of using it (English). In many respects these overlapped, and yet they were far from identical.

Making a literary vehicle out of the spoken language was more easily conceived than executed. Logically, it seemed to require the sorting out of native elements already present in the standard literary style, and then their reblending with other elements hitherto excluded from the printed page. But how was one to assemble an indigenous vocabulary? And what would it sound like in operation? The most obvious answer was to transfer the speech of an American (whatever that was) to the printed page, the chief consideration being verisimilitude. At first, the writer's ear had to furnish the evidence against which he could check and improve his mimetic powers. Only after various regional and social dialects had been learned and dialogue had been sufficiently refined were enough conventions available to permit stylization. This process of establishing a literary imitation of colloquial speech and then polishing it resembles the gradual stylistic refinement of language in the English Renaissance theater, a recent study of which, after describing the primitive heartiness of the early theater's popular style, designated the problem facing the next generation of playwrights: "To assimilate this raw speech into an organized style that would lend itself to more complex uses without, in the process, losing its vitality and its close kinship with the spoken word."

The fundamental question for all those working with the vernacular was how to eliminate the taint of vulgarity and of humor that normally accompanied popular speech. Taking a long view of the nineteenth century for a moment, one can trace the vernacular's increasing acceptance in the familiar descriptive terms "prose humor," "local color," and "realism." They signal the progressive flooding of the literary world with a common speech that for more and more readers is accepted as a literary norm. What was enjoyed with condescending amusement before the Civil War was encouraged after the war for its vivacious authenticity, then later as the literary manifestation of a militant attitude toward life.

Mark Twain's use of a boy as narrator in *Huckleberry Finn* provided American writers one important entry to the language and homely particulars of American life. In that story we hear no condescending adult voice by which Huck can be judged insufficient. His idiom is the standard. And because Huck is a boy, not only is his language natural to him, but his attitude toward the world of particulars around him is one of unremitting interest. His quiet concentration upon all that surrounds him invests the commonplace world with dignity, seriousness, and an unforeseen beauty that radiates through the very words he uses. An adult is tainted with stylistic original sin—double vision, awareness of tradition, vanity. Huck's style is prelapsarian in its innocence and single-minded directness. That is its excellence, but its limitation too, for although Huck saw deeply, his was a narrow vision. After the example of *Huckleberry Finn* writers had to learn how to overcome the limits of his restricting viewpoint.

As others have since, Mark Twain met the problem by avoiding it. In his subsequent work he either imitated *Huckleberry Finn* or he regressed to a mixed style where, like his admirers Stephen Crane and George Ade, he deliberately encouraged incongruities for their easy irony. Somewhat later Ring Lardner found a provisional solution. By using an illiterate ballplayer as his narrator, he managed to extend the range of experience of the vernacular voice, yet conserve its linguistic naïveté. The handicaps of this approach, however, were all too evident. Sherwood Anderson tried yet another tack, making simplicity in language a doctrinal virtue. But despite an abundance of faith, he lacked the technical control that could protect him from writing simplistic parodies of himself. All in all, the thoroughly puzzled American writers could not disentangle a stable idiom from the vernacular. Merely to recognize the importance of Mark Twain's contribution was not to understand how to adapt his example to the uses of a general American prose style. Although *Huckleberry Finn* was in the sky, the day remained cloudy.

By the last quarter of the century, technical improvements in the management of both dialect and standard dialogue necessitated the move toward stylization, toward a distinctive and cohesive mode of writing. Since perfect accuracy of reproduction in dialect was neither possible nor artistically desirable, at a certain point of sophistication the dialect writer was obliged to change his goal: rather than verisimilitude, he sought to achieve verbal artfulness. His attention shifted from the world "out there" to the prose surface. In order to free colloquial constituents from their naturalistic bondage, the writer had to form new literary conventions, an uncertain process with many a retreat and no clear success. Henry James produced work of special pertinence for solving the stalemate in which the realists like Mark Twain found themselves. He wished to give the impression in his narrative prose of a mind at work, to reveal the slow progress and convoluted recapitulations of thought. Having already produced a form of dialogue that for all its external simplicity bore a heavy psychological burden, James set to work some of the techniques he had developed for dialogue to produce a stylized version of the mind talking. The results sufficiently intrigued him that for a time he exaggerated them to see what further possibilities they might afford his prose style. Radical punctuation, fragmented expressions, and odd verbalisms resulted. James's practice supplied answers which Mark Twain's camp of vernacularists needed, the medium of transmission being Gertrude Stein.

With her abstract exercises in writing, Gertrude Stein drew the basic features of colloquial language out into the open, magnifying and underlining them. Although it was not precisely her intention, she offered colloquial language as free as possible of a subject matter, thus concentrating the attention of the student of style upon pure manner. The instruction provided by both her precepts and her copious examples helped Ernest Hemingway create a definitive style based upon the American colloquial tradition. In his first years as a writer we can watch him experimenting with the narrator whose presence ostensibly legitimizes the presence of the colloquial mode. He later concealed and sometimes withdrew the narrator, but at the same time he tinkered with his prose so that, whether the narrator were present or not, it retained its colloquial base.

On the basis of this summary then and in spite of genuine reservations about the possibility of discussing a national prose style, I believe one can still affirm the following propositions with some confidence:

1) American prose style changed significantly between 1825 and 1925.

2) On the whole the change was toward greater concreteness of diction and simplicity in syntax.

3) The change was initiated primarily in dialect pieces and in fictional dialogue.

4) Toward the end of the century writers became increasingly conscious of the techniques of colloquial writing.

5) These techniques were then stylized to accentuate the following characteristics of colloquial style:
a) stress on the individual verbal unit,
b) a resulting fragmentation of syntax, and
c) the use of repetition to bind and unify.

If one asks once more how Hemingway's prose and the prose of the twentieth century differ from that of Hawthorne and *his* century, the briefest answer would argue the greater verbal simplicity of the modern style. Long words are eliminated or infrequently used, and then as deliberate contrasts. The sentences themselves are shorter. What was hinged and stapled by semicolons in the earlier prose is broken up into a series of declarative sentences in the later. Fewer details are provided, and those offered are precise and concrete. References to a cultural and historical past are stripped away, and the haze of emotive words is dispelled. Primary colors are accented. The immediate material world claims all the reader's attention. The result is a sharp, hard focus. Hemingway's prose is not the ultimate prose by any means, but its lean, artful sufficiency based upon a vernacular diction and a colloquial manner had to be achieved before it could effloresce into more intricate structures.

Since this study traces a movement in colloquial prose that progressively simplifies and concentrates verbal expression, it may occur to the reader that some Southern writers have employed an oral style that is fundamentally expansive and opulent in nature. Although Southern writing can be as laconic as other American colloquial prose, it also indulges in that public oratory we habitually associate with the Southern politician, and which we often hear in the prose of Thomas Wolfe and William Faulkner, of Robert Penn Warren and William Styron, and even, ironically, of James Baldwin. Such prose, which is not embarrassed by the oratorical flourish, can be accommodated to the historical process which this study describes, for the oratorical mode shares the characteristics of the colloquial. Its exclamations, repetitions, uncertain backings and fillings, accumulations of synonyms, and rhetorical emphases all originate in the extemporaneousness of speech, the spontaneous jetting of language that maintains its equilibrium by constant movement forward rather than by a poised interrelationship among stable elements.

FROM HOWELLS TO HEMINGWAY

Walker Gibson

I did not say anything. I was always embarrassed by the words . . . .

When a new style swims into our ken, as Hemingway's did in the 1920s, it is new, or was new, in respect to a historical situation. People brought to their reading, just as they still do of course, a set of assumptions about how books ought to be written. No novelist would be interested in a reader who had never read a novel, or who had never experienced, as *he* has experienced, the going literature of the recent past. So Hemingway's assumed reader of the 1920s had an ear tuned to nineteenth century rhythms and attitudes; it was in their light that Hemingway's style appeared so fresh and exciting. It is still exciting, if not exactly fresh, a generation later, which is testimony enough to the power of a great writer.

But in order to remind ourselves of some of the stylistic expectations against which Hemingway was first read, and to some extent must still be read, it will be useful to contrast the opening of *A Farewell to Arms* (1929) with the opening of a standard sort of American novel of forty years earlier. The opening I have chosen, from W. D. Howells' *A Modern Instance* (1888), has some superficial resemblance in stage setting to Hemingway's opening that may make the contrast in style the more striking. In each case a narrator is introducing us to a scene as well as to himself, and both scenes include a *village* on a *plain*, in the *summer*, with a view of *mountains* and a *river*.

PASSAGE A (HOWELLS)

The village stood on a wide plain, and around it rose the mountains. They were green to their tops in summer, and in the winter white through their serried pines and drifting mists, but at every season serious and beautiful, furrowed with hollow shadows, and taking the light on masses and stretches of iron-grey crag. The river swam through the plain in long curves, and slipped away at last through an unseen pass to the southward, tracing a score of miles in its course over a space that measured but three or four. The plain was very fertile, and its features, if few and of purely utilitarian beauty, had a rich luxuriance, and there was a tropical riot of vegetation when the sun of July beat on those northern fields. They waved with corn and oats to the feet of the mountains, and the potatoes covered a vast acreage with the lines of their intense, coarse green; the meadows were deep with English grass to the

From *Tough, Sweet and Stuffy: An Essay on Modern American Prose Styles*, by Walker Gibson, Ch. 3, "Tough Talk: The Rhetoric of Frederic Henry," pp. 28–42. Copyright © 1966 by Indiana University Press. Reprinted by permission. Passage B: Reprinted by permission of Charles Scribner's Sons from *A Farewell to Arms*, page 3, by Ernest Hemingway. Copyright 1929 Charles Scribner's Sons; renewal copyright © 1957 by Ernest Hemingway. Notes have been omitted.

banks of the river, that, doubling and returning upon itself, still marked its way with a dense fringe of alders and white birches.

PASSAGE B (HEMINGWAY)
    In the late summer of that year we lived in a house in a village that looked across the river and the plain to the mountains. In the bed of the river there were pebbles and boulders, dry and white in the sun, and the water was clear and swiftly moving and blue in the channels. Troops went by the house and down the road and the dust they raised powdered the leaves of the trees. The trunks of the trees too were dusty and the leaves fell early that year and we saw the troops marching along the road and the dust rising and leaves, stirred by the breeze, falling and the soldiers marching and afterward the road bare and white except for the leaves.
    The plain was rich with crops; there were many orchards of fruit trees and beyond the plains the mountains were brown and bare. There was fighting in the mountains and at night we could see the flashes from the artillery. In the dark it was like summer lightning, but the nights were cool and there was not the feeling of a storm coming.

    Who are these two people talking to us?
    The narrator in Passage A (Howells) is concerned with making us see and know the landscape surrounding the village, and he can do this because he can occupy a position where *he* sees and knows this landscape intimately. Let us begin by locating this position, which is expressible in respect to both space and time. Physically, the narrator can speak as from a cloud, a balloon, floating wide-eyed over the plain. He sees large features of the scene— the mountains, the course of the winding river, the fields with their crops. It is a bird's-eye view. He also occupies a favorable position in time. He has been here before, he *knows*. He knows, for example, how the mountains look not only in summer (the *then* of the opening scene), but in winter as well. (Sentence A-2.) He knows (A-3), even though it is not at present visible, that the river slips away "through an unseen pass" to the southward. This is a speaker whose particular rhetorical personality, which would look very strange in a novel of the second half of the twentieth century, serves to inspire our confidence, partly from its very antiquity. Note that as assumed readers we date the speaker immediately, however vaguely, and date ourselves as well, by ruling out some twentieth-century suspicions and expectations. We are introduced to a familiar kind of traditional gentlemanly voice whose tones we associate with Standard Literature, and whose word we accept absolutely. This man knows what there is to know about this scene. We are in good hands.
    The man talking in Passage B speaks to us from an utterly different position. As he thinks back on his experience in the village—and note that it is *his* experience that he thinks back on—the positions he occupies are drastically more limited than those of our airborne observer in A. Everything described in B can be seen (or almost seen) from one place, the house where *he* lived. The language keeps reminding us of this limitation by returning to the speaker and his companions (*we*) and their vantage point for seeing and feeling. The house "looked across the river"; "we saw the troops"; "we could see the flashes"; "there was not the feeling of a storm coming." The

speaker's range is similarly limited in time; all he tells us about is the way things looked during one particular late summer as it became autumn. The other seasons, before he came to live in the village, or after he left, he presumably doesn't know about. We hear the familiar "flatness" of the voice addressing us, the speaker's refusal to say more than he knows from ordinary human experience. He is close-lipped. The simplicity of his style, the apparent simplicity of it, is of course notorious. You would not call this man genial. He behaves rather as if he had known us, the reader, a long time and therefore doesn't have to pay us very much attention. He is more tense, more intense, than A. And after all, we should observe, he is dealing with images of war, and not with a peaceful New England landscape.

So much for one reader's quick first impression of the two personalities addressing us and the positions from which they speak. But I propose a longer look at some grammatical and rhetorical peculiarities of these two speakers, returning often to their personalities and positions to ask how these have been created, and how we may refine our first impressions. How are these impressions justified by the language, if they are? How do details of wording force us to certain conclusions about the man we're being introduced to? If some of what follows seems alarmingly statistical and detailed, I would argue that only by such devices can we begin to understand the effort that went into these two creative acts.

Words, their size. Everybody knows that Hemingway's diction is characterized by short, simple, largely Anglo-Saxon words. Howells' vocabulary is more conventionally extensive. Actually, in the Howells passage, almost three-quarters of the words are monosyllables, while only one word out of twenty is longer than two syllables. It is hardly an elaborate or affected diction. Yet we recognize in Howells that there are particular words, especially the longer words, which for various reasons would be unthinkable in Hemingway. Among them are *beautiful, utilitarian, luxuriance*—and I shall have more to say about them below. For the present, we note that in passage B, the Hemingway passage, over four-fifths of the words (82 per cent) are of one syllable only, an extremely high proportion. What is more remarkable, only two words, or about one in a hundred, are more than two syllables in length. (These two are *afterward* and *artillery*, neither of them very formidable.) The rigorous selection, or limitation, in vocabulary that these figures imply is drastic, and certainly contributes largely to our sense of a laconic, hard-bitten, close-talking fellow. He is literally *curt*.

Modifiers. An important distinction in the way the two speakers choose words has to do with the frequency of their modifiers. What would we expect of a man who knows, who is magically airborne over the landscape, as against a speaker who is laconically reporting the facts of his own limited experience? We would expect that the former would be more free with his modifiers, would be, that is, willing to name the qualities and virtues of things, not just the things themselves. Actually there are about twice as many modifiers in the Howells as in the Hemingway. Some of Howells' adjectives, in particular, have obvious implications of value: *serious, beautiful, rich, utilitarian*. While many others are simply descriptive (if that is possible), such as *green, deep, dense*, every one of the modifiers in B is of the type that purports to avoid value and simply state facts, especially physical facts: *dry, white, blue, dusty, swiftly*, and so on.

Nouns and repetition. A count of nouns in the two passages results in almost identical figures. But because of a great difference in repetition of nouns, there is a difference in the actual repertoire the two writers use. There are 47 appearances of nouns in A, and because repetition is negligible there are 43 different nouns used. In Hemingway I count 46 noun appearances with a remarkable refrain of repetition. Fourteen nouns appear twice or three times; only 32 different nouns are to be found in the passage. The effect of this rather astonishing contrast is worth speculating on. It helps us, again, to understand why we could call the B narrator "close-lipped." He simply doesn't use many words! There is a critical suggestion to the speaker's personality, as if he were saying, I'm not one of your fancy writers, always scrabbling around for elegant variation. I say what I mean. If I mean the same thing twice, I *say* the same thing twice, and I don't care if it offends the so-called rules of so-called graceful prose.

Imagery, abstract and concrete. It is a commonplace about modern writers, and it may seem to be borne out by our analysis up to this point, that the more recent writers are concerned hardheadedly with things-as-they-are, with precise description rather than with the evaluative blur that we like to think characterizes the older literature. Everybody's passion nowadays for being "concrete" rather than "abstract" represents a fashionable general attitude. But, judging from the present evidence, the commonplace may not be true. Nobody knows, I suspect, how to distinguish concrete words from abstract in any very satisfactory way, but suppose we apply in all innocence this rule of thumb: which of our two speakers tells us more about the scene, supposing we wanted to paint a picture of it? There is no doubt that it is Howells. It is not simply Hemingway's paucity of nouns and modifiers that handicaps him as a scene-painter. It is his very choice of the nouns and modifiers that he does use. Where Hemingway writes *trees*, Howells names them—*alders, birches*. Where Hemingway refers to *crops* and *orchards*, Howells gives us *corn, oats*, and *potatoes*. It is true that Howells includes some words normally thought of as "abstract" (*features, beauty, luxuriance*), while Hemingway gives us plenty of "concrete" nouns, *pebbles* and *boulders, mountains, orchards, soldiers*. But the result is what matters, and in this case the result is that the language creates, in A, a narrator who *cares* about telling us what the landscape looked like, and in B we sense a narrator who cares about something else.

What else does he care about? Why does he, in spite of his superficial and apparent concreteness, tell us so little specifically about the scene? Because the scene, from his position, is not important except as it contributes to his own feelings, his remembered feelings. His recurrences to the act of personal viewing mentioned earlier (*We saw, we could see*) are reminders of the highly personal interest of this speaker. He is not concerned with having us see the landscape, but in having us understand *how he felt*. This is a very different aim; all his devices of grammar and rhetoric are chosen to achieve this aim.

Sentences, their size and structure. Again the short sentence in Hemingway is a commonplace observation, and it no doubt contributes to the curtness we have been noticing. Actually, in these two passages, the difference is only between an average length of 38 words and of 28 words—nothing very spectacular. Much more interesting is the grammatical structure of the sentences of each passage. In A we have both compound and compound-complex sentences, with considerable subordination of clauses. In B we have largely compound sentences made up of coordinate clauses strung together with *and*. (Sentence B-4 is a good example.) When we count up subordinate clauses in the two passages, we discover that in B there are only two, and they are informal and inconspicuous. "The dust they raised," for instance, gives us a modifying clause without the signal *that*, an omission common in oral speech. We are reminded that the narrator knows us, speaks familiarly, doesn't in fact go out of his way for us much. Modifying clauses in A, on the other hand, are crucially different. Here their formal qualities are directed not toward maintaining a pose of familiarity with a reader, but instead toward seriously clarifying for the reader, whom the speaker has only just met, what the landscape looked like. The second half of Sentence A-5, for example, offers us a subordinate clause of some elegance and considerable skill.

. . . the meadows were deep with English grass to the banks of the river, that, doubling and returning upon itself, still marked its way with a dense fringe of alders and white birches.

One may not wish to go so far as to say that the very phrasing here, in its leisurely meandering, doubles and returns upon itself like the river, but one would have to say, at least, that a subordinate clause of this kind, punctuated in this way, would look very odd in Hemingway. You do not talk this way to someone you know easily and intimately.

More spectacular in the Hemingway style, of course, are the successions of coordinate clauses linked by *and*. It is a highly significant grammatical expression, and its significance can be grasped if one tries irreverently to rewrite a coordinate Hemingway sentence in more traditional patterns of subordination. Here is the original sentence B-4, for instance:

The trunks of the trees too were dusty and the leaves fell early that year and we saw the troops marching along the road and the dust rising and leaves, stirred by the breeze, falling and the soldiers marching and afterward the road bare and white except for the leaves.

Now here is a version attempting to subordinate some of the clauses:

The leaves fell early that year, which revealed the dusty trunks of the trees and the marching troops on the road; when the troops went by, we saw the dust rise, while the leaves fell, stirred by the breeze, but after the soldiers had gone the road was bare and white except for the leaves.

The original B-6 reads this way:

There was fighting in the mountains and at night we could see the flashes from the artillery.

If we subordinate one of these clauses, we must state a relation between them
—for example the relation of logical cause:

We knew there was fighting in the mountains, for at night we could see the flashes
from the artillery.

Now the damage done to the original, in both cases, is of course cata-
strophic. In the original B-6, the speaker doesn't say how he knew there was
fighting in the mountains. It was just there, ominous, baldly stated. The
awareness of the fighting and the seeing of the flashes are all part of a huge
complex of personal feeling, and the connections between the various
sensations are left (deliberately of course) ambiguous. This is a highly refined example of the leave-it-up-to-the-reader technique that I found so
irritating in "Private World". . . .

This is why so many people do not know how to read. They have been taught to turn
books into abstractions.

There, as in Hemingway, the logical connection between the two uncon-
nected independent structures was unstated. But there is a difference. In
"Private World," the intended connection is plain. What in Hemingway
was a suggestive technique for implying several possible connections while
stating none, becomes merely a rhetorical gimmick for forcing the reader to
supply an obvious meaning. This is what we mean by the Misuse of a Style.

   The definite article. I have mentioned a difference in relation with their
assumed readers that the two speakers suggest. Whereas the speaker in A
keeps his distance, using what we think of as fairly formal discourse, the
speaker in B seems to have known the reader before and doesn't trouble himself to explain things as one must for an acquaintance one has just met. A
possible cause of this difference between the two speakers can be found in
the different ways they use a simple three-letter word—the word *the*. To be
statistical again, the incidence of the definite article in the Howells paragraph
comes to about 8 per cent; in the Hemingway passage it is about 18 per
cent, or almost one word out of every five. It is clearly the Hemingway
passage that is unconventional, labeling every other noun with *the*.

   What is the effect of such an extraordinary preoccupation?

In the late summer of that year we lived in a house in a village that looked across
the river and the plain to the mountains.

One's first naive response to that sentence might be some perfectly pardon-
able questions. "What year? What river, what plain, what mountains? I
don't know what you're talking about." Precisely: the *real* reader doesn't
know what the speaker is talking about, but the assumed reader doesn't
bother about that. *He* has been placed in a situation where he is expected to
assume that he does know what the speaker is talking about. It is as if, for
the assumed reader, a conversation had been going on before he opened the
book, a conversation that laid the groundwork for all this assumed intimacy.

Or it is as if—another analogy—we were suddenly plopped down in a chair listening to a man who has begun telling a story to another man who has just left the room. Curiously the story-teller confuses us with the friend who has just departed, and we find ourselves taking the place of this friend, yoked to the teller as he was. And of course, as always, we can't talk back.

The difference can be realized if again we try an irreverent revision, excising most of the definite articles:

Late in 1915, when I was an officer in the Italian army, my unit lived in a house in a northern Italian village that looked across a river toward some mountains.

In this version, the speaker makes no such assumptions about the common knowledge shared by himself and his assumed reader. Now he names the year and the locale, he defines who "we" are, and his consistent indefinite articles maintain a more distant posture with his reader.

My revision again, naturally, is disastrous. It does more than create distance between reader and speaker. Reading it, one has the impression that the narrator doesn't care much about what he's saying. It starts off like any old war reminiscence. But in Hemingway's version, for many more reasons than I've been able to express here, we feel already the excitement, or what I have to call the intensity, of the narrator. He is deeply involved in his feeling about what he is going to tell us, and perhaps one reason he can give that impression is that he can pretend not to have to worry very much about us, about cueing us in in the conventional way.

The first word of the Howells passage is *The*, but the quickest reading reveals the difference. Here the narrator is describing a scene as if we had never seen it before—as indeed we have not. We need not assume the same kind of intimate relation with the narrator; he keeps us relatively at a distance, and he does not use (as Hemingway does) the first person pronoun. Yet even the Howells narrator launches us somewhat *in medias res*, assuming we will not ask, of his first two words, "What village?" Again the removal of the definite article will show how a speaker can back off even further from his reader, beginning a wholly new relationship with new information: A village stood on a wide plain, and around it rose mountains. One feels, of that sentence, that it should be prefaced by "Once upon a time," and it may be that in telling a fairy story, part of the trick is to assume very little from your reader. Nor is there any effort, in the fairy story, to make the narrator or his tale sound "real." In fact the effort must be just the other way. In the Hemingway kind of story, quite a lot is implied, through intensity of tone, about how seriously, how real, we are to take all this. There is a scale of pretension we could trace, something like this:

Fairy story: Here's a little tale of something that (let's pretend) might have happened a long, long time ago in the Land of Nod.
Howells: Here is a story about people behaving much as people in life do behave; I hope you enjoy it.
Hemingway: This is how it really felt to me when it all happened. (Oh yes, if you insist; it's a *story*.)

My passages can't possibly justify all that. But if there is anything to such a scale, then the Hemingway rhetoric has the effect of including, as part of its fiction, the fiction that all this really happened to a narrator who felt intensely about it, and the reader is maneuvered into a position of sympathy with a person whose principal concern is not with the reader, not with the scene he is describing, but with himself and his own feelings. There is a consequent lift of the voice, a tension in the vocal chords. That is no armchair, relaxed and comfortable, that the Tough Talker occupies.

It will be useful now to summarize the Tough Talker's manner by means of a tentative definition of his personality and rhetoric. In doing so, we remember that our source is only the first 189 words of one Hemingway novel. Nor should we assume that the character described here is absolutely new to literature. What we do have here is an identifiable speaker (Frederic Henry by name), defined in an identifiable rhetoric, some of whose qualities we will be able to recognize in later prose.

A *description of a Tough Talker.* Frederic Henry is a hard man who has been around in a violent world, and who partially conceals his strong feelings behind a curt manner. He is in fact more concerned with those feelings than he is with the outward scenes he presents, or with cultivating the good wishes of the reader to whom he is introducing himself. He can ignore these traditional services to the reader because he assumes in advance more intimacy and common knowledge. (We are beyond explanations, beyond politenesses.) He presents himself as a believable human character, without omniscience: he knows only what he knows, and is aware of his limitations.

His rhetoric, like his personality, shows its limitations openly: short sentences, "crude" repetitions of words, simple grammatical structures with little subordinating. (I have no use for elegant variation, for the worn-out gentilities of traditional prose.) His tense intimacy with his assumed reader, another man who has been around, is implied by colloquial patterns from oral speech and by a high frequency of the definite article. He lets his reader make logical and other connections between elements. (You know what I mean; I don't have to spell it all out for *you.*) He prefers naming things to describing them, and avoids modification, especially when suggestive of value. All these habits of behavior suggest that he is self-conscious about his language—even about language generally. He is close-lipped, he watches his words.

This suspiciousness about language, only implied in our passage, deserves amplification particularly because it will concern us again later, in other writers. Part of the violent world that the Tough Talker has been around in is the violent verbal world, where words have been so abused that they have lost their lives. In a famous passage later on in *Farewell to Arms* Frederic Henry makes the point explicitly:

> I did not say anything. I was always embarrassed by the words sacred, glorious, and sacrifice, and the expression in vain. We had heard them, sometimes standing in the rain almost out of earshot, so that only the shouted words came through, and had read them, on proclamations, now for a long time, and I had seen nothing sacred, and the things that were glorious had no glory and the sacrifices were like the stockyards at Chicago if nothing was done with the meat except to bury it. There were

many words that you could not stand to hear and finally only the names of places had dignity. Certain numbers were the same way and certain dates and these with the names of the places were all you could say and have them mean anything. Abstract words such as glory, honor, courage, or hallow were obscene beside the concrete names of villages, and the numbers of roads, the names of rivers, the numbers of regiments and the dates.

Such a negative attitude toward language, however understandable and right in this novel, becomes deadly in later and less skillful hands. For some members of the Beat Generation all language became meaningless—a conviction peculiarly difficult for a writer to live with. The conviction may have had something to do with the poverty of beat style, and with the early demise of that movement. In any event, a self-conscious anxiety about the very reliability of words has become one of the crosses the modern writer has to bear. Fortunately it can be borne in many ways, from comedy to despair.

THE SUBJECTIVE STYLE: FAULKNER

Irena Kaluza

As a creator of an imaginative world complete in itself, with unforgettable characters and a profound sense of history and locality—William Faulkner is a truly objective writer. But the texture of his work is subjective in that he does not tell us *about* the world, its people and events, but conveys the *experience* of them directly and makes the reader participate in that experience. This refers not only to the stream-of-consciousness passages where the effect is to be expected, but permeates all of Faulkner's better work, including passages contributed by various narrators and even those professedly written from the point of view of an omniscient author.

It is the purpose of the present study to investigate Faulkner's texture-subjectifying technique and its double function of conveying experience directly and of imposing the writer's fictional world upon the reader. It can be assumed that the texture of a literary work—as an element most directly dependent on the medium, i.e., the language—can be investigated by examining some of its persistent linguistic patterns, especially those differing from similiar patterns as occurring in neutral language. We can thus formulate a working hypothesis that the study of Faulkner's texture-

From Irena Kaluza, "William Faulkner's Subjective Style," *Kwartalnik Neofilologiczny*, XI (1964), 13–29, at 13–15, 21–28. Printed by persmission of *Kwartalnik Neofilologiczny* and Irena Kaluza. Some of the notes have been omitted, and the remainder renumbered to run in sequence.

subjectifying technique can be identified with what may be called his Subjective Style.[1]

Since an examination of all persistently recurrent linguistic patterns in Faulkner's work is beyond the scope of the present paper, I have limited my considerations to the syntactic-structural patterns, a linguistic category which I believe to be most revealing for this kind of study. (This is, of course, an arbitrary choice and it is to be expected that a study of recurring semantic patterns, synonyms or images for instance, may yield rich and interesting results.) The selected structures will be described and then interpreted as stylistic categories, on the assumption that structural patterns can symbolically—by means of a system of formal contrasts—convey certain aspects of reality as interpreted by human consciousness, in the manner in which, say, *I am doing it* conveys an aspect of time different from *I do it.*

For practical reasons I have limited my material to five novels written between 1929–1936: *The Sound and the Fury* (1929), *As I Lay Dying* (1930), *Sanctuary* (1930), *Light in August* (1932), *Absalom, Absalom!* (1936). With the possible exception of *Sanctuary*, they are generally accepted as Faulkner's most impressive achievement.[2] The examples of sentences to be quoted in the paper have been chosen chiefly for their brevity and explicitness in illustrating particular features of Faulkner's grammar and rhetoric. It should be remembered, however, that in Faulkner's prose the phenomena I shall try to describe seldom occur in isolation: rather they form a tangled maze with the result that his syntax has often been dismissed as no syntax at all.

From the point of view of literary method Faulkner's texture-subjectifying technique consists in unravelling his material through the human mind, whether of an interior monologuist, a narrator or an omniscient author.

---

[1]Cf. the following definition of style proposed by Bernard Bloch: "The Style of a discourse is the message carried by the frequency-distributions and transitional probabilities of its linguistic features, especially as they differ from those of the same features in the language as a whole." Bernard Bloch, *"Linguistic Structure and Linguistic Analysis,"* in *Report of the Fourth Annual Round Table Meeting on Linguistics and Language Teaching* (Washington, D. C., 1953), p. 42. Quoted after Samuel R. Levin, *Linguistic Structures in Poetry,* Janua Linguarum, XXIII ('S-Gravenhage, 1962), p. 15.

The word "subjective" (and consequently "subjectifying") is used here as covering both senses given by COD: "1. (Philos.) belonging to, of, due to, the consciousness or thinking or perceiving subject or ego as opp. real or external things. . . . 2. (Of art and artists) giving prominence to or depending on personal idiosyncrasy or individual point of view, not producing the effect of literal and impartial transcription of external realities. . . ." (The third sense of "subjective" given by COD is irrelevant, as it refers to the grammatical concept of subject.)

[2]. . . The editions used in the present work are: *Absalom, Absalom!* [*AA*], New York, Modern Library, 1951; *As I Lay Dying* [*AD*], New York, Random House, 1946; *Light in August* [*LA*], Penguin Books, 1960: *Sanctuary* [*S*], Penguin Books, 1955; *The Sound and the Fury* [*SF*], London, Chatto & Windus, 1954; Appendix to *The Sound and the Fury* [*A to SF*], New York, Random House, 1946. . . .

The numerical reference after quotations consists of the number attached successively to each sentence on a given page, and of the number of the page itself; e.g., 18/97 = sentence no. 18 on page 97. . . .

Consequently the problems that confront him are:

(1) how to convey the private incoherencies of human consciousness,
(2) how to make them understandable and artistically meaningful, and
(3) how to make the reader participate in the fictional stream-of-consciousness.

Trying to give a partial answer to these questions (i.e., an answer involving the sentence structure only) I have found it convenient to divide my analysis into two parts:

(A) Sentence structure on grammatical level: linguistic devices of *fragmentation* as conveying the incoherencies of mental content;
(B) Sentence structure on rhetorical level: linguistic devices of *organization* as conveying mental process as a continuum. A great many of the devices contained in these two groups are also partly responsible, as we shall see, for that peculiar quality of Faulkner's work which makes the reader share the experience of the fictional world.

The technique of *Fragmentation* can best be understood by comparing Faulkner's unconventional sentences with normal structures and describing the deviations from the standard syntax of a Subject-Predicate sentence. These deviations can be grouped under three main headings: Disintegration of the Basic Elements of a Simple Sentence, Ambiguity in Grammatical Reference, and Lack of Grammatical Hierarchy in Relation between Syntactic Units.

*   *   *   *

A consideration of ambiguous *who-* and *which-* structures has already shown Faulkner experimenting with the formal means of subordination. This brings us to the last important group of fragmentation devices, namely to those characterized by the lack of grammatical hierarchy in relation between syntactic units. They can generally be said to represent lack of logic in undirected mental activity. The most frequent of them consists in overusing the coordinating conjunction *and* which in Faulkner plays the role of a Jack of all trades. Thus we often get a protracted polysyndetic string of simple sentences invariably joined by *and;* e.g.,

I put on my new suit *and* put my watch on *and* packed the other suit *and* the accessories *and* my razor *and* brushes in my handbag, *and* wrapped the trunk key into a sheet of paper *and* put it in an envelope *and* addressed it to Father *and* wrote the two notes *and* sealed them. *SF* 9/79

Here *and* is used seven times to join seven finite verbs to their subject *I* appearing only at the beginning of the sentence, and three times to join the nouns forming the object. Unattractive as such a sentence seems to be, it performs a special function in the novel. The person in whose mind all this occurs is contemplating suicide: his mind monotonously and impassively

registers the trivial little actions in their time sequence, but is really set on
other matters.

Even more striking are the patterns in which Faulkner puts a coordinating conjunction between syntactic units of formally unequal rank. Thus we
find a headword-modifier unit joined by *and* to a subject-verb unit in a
passage of quoted speech:

"...—woman whom he was to tell Grandfather thirty years afterwards he had found
unsuitable to his purpose and so set aside, though providing for her *and* there were a
few frightened half-breed servants with them who..." *AA* 1/247

As there is no comma before the *and* in question we expect the phrase *though
providing for her and* to continue with another word governed by *for*, for
instance *for her and the child*. Instead of that the coordinating conjunction
and introduces an independent syntactic unit of S-V pattern. Such "illogical"
structures are typical for Faulkner's narrators, who tell their stories
spontaneously and often are in a state of emotional tension. The very
significant absence of at least a comma to separate the two independent
structural units strengthens the dramatic effect of the material being delivered "in one breath."

Finally the rejection of grammatical hierarchy acquires the form of a refusal to use almost any connectives at all, e.g.,

The boy got in the water. He went on. He turned and looked at Luster again.
He went on down the branch.
The man said 'Caddie' up the hill. The boy got out of the water and went up the
hill. *SF* 39-44/14

In this passage Faulkner presents the working of the mind of an idiot who is
incapable of organizing the material logically in terms of cause-and-effect
relations or even in temporal sequence.

Let us now recapitulate the main features of Faulkner's *syntax of fragmentation* as differing from the normal sentence structure. Faulkner's
sentence structure is essentially chain-like, the syntactic units—often "fragmentary" and of vague grammatical reference—being placed indifferently
one after another, with few connectives or arbitrarily used connectives, so
that no distinction is made (and no formal connection either) between what
logic would differentiate as central and peripheral material, nor are time-,
space-, cause-and-effect relations clearly indicated. In this a-grammatical
maze the pronouns (when not ambiguously used) seem to provide the most
reliable signals of internal relationships. This is because the pronoun has
inflected forms indicating case, number and gender. ...[T]he high frequency
of pronoun occurrence is utilized by Faulkner stylistically; ...we can also
appreciate it as functional for his sentence structure.

As has been indicated, Faulkner's syntax of fragmentation conveys the
spontaneous, the disorderly and often incoherent mental content. In other
words, it conveys mental content dynamically as it enters consciousness,
whereas normal syntax presents it statically after it has been intellectualized
and logically arranged.

The syntax of fragmentation is also used by Faulkner to control the reader's response. Reproducing the immediacy of pre-rationalized consciousness, it makes the sympathetic reader share this immediacy and thus participate in the fictional world. The reader's involvement is also brought about by at least some of Faulkner's syntactic puzzles. These arouse our interest—for we want to know what happened and to whom—and make us cooperate with the author and share his world.

It will be generally agreed that, however fragmentary and even incoherent the mental content, it is experienced as a process, a continuum (hence the name of "stream-of-consciousness" attached to literature purporting to present the working of the mind, irrespective of technique). To render the continuum quality of mental processes Faulkner uses a technique of *Organization* of his linguistic material. (Incidentally some such unifying principle would be indispensable also from the point of view of aesthetics, to balance the principle of fragmentation.)

What syntactic devices are there at Faulkner's disposal to organize his linguistic material? Obviously he cannot use standard connectives and sequence signals, since the resulting language would then be static and conceptual, or to put it otherwise, the technique of fragmentation would hardly have come into being. So Faulkner's technique of organization utilizes certain devices which can be called rhetorical. Since we are concerned with these as they operate on a sentence-structure level, it is theoretically possible again to compare the resulting structures with the standard ones; but it is more useful to work out a self-contained system of those devices, rather than to make comparisons with standard usage.[3]

Faulkner's rhetorical devices as applied to the organization of his linguistic material, are based on repetition of words, morphologic forms and syntactic patterns. The resultant structures generally avoid symmetry, while intertwining various components in intricate patterns.

No separate examples of iterative words need be given here, since the device is usually combined with other rhetorical forms.

Repetitive morphologic forms are often used in differing syntactic functions. The best example here is...the verbal -*ing* form which, not being tied down to finite grammatical agreement, can function both as a verbal and an adjectival form, e.g.,

He moves. *Moving* that quick his coat, *bunching*, tongues *swirling* like so many flames. With *tossing* mane and tail and *rolling* eye the horse makes another short *curveting* rush and stops again, feet bunched, *watching* Jewel. *AD* 19-21/345

We have already discussed Faulkner's tendency to use the non-committal verbal -*ing* form as actualizing experience, and now we must evaluate its function on the rhetorical level. Here its effectiveness is due to the use of

---

[3]Cf. Samuel R. Levin: "... the second approach to style confines itself to studying elements within the message and sets up its own code,".... According to Levin, the approach was first advocated by Archibald A. Hill, in *Introduction to Linguistic Structures* (New York, 1958), pp. 406 ff.

morhologically stable material (i.e. words containing the same bound morphemes) in variable functions, so that the device of repetition, while binding the presented experience into continuity, is also endowed with an element of surprise.

Now when repetitive morphological forms are used in the same grammatical function as headwords of syntactic units, the result is parallelism of structure. This, I believe, is Faulkner's basic principle in organizing his linguistic material. The statement can be risked (based on random samples) that nearly all the sentences over thirty words long, and a great many shorter ones, will reveal some form of parallelism of structure, while there will be little formal subordination in them (only one out of two and a half the sentences numbering thirty words or more has subordinate clauses in it). In fact the number and variety of parallel structures in Faulkner deserves a separate study, and no more than a few main types can be presented in this paper. I have chosen those covering free adjuncts, absolute free adjuncts and whole sentences, as more typical than others.

In adjuncts we find the following arrangements:

Example I, two participial adjuncts paired:

Dewey Dell stops and slides the quilt from beneath them ...
          and draws it up over them to the chin,
                              smoothing it down
                              drawing it smooth. *A D* 14/374

Example II, two nominal adjuncts, the second with a highly characteristic cumulative modifier:

The lane went between back premises—
          unpainted houses with those gay and startling coloured garments on lines,
          a barn broken-backed, decaying quietly among rank orchard trees,
                              unpruned and weed-choked,
                              pink and white and murmurous
                              with sunlight and with bees. *SF* 1/132

More frequently to the paired adjuncts an adjunct (or adjuncts) of different form is added, introducing an element of variety to otherwise neatly repetitive structures:

Example III, two participial adjuncts interrupted by an adjectival one:

And then the road will begin,
                              curving away into trees,
                              empty with waiting,
                    saying New Hope three miles. *A D* 6/422

But parallelisms are by no means restricted to paired forms: they can appear in sets of three, four and even five segments.

Example IV, four participial adjuncts followed by a prepositional one:

The procession became three streams,
        thinning rapidly upon dawdling couples,
        swinging hands,
        strolling in erratic surges,
        lurching into one another with puppyish squeals,
        with the random intense purposelessness of children. *S* 23/136

In introducing the above four examples, I have at the same time pointed out some formal ways in which Faulkner diversifies his parallel structures. But there is more to observe. First of all, a long main clause will be amplified by short adjuncts (*Example I*) and vice versa (*Examples II* and *III*). Then, a neatly constructed antithetical main clause (*Example I*) may be balanced by an adjunct utilizing crossed alliteration together with a playing upon the form and function of words, as in

smoothing it *d*own,
drawing it *s*mooth. (*Example I*)

Still another shade of variety is provided by adjuncts of the same form placed one after another but referring to various elements in the sentence (*Example IV*, where the first adjunct refers to the opening independent clause, while the three remaining adjuncts of the same form can be said to refer to the object of the first adjunct).

Other important forms of parallelism can be detected in the organization of whole sentences. In order to reduce the quoted material, I shall draw examples of these forms from sentences utilizing at the same time the device of iterative words used in a similar syntactic function.

Example V:

Cash   looks up the road quietly, his head turning as we pass it
                        like an owl's head,
                    his face composed.
Pa   looks straight ahead, humped.
Dewey Dell looks at the road too,
then she   looks back at me, her eyes watchful and repudiant. . . *AD* 6/413

Observe how the iterative *looks* is supplied each time with a different prepositional or adverbial particle, to avoid monotony. Also, as with adjuncts, none of the parallel structures are neatly symmetrical. Indeed such trim groups as for instance—

Example VI:

I suppose they knew that he would have to come out some time:
I suppose they sat there and thought about those two pistols. *AA* 7/46

—occur very rarely.

    But, however great Faulkner's ingenuity in diversifying parallel structures, his repertoire, if based solely on repetition of identical forms, might have been exhausted and patterns repeated. So he resorts to structures which are only vaguely similar, pairing for instance two different adjuncts, as in—

Example VII, free adjunct (a) and absolute free adjunct (b):

It uncurled upon a nickel,
      (a) moist and dirty
      (b) moist dirt, ridged into her flesh. *SF* 22/125

or a phrase (c) and a clause (d), as in—

Example VIII:

The sound of bees diminished, sustained yet,
(c) as though instead of sinking into silence,
                         (d) silence merely increased between us,
(d) as water rises. *SF* 8/122

Of course such structures could hardly in themselves be perceived as parallel, so in order to cement them Faulkner again makes use of iterative words. By intertwining parallel or pseudo-parallel structures and iterative words or phrases, he creates new patterns of intertwined structure in which syntactic and semantic units seem to be treated, rhetorically, on the same level (a device very much in keeping with his tendency to disregard logical categories in language). To illustrate: in *Example VIII* it is the iterative connective *as* that helps to join *as though instead of sinking into silence* in pseudo-parallel structure with *as water rises.* Moreover the word *silence*, which finishes the third unit of the sentence, immediately generates the next unit with *silence* as subject. Further integration of the rhetorical pattern is achieved by a pattern of semantic- and length-opposition in verbs:
                    diminish—increase
                    sink   —rise,
and by persistent repetition of the [s] and [z] phonemes (onomatopoeic, as the sentence refers to the sound of bees). Generally it can be said that the more esoteric the type of structural parallelism, the more Faulkner utilizes special phonemic and semantic combinations to bring out the patterning in structure.

    A unit of intertwined structure, by its very nature of interlocked continuity, tends to generate the next unit, and that—automatically—the next one, and so on. A problem then arises how to terminate such a proliferating structure. Faulkner does it often by making the final unit or units differ in length and structure from the preceding ones. Consider *Example IX* as an illustration of Faulkner's rhetoric at work:

The lights were on in the car,
so   (b) I couldn't see anything
(a) while we ran between the trees
                      except my own face

                                and a woman across the aisle
                                with a hat sitting right on the top of her head,
                                with a broken feather in it,
                                (b) I could see the twilight again,
but
(a) when we ran out of the   that quality of light
     trees   as if time really had stopped for a while,
                                   with the sun hanging just under the horizon,
(b) and then we passed the
     marque   (a) where the old man had been eating out of the sack,
          and the road going on under the twilight
                         into   twilight
          and the sense of water peaceful and swift beyond. *SF* 26/167

The sentence opens with a short main clause, syntactically set apart from the "body" of the sentence. This body is composed of a firm framework of six clauses arranged in three parallel pairs and reinforced by precise word-correspondencies, and of repetitive interlocked modifiers attached in profusion to the first two subdivisions of the framework. Observe in the framework how variation is obtained in repetition by reversing the pattern, once it has been established. Thus the first two subdivisions have the dependent clause followed by the independent one, while the third reverses the pattern. In symbols the scheme can be presented as *a b, a b, b a*. Moreover a number of corresponding syntactic units utilize opposition or contrast, whether formal (*I couldn't see : I could see*) or semantic (*between the trees : out of the trees*). As for the modifying groups, they are linked by repetitive prepositional *with*-phrases, the first pair of them being interlocked. The sentence ends with a measured coda of parallel absolute structures. Like the initial main clause, the coda is syntactically set apart from the "body" of the sentence. Among the other unifying devices, the evenly spread words *light* and *twilight* should be observed, as well as the gradation in meaning of the prepositions *in, under, into, beyond,* joining the opening main clause with the final coda. Finally, consider how Faulkner manages to finish this long proliferating sentence. He obviously suggests finality by means of the verbless coda whose syntactic units are longer and structurally different from what goes before in the sentence. But there is more than that. In the above quoted series of prepositions the first three have "objects" of their own (*in the car, under the twilight, into twilight*) and consequently a precise grammatical function, while the last, *beyond* (an adverb?), has not any grammatical referent easy to locate and thus can be interpreted as a construction "into infinity." It is then followed by a "generalizing" construction which omits the definite article before the final *twilight: under twilight into twilight.* Observe that the meaning of the coda corroborates what is suggested by the form.

     Let us now recapitulate the main features of Faulkner's *technique of organization* as based on a system of rhetorical devices. The Faulknerian organization of linguistic material exploits a fertile and intricately developed technique of repetition. The repetition is applied to categories whose grammatical status is normally unequal: syntactic units, semantic units, morphological forms and phonemes, in such a way that, on the rhetorical level, they acquire a kind of equality as factors shaping the Faulknerian sentence. The technique yields an astonishing variety of patterns of simple and interlocked repetition. Indeed, the variety of pattern is so great that the reader, who has simply noticed that Faulkner "repeats words," may have read for some time before he notices how heavily Faulkner relies on repetition of structure. Moreover, by their very nature, Faulkner's repetitive structures have a tendency to generate similar new structures which appear in accretive and cumulative groups interwoven with the preceding structures.

What more effective stream of eloquence can language devise to express the spontaneous stream of consciousness, with its continuity, persistence and associative quality? Even the frequent objections to the annoying character of Faulkner's style themselves suggest a virtue. Our consciousness, too, can be annoying at times.

THE SENTENCE IN PROGRESS: JOYCE

David Hayman

With the inclusion of Joyce's addition to the second galley proofs of *Finnegans Wake*, our passage lacked but one syllable ("leaves") of the published sentence. Consequently, for the sake of brevity and clarity, I shall indicate below the variants from the two drafts within the formal unity of the printed version.

I could sit on safe side till the bark of Saint Grouseus for hoopoe's hours, *till heoll's* ~~horerisings~~ *hoerrisings*, laughing lazy at the sheep's lightning and turn a widamost ear *dre*amily to the drummling of snipers, hearing the wireless harps of sweet old Aerial and the mails across the nightrives (peepet! peepet!) and whippoorwilly in the woody (moor park! moor park!) as peacefed as a philopotamus, and crekking jugs at the grenoulls, leaving tea*leaves* for the trout and belleeks for the wary till I'd followed through my upfielded neviewscope the rugaby moon cumuliously godrolling himself westasleep amuckst the cloudscrums for to watch how carefully my nocturnal goosemother would lay her new golden sheegg for me down under in the shy orient.

Characteristically, Joyce's last changes lean heavily upon poetic devices. Both the rythmic and the visual patterns are visibly improved by the addition of the echoing "leaves," while the double *l* in "till" finds its reflection in

Reprinted by permission of the Modern Language Association from David Hayman, "From *Finnegans Wake*: A Sentence in Progress," *PMLA*, LXXIII (1958), 136–154, at 150–153. Notes have been omitted.

"heoll's" and "hoe*rr*isings." Of more consequence is the fact that the *o* and *e* in "hoop*oe*'s" gain in symbolic portent when combined with those in "heoll's hoerrisings" to form the first of an alternating departure-return series, *oe, eo, oe*. Throughout his sentence Joyce opposes *e*'s and especially double *e*'s to *o*'s and double *o*'s but only here does he associate them in this manner, employing them as rising and falling vitalities, new manifestations of the eternal conflict between darkness and light. Man's unity in diversity is then symbolized by a digraph. His state depends upon the precedence of one or the other letter. In "heoll" for example, *o* or the disk of light preceded by *e* or delphic dark wisdom is a symbol of the fall or light eclipsed by intellect. But this too is equivocal because *eo* is Greek for *dawn* or *daylight*. These same paradoxical interpretations may be applied to the *word* "heoll" which the Celts use to signify the Sun (*heol*), but whose most accessible meaning is "Hell-Sheol" or a combination of two conceptions of the afterworld.

Briefly then, Jaun is stating his desire to remain beside the sun's or Hell's horizon until the dawn when all arise or until Christ, the hound, will come to harrow, that is, "till," Hell. More poignant is the adolescent hero's acknowledgment of his duty to await Aeolus' (Eol's) arising or the sound of the bullroarers which will summon him to the test. Here, as though to demonstrate the debased state of the heroic currency, Joyce links the awesome voice of God to the clamor of newspaper and radio, that is, "Aerial" and the "mails." Perhaps the noise of that wind is vaguely present in "for hoopoe's hours, till heoll's hoerrisings," while the note of "horror" carried over from "*horer*isings" is intended to imply Jaun's mood. Such effects predominate in this last insertion, a penultimate piece of virtuosity. I believe that an identical love of effects motivated the late addition of "leaves" by which Joyce dotted a final *i*, applying a light touch of birdness ("teal"), a fortune-teller nuance, and a final alliterative twitch. For indeed he had long since completed this subdivision of his mighty structure, leaving little or nothing to chance or to the reader's innocent whim.

To sum up, in the case before us now, the story of a sentence's evolution is the tale of the gradual mobilization by the artist of all the tools available to him. Built, literally constructed, within a tactile framework of the established mysteries, myths, and symbols, the finished piece revolves like a carved bead about the central axis or universally accepted situation. While maintaining a static-kinetic balance through thirteen successive changes, while placing all movement in the future, while making it all tentative and equivocal, Joyce nevertheless suggests an infinite variety of actions and provides for a delicate variation in mood. Working under self-imposed restrictions, he produces skillfully manipulated paradoxes from which arise the synthetic experience of the reader. Here, the crucified Christ and the abstracted Buddha mix their respective roles and remain intact; terror is akin to peace; the sublime meets and occasionally submits to the inroads of the ridiculous; yet the finished product makes lively sense to men of our generation.

By approaching several levels of this sentence simultaneously, I have attempted to show how Joyce reconciled a variety of seemingly contradictory accounts of the hero's approach to the brink of the abyss, how he chose or

formed words and even arranged letters to fit his evolving pattern. I have
tried to indicate how Joyce managed to integrate a great mass of esoteric
knowledge into an experiential mold. In retrospect, the three aspects of
James Joyce's style best highlighted by this study are: the degree to which
this knowledge is organized and controlled, the essentially poetic nature
of the means, and finally the end which these means were intended to serve.

Joyce's new language demanded an even more rigid control than did the
stylistic quirks and symbolism of *Ulysses*. Even if we neglect the series of
parallels imposed by the author upon his chapter, section, and book, our
sentence remains an example of the extremes to which planning can go.
When he composed the first draft of his sentence, Joyce established a frame
of reference vague enough to support elaboration. At that point the aspects
fundamental to the action were present, but instead of splitting this unit in
order to make of it his armature, Joyce preferred to safeguard its primitive
integrity while elaborating by repetition the two final elements, "till" (or
the duration) and "the bark of the day" (or the objective). Thus, two drafts
later, three basically ambivalent thought units enjoyed equal emphasis:
Jaun's rest, the moon's journey (i.e., the nature of duration), and the Sun's
rebirth (i.e., the protagonist's motivation). In 1928, when Joyce became
aware of the need for further coordination, he recognized also the all-
inclusive nature of his primary element. Thereafter, he concentrated on the
elaboration of Jaun's nocturnal activities, which he modulated by means of
strong interior references to the other two aspects. As the expanding sentence demanded new organizing principles, Joyce systematically developed
such devices as the sensory climate of the sedentary decadent. An analysis
of the completed sentence reveals that Jaun's sense of touch is evoked in
the passages concerned with physical aspects of his lazy nocturnal activities;
his ears are treated to a variety of sounds; his taste buds are titillated by
the prospect of his picnic, of being "peacefed," of eating the "sheegg";
his eyes are pleased by the gentle prospects of the heavens and of the hunt;
and his nostrils are filled by the odor of corruption which pleases his age—
the stench of the hoopoe's nest, of "sheegg," and of the crime, his over-
cultivated and abandoned heritage. Meanwhile, Joyce tied Jaun to the soil
of the book, elaborated and skillfully joined together the major motifs.
Imperceptibly, he superimposed upon the original triple division a four-part
series of balanced opposites, a résumé of *Finnegans Wake*'s book structure.
Even though the last of these parts to be developed stands first in the order
of the sentence, there is every indication that Joyce had in mind a minutely
organized progression of ideas. Thus, the complex rise-fall, heaven-hell
evocations, whose generalized impersonality recalls the larger revolutions of
the cycle, blend smoothly into overtones of the heroic crime, the creative-
destructive act of the Father. This last is followed by the black-white,
good-evil structure of the brother battle with its lunar aspects. Finally,
in Part IV of the sentence as in Part IV of the book, Joyce briefly elaborates
the maternal echo of the Father's act as the female sows the seed of her own
dissolution.

The elaboration of the paragraph follows roughly the same pattern as
does the development of the sentence. Coordination works two ways:

echoes of the last-judgment motif are added to the sentence before ours in the course of the heavy revision of draft six, "breezes ... do be devils to flirt." The fox-hunting motif with its John Peel elements is supported first by the addition, "I'll nose a blue fonx" (Draft 14), and later by "the fox! has broken at the coward sight ..." (Draft 18). Sooner or later all the themes and background elements are held in common by the sentence and the paragraph. If, as I mentioned above, the germ of our sentence follows the essential movement of the germ paragraph, the completed sentence is ideationally an echo of the paragraph as it now stands.

The movement of the preceding sentence parallels that of our own, consisting first of a statement of Jaun's desire to stay put, "leaning on my cubits," which is followed by a description of how he plans to pass the first five or six hours of the night (until "twoohoo the hour") gathering in the natural riches ("pinching stopandgo jewels" and "catching dimtop brilliants"). It concludes, as does the paragraph, on an ambiguous note of terror and peril: he fears the owl's cry "twoohoo" and the breezes that "do be devils to play flirt." The sentence we have been studying prolongs Jaun's projected stay till daybreak at which time the predicted sunrise will bring material or spiritual success or the "golden sheegg." Joyce begins our sentence on the same suppressed note of terror which punctuated the preceding one, but here he reverses the emotional progression, ending on a series of pleasant associations, that is, the sunrise as glory. Jaun's fears are sufficiently sublimated by this to permit him to expatiate in the second part of the paragraph on his future success.

Joyce's interest in narration is so secondary that, once the narrative content of a passage or of a chapter has been mapped out, he deliberately covers up the marks of his artistic act, turning his attention to the thickening of effects, and to the rarefication of nuances by means of subtle transitionary devices, shifts of interior mood and psychology. Here perhaps we have a major key to the essential novelty of Joyce's sentence.

In the conventional novel the sentence tends to be a linear construction. The reader lets his eyes follow its development and draws from it material capable of preparing him for what is to come. In our sentence, however, Joyce is dealing with a poetic moment of doubt, a pause, which can hardly be isolated from all other such moments in man's history. Jaun's hesitation can be considered only in conjunction with the mass of experience that went into the epiphany of its revelation: the total being, a semimystical combination of Braman-Atman, the self-nonself of man. Joyce's sentence, therefore, as I have tried to demonstrate, does not in any real sense advance the action or the argument of the paragraph. His "action" is essentially static, an embroidery about a theme or an instant. His book is broken up into sentences very much like the one we have examined. These, in the last analysis, resemble nothing more than views of a cross section of some organism seen under varying lighting conditions and from a variety of different angles. The sentence, therefore, tends to atomize *the* meaning in favor of the *many possible* meanings rendering an *impression* to which all *ideas* are secondary. In spite of its total union with its context, the minor organism has a life of its own. The reader approaches it well supplied with images and impressions gathered from his experience with other parts of the book, but he is obliged to isolate this element, to subject it to a searching scrutiny before he can safely replace it in its context.

SUGGESTIONS FOR RESEARCH

1. Examine the various methods which have been employed to study nineteenth-century prose style, attempting to determine which have the most value.

2. Discover what certain writers have had to say about style, and examine their writings for evidence of their theories. John Henry Newman and Robert Louis Stevenson would offer excellent subjects.

3. Study the evolution of a writer's style; see Barnett (1964) on Lamb. For example, Ruskin changed from a writer on primarily aesthetic matters to a social and economic critic, with a corresponding alteration of style. Trace the evolution of his style. Was the change abrupt or gradual?

4. Study the oratory of nineteenth-century political leaders (for example, Disraeli and Lincoln). What stylistic and structural strategies do they employ in common, and what techniques particularly differentiate them? Compare their methods to those employed by controversialists in written prose (Arnold, Emerson, and the like). Compare them to their counterparts in previous and succeeding centuries.

5. Lewis (1894) asserts: "The unity of the paragraph becomes nearly unimpeachable in such men as Addison, Shaftesbury, Bolingbroke, Johnson, Hume, Burke. Only the best paragraphers of the nineteenth century, Macaulay, for example, surpass these authors in this respect." But Lewis also avers: "The better paragraphs of the nineteenth century are far more organic, far more highly organized, than the better ones of the eighteenth." The subject needs extensive sifting. Begin by comparing a few paragraphs by eighteenth- and nineteenth-century prose writers. Study closely the paragraphs of a piece of writing by one author or the paragraphs in one author's works, working toward a knowledge of the development of the paragraph in the century. A suggested approach is to study the discussions in the "Symposium on the Paragraph" (1966), decide on a method of paragraph description, and then begin to compare paragraphs by different authors.

6. Study the variety of styles in one short piece of writing. For example, how would you describe the first paragraph of Hazlitt's essay on Hamlet? It is cumulative in structure, a main statement followed by fourteen modifications (relative clauses and appositives) plus one adverbial clause at the end. But is it Senecan "trailing"? Now look at the second paragraph, especially the first six sentences. Is this Senecan "curt"? And now the seventh sentence—what structure has it?

7. Statistical studies are urgently needed if the history of prose style is ever to achieve relative accuracy. The raw material of numerical data is so generally lacking that it is no wonder so many descriptive studies are practically useless, and critical evaluation is severely hampered by the lack of a mass of facts upon which to work. Select some numerical study as a guide— for example, Milic (1967b) or the essays in Leed (1966) or Doležel and Bailey (1969)—and describe statistically a piece of writing in the period. You might also read Ullmann's (1964, pp. 118–119) cautions about the statistical approach.

8. Extend Ohmann's (1965, this chapter) method of analyzing Arnold to other Victorian prose writers.

9. Some critics have argued that Victorian prose possessed more formal excellence than did Elizabethan prose and more range than did Augustan prose. Can these beliefs be substantiated?

10. Did a change in prose style occur toward the end of the Victorian period? What kind?

11. Macaulay's style has been called "the old *Edinburgh Review* style." Trace the antecedents of that style up to Macaulay, and then beyond him into the Victorian period and the twentieth century.

12. Much has been written about James's revisions. Study the revisions of another writer and compare them to James's.

13. Earle (1891) believes that all of the "well-marked styles" of the nineteenth century are based on one type—Dr. Johnson's. Establish the essential characteristics of Johnson's prose and examine some short passages by nineteenth-century stylists for likenesses. (Keep in mind that Johnson wrote in more than one style.)

14. Much of the criticism of twentieth-century prose lacks sufficient substantiation to be fully convincing. Is Schorer (1941) right, for example, that *For Whom the Bell Tolls* was written in a more varied and loose syntax than were Hemingway's earlier novels? Are the stylistic studies of contemporary prose as discerning and well substantiated as, say, the studies of seventeenth-century prose?

15. Historians and critics of the nineteenth and especially twentieth century tend to treat the styles of writers of those centuries as *sui generis*—as though traditional modes of expression had vanished. Examine the works of modern writers as Ciceronian, Senecan, and so on. For example, the "curt" style of the sixteenth and seventeenth centuries is sometimes called "laconic." Hemingway's and Beckett's styles have also been described as laconic. How do these recent writers resemble earlier, "pointed" writers?

16. The historical origins of the style of the twentieth-century novel are practically unexplored. Bridgman (1966) is a notable exception. What other books and articles offer valuable contributions to our knowledge of the place of twentieth-century prose style in the continuity of style? Begin to gather your own evidence by assessing existing studies and by comparing earlier novelists with modern novelists and studies of earlier periods—for example, Teets (1964) on the Elizabethan novel—with studies of the modern novel.

17. The twentieth century is sometimes referred to as the age of plain and utilitarian prose; yet a great amount of high-quality "poetic" prose has

been written since 1900. The subject has not been neglected, but much work needs to be done in description, definition, and evaluation. A significant book could be written assessing the present state of our knowledge of "poetic" style in the century. Numerous specific, close studies are needed also if we are to accumulate enough reliable description to enable us to understand and evaluate what has been written "poetically" in prose during the century. What book or essay best defines "poetic" prose? What is the best book or essay which analyzes a piece of poetic prose? Once these tasks have been accomplished, you are ready to begin to relate this prose to the long history of similar prose.

18. What is Faulkner's habitual syntax? (Does he have one?) Or Virginia Woolf's? Or Thomas Wolfe's? Or Henry Green's? What relation does their syntax have to the over-all structure and meaning of their writings? Brooks and Warren (1959) have found a connection between the sentence structure and the world portrayed in Hemingway's "The Killers." Where else do you find such an organic relationship between style and content in twentieth-century prose? See Follett (1937) and Dupee (1962). What relationships do you discern between contemporary "organic" stylists and earlier such stylists?

19. Relate a modern system of grammatical description to an older and traditional description—for example, Senecan—and apply it to a piece of recent prose.

20. Comparative stylistics offers some of the most fruitful investigations into style. Various studies have dealt with two cultures (Hemingway and Haiku), with a poet and a novelist (Blake and Gulley Jimson), or with national contemporaries (Faulkner and Stein). Fewer studies have endeavored to relate modern prose stylists to the continuity of style. Make a list of all such comparative historical studies which you can locate—for example, Bridgman (1966) and Dobrée (1934)—and examine their assumptions and methods. Which seems to offer the more reliable approach? Make a list of possible stylistic comparisons which you might explore in the future.

21. Many prose writers are also poets. Make a list of those who are, and then select one to compare his prose and poetry. How many notable prose writers have been insufficiently compared? D. H. Lawrence? What study offers the best guide to such a comparison? See Bouma (1956).

22. Study the early and late styles of an individual author. For example, there is a dissertation on Conrad's early style, Ordoněz (1963). What developments occurred as Conrad matured? And Hemingway? Faulkner? E. B. White? Santayana? What parallels do you discover in the development of the styles of earlier writers?

23. Obscurity as a deliberate stylistic device has received some attention in studies of recent prose. Continue the investigation, including past writers who employed "difficulty" as a style (for example, De Quincey).

24. Can the arguments by D. C. Allen (1948), Croll (1914), and others concerning the "libertine" or neo-Stoic base of the Anti-Ciceronian style be applied to twentieth-century style in any way?

25. Study the schemes and tropes in a piece of recent prose. How frequently do you find instances of either, and what types tend to predominate?

26. Is there any modern writer who employs the a-logical style? Characterize his particular brand of a-logicality. Compare him with earlier a-logical stylists, for example, Donne.

27. There has been some study of the *cursus* in older prose, but practically none in modern. What authors employ the *cursus*, and in what patterns and frequency?

28. See Staton (1958) in Chapter III of this volume. Apply the three "characters" to modern prose as a way of distinguishing among the many varieties. See also Bridgman (1966).

29. Henry James's prose has been described by one critic as "involuted." The word *involute* means "to roll inward from two ends." Can you find any examples in James?

30. Study Hemingway's connectives, especially his use of *and*. Examine a variety of his works from early in his career to late.

31. There has been little study of parodies. What makes an effective parody? Study, for example, those in *Vanity Fair* during the 1920's, such as Donald Ogden Stewart's rewriting of "Bedtime Stories for Grown-ups" (April 1921) in the styles of Sinclair Lewis, James Branch Cabell, and Theodore Dreiser or Samuel Hoffenstein's "Love in Lettuce, Ohio: A Drama Recounted in the Manner of the Realistic Middle-Western Novelist" (September 1924). Tindall (1959) describes the chapter "Oxen in the Sun" of Joyce's *Ulysses* as a "more or less chronological sequence of parodies. ... Some of these parodies are mediocre, some brilliant—those of Swift, ... Sterne, ... and Carlyle, ... in particular." Is Tindall's evaluation correct?

32. In his autobiography, William Carlos Williams describes the style of his *In the American Grain:* "The Tenochtitlan chapter was written in big, square paragraphs like Inca masonry. Raleigh was written in what I conceived to be Elizabethan style; the Eric the Red chapter in the style of the Icelandic saga," and so on. How well did Williams achieve his aims in the various chapters?

33. In *The Armies of the Night*, Norman Mailer writes that his "style changed for every project." Compare Mailer's style from his earliest to his latest books.

SELECTIONS FOR ANALYSIS

WILLIAM WORDSWORTH (1770–1850)
From Preface to Lyrical Ballads

The principal object, then, proposed in these Poems was to choose incidents and situations from common life, and to relate or describe them, throughout, as far as was possible in a selection of language really used by men, and, at the same time, to throw over them a certain colouring of imagination, whereby ordinary things should be presented to the mind in an unusual aspect; and, further, and above all, to make these incidents and situations interesting by tracing in them, truly though not ostentatiously, the primary laws of our nature: chiefly, as far as regards the manner in which we associate ideas in a state of excitement.   Humble and rustic life was generally chosen, because, in that condition, the essential passions of the heart find a better soil in which they can attain their maturity, are less under restraint, and speak a plainer and more emphatic language; because in that condition of life our elementary feelings co-exist in a state of greater simplicity, and, consequently, may be more accurately contemplated, and more forcibly communicated; because the manners of rural life germinate from those elementary feelings, and, from the necessary character of rural occupations, are more easily comprehended, and are more durable; and, lastly, because in that condition the passions of men are incorporated with the beautiful and permanent forms of nature.   The language, too, of these men has been adopted (purified indeed from what appear to be its real defects, from all lasting and rational causes of dislike or disgust) because such men hourly communicate with the best objects from which the best part of language is originally derived; and because, from their rank in society and the sameness and narrow circle of their intercourse, being less under the influence of social vanity, they convey their feelings and notions in simple and unelaborated expressions.   Accordingly, such a language, arising out of repeated experience and regular feelings, is a more permanent, and a far more philosophical language, than that which is frequently substituted for it by Poets, who think that they are conferring honour upon themselves and their art, in proportion as they separate themselves from the sympathies of men, and indulge in arbitrary and capricious habits of expression, in order to furnish food for fickle tastes, and fickle appetites, of their own creation.

From *Anglistica*, vol. 9, W. J. B. Owen, ed., *Wordsworth's Preface to 'Lyrical Ballads'* (Copenhagen: Rosenkilde and Bagger, 1957), pp. 115–116. Reprinted by permission of Rosenkilde and Bagger.

WILLIAM HAZLITT (1778–1830)
From **Characters of Shakespear's Plays**

Hamlet

This is that Hamlet the Dane whom we read of in our youth, and whom we may be said almost to remember in our after years; he who made that famous soliloquy on life, who gave the advice to the players, who thought "this goodly frame, the earth," a sterile promontory, and "this brave o'er-hanging firmament, the air, this majestical roof fretted with golden fire," "a foul and pestilent congregation of vapours;" whom "man delighted not, nor woman neither;" he who talked with the grave-diggers, and moralised on Yorick's skull; the school-fellow of Rosencrans and Guildenstern at Wittenberg; the friend of Horatio; the lover of Ophelia; he that was mad and sent to England; the slow avenger of his father's death; who lived at the court of Horwendillus five hundred years before we were born, but all whose thoughts we seem to know as well as we do our own, because we have read them in Shakespear.

Hamlet is a name; his speeches and sayings but the idle coinage of the poet's brain. What then, are they not real? They are as real as our own thoughts. Their reality is in the reader's mind. It is *we* who are Hamlet. This play has a prophetic truth, which is above that of history. Whoever has become thoughtful and melancholy through his own mishaps or those of others; whoever has borne about with him the clouded brow of reflection, and thought himself "too much i' th' sun;" whoever has seen the golden lamp of day dimmed by envious mists rising in his own breast, and could find in the world before him only a dull blank with nothing left remarkable in it; whoever has known "the pangs of despised love, the insolence of office, or the spurns which patient merit of the unworthy takes;" he who has felt his mind sink within him, and sadness cling to his heart like a malady, who has had his hopes blighted and his youth staggered by the apparitions of strange things; who cannot be well at ease, while he sees evil hovering near him like a spectre; whose powers of action have been eaten up by thought, he to whom the universe seems infinite, and himself nothing; whose bitterness of soul makes him careless of consequences, and who goes to a play as his best resource to shove off, to a second remove, the evils of life by a mock representation of them—this is the true Hamlet.

From William Hazlitt, *Lectures on the Literature of the Age of Elizabeth, and Characters of Shakespear's Plays* (London: Bell & Daldy, 1870), pp. 73–75.

THOMAS DE QUINCEY (1785–1859)
From On the Knocking at the Gate in Macbeth

In "Macbeth," for the sake of gratifying his own enormous and teeming faculty of creation, Shakspere has introduced two murderers: and, as usual in his hands, they are remarkably discriminated: but—though in Macbeth the strife of mind is greater than in his wife, the tiger spirit not so awake, and his feelings caught chiefly by contagion from her—yet, as both were finally involved in the guilt of murder, the murderous mind of necessity is finally to be presumed in both. This was to be expressed; and on its own account, as well as to make it a more proportionable antagonist to the un-offending nature of their victim, "the gracious Duncan," and adequately to expound "the deep damnation of his taking off," this was to be expressed with peculiar energy. We were to be made to feel that the human nature— *i.e.*, the divine nature of love and mercy, spread through the hearts of all creatures, and seldom utterly withdrawn from man—was gone, vanished, extinct, and that the fiendish nature had taken its place. And, as this effect is marvellously accomplished in the *dialogues* and *soliloquies* themselves, so it is finally consummated by the expedient under consideration; and it is to this that I now solicit the reader's attention. If the reader has ever witnessed a wife, daughter, or sister, in a fainting fit, he may chance to have observed that the most affecting moment in such a spectacle is *that* in which a sigh and a stirring announce the recommencement of suspended life. Or, if the reader has ever been present in a vast metropolis on the day when some great national idol was carried in funeral pomp to his grave, and, chancing to walk near the course through which it passed, has felt powerfully, in the silence and desertion of the streets and in the stagnation of ordinary business, the deep interest which at that moment was possessing the heart of man—if all at once he should hear the death-like stillness broken up by the sound of wheels rattling away from the scene, and making known that the transitory vision was dissolved, he will be aware that at no moment was his sense of the complete suspension and pause in ordinary human concerns so full and affecting as at that moment when the suspension ceases, and the goings-on of human life are suddenly resumed. All action in any direction is best expounded, measured, and made apprehensible, by reaction. Now apply this to the case in "Macbeth." Here, as I have said, the retiring of the human heart and the entrance of the fiendish heart was to be expressed and made sensible. Another world has stepped in; and the murderers are taken out of the region of human things, human purposes, human desires. They are transfigured: Lady Macbeth is "unsexed"; Macbeth has forgot that he was born of woman; both are conformed to the image of devils; and the world of devils is suddenly revealed. But how shall this be conveyed and made palpable? In order that a new world may step in, this world must for a time disappear. The murderers, and the murder, must be insulated—cut off by an immeasurable gulf from the ordinary tide and succession of human

From Milton Haight Turk, ed., *Selections from De Quincey* (Boston and London: Ginn, 1902), pp. 398–400.

affairs—locked up and sequestered in some deep recess; we must be made sensible that the world of ordinary life is suddenly arrested—laid asleep—tranced—racked into a dread armistice; time must be annihilated; relation to things without abolished; and all must pass self-withdrawn into a deep syncope and suspension of earthly passion. Hence it is that, when the deed is done, when the work of darkness is perfect, then the world of darkness passes away like a pageantry in the clouds: the knocking at the gate is heard, and it makes known audibly that the reaction has commenced; the human has made its reflux upon the fiendish; the pulses of life are beginning to beat again; and the re-establishment of the goings-on of the world in which we live first makes us profoundly sensible of the awful parenthesis that had suspended them.

HENRY DAVID THOREAU (1817–1862)
From A Week on the Concord and Merrimack Rivers

A perfectly healthy sentence, it is true, is extremely rare. For the most part we miss the hue and fragrance of the thought; as if we could be satisfied with the dews of the morning or evening without their colors, or the heavens without their azure. The most attractive sentences are, perhaps, not the wisest, but the surest and roundest. They are spoken firmly and conclusively, as if the speaker had a right to know what he says, and if not wise, they have at least been well learned. Sir Walter Raleigh might well be studied if only for the excellence of his style, for he is remarkable in the midst of so many masters. There is a natural emphasis in his style, like a man's tread, and a breathing space between the sentences, which the best of modern writing does not furnish. His chapters are like English parks, or say rather like a western forest, where the larger growth keeps down the underwood, and one may ride on horse-back through the openings. All the distinguished writers of that period, possess a greater vigor and naturalness than the more modern,—for it is allowed to slander our own time,—and when we read a quotation from one of them in the midst of a modern author, we seem to have come suddenly upon a greener ground, a greater depth and strength of soil. It is as if a green bough were laid across the page, and we are refreshed as by the sight of fresh grass in mid-winter or early spring. You have constantly the warrant of life and experience in what you read. The little that is said is eked out by implication of the much that was done. The sentences are verduous and blooming as evergreen and flowers, because they are rooted in fact and experience, but our false and florid sentences have only the tints of flowers without their sap or roots. All men are really most attracted by the beauty of plain speech, and they even write in a florid style in imitation of this. They prefer to be misunderstood rather than to come short of its exuberance. Hussein Effendi praised the epistolary style

From Henry David Thoreau, *A Week on the Concord and Merrimack Rivers* (Apollo edition; New York: Thomas Y. Crowell, 1961), pp. 123–125.

of Ibrahim Pasha to the French traveller Botta, because of "the difficulty of understanding it; there was," he said, "but one person at Jidda who was capable of understanding and explaining the Pasha's correspondence." A man's whole life is taxed for the least thing well done. It is its net result. Every sentence is the result of a long probation. Where shall we look for standard English, but to the words of a standard man? The word which is best said came nearest to not being spoken at all, for it is cousin to a deed which the speaker could have better done. Nay, almost it must have taken the place of a deed by some urgent necessity, even by some misfortune, so that the truest writer will be some captive knight, after all. And perhaps the fates had such a design, when, having stored Raleigh so richly with the substance of life and experience, they made him a fast prisoner, and compelled him to make his words his deeds, and transfer to his expression the emphasis and sincerity of his action.

EDGAR ALLAN POE (1809–1849)
From The Poetic Principle

While the epic mania—while the idea that, to merit in poetry, prolixity is indispensable—has, for some years past, been gradually dying out of the public mind, by mere dint of its own absurdity—we find it succeeded by a heresy too palpably false to be long tolerated, but one which, in the brief period it has already endured, may be said to have accomplished more in the corruption of our Poetical Literature than all its other enemies combined. I allude to the heresy of *The Didactic*. It has been assumed, tacitly and avowedly, directly and indirectly, that the ultimate object of all Poetry is Truth. Every poem, it is said, should inculcate a moral; and by this moral is the poetical merit of the work to be adjudged. We Americans especially have patronized this happy idea; and we Bostonians, very especially, have developed it in full. We have taken it into our heads that to write a poem simply for the poem's sake, and to acknowledge such to have been our design, would be to confess ourselves radically wanting in the true Poetic dignity and force—but the simple fact is, that, would we but permit ourselves to look into our own souls, we should immediately there discover that under the sun there neither exists nor *can* exist any work more thoroughly dignified—more supremely noble than this very poem—this poem *per se*—this poem which is a poem and nothing more—this poem written solely for the poem's sake.

  With as deep a reverence for the True as ever inspired the bosom of man, I would, nevertheless, limit, in some measure, its modes of inculcation. I would limit to enforce them. I would not enfeeble them by dissipation. The demands of Truth are severe; she has no sympathy with the myrtles.

From John Brooks Moore, ed., *Selections from Poe's Literary Criticism* (New York: F. S. Crofts, 1926), pp. 6–8. Reprinted by permission of Appleton-Century-Crofts.

All *that* which is so indispensable in Song, is precisely all *that* with which *she* has nothing whatever to do. It is but making her a flaunting paradox, to wreathe her in gems and flowers. In enforcing a truth, we need severity rather than efflorescence of language. We must be simple, precise, terse. We must be cool, calm, unimpassioned. In a word, we must be in the mood which, as nearly as possible, is the exact converse of the poetical. *He* must be blind indeed who does not perceive the radical and chasmal differences between the truthful and the poetical modes of inculcation. He must be theory-mad beyond redemption who, in spite of these differences, shall still persist in attempting to reconcile the obstinate oils and waters of Poetry and Truth.

MATTHEW ARNOLD (1822-1888)
From Essays in Criticism

The Literary Influence of the Academies
I say that is extravagant prose; prose too much suffered to indulge its caprices; prose at too great a distance from the centre of good taste; prose, in short, with the note of provinciality. People may reply, it is rich and imaginative; yes, that is just it, it is *Asiatic* prose, as the ancient critics would have said; prose somewhat barbarously rich and overloaded. But the true prose is Attic prose.

Well, but Addison's prose is Attic prose. Where, then, it may be asked, is the note of provinciality in Addison? I answer, in the commonplace of his ideas. This is a matter worth remarking. Addison claims to take leading rank as a moralist. To do that, you must have ideas of the first order on your subject—the best ideas, at any rate, attainable in your time—as well as be able to express them in a perfectly sound and sure style. Else you show your distance from the centre of ideas by your matter; you are provincial by your matter, though you may not be provincial by your style. It is comparatively a small matter to express oneself well, if one will be content with not expressing much, with expressing only trite ideas; the problem is to express new and profound ideas in a perfectly sound and classical style. He is the true classic, in every age, who does that. Now Addison has not, on his subject of morals, the force of ideas of the moralists of the first class—the classical moralists; he has not the best ideas attainable in or about his time, and which were, so to speak, in the air then, to be seized by the finest spirits; he is not to be compared for power, searchingness, or delicacy of thought to Pascal or La Bruyère or Vauvenargues; he is rather on a level, in this respect, with a man like Marmontel. Therefore, I say, he has the note of provinciality as a moralist; he is provincial by his matter, though not by his style.

From Matthew Arnold, *Essays in Criticism: First Series* (London and New York: Macmillan, 1898), pp. 63–65. A footnote has been omitted.

HENRY JAMES (1843–1916)
From Essays in London and Elsewhere

Criticism

If literary criticism may be said to flourish among us at all, it certainly flourishes immensely, for it flows through the periodical press like a river that has burst its dikes. The quantity of it is prodigious, and it is a commodity of which, however the demand may be estimated, the supply will be sure to be in any supposable extremity the last thing to fail us. What strikes the observer above all, in such an affluence, is the unexpected proportion the discourse uttered bears to the objects discoursed of—the paucity of examples, of illustrations and productions, and the deluge of doctrine suspended in the void; the profusion of talk and the contraction of experiment, of what one may call literary conduct. This, indeed, ceases to be an anomaly as soon as we look at the conditions of contemporary journalism. Then we see that these conditions have engendered the practice of "reviewing"—a practice that in general has nothing in common with the art of criticism. Periodical literature is a huge, open mouth which has to be fed—a vessel of immense capacity which has to be filled. It is like a regular train which starts at an advertised hour, but which is free to start only if every seat be occupied. The seats are many, the train is ponderously long, and hence the manufacture of dummies for the seasons when there are not passengers enough. A stuffed mannikin is thrust into the empty seat, where it makes a creditable figure till the end of the journey. It looks sufficiently like a passenger, and you know it is not one only when you perceive that it neither says anything nor gets out. The guard attends to it when the train is shunted, blows the cinders from its wooden face and gives a different crook to its elbow, so that it may serve for another run. In this way, in a well-conducted periodical, the blocks of *remplissage* are the dummies of criticism —the recurrent, regulated breakers in the tide of talk. They have a reason for being, and the situation is simpler when we perceive it. It helps to explain the disproportion I just mentioned, as well, in many a case, as the quality of the particular discourse. It helps us to understand that the "organs of public opinion" must be no less copious than punctual, that publicity must maintain its high standard, that ladies and gentlemen may turn an honest penny by the free expenditure of ink. It gives us a glimpse of the high figure presumably reached by all the honest pennies accumulated in the cause, and throws us quite into a glow over the march of civilization and the way we have organized our conveniences. From this point of view it might indeed go far towards making us enthusiastic about our age. What is more calculated to inspire us with a just complacency than the sight of a new and flourishing industry, a fine economy of production? The great business of reviewing has, in its roaring routine, many of the signs of blooming health, many of the features which beguile one into rendering an involuntary homage to successful enterprise.

From Henry James, *Essays in London and Elsewhere* (New York: Harper and Brothers, 1893), pp. 259–261.

Yet it is not to be denied that certain captious persons are to be met who are not carried away by the spectacle, who look at it much askance, who see but dimly whither it tends, and who find no aid to vision even in the great light (about itself, its spirit, and its purposes, among other things) that it might have been expected to diffuse.

GEORGE BERNARD SHAW (1856–1951)
From Our Theatres in the Nineties

The advantage of having a play criticized by a critic who is also a playwright is as obvious as the advantage of having a ship criticized by a critic who is also a master shipwright. Pray observe that I do not speak of the criticism of dramas and ships by dramatists and shipwrights who are not also critics; for that would be no more convincing than the criticism of acting by actors. Dramatic authorship no more constitutes a man a critic than actorship constitutes him a dramatic author; but a dramatic critic learns as much from having been a dramatic author as Shakespear or Mr Pinero from having been actors. The average London critic, for want of practical experience, has no real confidence in himself: he is always searching for an imaginary "right" opinion, with which he never dares to identify his own. Consequently every public man finds that as far as the press is concerned his career divides itself into two parts: the first, during which the critics are afraid to praise him; and the second, during which they are afraid to do anything else. In the first, the critic is uncomfortably trying to find faults enough to make out a case for his timid coldness: in the second, he is eagerly picking out excellences to justify his eulogies. And of course he blunders equally in both phases. The faults he finds are either inessential or are positive reforms, or he blames the wrong people for them: the triumphs of acting which he announces are stage tricks that any old hand could play. In criticizing actresses he is an open and shameless voluptuary. If a woman is pretty, well dressed, and self-satisfied enough to be at her ease on the stage, he is delighted; and if she is a walking monument of handsome incompetence, so much the better, as your voluptuary rarely likes a woman to be cleverer than himself, or to force him to feel deeply and think energetically when he only wants to wallow in her good looks. Confront him with an actress who will not condescend to attack him on this side who takes her work with thorough seriousness and self-respect—and his resentment, his humiliation, his sense of being snubbed, break out ludicrously in his writing, even when he dare not write otherwise than favorably. A great deal of this nonsense would be taken out of him if he could only write a play and have it produced. No dramatist begins by writing plays merely as excuses for the exhibition of pretty women on the stage. He comes to that ultimately perhaps; but at first he does his best to create real characters and make them pass

From Bernard Shaw, *Our Theatres in the Nineties* (Vol. 1; London: Constable, 1932), pp. 248–250. Reprinted by permission of The Society of Authors, for the Bernard Shaw Estate.

through three acts of real experiences. Bring a critic who has done this face to face with the practical question of selecting an actress for his heroine, and he suddenly realizes for the first time that there is not such a galaxy of talent on the London stage as he thought, and that the handsome walking ladies whom he always thought good enough for other people's plays are not good enough for his own. That is already an immense step in his education. There are other steps, too, which he will have taken before the curtain falls on the first public representation of his play; but they may be summed up in the fact that the author of a play is the only person who really wants to have it well done in every respect, and who therefore has every drawback brought fully home to him. The man who has had that awakening about one play will thenceforth have his eyes open at all other plays; and there you have at once the first moral with the first technical qualification of the critic—the determination to have every play as well done as possible, and the knowledge of what is standing in the way of that consummation. Those of our critics who, either as original dramatists or adapters and translators, have super-intended the production of plays with paternal anxiety, are never guilty of the wittily disguised indifference of clever critics who have never seen a drama through from its first beginnings behind the scenes. Compare the genuine excitement of Mr Clement Scott, or the almost Calvinistic serious-ness of Mr William Archer, with the gaily easy what-does-it-matterness of Mr Walkley, and you see at once how the two critic-dramatists influence the drama, whilst the critic-playgoer only makes it a pretext for entertaining his readers. On the whole there is only as much validity in the theory that a critic should not be a dramatist, as in the theory that a judge should not be a lawyer nor a general a soldier. You cannot have qualifications without experience; and you cannot have experience without personal interest and bias. That may not be an ideal arrangement; but it is the way the world is built; and we must make the best of it.

WALTER PATER (1839–1894)
From Style

Such is the matter of imaginative or artistic literature—this transcript, not of mere fact, but of fact in its infinite variety, as modified by human prefer-ence in all its infinitely varied forms. It will be good literary art not because it is brilliant or sober, or rich, or impulsive, or severe, but just in proportion as its representation of that sense, that soul-fact, is true, verse being only one department of such literature, and imaginative prose, it may be thought, being the special art of the modern world. That imaginative prose should be the special and opportune art of the modern world results from two impor-tant facts about the latter; first, the chaotic variety and complexity of its interests, making the intellectual issue, the really master currents of the present time incalculable—a condition of mind little susceptible of the

From H. G. Rawlinson, ed., *Selected Essays of Walter Horatio Pater* (London: Macmillan, 1927), pp. 6–7. A footnote has been omitted. Reprinted by permission of Macmillan London and Basingstoke.

restraint proper to verse form, so that the most characteristic verse of the nineteenth century has been lawless verse; and secondly, an all-pervading naturalism, a curiosity about everything whatever as it really is, involving a certain humility of attitude, cognate to what must, after all, be the less ambitious form of literature. And prose thus asserting itself as the special and privileged artistic faculty of the present day, will be, however critics may try to narrow its scope, as varied in its excellence as humanity itself reflecting on the facts of its latest experience—an instrument of many stops, meditative, observant, descriptive, eloquent, analytic, plaintive, fervid. Its beauties will be not exclusively "pedestrian"; it will exert, in due measure, all the varied charms of poetry, down to the rhythm which, as in Cicero, or Michelet, or Newman, at their best, gives its musical value to every syllable.

JOSEPH CONRAD (1857–1924)
From Preface to The Nigger of the "Narcissus"

Fiction—if it at all aspires to be art—appeals to temperament. And in truth it must be, like painting, like music, like all art, the appeal of one temperament to all the other innumerable temperaments whose subtle and resistless power endows passing events with their true meaning, and creates the moral, the emotional atmosphere of the place and time. Such an appeal to be effective must be an impression conveyed through the senses; and, in fact, it cannot be made in any other way, because temperament, whether individual or collective, is not amenable to persuasion. All art, therefore, appeals primarily to the senses, and the artistic aim when expressing itself in written words must also make its appeal through the senses, if its high desire is to reach the secret spring of responsive emotions. It must strenuously aspire to the plasticity of sculpture, to the colour of painting, and to the magic suggestiveness of music—which is the art of arts. And it is only through complete, unswerving devotion to the perfect blending of form and substance; it is only through an unremitting never-discouraged care for the shape and ring of sentences that an approach can be made to plasticity, to colour, and that the light of magic suggestiveness may be brought to play for an evanescent instant over the commonplace surface of words: of the old, old words, worn thin, defaced by ages of careless usage.

The sincere endeavour to accomplish that creative task, to go as far on that road as his strength will carry him, to go undeterred by faltering, weariness or reproach, is the only valid justification for the worker in prose. And if his conscience is clear, his answer to those who in the fulness of a wisdom which looks for immediate profit, demand specifically to be edified, consoled, amused; who demand to be promptly improved, or encouraged, or fright-

From Joseph Conrad, *The Nigger of the "Narcissus": A Tale of the Sea* (London and Toronto: J. M. Dent & Sons, n.d.; Paris: J. M. Dent et Fils, 1923), pp. ix–x. Reprinted by permission of J. M. Dent & Sons Ltd. Acknowledgment is also made to the Trustees of the Joseph Conrad Estate.

ened, or shocked, or charmed, must run thus:—My task which I am trying
to achieve is, by the power of the written word to make you hear, to make
you feel—it is, before all, to make you *see*. That—and no more, and it is
everything. If I succeed, you shall find there according to your deserts:
encouragement, consolation, fear, charm—all you demand—and, perhaps,
also that glimpse of truth for which you have forgotten to ask.

To snatch in a moment of courage, from the remorseless rush of time,
a passing phase of life, is only the beginning of the task. The task approached in tenderness and faith is to hold up unquestioningly, without
choice and without fear, the rescued fragment before all eyes in the light
of a sincere mood. It is to show its vibration, its colour, its form; and
through its movement, its form, and its colour, reveal the substance of its
truth—disclose its inspiring secret: the stress and passion within the core of
each convincing moment. In a single-minded attempt of that kind, if one be
deserving and fortunate, one may perchance attain to such clearness of
sincerity that at last the presented vision of regret or pity, of terror or mirth,
shall awaken in the hearts of the beholders that feeling of unavoidable
solidarity; of the solidarity in mysterious origin, in toil, in joy, in hope, in
uncertain fate, which binds men to each other and all mankind to the visible
world.

MARK TWAIN (1835-1910)
From How to Tell a Story

The Humorous Story an American Development—Its Difference from Comic and Witty Stories

I do not claim that I can tell a story as it ought to be told. I only claim to
know how a story ought to be told, for I have been almost daily in the company of the most expert story-tellers for many years.

There are several kinds of stories, but only one difficult kind—the
humorous story is American, the comic story is English, the witty story is
French. The humorous story depends for its effect upon the *manner* of the
telling; the comic story and the witty story upon the *matter*.

The humorous story may be spun out to great length, and may wander
around as much as it pleases, and arrive nowhere in particular; but the comic
and witty stories must be brief and end with a point. The humorous story
bubbles gently along, the others burst.

The humorous story is strictly a work of art—high and delicate art—and
only an artist can tell it; but no art is necessary in telling the comic and the
witty story; anybody can do it. The art of telling a humorous story—
understand, I mean by word of mouth, not print—was created in America,
and has remained at home.

From Mark Twain, *'How to Tell a Story' and Other Essays* (New York and London:
Harper and Brothers, 1902), pp. 3-4.

The humorous story is told gravely; the teller does his best to conceal the fact that he even dimly suspects that there is anything funny about it; but the teller of the comic story tells you beforehand that it is one of the funniest things he has ever heard, then tells it with eager delight, and is the first person to laugh when he gets through. And sometimes, if he has had good success, he is so glad and happy that he will repeat the "nub" of it and glance around from face to face, collecting applause, and then repeat it again. It is a pathetic thing to see.

T. S. ELIOT (1888-1965)
From Selected Essays

Tradition and the Individual Talent

Yet if the only form of tradition, of handing down, consisted in following the ways of the immediate generation before us in a blind or timid adherence to its successes, "tradition" should positively be discouraged. We have seen many such simple currents soon lost in the sand; and novelty is better than repetition. Tradition is a matter of much wider significance. It cannot be inherited, and if you want it you must obtain it by great labour. It involves, in the first place, the historical sense, which we may call nearly indispensable to any one who would continue to be a poet beyond his twenty-fifth year; and the historical sense involves a perception, not only of the pastness of the past, but of its presence; the historical sense compels a man to write not merely with his own generation in his bones, but with a feeling that the whole of the literature of Europe from Homer and within it the whole of the literature of his own country has a simultaneous existence and composes a simultaneous order. This historical sense, which is a sense of the timeless as well as of the temporal and of the timeless and of the temporal together, is what makes a writer traditional. And it is at the same time what makes a writer most acutely conscious of his place in time, of his own contemporaneity.

No poet, no artist of any art, has his complete meaning alone. His significance, his appreciation is the appreciation of his relation to the dead poets and artists. You cannot value him alone; you must set him, for contrast and comparison, among the dead. I mean this as a principle of aesthetic, not merely historical, criticism. The necessity that he shall conform, that he shall cohere, is not onesided; what happens when a new work of art is created is something that happens simultaneously to all the works of art which preceded it. The existing monuments form an ideal order among themselves, which is modified by the introduction of the new (the really new) work of art among them. The existing order is complete before the new work arrives; for order to persist after the supervention of novelty, the *whole* existing order must be, if ever so slightly, altered; and so the relations, proportions, values of each work of art toward the whole are readjusted; and this is conformity between the old and the new. Whoever has approved this idea of order, of the form of European, of English litera-ture will not find it preposterous that the past should be altered by the present as much as the present is directed by the past. And the poet who is aware of this will be aware of great difficulties and responsibilities.

GEORGE SANTAYANA (1863–1952)
From Soliloquies in England and Later Soliloquies

Imagination
In the *Mahabharata*, a learned friend tells me, a young champion armed for the combat and about to rush forward between the two armies drawn up in battle array, stops for a moment to receive a word of counsel from his spiritual adviser—and that word occupies the next eighteen books of the epic; after which the battle is allowed to proceed. These Indian poets had spiritual minds, they measured things by their importance to the spirit, not to the eye. They despised verisimilitude and aesthetic proportion; they despised existence, the beauties of which they felt exquisitely nevertheless, and to which their imagination made such stupendous additions. I honour their courage in bidding the sun stand still, not that they might thoroughly vanquish an earthly enemy, but that they might wholly clarify their own soul. For this better purpose the sun need not stand still materially. For the spirit, time is an elastic thing. Fancy is quick and brings the widest vistas to a focus in a single instant. After the longest interval of oblivion and death, it can light up the same image in all the greenness of youth; and if cut short, as it were at Pompeii, in the midst of a word, it can, ages after, without feeling the break, add the last syllable. Imagination changes the scale of everything, and makes a thousand patterns of the woof of nature, without disturbing a single thread. Or rather—since it is nature itself that imagines—it turns to music what was only strain; as if the universal vibration, suddenly ashamed of having been so long silent and useless, had burst into tears and laughter at its own folly, and in so doing had become wise.

From George Santayana, *Soliloquies in England and Later Soliloquies* (New York: Charles Scribner's Sons, 1923), pp. 125–126. Reprinted by permission of Charles Scribner's Sons.

D. H. LAWRENCE (1885–1930)
From **Studies in Classic American Literature**

The Spirit of Place

Let us look at this American artist first. How did he ever get to America, to start with? Why isn't he a European still, like his father before him?

Now listen to me, don't listen to him. He'll tell you the lie you expect. Which is partly your fault for expecting it.

He didn't come in search of freedom of worship. England had more freedom of worship in the year 1700 than America had. Won by Englishmen who wanted freedom, and so stopped at home and fought for it. And got it. Freedom of worship? Read the history of New England during the first century of its existence.

Freedom anyhow? The land of the free! This the land of the free! Why, if I say anything that displeases them, the free mob will lynch me, and that's my freedom. Free? Why I have never been in any country where the individual has such an abject fear of his fellow countrymen. Because, as I say, they are free to lynch him the moment he shows he is not one of them.

No, no, if you're so fond of the truth about Queen Victoria, try a little about yourself.

Those Pilgrim Fathers and their successors never came here for freedom of worship. What did they set up when they got here? Freedom, would you call it?

They didn't come for freedom. Or if they did, they sadly went back on themselves.

All right then, what did they come for? For lots of reasons. Perhaps least of all in search of freedom of any sort: positive freedom, that is.

They came largely to get *away* that most simple of motives. To get away. Away from what? In the long run, away from themselves. Away from everything. That's why most people have come to America, and still do come. To get away from everything they are and have been.

"Henceforth be masterless."

Which is all very well, but it isn't freedom. Rather the reverse. A hopeless sort of constraint. It is never freedom till you find something you really *positively want to be*. And people in America have always been shouting about the things they are *not*. Unless of course they are millionaires, made or in the making.

Benjamin Franklin

The Perfectibility of Man! Ah heaven, what a dreary theme! The perfectibility of the Ford car! The perfectibility of which man? I am many men. Which of them are you going to perfect? I am not a mechanical contrivance.

Education! Which of the various me's do you propose to educate, and which do you propose to suppress?

Anyhow I defy you. I defy you, oh society, to educate me or to suppress me, according to your dummy standards.

The ideal man! And which is he, if you please? Benjamin Franklin or Abraham Lincoln? The ideal man! Roosevelt or Porfirio Diaz?

There are other men in me, besides this patient ass who sits here in a tweed jacket. What am I doing, playing the patient ass in a tweed jacket? Who am I talking to? Who are you, at the other end of this patience?

Who are you? How many selves have you? And which of these selves do you want to be?

Is Yale College going to educate the self that is in the dark of you, or Harvard College?

The ideal self! Oh, but I have a strange and fugitive self shut out and howling like a wolf or a coyote under the ideal windows. See his red eyes in the dark? This is the self who is coming into his own.

The perfectibility of man, dear God! When every man as long as he remains alive is in himself a multitude of conflicting men. Which of these do you choose to perfect, at the expense of every other?

Old Daddy Franklin will tell you. He'll rig him up for you, the pattern American. Oh, Franklin was the first downright American. He knew what he was about, the sharp little man. He set up the first dummy American.

GERTRUDE STEIN (1874–1946)
From Lectures in America

Poetry and Grammar

So now to come to the real question of punctuation, periods, commas, colons, semi-colons and capitals and small letters.

I have had a long and complicated life with all these.

Let us begin with these I use the least first and these are colons and semi-colons, one might add to these commas.

When I first began writing, I felt that writing should go on, I still do feel that it should go on but when I first began writing I was completely possessed by the necessity that writing should go on and if writing should go on what had colons and semi-colons to do with it, what had commas to do with it, what had periods to do with it what had small letters and capitals to do with it to do with writing going on which was at that time the most profound need I had in connection with writing. What had colons and semi-colons to do with it what had commas to do with it what had periods to do with it.

What had periods to do with it. Inevitably no matter how completely I had to have writing go on, physically one had to again and again stop sometime and if one had to again and again stop some time then periods had to exist. Beside I had always liked the look of periods and I liked what they did. Stopping sometime did not really keep one from going on,

From Gertrude Stein, *Lectures in America* (New York: Random House, 1935), pp. 216–217. Copyright, 1935, by The Modern Library, Inc. Reprinted by permission of Random House, Inc.

it was nothing that interfered, it was only something that happened, and as it happened as a perfectly natural happening, I did believe in periods and I used them. I really never stopped using them.

From Composition as Explanation

The problem from this time on became more definite.

It was all so nearly alike it must be different and it is different, it is natural that if everything is used and there is a continuous present and a beginning again and again if it is all so alike it must be simply different and everything simply different was the natural way of creating it then.

In this natural way of creating it then that it was simply different everything being alike it was simply different, this kept on leading one to lists. Lists naturally for a while and by lists I mean a series. More and more in going back over what was done at this time I find that I naturally kept simply different as an intention. Whether there was or whether there was not a continuous present did not then any longer trouble me there was or there was not, and using everything no longer troubled me if everything is alike using everything could no longer trouble me and beginning again and again could no longer trouble me because if lists were inevitable if series were inevitable and the whole of it was inevitable beginning again and again could not trouble me so then with nothing to trouble me I very completely began naturally since everything is alike making it as simply different naturally as simply different as possible. I began doing natural phenomena what I call natural phenomena and natural phenomena naturally everything being alike natural phenomena are making things be naturally simply different. This found its culmination later, in the beginning it began in a center confused with lists with series with geography with returning portraits and with particularly often four and three and often with five and four. It is easy to see that in the beginning such a conception as everything being naturally different would be very inarticulate and very slowly it began to emerge and take the form of anything, and then naturally if anything that is simply different is simply different what follows will follow.

H. L. MENCKEN (1880–1956)
From Prejudices

Literature and the Schoolma'm
With precious few exceptions, all the books on style in English are by writers quite unable to write. The subject, indeed, seems to exercise a

special and dreadful fascination over schoolma'ms, bucolic college professors, and other such pseudo-literates. One never hears of treatises on it by George Moore or James Branch Cabell, but the pedagogues, male and female, are at it all the time. In a thousand texts they set forth their depressing ideas about it, and millions of suffering high-school pupils have to study what they say. Their central aim, of course, is to reduce the whole thing to a series of simple rules—the overmastering passion of their melancholy order, at all times and everywhere. They aspire to teach it as bridge whist, the American Legion flag-drill and double-entry bookkeeping are taught. They fail as ignominiously as that Athenian of legend who essayed to train a regiment of grasshoppers in the goose-step.

For the essence of a sound style is that it cannot be reduced to rules— that it is a living and breathing thing, with something of the devilish in it— that it fits its proprietor tightly and yet ever so loosely, as his skin fits him. It is, in fact, quite as securely an integral part of him as that skin is. It hardens as his arteries harden. It has *Katzenjammer* on the days succeeding his indiscretions. It is gaudy when he is young and gathers decorum when he grows old. On the day after he makes a mash on a new girl it glows and glitters. If he has fed well, it is mellow. If he has gastritis it is bitter. In brief, a style is always the outward and visible symbol of a man, and it cannot be anything else. To attempt to teach it is as silly as to set up courses in making love. The man who makes love out of a book is not making love at all; he is simply imitating someone else making love. God help him if, in love or literary composition, his preceptor be a pedagogue!

PETER QUENNELL (1905–
From Baudelaire and the Symbolists

Stéphane Mallarmé
Like leaves imprisoned beneath thick ice, which the poet mentions in a passage I have transcribed above, Mallarmé's *concetti*, his *Petits Vers*, inscriptions for fans, enigmatic and melodious stanzas to be copied into the pages of an album, verse epistles, rhyming envelopes, are less fluttering and ephemeral than from the nature of such productions we usually expect. Imagine a clear sheet of ice, solid, unflawed, allowing the passer-by to look down and examine its depths, the ingenuous aspirations which lay immobilised there, the combed-out tresses of the stream, drowned refuse and all the wrack and wastage of circumstance.... Yet under this translucent covering, to-and-fro moves an inconstant, small brilliant flame, glowing through its coffin-lid, momentarily transforming the icy, motionless fronds among which it is immured. "Il détient le génie, la puissance, la gloire," Mallarmé said, after visiting Victor Hugo, "mais il lui manque une petite flamme que j'ai et que je voudrais lui donner." The consciousness of genius, Mallarmé's preoccu-

From Peter Quennell, *Baudelaire and the Symbolists* (London: Chatto & Windus, 1929), pp. 212 214. Reprinted by permission of George Weidenfeld & Nicholson Ltd., publishers.

pation with the Word, its lofty obsession,—"donner un sens plus pur aux mots de la tribu",—so irradiates his verse that although, during his search for a poetic formula which should have enabled him to put his hands on the essential part of every poet's inspiration—(the long-drawn melancholy cadence of Baudelaire's autumnal dirge, what critics have called his *miaulement* or voluptuous feline wail)—he seems to have destroyed the sententious magniloquence of the ancient poetry by excluding its rhetorical basis, equally he would seem to have re-endowed it with that interior dispassionate glow which, if it had not altogether lost, it was then in some great danger of losing.   Convinced that literary expression had grown too elastic, that its channels were too accommodating, the writer was concerned to erect fresh obstacles, since we can best achieve solitude by retreating on to a plane where the larger number of our contemporaries will not care to follow.   Yet it was no mere immunity from latterday contacts that Mallarmé sought; the sympathies which actuated him had little or nothing in common with that cultivated depravation of literary taste, summed up in the protagonist of Huysmans' lugubrious romance.   Mallarmé, we should remember, was a student of English verse; he had learned to appreciate the magical *immediacy* of effect which is the occasional, precarious and hard-won privilege of certain English writers.   After a thousand beauties, so many of them cumulative, which the fulness of time brings into being, which their context gradually matures, the sudden emergence of some felicitous image, springing like a group of sea-gods where a moment earlier there was vacancy, flowering like a wave where we could distinguish only the bare, uneventful swelling and subsiding movement of the verse, is startling and peculiarly delightful to a foreign ear:

> He...
> ... question'd every gust of rugged wings
> That blows from off each beaked Promontory,
> They knew not of his story
> And sage Hippotades their answer brings,
> That not a blast was from his dungeon stray'd,
> *The air was calm and on the level brine*
> *Sleek Panope and all her sisters play'd.*

EDMUND WILSON (1895–   )
From Axel's Castle

Gertrude Stein
Sometimes these writings of Gertrude Stein make us laugh: her humor is perhaps the one of her qualities which comes through in her recent books most clearly; and I should describe them as amusing nonsense, if "nonsense" were not a word which had so often been used in derogation both of the

From Edmund Wilson, *Axel's Castle: A Study in the Imaginative Literature of 1870–1930* (New York: Charles Scribner's Sons, 1931), pp. 244–245.   Reprinted by permission of the publisher.

original Symbolists and of the contemporary writers dealt with in this book. If I should say that Miss Stein wrote nonsense, I might be thought to be implying that she was not serious or that she was not artistically successful. As a matter of fact, one should not talk about "nonsense" until one has decided what "sense" consists of—and one cannot investigate this without becoming involved in questions which go to the bottom of the whole Symbolist theory and throw further light on the issues it raises.

The original Symbolists supposed themselves to be defending the value of suggestion in literature as against the documentation of Naturalism and the logic of rationalism—and both they and their opponents seemed to tend to take it for granted that the suggestion was all on one side and the sense all on the other. We have already noted this tendency in Valéry, in Eliot and in Yeats, and we have stumbled over the difficulties it leads to. Now, as a matter of fact, all literature, all writing, all speech, depends equally upon suggestion; the "meaning" of words is what they suggest. Speaking accurately, it is impossible to say that one kind of writing suggests, whereas another kind proves or states. Any literary work, if it accomplishes its purpose, must superinduce in the reader a whole complex of what we are accustomed to call thoughts, emotions and sensations—a state of consciousness, a state of mind; it depends for its effectiveness upon a web of associations as intricate and in the last analysis as mysterious as our minds and bodies themselves. Our words themselves are the prime symbols, and the only originality of the Symbolists consisted in reminding people of the true nature and function of words. It is of course possible to think of words abstractly so that they shall seem to have pure definite meanings, but the fact remains that as soon as we begin to use them, we cannot help pouring them full of suggestion by our inflections, our pauses, our tones or by their order and collocation on the page, and in any case by selecting them in such a way as to bring out certain previous associations.

JOSEPH WOOD KRUTCH (1893–1970)
From Five Masters

Richardson

"Clarissa" trembles on the edge of the ridiculous. Pomposity, smugness, and fatuity are always just around the corner. And yet it would not be fair to dismiss it as merely pompous, smug or fatuous. In it there is a remarkable refinement of observation, and an amazing insight into all the corners of a small but ardent mind. Richardson's sympathies, for all the narrowness of their range, were extraordinarily acute and so completely does he live in and through the soul of Clarissa that one is compelled to admit that one at least knows what Dr. Johnson meant when he said that there was "more knowledge of the human heart" in one letter of "Clarissa" than in all of the

From Joseph Wood Krutch, *Five Masters: A Study in the Mutations of the Novel* (New York: Jonathan Cape & Harrison Smith, 1930), pp. 155–156. Reprinted by permission of Joseph Wood Krutch.

novels of Fielding. In it readers could recognize themselves to an extent which was impossible in any previous novel. Experiences such as might possibly happen to them were here happening to people like themselves and they could live with Clarissa on the terms of an intimacy impossible in the case of any other heroine of fiction. No one could possibly *behave* like Don Quixote or Robinson Crusoe, but thousands must have asked themselves what Clarissa (or Lovelace!) would have done under these circumstances or those.

Thus their creator at once restricted and enlarged the field of fiction. He eliminated all extraordinary adventures and all passions more exalted than those within the range of the more ordinary sort of person but he examined the emotions appropriate to bourgeois existence with a minuteness never known before and he did for the middle class heart what Defoe had done for the externals of daily life—he examined, that is to say, all its little hopes, scruples, and perturbations, with an eye which delighted to note and to respect them. Hence it was thanks more to his influence than to that of any other man that the novel could become, as it has, a dominant influence in moulding the opinions, the manners, and the modes of feeling cultivated by a very large section of any literate public.

VIRGINIA WOOLF (1882–1941)
From The Second Common Reader

How Should One Read a Book?

"We have only to compare"—with those words the cat is out of the bag, and the true complexity of reading is admitted. The first process, to receive impressions with the utmost understanding, is only half the process of reading; it must be completed, if we are to get the whole pleasure from a book, by another. We must pass judgment upon these multitudinous impressions: we must make of these fleeting shapes one that is hard and lasting. But not directly. Wait for the dust of reading to settle; for the conflict and the questioning to die down; walk, talk, pull the dead petals from a rose, or fall asleep. Then suddenly without our willing it, for it is thus that Nature undertakes these transitions, the book will return, but differently. It will float to the top of the mind as a whole. And the book as a whole is different from the book received currently in separate phrases. Details now fit themselves into their places. We see the shape from start to finish; it is a barn, a pig-sty, or a cathedral. Now then we can compare book with book as we compare building with building. But this act of comparison means that our attitude has changed; we are no longer the friends of the writer, but his judges; and just as we cannot be too sympathetic as friends, so as judges we cannot be too severe. Are they not criminals, books that have wasted our

From "How Should One Read a Book?" in *The Second Common Reader*, pp. 190–192, by Virginia Woolf, copyright, 1932, by Harcourt, Brace & World, Inc.; renewed, 1960, by Leonard Woolf. Reprinted by permission of Harcourt Brace Jovanovich, Inc. Acknowledgment is also made to Quentin Bell, Angelica Garnett and the Hogarth Press.

time and sympathy; are they not the most insidious enemies of society, corrupters, defilers, the writers of false books, faked books, books that fill the air with decay and disease? Let us then be severe in our judgments; let us compare each book with the greatest of its kind. There they hang in the mind the shapes of the books we have read solidified by the judgments we have passed on them—*Robinson Crusoe*, *Emma*, *The Return of the Native*. Compare the novels with these—even the latest and least of novels has a right to be judged with the best. And so with poetry—when the intoxication of rhythm has died down and the splendour of words has faded a visonary shape will return to us and this must be compared with *Lear*, with *Phèdre*, with *The Prelude*; or if not with these, with whatever is the best or seems to us to be the best in its own kind. And we may be sure that the newness of new poetry and fiction is its most superficial quality and that we have only to alter slightly, not to recast, the standards by which we have judged the old.

GEORGE ORWELL (1903–1950)
From Shooting an Elephant and Other Essays

Politics and the English Language

Most people who bother with the matter at all would admit that the English language is in a bad way, but it is generally assumed that we cannot by conscious action do anything about it. Our civilization is decadent and our language—so the argument runs—must inevitably share in the general collapse. It follows that any struggle against the abuse of language is a sentimental archaism, like preferring candles to electric light or hansom cabs to aeroplanes. Underneath this lies the half-conscious belief that language is a natural growth and not an instrument which we shape for our own purposes.

Now, it is clear that the decline of a language must ultimately have political and economic causes: it is not due simply to the bad influence of this or that individual writer. But an effect can become a cause, reinforcing the original cause and producing the same effect in an intensified form, and so on indefinitely. A man may take to drink because he feels himself to be a failure, and then fail all the more completely because he drinks. It is rather the same thing that is happening to the English language. It becomes ugly and inaccurate because our thoughts are foolish, but the slovenliness of our language makes it easier for us to have foolish thoughts. The point is that the process is reversible. Modern English, especially written English, is full of bad habits which spread by imitation and which can be avoided if one is willing to take the necessary trouble. If one gets rid of these habits one can think more clearly, and to think clearly is a necessary first step towards political regeneration: so that the fight against bad English is not frivolous and is not the exclusive concern of professional writers.

From "Politics and the English Language" in *Shooting an Elephant and Other Essays*, pp. 77–78, by George Orwell, copyright, 1945, 1946, 1949, 1950, by Sonia Brownell Orwell. Acknowledgment is also made to Secker & Warburg Ltd. Reprinted by permission of Harcourt Brace Jovanovich, Inc., and A. M. Heath & Co., Ltd.

E. B. WHITE (1899–   )
From The Second Tree from the Corner

The Wonderful World of Letters

In the same envelope with the calculator, we received another training aid for writers—a booklet called "How to Write Better," by Rudolf Flesch. This, too, we studied, and it quickly demonstrated the broncolike ability of the English language to throw whoever leaps cocksurely into the saddle. The language not only can toss a rider but knows a thousand tricks for tossing him, each more gay than the last. Dr. Flesch stayed in the saddle only a moment or two. Under the heading "Think Before You Write," he wrote, "The main thing to consider is your *purpose* in writing. Why are you sitting down to write?" And Echo answered: Because sir, it is more comfortable than standing up.

Communication by the written word is a subtler (and more beautiful) thing than Dr. Flesch and General Motors imagine. They contend that the "average reader" is capable of reading only what tests Easy, and that the writer should write at or below this level. This is a presumptuous and degrading idea. There is no average reader, and to reach down toward this mythical character is to deny that each of us is on the way up, is ascending. ("Ascending," by the way, is a word Dr. Flesch advises writers to stay away from. Too unusual.)

It is our belief that no writer can improve his work until he discards the dulcet notion that the reader is feeble-minded, for writing is an act of faith, not a trick of grammar. Ascent is at the heart of the matter. A country whose writers are following a calculating machine downstairs is not ascending—if you will pardon the expression—and a writer who questions the capacity of the person at the other end of the line is not a writer at all, merely a schemer. The movies long ago decided that a wider communication could be achieved by a deliberate descent to a lower level, and they walked proudly down until they reached the cellar. Now they are groping for the light switch, hoping to find the way out.

From pp. 166–167, *The Second Tree from the Corner*, by E. B. White. Copyright, 1951, by E. B. White. Reprinted by permission of Harper & Row, Publishers, Inc.

GENERAL SUGGESTIONS FOR RESEARCH

1. Baker (1967) has attempted to define four types of syntax by which to trace the changes in poetry from 1870 to 1930: normal, dislocated, elaborated, and fragmentary. Employ the same scheme to describe the syntax of some prose writer. Try to indicate where and how Baker's system relates to traditional types.

2. Apply Frye's (1947) distinction between the "recurring" rhythm of poetry and the prose "semantic" rhythm of "continuity" to a comparison of two prose writers. How useful is the method in showing the difference between two prose writers? For a recent application of Frye's theory, see Duffy (1967) on Pater.

3. Using the concepts of "micro-context" and "macro-context," describe a selected text, trying to employ together the terminology and tools of traditional and current prose-style analysis. See Riffaterre (1960) and Ullmann (1964, pp. 126–129).

4. Relate Christensen's (1967) method of analysis to traditional schemes for the analysis of a piece of prose. His system of numbering the elements of the sentence in their relation to the subject-verb core offers a possible way of more concretely describing Ciceronian, Senecan, and other styles.

5. After the manner of Ullman (1957 and 1963), study the role of a similar stylistic element in the structures of two prose works written at different times. Such a study by itself will not reveal much about the continuity of prose, but it will contribute to the accumulation of evidence for future synthesis.

6. Very little has been written about punctuation and the history of prose style; see Walcutt's (1962) excellent study questions following the selections. Select several short passages for close analysis of the punctuation, as a beginning to a history of the subject.

7. The psychological approach to style has received strong impetus in recent years from Spitzer's (1948) "philological circle" method: first, read a text repeatedly until you discern some stylistic peculiarity; second, look for a psychological explanation of this feature; third, find corroboration in the author's life and mind. Apply this method to a twentieth-century author, attempting simultaneously to connect your description of the stylistic

peculiarity to the traditions of style and stylistic criticism. The psychological approach to style has been supported interestingly lately by Holland (1965); see also the rejoinder by Harris (1966). Investigate the relevance of Holland's approach to the history of prose style.

8. Evaluate histories of prose style which generalize about the progress of prose style through writers who are in fact idiosyncratic.

9. Political style needs more study. Read Postman *et al.* (1970), reviewed by Ohmann (1971), and Seaman (1968), and apply their methods to the analysis of a political speech.

10. Study various statistical analyses of style and apply the techniques to a piece of prose. See Doležel and Bailey (1969) and Bailey and Doležel (1968).

A CONTEXTUAL METHOD FOR THE DESCRIPTION OF PROSE STYLE

OUTLINE WITH BIBLIOGRAPHY

(For full bibliographical data, see the Annotated Bibliography.)

This approach derived originally from Enkvist *et al.* (1964), which in turn looks back to J. R. Firth, M. A. K. Halliday, and the "levels-and-categories method." A recent systematic presentation of this approach, though restricted to the style of conversation, journalism, legal documents, and so forth, rather than to literary analysis, is Crystal and Davy (1970).

Bibliographies: Bailey and Burton (1968), Bailey and Doležel (1968), Milic (1967c), *Style* (University of Arkansas, Annual Bibliography, winter issue).

Other Methodological Sources: Chatman and Levin (1967), Corbett (1966), Doležel and Bailey (1969), Fowler (1966), Freeman, D. C. (1970), Gibson (1966, "Styles and Statistics: A Model T. Style Machine"), Hough (1969), Lodge (1967), Love and Payne (1969), Milic (1967b), Riffaterre (1959).

I. Contexts
   A. **Biographical, Historical, Cultural** All information about the social, political, economic, religious, and literary circumstances to which a writer responds is relevant to the description of style. For example, Ohmann (1962) studied Shaw's attitudes toward his age as essential to a full understanding of his linguistic choices. A good theoretical study of the relationship between these large contexts and language is Wellek and Warren (1942).
   B. **Literary** See A above.
   C. **Linguistic**
      1. **Period**
      2. **Dialect**
      3. **Subject Matter**
      4. **Spoken-Written**

    5. Formality (Anglo-Saxon-Latinate, concrete-abstract)
Barfield (1967), Baugh (1967), Bloomfield and Newmark (1963), Brook (1964), Chomsky (1965), Clark, J. W. (1964), Francis, N. (1965), Gordon (1966), Greenough and Kittredge (1962), Groom (1934), Jespersen (1948), Kellner (1892), McIntosh *et al.* (1965), McKnight (1923), *The Oxford English Dictionary* (1933), Partridge (1950), Perrin (1959), Pyles (1952), Rigg (1968), Robertson and Cassidy (1954), Schlauch (1964), Serjeantson (1936), Thomas, O. (1965), *Webster's Third New International Dictionary of the English Language* (1961), Wright (1898–1905).

II. Individual Characteristics
  A. Syntax
    1. Sentence Length (longest, shortest, average)
    2. Sentence Types
      a. Functional (statement, question, command, exclamation)
      b. Grammatical Christensen (1967, "A Generative Rhetoric of the Sentence"), Perrin (1959).
      c. Rhetorical Type (regular, dislocated, elaborated, fragmented) Baker (1967).
      d. Rhetorical Type (curt, loose, baroque, periodic, balanced *or* Senecan, Ciceronian, Euphuistic, plain) Adolph (1968), Croll in Patrick *et al.* (1966), Potter (1965), Williamson (1951).
    3. Clausal-Phrasal Aurner (1923b), Miles (1967), Scott and Chandler (1932).
    4. Connectives (sentence openers) Christensen (1967, "Sentence Openers"), Milic (1967b).
    5. Schemes Corbett (1965), Leech (1966), Riedel (1969).
    6. Rhythm (cursus) Baum (1952).
    7. Deep-Surface Structure Ohmann (1966).
    8. Punctuation Menikoff (1970), Walcutt (1962).
  B. Lexis
    1. Collocation and Set Adolph (1968, pp. 253ff).
    2. Nominal-Verbal Gerwig (1894), Thomas, O. (1965, Chs. 4–5), Wells (1960), Wilson, J. (1956).
    3. Tropes Brower (1951, Ch. 3), Corbett (1965, 1969).
    4. Imagery Brower (1951, Ch. 2), Roberts (1969, Ch. 9).
  C. Sound (alliteration, assonance) Brower (1951, Ch. 4), Corbett (1969 on schemes), Wellek and Warren (1942), "Euphuism" in Glossary.

III. Greater-Than-Sentence Stylistics: Paragraph and Whole Discourse
Burke, V. M. (1968), Levin, G. (1964), Lewis (1894), Roberts (1969), Watt (1960).
  A. Traditional Structural Principles Scott and Denney (1894), Wendell (1891).
  B. Thought Structure (argument, exposition, description, narration) Brooks and Warren (1958).
  C. Sentence-Length Pattern

   D. Sentence-Type Pattern   Christensen (1967, "A Generative Rhetoric of the Paragraph").
   E. Word Patterns   Guerin *et al.* (1966).
   F. Sound Patterns   Saintsbury (1912).
   G. Point of View   Booth (1961), Roberts (1969, Ch. 10).
   H. Tone   Chatman (1969), Lodge (1967), Ohmann (1962), Roberts (1969, Ch. 11).

IV. Establishment of a Norm (comparison with other texts)   Craddock (1968), Halliday (1962), Hayes (1968).

V. Two Historical Types: Plain-Utilitarian, Ornate-Expressive   Adolph (1968), Boulton, M. (1954), Chambers, R. W. (1932), Gordon (1966).

SAMPLE DESCRIPTION

The contextual method is applied below to one paragraph from Chapter 20, "Adam Visits the Hall Farm," of *Adam Bede* by George Eliot. The text is from an edition published by Holt, Rinehart and Winston, reprinted from an edition first published by William Blackwell and Sons (London and Edinburgh, 1867). Those items of the Outline which pertain specifically to this passage are utilized in the analysis.

[1]Adam walked round by the rick-yard, at present empty of ricks, to the little wooden gate leading into the garden—once the well-tended kitchen-garden of a manor-house; now, but for the handsome brick wall with stone coping that ran along one side of it, a true farmhouse garden, with hardy perennial flowers, unpruned fruit-trees, and kitchen vegetables growing together in careless, half-neglected abundance. [2]In that leafy, flowery, bushy time, to look for any one in this garden was like playing at "hide-and-seek." [3]There were the tall hollyhocks beginning to flower, and dazzle the eye with their pink, white, and yellow; there were the syringas and Gueldres roses, all large and disorderly for want of trimming; there were leafy walls of scarlet beans and late peas; there was a row of bushy filberts in one direction, and in another a huge apple-tree making a barren circle under its low-spreading boughs. [4]But what signified a barren patch or two? [5]The garden was so large. [6]There was always a superfluity of broad beans—it took nine or ten of Adam's strides to get to the end of the uncut grass walk than ran by the side of them; and as for other vegetables, there was so much more room than was necessary for them, that in the rotation of crops a large flourishing bed of groundsel was of yearly occurrence on one spot or other. [7]The very rose-trees, at which Adam stopped to pluck one, looked as if they grew wild; they were all huddled together in bushy masses, now flaunting with wide open petals, almost all of them of the streaked pink-and-white kind, which doubtless dated from the union of the houses of York and Lancaster. [8]Adam was wise enough to choose a compact Provence rose that peeped out half-smothered by its flaunting scentless neighbours, and held it in his hand—he thought he should be more at ease holding something in his hand—as he walked on to the far end of the garden, where he remembered there was the largest row of currant-trees, not far off from the great yew-tree arbour.

CONTEXTS

Biographical, Historical, Cultural

Of the most powerful influences on the life of Marian Evans (George Eliot)—the high role of duty, the influence of her father, the loss of her religious faith before she was twenty years old—only the first is directly relevant to the passage. The historical and cultural background is more apparent. The novel presents a traditional society in which everyone knows his place and his duty. The lush, bushy garden where Adam finds Hetty Sorrel, where even the vegetables run wild, suggests the riotous emotions arising within Hetty for Arthur Donnithorne in opposition to settled society. This large social context is contained within an even larger cosmos of the Creation and the Judgment of Man. The scene takes place in a fecund garden, in the middle of which is an apple tree. Two people are there, Adam Bede and Hetty, though we see only Adam at this moment. Here is one of the central myths of Christianity, its God the Creator and Judge of all things, the Garden of Eden, and the Fall of our Original Parents (though in the novel only Eve-Hetty sins), through whose disobedience all mankind was corrupted. The moral context of the Garden of Eden resonates with the author's sense of the effect of deeds upon the community. Arthur Donnithorne's "thoughtless seduction of Hetty Sorrel," writes Walter Allen in *George Eliot* (New York, 1967), "not only leads to her murder of her baby and her imprisonment and to Adam's wretchedness, it also brings shame on the Poysers and very nearly their departure from Hayslope. In other words, it disrupts a whole community. Nothing can be the same again."

Literary

The novel follows the tradition of the omniscient narrator—the tradition of Fielding and Thackeray—in which the author, directly involved as story-teller, relates an action long after its conclusion, as though she were God, in full knowledge and judgment of the actions and thoughts of the characters. George Eliot is especially present in *Adam Bede* (increasingly less present in her later novels), not only through direct narration and description, but through direct authorial comment. The obvious connection of this paragraph with the omniscient-narrator tradition is revealed in such comments as the analogy of the pink-and-white roses with the houses of York and Lancaster (not a thought of which Adam is capable) and the direct observation that "Adam was wise enough."

The passage also reflects the realistic tradition which aspires, in Eliot's own words, "to give a faithful account of men and things," as true as history, the "rare, precious quality of truthfulness that I delight in so many Dutch paintings." This minute scene, in which the setting is concretely set forth, is part of the picture of society Eliot slowly builds up (what Professor Van Ghent calls "the massively slow movement" of the novel). But it is not a mere photograph of the actual; as we have seen and will see further, the novel and the passage reveal a society that is a closely woven moral web involving not only all the elements of the present, but of the past as well.

Mr. Irwine, a character in the novel, speaks for the author when he says: "Consequences are unpitying. Our deeds carry their terrible consequences, quite apart from any fluctuations that went before—consequences that are hardly ever confined to ourselves."

Linguistic

Period
Unfortunately, very little is firmly known about the linguistic context of the nineteenth century. The state of knowledge about the style of the period is so rudimentary that few generalizations can be supported with the evidence necessary for conviction. In the opinion of some stylistic historians, the period is one of individualism, when every writer's style was *sui generis.* Others perceive steady continuity from the seventeenth and eighteenth centuries. John Earle in *English Prose* (New York, 1891), for example, believes that the nineteenth century "has been remarkable for the great number of well-marked styles that have appeared. . . . But they are all based upon one recognized type; the Johnsonian style is at the root of them all." Since an abundance of evidence can be found to support both theses, we must wait until we have a great deal more statistical information before we can generalize about the period's linguistic features.

Dialect
The passage is clearly not in dialect. The novel contains dialect (as in Adam's "it'ud ha' been too heavy for your little arms"), but this passage is in the standard English of well-educated persons—indeed, of George Eliot.

Subject Matter
The subject matter directly affects the linguistic features of the paragraph. As description it appropriately contains the concrete details necessary to render the scene visual—*wooden gate, Provence rose,* and so on. As symbol it effectively suggests the Biblical Garden through these details, while it ironically reverses Adam's situation.

Spoken-Written
The passage is written English (which contemporary linguists refer to as *langue*), clearly distinguishable from spoken English (*parole*). The last sentence especially offers an emphatic illustration of written English in its elaborate syntax and sustained, suspended thought of composed utterance. George Eliot, writer, is plainly present here.

Formality
On the other hand, the passage's formality is lessened by the preponderance of Anglo-Saxon (*walked, empty, wooden*) and concrete or count-noun (*Adam, ricks, gate*) words, rather than Latinate and abstract words. And even the Latinate words (*kitchen, wall*) resemble short Anglo-Saxon words. This concreteness and the simplicity of diction, furthermore, are appropriate to the setting and characters of Adam and Hetty.

INDIVIDUAL CHARACTERISTICS

Syntax

Sentence Length
Perhaps the most obvious characteristic of the paragraph syntactically is its sentence-length variety. The longest sentence contains 70 words, the shortest 5. The average is 45, which is long, compared, for example, to the average of 41 in Hooker's *Ecclesiastical Polity*, notable for its long sentences.

Sentence Types
This extreme variety is exhibited, however, in only one of the four sentence types. Grammatically, there are three simple sentences, one complex, one compound (Sentence 3 is composed of four sentences connected by semicolons), and three compound-complex. All of the sentences are statements, except Sentence 4 (the second-shortest sentence in the paragraph), which is interrogative. The connectives offer a mixture of hypotaxis and parataxis, with a tendency to begin new clauses not with a conjunction, but with a new S-V following a period or semicolon. I will note two ways of treating a sentence rhetorically. One, employed by William Baker in *Syntax in English Poetry, 1870–1930* (Berkeley, 1968), describes a sentence as either regular (S-V-O), elaborated (for which he has such arbitrary criteria as five finite verbs in a sentence), dislocated (the disarrangement of the regular S-V-O order), and fragmented. This paragraph contains all regular sentences by his criteria. The second rhetorical approach to sentences is the one long-established by scholars of seventeenth-century style—curt, loose, periodic, balanced (or Senecan, Ciceronian, Euphuistic). The sentences in this paragraph are all of the loose type.

Connectives (sentence openers)
The sentence openers further reveal this structure. Five of the sentences begin S-V. A sixth opens with a conjunction followed by the S-V, and a seventh opens with the subject followed by a brief modifying clause before the verb. Sentence 2, however, opens with a prepositional phrase prior to the S-V, but even it is very short.

Schemes
These basic syntactical structures are embellished somewhat by the schemes (from classical rhetorical origins, deviations from normal order) of triads (in the first three sentences—for example, in Sentence 1: *flowers, fruit-trees, vegetables*) and anaphora in Sentence 3 (repetition of words at the beginning of successive clauses). The author employs no *cursus* (cadences at the ends of sentences).

Punctuation
The punctuation is mainly logical, in accordance with modern rules. But notice the several expressive commas (for example, in Sentence 3: "flower, and dazzle"), reminiscent of the older freedom in punctuation through the eighteenth century.

Lexis

Collocation and Set
Collocation accounts for the tendency of certain words to associate with certain other words. The grouping of certain words in a text is a set. Thus in this text, the situation naturally associates words common to a garden. The collocations are quite ordinary for the particular setting—*gate*, *flowers*. There are no coined words, recent borrowings, slang, though there are some seminaturalized foreign words which may seem ostentatiously learned (*Gueldres* and *Provence*) and inappropriate to Adam. There are few metaphors (one of the tropes of classical rhetoric), and these are quite simple (the simile in Sentence 2 and the metaphors of the huddling-peeping roses in Sentences 7 and 8). Only the historical analogy of the houses of York and Lancaster is subtle and difficult. On the other hand, the passage as a whole is complex, because it is both symbolical and ironical: the garden suggests the Paradisal Garden, but this Adam will not pluck the rose Hetty.

Imagery
The imagery is appropriately concrete, mainly visual (a dozen visual images in the first sentence alone). Ominously the garden, although packed with flowers, is scentless, except for the Provence rose.

Nominal-Verbal
In quantity the passage is nominal. But quantity is not the only criterion, and possibly not the most important. Robert Adolph in *The Rise of Modern Prose Style* (Cambridge, Mass., 1968) distinguishes between the "nominal operative" and "verbal descriptive" styles. In the former style, verbs are mere logical indicators, unaffected by context or subject matter, while nouns have invariable meanings and do the work of verbs, and adjectives are impersonal and for distinctions only. In the "verbal descriptive" style, on the other hand, the verbs are descriptive, evaluative, and affected by contexts, while nouns and adjectives are spontaneous, idiosyncratic, and affected by contexts, and syntax is more complex, more subordinate, expressing the point of view of narrator or speaker. With these definitions as our guide, we can say that the passage is verbal descriptive, since the context does affect nouns, adjectives, and verbs (the half-smothered rose, the barren circle) and syntax (the embedded clause in Sentence 7), partly expressive of Adam's point of view, partly of the author's. Yet the collocations are ordinary, and many of the verbs are not descriptive or evaluative or imperative, but forms of "to be."

GREATER-THAN-SENTENCE STYLISTICS: PARAGRAPH AND WHOLE DISCOURSE

Traditional Structural Principles (logical structure)
The paragraph moves from the general (garden) to the specific (rose-Hetty).

Thought (Narrative) Structure

The narrative is composed of two intertwining parts: (1) the movement of Adam from rick-yard to garden across the garden to Hetty (Sentences 1, 6, 7, and 8), during which time he plucks the Provence rose; and (2) the description of the garden (in all of the sentences). It is appropriate that a man like Adam should walk directly across the garden and that he should pick not the gaudy, open, mixed-color roses, but the obscure, almost smothered, single-color odorous Provence rose.

Sentence-Length and Sentence-Type Pattern

The syntactical type and sentence length are also organically relevant. Precisely in the middle of the paragraph, preceded and followed by long and relatively complex sentences, two short, staccato sentences, first a question and then an answer (both ironic), accentuate the moral issue.

Word Patterns

The imagery is arranged in two patterns, each containing an antithesis. On the one hand, there are more than 20 references to abundance and fecundity, from *abundance* itself to *bushy* (repeated significantly three times). In contrast, 4 references ominously point up the sterility potential in an abused fertility. The *barren circle* and *barren patch* under the apple tree, a significant repetition, compel us to consider within the context of the Biblical Fall of Eve the implications of the question, "But what signifies a barren patch or two?" For Hetty will bear and then murder her illegitimate child, an act which deeply affects the entire community. The second pattern in the imaginal design is that of naturalness versus artificiality (freedom versus restraint). This pattern, in support of the first and primary pattern of abundance versus barrenness, emphasizes the neglected, disorderly, *unpruned* nature of the lush garden where Adam finds Hetty, and the ineffectiveness of the wooden gate and brick wall. Hetty, as *leafy*, *flowery*, and *bushy*, as *careless* and *uncut* as the garden, will break through the gates and walls of social order and duty, to end in the barren circle of prison and disgrace.

Point of View

A final comment on the point of view of the paragraph will serve to connect the various elements together. There is some confusion as to the point of view in the paragraph. A recent writer would have presented the entire scene through the sensibility of Adam, designing everything to express his reactions at the moment. Had the passage been focused that way, we could have related the syntactical and lexical designs to what Adam was feeling. In Sentence 7 the author seems to come close to this method, when we seem to look through Adam's eyes as he plucks the rose, but the analogy at the end of the sentence reminds us that we are in direct contact with the author and that we are observing Adam and Hetty from the author's omniscient, symbolic, and ironic perspective. Thus the description of the text is necessarily partly revealing of the dramatic instance and partly of the mind and recurrent style of George Eliot.

GLOSSARY OF HISTORICAL AND CRITICAL TERMS

ACULEATE Relating to an exaggerated ingeniousness (through sententiousness, figures of repetition, and so on) or artificial formality. See "Aculeate Style and the Cult of Form" in Williamson (1951).

ALLITERATION A **SCHEME** of **REPETITION** in which initial letters or sounds are repeated in two or more closely associated words or stressed syllables. Closely related to **EUPHUISM** (as is *assonance*): "Euphuism ... is basically a style founded upon patterns of sounds" (Toor, 1966). See **PARALLELISM**.

A-LOGICAL Relating to the absence of logic. Rooney (1962–1963) compares Donne's "Second Prebend Sermon" to El Greco's *St. Andrew and St. Francis*, "where the divisions in the canvas ... are made quite clear, only to have the symmetry exploded by startlingly excessive emphases." See **BAROQUE** and the writings of Croll.

ANACOLUTHON A broken sentence, common in Greek prose. As late as the seventeenth century, since English grammar was still unformed, authors followed **CLASSICAL SYNTAX**. "That other leading city of Greece, Lacedaem ... it is to be wondered how museless and unbookish they were" (Milton).

ANAPHORA A **SCHEME** of **REPETITION** in which a word or group of words is repeated at the beginning of successive clauses; employed for emphasis and for rhythmical and emotional effect. "Never was there such a town as ours, I thought, as we fought on the sandhills with rough boys or dared each other to climb up the scaffolding of half-built houses soon to be called Laburnum Beaches. Never was there such a town, I thought, for the smell of fish and chips on Saturday evenings" (Dylan Thomas, "Quite Early One Morning").

ANGLO-FRENCH Relating to the French influence on English style, which began in 1066 with William the Conqueror's victory at Hastings. The importance and extent of this influence are debatable. A vast amount of literature in twelfth-century English was written in French, but some historians believe that the initial impact of Norman French on the English language was slight, since the great bulk of French words was borrowed after French ceased to be spoken as a native language in England (c. 1250). Prins (1952), in contrast, stresses the importance of French: "What happened then was rather that a happy blend ... was gradually evolved, and the Prayer Book of 1549 is a good exponent of this resulting style ... Anglo-Saxon, French and Latin being equally present in vocabulary, phraseonomy and style." N. Davis (1961) argues that the French example was important "in ordering the construction of sentences," and detailed support for this contention may be found in Workman (1940). Gordon (1966), who, in contrast, minimizes the French influence, describes a new type of French-based prose which does not contribute to order: the heaping up of additional thoughts onto the initial statement, connected by French-derived linking words (*lequel*, the which; *dont*, and therefore): "In the new trailing sentence the unity and coherence have gone. The syntax is disjointed. The reason for an action follows the action in a kind of explanatory afterthought. Each clause seems to generate the next one, which gives no impression of its having been in the writer's mind when he began the sentence."

ANGLO-LATIN Relating primarily to prose written in Latin in England during the Old English and Middle English periods. Because of the classical-rhetorical foundation of English education and the large number of translations from the Latin into English, the influence of Latin on English style was profound. See **CLASSICAL SYNTAX** and **RHETORIC**.

ANGLO-SAXON Relating to the Old English period. In the fifth and sixth centuries, the Teutonic tribes (Angles, Saxons, and Jutes) conquered Britain. From the Angles came the name *England* (Angle-land). Most of the common words of the language, the core of functioning English vocabulary, are of Anglo-Saxon origin. Some of the prose writers during this period (to c. 1100) are King Alfred, Aelfric, and Wulfstan. "During the late tenth and eleventh centuries, the classical period of Old English prose, many writers were active and much good prose was written. Homiletic prose in particular reached heights of achievement comparable to the masterpieces of modern times. Historical prose, too, flourished, and a beginning was made with scientific prose. Moreover, prose writers even ventured into the realm of fiction, territory hitherto monopolized by verse. Had this rapid development kept up, the twelfth and thirteenth centuries might have been as glorious in English literature as they actually were in Icelandic. But William of Normandy won at Hastings" (Kemp Malone in Baugh *et al.*, 1967).

ANTI-CICERONIANISM A stylistic movement in antiquity and in the seventeenth century virtually synonymous, according to Croll and his followers, with **ATTIC** (*genus humile*), **SENECAN**, and **BAROQUE** (Croll's word for the Attic prose of the seventeenth century). Whatever the label, the Crollians conceive of the style as the basis of seventeenth-century plain style and therefore of scientific, Restoration, and modern prose. This position was formidably challenged by R. F. Jones (1930, 1931, 1932), who described the style advocated by the scientists as being in opposition to the Senecan style. Agreeing mainly with Jones, Adolph (1968) questions "first, whether the 'moderns' were influenced by ancient and contemporary Anti-Ciceronians; and second, whether Croll's identification of seventeenth-century Anti-Ciceronianism with the ancient *genus humile* is correct. Indeed, was there ever such a thing as 'Anti-Ciceronianism' at all, either in antiquity or the seventeenth century?" Adolph concludes that Anti-Ciceronianism did not influence "English scientists and the Restoration at all."

ANTITHESIS The juxtaposition of contrasting ideas, often in parallel structure, a classical **SCHEME** of construction (**BALANCE**). "We have just enough religion to make us hate, but not enough to make us love one another" (Swift).

APHORISTIC An *aphorism* is a brief statement of a truth or principle (to be distinguished from *proverb* and *maxim*). An aphoristic style, characterized by a large number of short, effectively phrased sentences expressing weighty truths, is associated with the **CURT** style of **ANTI-CICERONIANISM**. See **ATTIC**, **GNOMIC**, and **POINTED**.

ASIATIC " 'Asiatic' describes the florid, oratorical style of Cicero's early orations or any style ancient or modern distinguished by the same copious periodic form and the Gorgianic figures that attend upon it" (Croll, 1921).

ASYNDETON The omission of conjunctions between parts of a sentence; part of the **NATIVE TRADITION** and a classical rhetorical **SCHEME**. "I have done.

You have heard me. The facts are before you. I ask for your judgment" (conclusion of Aristotle's *Rhetoric*). Asyndeton is also a characteristic of **SENECAN** *stile coupé* as described by Croll (1929)—the omission of the ordinary syntactic ligatures. "Here we are but *Viatores*, Passengers, way-faring men; This life is but the high-way, and thou canst not build thy hopes here; Nay, to be buried in the high way is no good marke" (Donne as quoted in Webber, 1962). See **PARATAXIS**.

ATTIC Croll's (1921) early expression for **ANTI-CICERONIANISM**. By "Attic," he designated at least two styles: one curt; the other loose and informal. Both were reactions against sixteenth-century emphases on conventional form, genre, and tradition, in favor of, Croll believed, an instrument of maximum expressiveness, in which the mind in process of thinking took precedence. A good background introduction to the subject is "Preface to Anti-Ciceronianism" in Williamson (1951). Cicero in the *Orator* described the Attic style as restrained, plain, in short and concise clauses, packed with apposite maxims (*acutae sententiae*) and **WIT**, while rigorously excluding **GORGIAN** symmetry and **PERIODIC** structure. Erasmus associated the style especially with brevity, wit, and sententious density of matter.

ATTIC

(disjunctive composition either asyndetic or loosely syndetic)

CURT (Brief, com- ◄──────── SENECA ────────► LOOSE (Adds length
pact expression,   and connection to its
short and abrupt in   members.)
movement.)

TACITUS (More compressed,
truncated, asymmetrical
expression.)

AUGUSTAN Relating to the age of Emperor Augustus of Rome, notable for the perfection of letters and learning (Virgil, Horace). Loosely applied to any period noted for the polish and refinement of its literature, such as the age of Addison, Steele, and Pope (**NEO-CLASSICAL**).

AUREATE Relating to a striving after the resplendent and the recondite. A highly favorable term in the fourteenth and fifteenth centuries, but by the nineteenth century it became pejorative, as in *The Cambridge History of English Literature* for 1908, where aureate style is equated with "heavily pompous diction." See **ORNATE** and Conley (1966).

BALANCE [1] In the sentence (a classical **SCHEME** of construction): noticeable equality in length and/or similarity in movement of the constructions. The chief characteristic of **EUPHUISM**. The balanced sentence may express two similar thoughts in **PARALLELISM** or two opposing thoughts in **ANTITHESIS**. [2] In elements of composition larger than the sentence: proportion among the various elements of a piece of writing. See **SCHEMATIC**.

BAROQUE Croll (1929) uses the term to describe a mode of expression characteristic of all the arts during the Renaissance and having the qualities of expressiveness rather than formal beauty, of energy of mind seeking truth. Croll identifies two types of the baroque: first, the **SENECAN** style, also called *période coupé* or *stile coupé*, "serried" or "curt" style; and second, the "loose" period or style ("trailing," "linked," or "libertine"). The characteristics of the **CURT** style, according to Croll, are freedom of syntactical members; lack of syntactic ligatures; shortness of members; a statement of the whole idea of the period in the first member; deliberate asymmetry of the members. Williamson disagrees with the last argument, in that he discerns connections between the **SCHEMATIC** or Euphuistic style and the **POINTED** or Senecan style; see the detailed analysis "Schematic Prose and Pointed Prose" in Williamson (1951). From Croll (1929): "Men must beware of running down steep places with weighty bodies; they once in motion, *suo feruntur pondere*; steps are not then voluntary" (Sir Henry Wotton). "Tis not worth the reading, I yield it. I desire thee not to lose time in perusing so vain a subject, I should peradventure be loth myself to read him or thee so writing; 'tis not *operae pretium*" (Burton, *The Anatomy of Melancholy*). "No armour can defend a fearful heart. It will kill itself within" (Felltham, *Resolves*). "To see ourselves again we need not look for Plato's year: every man is not only himself; there have been many Diogenes, and as many Timons, though but few of that name; men are lived over again; the world is now as it was in ages past; there was none then but there hath been some since that parallels him, and is, as it were, his revived self" (Browne, *Religio Medici*). The other type of baroque style is the **LOOSE**, "in which the members are usually connected by syntactic ligatures, and in which, therefore, both the members and the period as a whole may be, and in fact usually are, as long as in the Ciceronian style, or even longer." The style typically moves by addition to the main idea stated at the beginning. Connection is by coordinating conjunctions, and there is frequent use of absolute-participle construction. The style reflects spontaneous and unpremeditated development or accumulation of thought in process. "I could never perceive any rational consequence from those many texts which prohibit the children of Israel to pollute themselves with the temples of the heathens; we being all Christians, and not divided by such detested impieties *as* might profane our prayers, or the place wherein we make them; *or that* a resolved conscience may not adore her Creator anywhere, *especially* in places devoted to his service; *where*, if their devotions offend him, mine may please him; if theirs profane it, mine may hallow it" (Browne, *Religio Medici*). Here is a summary of Croll's analysis of the passage: The period begins with a statement complete in itself, which does not syntactically imply anything to follow it; an absolute participle carries on, in the second member. Thereafter the connectives are chiefly subordinating conjunctions. Observe particularly the use of *as*, *or that*, and *where*: how slight these ligatures are in view of the length and mass of the members they must carry. They are frail and small hinges for the weights that turn on them; and the period abounds and expands in nonchalant disregard of their tight, frail logic. "For as knowledges are now delivered, there is a kind of contract of error between the deliverer and the receiver: for he that delivereth knowledge desireth to deliver it in such form as may be best believed, and not as may be best examined; and he that receiveth knowledge desireth rather present satisfaction than expectant inquiry; and so rather not to doubt than not to err: glory making the author not to lay open his weakness, and sloth making the disciple not to know his strength" (Bacon, *The Advancement of Learning*). "I would gladly know how Moses, with an actual fire, calcined or burnt the golden calf into powder: for that mystical metal of gold, whose solary and celestial nature I admire, exposed unto the violence of fire, grows only hot, and liquefies, but consumeth not; so when the consumable and the volatile pieces of our bodies shall be refined into a more impregnable and fixed temper, like gold, though they suffer from the action of flames, they shall never perish, but lie immortal in the arms of fire" (Browne, *Religio Medici*). Croll emphasizes the distinct difference between baroque and Ciceronianism. Whereas the order of development in the oratorical Ciceronian period is round or circular, in the sense that members are placed with reference to the central or climactic member that they point forward or back to, the curt and loose periods avoid roundness and seek to express first the experience or idea. One more characteristic of the baroque sentence stresses the opposition to the Ciceronian style: a member often depends not upon the general idea or main words of a preceding member, but upon its final phrase or word alone. "As there were many reformers, so likewise many reformations: every country proceeding in a particular way and method, according as their national interest, together with their constitution and clime, inclined them: some angrily and with extremity; others calmly and with mediocrity, not rending, but easily dividing, the community, and leaving an honest possibility of a reconciliation;—*which* though peaceable spirits do desire, and may conceive that revolution of time and the mercies of God may effect, yet that judgment that shall consider the present antipathies between the two extremes,— their contrarities in condition, affection, and opinion,—may with the same hopes expect a union in the poles of heaven" (Browne, *Religio Medici*). Croll analyzes the passage thus: "Here the word *which* introduces a new development of the idea, running to as much as five lines of print; yet syntactically it refers only to the last preceding word *reconciliation*. The whole long passage has been quoted, however, not for this reason alone, but because it illustrates so perfectly all that has been said of the order and connection of the loose period. It begins, characteristically, with a sharply formulated complete statement, implying nothing of what is to follow. Its next move is achieved by means of an absolute-participle construction. This buds off a couple of appositional members; one of these budding again two new members by means of dangling participles. Then a *which* picks up the trail, and at once the sentence becomes involved in the complex, and apparently tight, organization of a *though ... yet* construction. Nevertheless it still moves freely, digressing as it will, extricates itself from the complex form by a kind of *anacoluthon* (in the *yet* clause), broadening its scope, and gathering new confluents, till it ends, like a river, in an opening view." Croll's choice of the term baroque is unfortunate because of the confusion it creates in distinguishing between **ORNATE** and **PLAIN** styles, particularly by his association of baroque with **ATTIC**, which means for Croll what the seventeenth century called the *plain style* and antiquity, the *genus humile*. Clearer, but opposite, usages of the term may be found in Gordon (1966) and Highet (1949). Gordon limits the term to Donne, Brown, and Taylor, while Highet includes both Senecan and Ciceronian styles. A major clarification of the baroque in prose in relation to plain style is Adolph (1968), a study of the sources and nature of the plain style in the seventeenth century. Adolph argues persuasively that the rise of the new plain style is in reaction against Senecan baroque.

BIBLE, KING JAMES or AUTHORIZED VERSION Composed from 1604 to 1611 by fifty-four scholars working in six groups; the immense success of this piece of collective scholarship is attested by its persistence for so many hundreds of years. As Saintsbury (1912) has written, "The astounding skill with which they took the best from everything, and added better of their own, can only be appreciated by actual comparison of the different texts." But their success also derives from their adherence to a long tradition, following the general lines of English prose up to that time, and from their close dependence on Tyndale (and Coverdale to a lesser extent). The primary credit for the greatness of the Authorized Version, according to Brooke (1967), "rests with Tyndale and Coverdale, and after them with the long series of ardent men, of whom King James's translators were the last, who for eighty years probed and polished its phrases."

CAROLINE Relating to the reign of Charles I (1625–1649). Milton began to write during this period, and it was also the age of Burton and Browne.

CICERONIANISM Combines (1) periodicity: the cumulative, comprehensive sentence (Cicero's special expression); (2) **BALANCE: PARALLELISM (ISOCOLON and PARISON) and ANTITHESIS**; and (3) tight and frequent syntactical ligatures between sentences and parts of sentences. "Now if nature should intermit her course, and leave altogether though it were but for a while the observation of her own laws; ... if the moon should wander from her beaten way, the times and seasons of the year blend themselves by disordered and confused mixture, the winds breathe out their last gasp, the clouds yield no rain, the earth be defeated of heavenly influence, the fruits of the earth pine away as children at the withered breasts of their mother no longer able to yield them relief: what would become of man himself, whom these things now do all serve?" (Richard Hooker, *The Laws of Ecclesiasticall Politie*) See **PERIODIC**.

CLASSICAL ORATORY (STRUCTURE) See **RHETORIC**.

CLASSICAL RHETORIC See **RHETORIC**.

CLASSICAL SYNTAX Latin and Greek significantly influenced English syntax in the following ways: (1) employment of the **TROPES** and **SCHEMES**, especially of balanced sentences, clauses counterweighing clause; (2) freedom in order of words, resulting in the **PERIODIC** sentence; (3) certain favorite cadences (*clausulae*) for the ends of sentences (see **CURSUS**); (4) the use of *which* for *this* or *him*; (5) the use of the correlatives *tantus* and *quantus* ("For look how much right the king ... so much right hath ..."); (6) the absolute construction of the participle, creating sentences of intricately related clauses (as in the fantastic sentence in Sidney's *Arcadia*, Argalus and Parthenia section, beginning, "But then, Demagoras assuring himself ..."); (7) placement of adjectives after nouns ("court martial"); (8) various constructions such as "each of them hath his proper to him bounds" (after the Latin *fines sibi proprias*) and "It happened this young imp to arrive," where "imp" is apparently in an inflected case as subject of the infinitive.

COLLOCATION One of the fundamental linguistic categories for the formal description of lexis, "set up to account for the tendency of certain items in a language to occur close to each other.... For example, the item 'economy' is likely to occur in the same linguistic environment as items such as 'affairs,' 'policy'.... These items are termed the *collocates* of 'economy' which, because it is the item under examination, is itself termed the *nodal item* .... Collocation is an important concept to have in mind when studying the language of literature. This is because the creative writer often achieves some of his effects through the interaction between usual and unusual collocations, and through the creation of new, and therefore stylistically significant, collocations" (Spencer and Gregory, 1964). Adolph (1968, Ch. 6) has employed collocation effectively in defining Restoration syntax and language.

COLLOQUIAL Relating to expression that is appropriate to informal conversation. Characterized by vernacular diction and simple syntax. Bridgman (1966) describes the significant change in American prose style from 1825 to 1925 toward a colloquial style. In a larger context, the colloquial style is a part of the long *native tradition* of **PLAIN, IDIOMATIC,** vernacular prose, which is as old as Alfred. "She was a big one, and she was coming in a hurry, too, looking like a black cloud with rows of glowworms around it; but all of a sudden she bulged out, big and scary, with a long row of wide-open furnace doors shining like red-hot teeth, and her monstrous bows and guards hanging right over us" (Mark Twain, *Huckleberry Finn*).

CONCEIT In general, an ingenious, fanciful thought or expression. More specifically, a striking or elaborately extended metaphor, paradox, or pun. Especially characteristic of **POINTED** prose. See **PARADOX** and **WIT**.

CONSTITUENT *Immediate Constituent (IC)*: One of the two or more constituents from which any construction is directly formed. In "his old enemy shot the gun," "his old enemy" and "shot the gun" are the two IC's of the sentence; "his," "old," and "enemy" are the IC's of the subject; "shot" and "the gun" are the IC's of the predicate; "the" and "gun" are the IC's of the object of the verb. See **HEAD, NOUN CLUSTER**, and **VERB CLUSTER**. *Ultimate Constituent (UC)*: Each of the separate morphemes that enter into a construction and are incapable of further division or analysis. The sentence which is embedded, traditionally called the *dependent clause*, is called a constituent sentence by transformationalists. See **TRANSFORMATIONAL GRAMMAR.**

CONTEXT   The environment of a word or phrase that helps to determine its function and to define its meaning.   This environment ranges from phonemic, morphemic, lexical, and syntactic levels to considerations of point of view, genre, and cultural beliefs.   See Spencer and Gregory (1964) on context and "placing the text."

COORDINATE SENTENCE   See **POLYSYNDETON.**

CURSUS   Originating in ancient Greece, the *cursus* were special rhythmical effects or cadences (*clausulae*) at the ends of sentences intended especially to signal a pause.   For this purpose certain rhythmical sequences were favored, and these were called *cursus*, the word implying a "run."   The three main types were (1) *cursus planus*: "mercy and pity," "beauty ascendant" (5 syllables, 2 stresses); (2) *cursus tardus*: "them that be penitent," "beauty conspicuous" (6 syllables, 2 stresses); and (3) *cursus velox*: "lose not the things eternal," "beautiful inspiration" (7 syllables, 2 stresses).   Baum (1952) tabulated 3,400 cadences in English writing and found the following cadences the most frequent: "mortal life" (3–2), "quick and the dead" (4–1), "Holy Spirit" (4–2), "strength and protection (5–2).

CURT   Relating to *stile coupé* or *période coupé*. See **SENECAN** and **BAROQUE.**

DECADENCE   A literary movement originating in nineteenth-century France which emphasized the superiority of the artist over bourgeois society, the autonomy of art, and the search for new sensations.   An example of the prose of the movement is George Moore's *Confessions of a Young Man.*

DEEP STRUCTURE   The simple or basic sentences underlying a complex sentence. See **SURFACE STRUCTURE**, Thomas, O. (1965), and Ohmann (1965, 1966).

DELIBERATIVE   [1] Relating to one of the three kinds of speeches (see **FORENSIC** and **EPIDEICTIC**), also known as *hortative* or *advisory*, in which one deliberates about public affairs, especially to persuade an audience to do something in the future. [2] A descriptive term used by H. Brown (1966) to denote the climactic movement of the **PERIODIC** sentence and the organization of classical oratory (**CICERONIANISM**).   Brown illustrates the style by three quotations: one from Demosthenes, one from Thucydides, and one from George Eliot's *Middlemarch*.

DIACHRONIC   Relating to the study of linguistic features through their historical evolution or development. See **SYNCHRONIC.**

DISPOSITIO   The second part of classical **RHETORIC**, which pertains to the effective organization of a discourse.   Aristotle emphasized two essential parts of a speech—the statement of the case and the proof of it—but he included also an introduction and a conclusion, to make four parts.   Latin rhetoricians added two more parts, to make six: (1) *exordium*, introduction; (2) *narratio*, statement of the problem; (3) *divisio*, outline of the argument; (4) *confirmatio*, proof of the argument; (5) *confutatio*, refutation of opposing arguments; and (6) *peroratio*, conclusion.   This arrangement was, of course, treated flexibly to meet varied circumstances.

ELIZABETHAN   Relating to the reign of Queen Elizabeth I (1558–1603).   Notable prose writers of the period were Sidney, Shakespeare, Raleigh, and Jonson.

ELOCUTIO   The third part of classical **RHETORIC**, meaning "style." Rhetoricians generally agreed in naming three levels of style: (1) low or plain (*attenuata, subtile*); (2) middle or forcible (*mediocris, robusta*); and (3) high or florid (*gravis, florida*). See Staton (1958). Naturally, considerations of style involve choice of words and arrangement of words into sentences, and the rhetoricians isolated numerous types called **TROPES** and **SCHEMES**.

EMBED   To insert one clause into another, interrupting it. "I remember well indeed the scruple I felt—the real delicacy—about betraying that *I* had, in the pride of my power, since our other meeting, stood, as their phrase went, among romantic scenes; but they were themselves the first to speak of it, and what, moreover, came home to me was that the coming and going of their friends in general— Brookbridge itself having even at that period one foot in Europe—was such as to place constantly before them the pleasure that was only postponed" (Henry James, " 'Europe' ").

ENGLISH LITERATURE, HISTORICAL PERIODS   English literature is usually broken down into the following periods. (American literature, from the seventeenth and eighteenth centuries on, is usually divided in a similar fashion.)

Old English (Anglo-Saxon)	Fifth Century–1100
Middle English	1100–1500
Renaissance	1500–1642
Early Tudor	1500–1557
Elizabethan	1557–1603
Jacobean and Caroline	1603–1642
Puritan (Commonwealth, 1649–1660)	1642–1660
Restoration	1660–1700
Neo-Classical (Age of Pope)	1700–1750
Neo-Classical and beginning of Romantic	1750–1798
Romantic	1798–1832
Victorian	1832–1870
Late Victorian and *Fin de Siècle*	1870–1900
Twentieth Century	1900–

These divisions are highly arbitrary and artificial, especially when related to the evolution of style, which is fluid and gradual, with tendencies fluctuating in prominence. The development of English as a language is more safely indicated by only three periods: Old English, from the beginnings to about 1100; Middle English, 1100 to 1500; Modern English, 1500 to today (Early Modern English, 1500 to 1700; Late Modern English, 1700 to today).

EPIDEICTIC   Relating to one of the three kinds of persuasive discourses (see **FORENSIC** and **DELIBERATIVE** [1]), also called *ceremonial*, in which the speaker attempts to please or inspire an audience. An example is Pericles' "Funeral Oration."

EPIGRAMMATIC   An *epigram* is a brief, clever, **POINTED** remark typically characterized by **ANTITHESIS**, **WIT**, and satire. An epigrammatic style is one in which these characteristics are marked. "The Puritans hated bear-baiting, not because it gave pain to the bear, but because it gave pleasure to the spectators" (Macaulay, *History of England*).

EUPHUISM   "All agree that Euphuism is a style based on **SCHEMES** as opposed to **TROPES**. Among the schemes the basic constituents are the schemes of **BALANCE: ISOCOLON, PARISON**, and **PAROMOION**. These are further reinforced by the schemes of sound patterns: *similiter cadens* (homoioteleuton), assonance, **ALLITERATION**, polyptoton.... Though these figures of sound are statistically the most frequent, the balance or paralleling of assertions ... seems to be most basic to the style pattern and to reflect very closely the thought habits underlying it" (Duhamel, 1948). Williamson (1951), following Croll and Clemons (1916), adds, as a second essential aspect of Euphuism, the constant use of simile. **ANTITHESIS** is a third characteristic. The opposition of Euphuism to **CICERO-NIANISM**, especially to periodicity, is clear. Two examples taken from Toor (1966) follow: the first from Alfred's translation of Boethius' *De Consolatione Philosophiae* (together with Toor's analysis); the second from Lyly's *Euphues and His England*.

Alfred: "A fairly elaborate pattern is maintained through the following excerpt that appears early in the work: 'Ic wende þ ic þe geo gelæred hæfde þ þu hi oncnawan cuðe, 7 ic wisse þ þu hi onscunedest ða ða þu hi hæfdest, ðeah þu hiora bruce. Ic wisse þæt ðu mine cwidas wið hiora willan oft sædest, ac ic wat þ nan gewuna ne mæg nanum men bion unwended þ þ mod ne sy be sumū dæle onstyred.' The first sentence contains two balancing clauses, the first beginning 'Ic wende,' and the other 'ic wisse.' This pattern is repeated in the next sentence beginning 'Ic wisse,' while the second clause starts 'ic wat.' These introductory phrases are followed in each instance by the same conjunctions and then similar parts of speech: 'Ic wende þ ic/ic wisse þ þu/Ic wisse þæt ðu/ic wat þ nan.' The first sentence as well uses initial vowel repetition in 'þu hi *o*ncnawan . . . þu hi *o*nscunedest,' and the second sentence uses fairly subtle alliteration: '*c*widas,' '*w*illan,' and '*g*ewuna.'"

Lyly: "Blessed is that Land, that hath all commodities to encrease the common wealth, happye is that Islande that hath wise counsailours to maintaine it, vertuous courtiers to beautifie it, noble Gentle-menne to aduance it, but to haue suche a Prince to gouerne it, as is their Soueraigne queene, I know not whether I should thinke the people to be more fortunate, or the Prince famous, whether their felicitie be more to be had in admiration, that haue such a ruler, or hir vertues to be honoured, that hath such royaltie."

Croll in effect argues that Euphuism follows the **GORGIAN-ISOCRATIC** tradi-tion, which he traces through medieval literature in Latin, where the Gorgianic schemes became the main, often the only, resource for adornment and heightening discourse. A more recent study has confirmed Croll's placement of Euphuism in an ancient classical tradition: Toor (1966) has shown that Euphuism made its first appearance in the earliest literary prose in the English language, based on classical-rhetorical models (especially the **SCHEMES**). The following passage from Ascham's *Toxophilus* illustrates most of the devices of the style (I have arranged the excerpt to dramatize the schematic arrangement and balancing devices):

My mind is, in profiting and pleasing every man,
                  to hurt or displease no man,
    intending none other purpose,
    but that youth might be stirred to labor,
                        honest pastime,
                        and virtue,
    and as much as lieth in me, plucked from idleness,
                        unthrifty games,
                        and vice:
which thing I have labored only in this book,
showing how fit shooting is for all kinds of men;
    how honest a pastime for the mind;
    how wholesom as exercise for the body;
    not vile for great men to use,
    not costly for poor men to sustain,

not lurking in holes and corners for ill men at their pleasure to misuse it,
but abiding in the open sight and face of the world,
for good men, if at fault, by their wisdom to correct it.

EXPRESSIONISM Part of the revolt against **REALISM** by dislocation and distortion of normal time sequence and of the objects and events of the outer world, for example, Joyce's *Ulysses* and *Finnegans Wake*.

FAMILIAR ESSAY Two primary traditions, after Montaigne and after Bacon, have constituted the genre. Montaigne's essays are usually described as friendly, personal, informal writing about any subject, but especially having to do with the inner man and his response to experiences of all sorts. *Essai* means "trying or experiencing a thing," and Montaigne's *Essais* of 1580 generally present Montaigne exploring himself: "I am myself the subject of my book." The other tradition, associated with Bacon's *Essays* (the first ten published in 1580), reflects upon life derived from experience or learning, especially from the Romans Cicero and Seneca and from the Bible, in an **APHORISTIC** style. The self hardly comes in. Bacon's purpose is to instruct rather than entertain, so that his tone is usually impersonal and didactic, stately and authoritative, compared to Montaigne's. See Dobrée (1946) and Walker (1966).

FIGURES OF SPEECH Language which departs from what is generally understood to be the standard construction or meaning. The rhetoricians called these **SCHEMES** (deviations from the ordinary, SVO arrangement of words: anastrophe, **ANTITHESIS**, and so on) and **TROPES** (deviations from the ordinary signification of a word: metaphor, hyperbole, and the like).

FIGURISTS One of the three Renaissance schools of rhetoric; focused primarily on the study of **SCHEMES** and **TROPES**. See **RAMISTS** and **TRADITIONALISTS**.

FORENSIC One of the three kinds of persuasive discourse (see **DELIBERATIVE** [1] and **EPIDEICTIC**), also called *legal* or *judicial*, in which a person seeks to defend or condemn someone's actions, for example, Newman's *Apologia Pro Vita Sua*.

GEORGIAN [1] Relating to the reigns of the four Georges (1714-1830) and covering a wide range of prose writers in the novel, from Defoe to Scott. [2] A period adjective which became current within a year or two of the accession of George V in 1910 and which refers to the half-decade preceding World War I. Some prose writers of the period are Conrad (*Victory*, 1915) and Galsworthy (*The Patrician*, 1911).

GNOMIC Relating to the **SENTENTIOUS** and **APHORISTIC** treatment of ethical questions. "The Healthy know not of their Health, but only the sick" (Carlyle, *Characteristics*).

GONGORISM Derived from Gongora, a Spanish poet (d. 1627). An intricate, highly affected style full of neologisms, **PUNS, PARADOXES, CONCEITS**, and inversions of word order.

GORGIAN Derived from Gorgias, an ancient Greek, the father of a style which can become exceedingly artificial; composed of elaborations of **ANTITHESES** and **PARALLELISMS**, accentuated by excesses of **ALLITERATION** and assonance and by boldness in **FIGURES OF SPEECH** and imagery. Ancestor of **EUPHUISM**. "Shameful was your sowing, baneful was your reaping" (revealing Gorgias' use of poetic metaphor, alliteration, balanced antithesis, and close parallelism in sound). See Kennedy (1963) and Denniston (1952).

GOTHIC Relating to a type of novel, inaugurated by Walpole's *Castle of Otranto* (1764), in which the aim is to exploit terror. Other novels in the genre are

Radcliffe's *The Mysteries of Adolpho* (1794) and Lewis's *The Monk* (1797). In style, *gothic* is often used to refer to anticlassical expression, that is, extravagant, wild, free, primitive expression.

GRAND   Relating to a kind of style. One way to approach this elusive term is through the ancient doctrine of the three "characters" of style: low, middle, and lofty. See Staton (1958).

GREAT VOWEL SHIFT   The change in the pronunciation of the complex vowels of English that took place during the sixteenth and seventeenth centuries.

HEAD   One of the two *Immediate* **CONSTITUENTS** of a structure of modification, the other being a **MODIFIER**. The head is that member of such a structure which can perform by itself the syntactic function performed by the whole structure without radical alteration of the lexical meaning of the whole.

HOPPING   Relating to **SENECAN** or **POINTED** style; brief, condensed sentences, full of points, aphorisms, antitheses, and asymmetry. See **LIPSIUS**.

HYPOTAXIS   The subordinate or dependent arrangement or relationship of clauses, phrases, and so on. Opposed to **PARATAXIS**. English syntax has developed broadly from a predominantly paratactical order to a hypotactical order, tending in the extreme to produce the dense texture of Henry James's later prose. "There was at last, with everything that made for it, an occasion when he got from Kate, on what she now spoke of as his eternal refrain, an answer of which he was to measure afterwards the precipitating effect" (*The Wings of the Dove*).

IDIOMATIC   Relating to a style characterized by expressions peculiar to a particular language and not readily translatable from its grammatical construction or the meaning of its component parts. "The kid came out and had to kill five bulls because you can't have more than three matadors, and the last bull he was so tired he couldn't get the sword in. He couldn't hardly lift his arm" (Hemingway, *Tender Buttons*).

IMMEDIATE CONSTITUENT   See **CONSTITUENT**.

INDENTURE   H. Brown's (1966) term for the style of legal documents and private formal messages, in which the sentence is stretched to include the whole content of the document.

INKHORN TERM   A phrase applied contemptuously in Elizabethan times to learned words newly coined or brought into English from other languages, especially from Latin. "Pondering, *expending*, and *revoluting* with my selfe, your *ingent affabilitie*, and *ingenious capacity* for *mundane* affairs: I cannot but *celebrate* and *extol* your *magnificat dexteritie* above all other" (quoted by Thomas Wilson in his *Arte of Rhetorique* [1553] as an example of new words in his day).

INVENTIO   The first part of classical **RHETORIC**; the method of finding arguments and generating ideas to support a case or point of view. According to Aristotle, there were two kinds of persuasion: (1) the nonartistic, which did not require invention, such as laws, witnesses, and contracts; and (2) the artistic. Again according to Aristotle, there were three types of artistic persuasion: (1) rational (*logos*); (2) emotional (*pathos*); and (3) ethical (*ethos*). Furthermore, Aristotle devised the "topics" (Greek *topoi*) to aid the speaker in discovering content for the three modes of persuasion. The *topic* was a storehouse on a given subject, providing aids to developing a line of argument.

ISOCOLON   A type of **PARALLELISM** having corresponding members—phrases, clauses, sentences—of equal length. "The vulgar, who are not in the secret, will admire the look of preternatural health and vigor; and the fashionable, who regard only appearances, will be delighted with the imposition" (Hazlitt, "On Familiar Style").

ISOCRATIC   Derived from Isocrates, one of the most influential of Greek rhetoricians.   He developed an artistic prose style based on the **ANTITHESIS** and **PARALLELISM** of Gorgias (see **GORGIAN**), but stressing the **PERIODIC** sentence more, to which Cicero (see **CICERONIANISM**) was indebted.   While Gorgias relied on striking words and phrases (through **ALLITERATION**, assonance, and metaphor), Isocrates subordinated individual words and clauses to a larger unity.   "Yes, and I so impressed my hearers by my statement of the case that not one of them thought of applauding my oratory or the finish and the purity of my style, as some are wont to do, but instead they marvelled at the truth of my arguments, and were convinced that only on certain conditions could you and the Athenians be made to cease from your contentious rivalry" (Isocrates, "To Philip").   See Nordin's Introduction to Isocrates' *Orations*, 3 vols.   (Loeb Classical Library, Cambridge, Mass.).

JACOBEAN   Relating to the reign of James ("Jacobus") I (1603–1625).   Important prose of the period: Bacon, Donne, the King James translation of the Bible.
JUNCTURE   The connection or transition between utterances or parts of utterances, as between sounds, syllables, words, phrases, and sentences.   Modern English is considered to have four junctures: (1) open (or plus) juncture, a slight pause between syllables or words, as in the different pronunciation of "nitrates" and "night rates," symbolized by the + sign; and three terminal junctures (2) rising ↗, (3) falling ↘, and (4) level →.

KERNEL   In generative-transformational grammar, relating to a nonderived sentence (a basic simple sentence), as "The girl sat down" and "The girl is pretty."   "The pretty girl sat down," derived from the other two sentences, is called a *transform*.   See **TRANSFORMATIONAL GRAMMAR**, **SURFACE STRUCTURE**, and **MATRIX**.   See Craddock (1968) for an analysis of the kernel sentences and transforms of the historians Robertson and Gibbon.

LIBERTINISM   Croll's (1914) label for the neo-Stoic philosophical base of **ANTI-CICERONIANISM** or the **ATTIC** style.
LIPSIUS   "The standard-bearer of **SENECAN** style" (see "Lipsius: His Hopping Style" in Williamson, 1951).   "To conclude, let them understand I have written many other things for others; but this book chiefly for my self; the former for fame, but this for profit.   That which one heretofore said bravely and acutely; the same I now truly proclaim.   To me a few Readers are enough, one is enough, none is enough.   All that I desire is, that whosoever opens this book, may bring with him a disposition to profit, and also to pardon" (Lipsius, *De Constantia*).
LOOSE   Relating, generally, to the "cumulative" sentence, a structure which is grammatically complete before the end of the sentence, such as an independent clause followed by a dependent clause.   It is basically construction by addition and modification to and following the main clause.   "The typical sentence of modern English" (Christensen, 1967).   Croll (1929) divided **BAROQUE**, and Williamson (1951) **SENECAN**, into **CURT** and **LOOSE**.

MARIVAUDAGE   Derived from the eighteenth-century novelist and playwright Pierre de Marivaux; a style characterized by psychological subtlety and stylistic elegance approaching affectation.   James and Faulkner often illustrate this type of writing.
MATRIX   The basic sentence, traditionally called an *independent clause*, is called a matrix by most transformationalists.   See **DEEP STRUCTURE** and **TRANSFORMATIONAL GRAMMAR**.

METALINGUISTICS   The linguistic study concerned with the interrelationship of linguistic and other cultural factors in a society.

METAPHYSICAL   Relating to a kind of style.   Umbach (1945) describes Donne's metaphysical style as the "frequent use of strange figures of rhetoric," the "ingenious straining after wit," the "exaggerated importance given to certain words and expressions," the "packing of authorities," and the "numerous, sometimes illogical, and often unnecessarily detailed divisions and sub-divisions."   See Webber (1965) for a quite different description of the metaphysical style of Andrewes.

MIDDLE ENGLISH   Spoken and written English in the period following the Norman Conquest and preceding the Early Modern period beginning with the Renaissance.   The approximate dates most commonly given are 1100–1500.   The period is often divided into Early (1066–1350) and Late (1350–1500).   Notable prose of the period includes voyages (Mandeville's *Travels*), the Wycliffe translation of the Bible, and romances (Malory's *Le Morte d'Arthur*).

MODIFIER   One of the **CONSTITUENTS** of a structure of modification, the other being the **HEAD**.   The head can be identified as the element which can be substituted for the whole structure.

MORPHEME   The basic unit of meaning in any language.   Late Modern English has three kinds of morphemes: (1) free word simple (*Dick, cow*); (2) bound syllabic (the *-ly* of *quickly*); and (3) bound phonemic (the /z/ of *boy's*.   See **PHONEME** and **STRING**.

NATIVE TRADITION   See the selection by Gordon in Chapter I of this volume. Here is a different view: "The simple colloquial or aggregative sentence, with sprawling members, loosely connected by temporal and co-ordinating conjunctions, unemphatic in effect.   It uses the simplest kind of amplification—cataloguing, the heaping of synonyms, words of similar meaning, or phrases of similar construction; for oral ornament it employs alliteration and synonymous wordpairs.   It was essentially a polysyndetic and highly co-ordinated style.   In a more disciplined form the English Bible transmits, through Tyndale, the native tradition of prose as shaped in the fifteenth century" (Williamson, 1951).   R. W. Chambers (1932) traces the native tradition—in his view, the primary English style—back to Alfred.   Krapp (1915) traces the development of artistic or schematic prose out of the native tradition from Wycliffe to Bacon.   See **LOOSE**.

NATURALISM   A literary tradition usually used in criticism of the novel, represented by Guy de Maupassant, Theodore Dreiser, and Eugene O'Neill and characterized by an inclusiveness of subject and a scientific, detached, and impersonal tone.   It closely resembles **REALISM**, but it tends to concentrate more on the sordid and to present life deterministically.

NEO-CLASSICAL   Relating to prose written between Dryden and Dr. Johnson (Addison, Swift, Goldsmith, and so on).   In style, connotes polish and refinement.

NOMINAL   "Linguists distinguish 'nominal' from 'verbal' styles.   Nominal style is more impersonal, more esoteric or technical, and has fewer clauses and complex sentences and less variety of sentence patterns. . . .   In a nominal style the verbs are chiefly operative, mere markers to indicate distinctions and logical processes to the reader" (Adolph, 1968).   See Wells (1960).   See **VERBAL**.

NOUN CLUSTER   A noun with its modifiers.   See **CONSTITUENT**.

ORGANIC   Relating to a style derived from the nature of the work's subject or the disposition of the author, rather than from rules externally imposed. Twentieth-century prose is particularly notable for its unity of style and content, the reflection of the subject in the style, as in Joyce's *Ulysses* and Faulkner's *The Sound and the Fury*.   But the technique is not absent in the literature of the past, even in nonfiction prose. See, for example, Houghton (1945) for an analysis of passages from Newman as expressions of "felt experience" or Sister Schuster (1955) for an explanation of the appropriateness of the individual styles of More and Bacon to their particular philosophies of life. Brooks and Warren (1959) point out that Hemingway's sentence structure in "The Killers" reflects not only the characters and the immediate situation but also "a dislocated and ununified world."

ORNATE   Relating to the following types of style: **CICERONIANISM, EUPHU-ISM, BAROQUE**, and **GOTHIC**. The characteristics are **SCHEMATIC PARAL-LISM**, cadenced **ANTITHESIS**, verbal elaboration and elegance, packed **WIT**, **SENTENTIOUS** manner, and expressiveness. Writers in the ornate tradition are Berners, North, Lyly, Donne, Browne, Taylor, Milton, Gibbon, Johnson, Burke, Landor, De Quincey, Ruskin, Pater, Santayana, Woolf, Thomas, Faulkner, and Joyce.

PARADOX   A rhetorical device in which a seemingly contradictory or absurd statement is actually true; a common element in the verbal ingenuity of **POINTED** prose.

PARALLELISM   A type of **BALANCE** in which similar thoughts are similarly structured in a pair or series of related words, phrases, or clauses; the setting forth of equivalent things in coordinate grammatical structure. The three types, in order of increasing parallelism, are **ISOCOLON, PARISON**, and **PAROMO-ION**. See **ANTITHESIS**. Parallelism and antithesis constitute the main characteristics of **SCHEMATIC** or **EUPHUISTIC** prose.

PARATAXIS   The independent arrangement of clauses and phrases without connectives. Opposed to **HYPOTAXIS**. See **ASYNDETON**.

PARISON   A type of **PARALLELISM** making corresponding members syntactically parallel, with each word in one member answering to a corresponding word in the other. "When they desire to borrow, they employ the base and supplicating style of the slave in the comedy; but when they are called upon to pay, they assume the royal and tragic declamation of the grandsons of Hercules" (Gibbon, *The Decline and Fall*).

PAROMOION   A type of **PARALLELISM** in which there is a similarity of sound between words or syllables. Special types: like endings (homoioteleuton); like beginnings (**ALLITERATION**); repetition of words with inversion (antimetabole); likeness of words with difference of meaning (paronomasia); repetition of the same stem with a different inflexion (polyptoton). According to Williamson (1951), paromoion was "the essential feature" of **EUPHUISM**. "Ye rise for religion: what religion taught you that? If ye were offered persecution for religion, ye ought to flee; so Christ teacheth you, and yet you intend to fight. If ye would stand in the truth, ye ought to suffer like martyrs; and ye would slay like tyrants. Thus for religion ye keep no religion; and neither will follow the counsel of Christ, nor the constancy of martyrs" (Sir John Cheke, *The Hurt of Sedition*).

PERIOD   According to Croll, the grammatical term *sentence* and the rhetorical term *period* are identical. "Period names the rhetorical, or oral, aspect of the same thing that is called in grammar a sentence; and in theory the same act of composition that produces a perfectly logical grammatical unit of sound. But, in fact, no utterance ever fulfils both of these functions perfectly, and either one or the other of them is always foremost in a writer's mind" (Croll, 1929).

PERIODIC   Relating to a sentence in which the sense is delayed until almost the end. "It was partly at such junctures as these and partly at quite different ones that with the turn my matters had now taken, my predicament, as I have called it, grew most sensible" (Henry James). See **CICERONIANISM**.

PHONEME   The minimum unit of distinctive sound in a language, functioning to

distinguish utterances from one another. The English phonemes /d/ and /b/
distinguish the words *dig* and *big*. See **MORPHEME**.

PHONEMICS   A phonemic system or the study of phonemic systems.

PHONETICS   The branch of linguistics dealing with the analysis, description, and
classification of speech sounds, including the physiological processes and the physical attributes.   The system of sounds in a language, more finely described than
the **PHONEMES**.

PHONOLOGY   **PHONEMICS** and **PHONETICS** taken together. The history of
the sound changes that have occurred in the evolution of a language.

PLAIN   Relating to a type of style.   "The English Plain Style existed before Wyclif
and continues beyond Bunyan, still running concurrently with the 'artificial' and
'unnatural' writing which makes up the history of English literary prose. Merchants, artisans, seamen, farmers, scholars; letters, accounts of transaction, descriptions of travels, instructions and practical and moral advice.   All these
furnish examples of sincere, more or less lucid communication of information and
misinformation, request, order, and opinion which make plain style prose 'the
great intellectual machine of civil life'" (Coleman, 1962). Plain style is so much a
matter of degree and comparison that it cannot be defined properly in a short
space. In general, it is a style relatively free of metaphor, simile, hyperbole,
ANTITHESIS, PUN, and all the host of rhetorical **FIGURES OF SPEECH**. It is
Tillotson in contrast to Donne. Tillotson: "The principles of religion, the belief
of a God and another life: by obliging men to be virtuous, do really promote
their temporal happiness. And all the privilege that atheism pretends to, is to
let men loose to vice, which is naturally attended with temporal inconveniences."
Donne: "Poor intricated soule! Riddleing, perplexed, labyrinthicall soule! Thou
couldest not say, that thou beleevest not in God, if there were not God; thou
couldest not beleeve in God, if there were not God; if there were no God, thou
couldest not speak, thou couldest not thinke, not a word, not a thought, no not
against God . . ." (the sentence continues for several more lines). It is a style, then,
which chooses simplicity over ornament.   But observe the triads and even a
quadruple in this famous sentence from Sprat's *History of the Royal Society*, one
of the greatest of all plain-style manifestos: "They have exacted from all their members a close, naked, natural way of speaking, positive expressions, clear senses,
a native easiness, bringing all things as near the mathematical plainness ... and
preferring the language of artisans, countrymen, and merchants before that of
wits or scholars."   See **NATIVE TRADITION** and the Introduction to this
volume.

POINTED   Related to the **SENECAN** or **ATTIC** style; compact and pregnant. See
CURT and **BAROQUE**.

POLYSYNDETON   A classical **SCHEME**, the repetition of connectives or conjunctions. See **ASYNDETON**. "The car was going a wild forty-five miles an hour
across the open *and* as Macomber watched, the buffalo got bigger *and* bigger until
he could see the gray, hairless, scabby look of one huge bull *and* how his neck was
a part of his shoulders *and* the shiny black of his horns as he galloped a little
behind the others that were strung out in that steady plunging gait; *and* then . . . ."
(Hemingway, "The Short Happy Life of Francis Macomber"). Polysyndeton is an
element in the historical continuity of the sentence: "Another characteristic of
Old English syntax is a fondness for clauses linked together by the conjunction
and" (Brook, 1964). 1100: "þa stod Drihtnes engel wiþ hig, *and* Godes beorhtnes
him ymbescean; *and* hi him mycelum ege adredon." 1380: "*And* loo! the aungel
of the Lord stood by sydis hem, *and* the clerenesse of God schynede aboute hem;
and thei dredden with greet drede." 1750: "*And* behold an angel of the Lord stood

by them *and* the brightness of God shone round about them: *and* they feared with a great fear." See the selection by Gordon in Chapter I of this volume.

PROPHETIC H. Brown's (1966) label for two stylistic varieties: *coupé* (**CURT** or terse) and *décousu* (copious or **LOOSE**). Brown describes the curt style as **SENTENTIOUS, PARADOXICAL**, brief, concentrated, sometimes disjointed, elliptical, and metaphorical. Some of the writers he cites as belonging to the curt style are the authors of the Prophetic books of the Bible, Seneca, Bacon, Emerson, Arnold Bennett, Lamb, and Carlyle. As loose writers, he cites Browne, Montaigne, Burton, Lamb, Carlyle, Browning, Meredith, Wyndham Lewis, and Joyce. His arguments and examples should be carefully compared with those of Williamson (1951) and Croll (1929). Williamson treats Brown's two types as two aspects of the **SENECAN** style; Croll calls the two **BAROQUE**.

PUN A classical **TROPE**, a play on words, characteristic of **POINTED** prose, especially antanaclasis (repetition of a word in two different senses) and paronomasia (words alike in sound but different in meaning).

PURITAN (COMMONWEALTH) Relating to the period from the end of the Civil War in 1649 to the Restoration in 1660. Notable prose writers were Browne, Fuller, Milton, and Walton.

RAMISTS Derived from Peter Ramus, notable in the history of classical **RHET-ORIC** for his effort to reduce rhetoric to style and delivery and to transfer invention and disposition to the sphere of logic as part of his advocacy of the **PLAIN** style. The Ramists constituted the third main group of Renaissance rhetoricians. See **FIGURISTS** and **TRADITIONALISTS**.

REALISM Howells described the aim of realism as the truthful, neutral depiction of life, in harmony with the scientific spirit. More specifically, realism is the employment of infinite detail to convey the natural, everyday happenings of people's lives. See **NATURALISM** and **EXPRESSIONISM**.

REGIONALISM The speech variety, as distinct from dialect, of a language, which does not hinder communication or necessitate the adoption of a spoken standard. Appalachian is a regionalism of American English.

RENAISSANCE In England, the sixteenth century primarily. See **ELIZA-BETHAN**.

REPETITION The classical **SCHEME** of reiterating or rephrasing a word or phrase for emphasis. Much of the power of prose depends on the repetition of important words, phrases, images, and metaphors in the same or a different context. **ANAPHORA** is one among many schemes of repetition. In a larger context, a writer writes for a reader able to make imaginative connections, to see one incident in the terms of another, so that each scene comes to have a cumulative as well as an immediate significance.

RESTORATION The period from the restoration of the Stuart line (Charles II) to the English throne in 1660 at the end of the Commonwealth (see **PURITAN**) until the end of the seventeenth century. Major prose writers were Dryden, Pepys, and Temple.

RHETORIC The word derives ultimately from the Greek *rhēma* (a word) and *rhētor* (a teacher of oratory) and immediately from the French *rhetorique*. The art of rhetoric—the use and manipulation of words—was formulated in fifth-century Greece. For long periods, it was the central discipline in schools; and it lasted as a vital school subject until sometime in the nineteenth century. It has always been associated primarily with the art of persuasive discourse and divided, mainly for pedagogical reasons, into five parts: inventio, dispositio, elocutio, memoria, and pronuntiatio. See **INVENTIO, DISPOSITIO, ELOCUTIO, TROPE**, and **SCHEME**.

whereby an artist urges his material into form more continuously and perhaps at a deeper level than by the conscious employment of stylistic devices. Not that one can divorce syntax from other stylistic categories. Many of the formal rhetorical schemes (asyndeton, anaphora, and the like) belong explicitly to the domain of syntax; they are methods of arranging words, and are so labeled by traditional analysts. A metaphor, any image, must assume *some* syntactic embodiment. Vocabulary itself not merely conforms to syntactic patterns, it often dictates them; and concern with syntax will on occasion prove identical with concern for grammar. Nevertheless, to read for syntax is to alert oneself to something distinct: the ways an author yokes his phrases together or splits them apart; the size, shape, and texture of the phrases themselves; the kinds he shuns as well as those he prefers, the degrees of likeness or unlikeness among them."

TACITUS   First translated into English in 1591, Tacitus was (along with Seneca—see **SENECAN**) one of the models of **ANTI-CICERONIANISM**: abruptly terse, brief to the point of obscurity. "In general, the curt Senecan style is an essay style marked by the cultivation of brevity, staccato form, and point; its rhythm is spasmodic: in particular, the Tacitean variety is an extreme development of this style" (Williamson, 1951). Adolph (1968) devotes a full chapter to an analysis of Tacitus' style. See **CURT** and **ATTIC**.

TRADITIONALISTS   One of the three schools of rhetoric during the Renaissance; emphasized the full five parts of rhetoric: invention, arrangement, style, memory, and delivery. See **FIGURISTS** and **RAMISTS**.

TRANSFORMATIONAL GRAMMAR   A theory treating most sentences as derivations of more basic sentences, with rules for deriving them. See **KERNEL, DEEP STRUCTURE,** and **SURFACE STRUCTURE.**

TROPE   Derived from the Greek *tropein* (to turn). One of the two classical types of **FIGURES OF SPEECH** in classical **RHETORIC** (see **SCHEME**): a deviation from the ordinary and principal signification of a word, a transference of meaning, for example, irony and metaphor.

ULTIMATE CONSTITUENT   See **CONSTITUENT.**

VERBAL   "In the verbal style . . . verbs are descriptive or, more rarely, evaluative, imperative, or interjections. They are affected by their contexts. . . . The verbal descriptive style will contain more complex sentences and subordinate qualifying elements expressing the point of view of the speaker" (Adolph, 1968). See **NOMINAL.**

VERB CLUSTER   A verb with its modifiers. See **CONSTITUENT.**

VICTORIAN   Relating to the reign of Queen Victoria (1837–1901), according to some; others date the period from the First Reform Bill (1832). The subtitle of Houghton's *The Victorian Frame of Mind: 1830–1870* indicates still another dating. Notable novelists of the period are Dickens, Eliot, Thackeray, Meredith, and Hardy. Nonfiction writers include Newman, Arnold, Ruskin, and Pater.

WIT   Verbal banter and word-play; characteristic of **POINTED** prose. See **PARADOX.**

BIBLIOGRAPHY
BY PERIOD

(**For full bibliographical data, see the Annotated Bibliography.**)

I. **General Studies** Aurner (1923b), Bailey and Burton (1968), Baugh (1967), Bloomfield and Newark (1963), Boulton, M. (1954), Bridgman (1966), Brook (1964), Brownell (1914), Burke, V. M. (1968), Coleman (1962), Conley (1966), Corbett (1965), Craik (1893–1896), Denniston (1952), Earle (1891), Enkvist *et al.* (1964), Francis, J. H. (1957), Frye (1947), Gerwig (1894), Gordon (1966), Graves and Hodge (1943), Highet (1949), Howes (1961), Jespersen (1894, 1948, 1949), Kellner (1892), Lewis (1894), Mellinkoff (1963), Milic (1966, 1967a, 1967c), Nist (1966), Poirier (1966), Potter (1965), Read (1928), Robertson and Cassidy (1954), Saintsbury (1892, 1912), Schlauch (1955, 1964), Scott (1910), Scott and Chandler (1932), Sherman (1888, 1892, 1893), Sprott (1955), Sutherland (1957), Tempest (1939), Thompson, J. A. K. (1956), Vallins (1957), Warburg (1965), Wright (1898–1905).

II. **From Alfred to More** Andrew (1940), Aurner (1923a), Baldwin (1928), Bennett H. S. (1945), Bennett, J. R. (1968a), Bethurum (1932a, 1932b, 1935, 1957), Chambers, R. W. (1932), Clark, C. (1968), Clark, D. L. (1959), Clark, J. W. (1964), Davis, N. (1955, 1961), Greenfield (1965), Hargreaves (1966), Humbert (1944), Krapp (1915), McKeon (1952), Morgan, M. M. (1952–1953), Muir (1935), Nichols, A. E. (1965a), Prins (1952), Schlauch (1950, 1952), Stone (1963), Toor (1966), Visser (1963, 1966), Wilson, H. P. (1956), Wilson, R. M. (1959), Workman (1940), Wyld (1936), Zeeman (1955, 1956).

III. **From More to Milton** Adolph (1968), Allen, D. C. (1948), Allen, W. S. (1963), Atwood (1965), Auerbach (1953), Baldwin (1939), Barish (1956, 1958, 1960), Bland (1957), Bowers (1968), Bowman (1964), Brooke (1967), Browne (1961), Bryan (1968), Burke, P. B. (1967), Challis (1965), Clark, D. L. (1951), Cleaveland (1911), Cope (1956), Craig, H. (1936), Crane, M. (1951), Crane, W. G. (1937), Croll (1914, 1921, 1923, 1924, 1929), Croll and Clemons (1916), Doherty (1965), Duhamel (1948), Dunn (1956), Fisch (1952), Grainger (1907), Harkness (1918), Hendrickson (1905), Highet (1949), Howell (1946), Joseph (1947), Kaula (1966), King, J. R. (1956), King, W. N. (1955), Krapp (1915), Lowes (1936), MacDonald (1943), Mandeville (1961), Matthiessen (1931), Miller (1939), Mitchell (1932), Moloney (1959), Morgan, E. (1951), Oliver (1945), Ong (1958,

251

form of the English prose structure in the translation of the Authorized Version."

Allott, Kenneth, and Miriam Allott, eds. 1956. *Victorian Prose 1830–1880.* The Pelican Book of English Prose, Vol. V. London. "Introduction."

Andrew, S. O. 1940. *Syntax and Style in Old English.* Cambridge. Distinguishes three different kinds of order for Old English—common order, conjunctive order, and demonstrative order—the difference consisting in the presence or absence of a conjunction or a demonstrative pronoun. Ch. 11 seeks to show that the supposed "paratactic" structure of Old English, whether in prose or verse, is an illusion.

Antrim, Harry T. 1965. "Faulkner's Suspended Style," *UR,* XXXII, 122–128. "What we might call Faulkner's 'suspended style' is a way of showing the possibility inherent in any given instant, and the style's parentheses, negations, recapitulations, and qualifications are indicative of an attempt to show how the past, continually shifting and changing in the re-creation, nonetheless proceeds inexorably to a qualification and conditioning of the present."

Atkins, John. 1952. *The Art of Ernest Hemingway: His Work and Personality.* London and New York. Ch. 4, "That Famous Style."

Atwood, Norman. 1965. "The Influence of Ancient, Medieval, and Early Renaissance Stylistic Theory and Practice Concerning Prose upon the Style of *The Hurt of Sedition* (1549) by Sir John Cheke." *DA,* XXIX, 252A, Columbia University. Contemporaries would have found his style "a noble attempt to regain for English oratory the lost province of the Ciceronian high style."

Auerbach, Erich. 1953. *Mimesis: The Representation of Reality in Western Literature.* Princeton. Ch. 13 analyzes Shakespeare's use of mixed styles in *Henry IV,* Part 2. Ch. 20 analyzes a piece of narrative prose from the fifth section of Part 1 in Virginia Woolf's *To the Lighthouse.*

Aurner, R. R. 1923a. *Caxton and the English Sentence.* Wisconsin Studies in Language and Literature, No. 18, 23–59. "His prefaces and epilogues are composed of long masses of structure which are rambling, unorganized, loose, and formless to the last degree."

    1923b. "The History of Certain Aspects of the Structure of the English Sentence," *PQ,* II, 187–208. Aurner employs an elaborate system of clausal-phrasal notation supported by diagrams and figures in discussing Caxton, Lyly, Bacon, Dryden, Addison, Johnson, and Macaulay.

Axton, William F. 1962. "Dramatic Style in Dickens' Novels." *DA,* XXII, 2788–2789, Princeton University. A stylistic study of Dickens' "theatricality."

Babb, Howard S. 1962. *Jane Austen's Novels: The Fabric of Dialogue.* Columbus. Ch. 1, "Jane Austen's Style: The Climate of the Dialogues."

Bailey, Richard W., and Dolores M. Burton. 1968. *English Stylistics: A Bibliography.* Cambridge, Mass. Reviewed by Louis Milic, *Style,* II (1968), 239–243.

Bailey, Richard W., and Lubomír Doležel. 1968. *An Annotated Bibliography of Statistical Stylistics.* Ann Arbor.

Baker, William E. 1967. *Syntax in English Poetry, 1870–1930.* Berkeley.

Baldanza, Frank. 1959. "Faulkner and Stein: A Study in Stylistic Intransigence," *GR,* XIII, 274–286. Comparing *Absalom, Absalom!* and *The Making of Americans,* Baldanza finds "arresting" the "profound similarity of many of their stylistic devices."

    1961. "D. H. Lawrence's Song of Songs," *MFS,* VII, 106–114. On Biblical rhythms in Lawrence's prose.

Baldwin, Charles Sears. 1928. *Medieval Rhetoric and Poetic.* London and New

York. Presents the salient tendencies and the actual theory and practice of composition to 1400.

1939. *Renaissance Literary Theory and Practice*. New York. Takes up the history of rhetoric and poetic where his 1928 volume left off and carries it to 1600. Ch. 3, "Imitation of Prose Forms, Ciceronianism, Rhetorics."

Barber, C. L. 1962. "Some Measurable Characteristics of Modern Scientific Prose," *Contributions to English Syntax and Philology*. Goteborg.

Barfield, Owen. 1967. *History in English Words*. Rev. ed. Grand Rapids.

Barish, Jonas A. 1956. "The Prose Style of John Lyly," *ELH*, XXIII, 14–35. Highly critical of Croll's (Introduction to Croll and Clemons, 1916) excessive emphasis on Lyly's devices of sound-design and of his understanding of Lyly's use of antithesis. Disagrees with Williamson's (1951) positing of two styles in Lyly ("schematic" and "pointed") by emphasizing the essential unity in *Euphues* and Lyly's dramatic prose through the basic logicality of his style.

1958. "Baroque Prose in the Theater: Ben Jonson," *PMLA*, LXXIII, 184–195. Revised as Ch. 2 in his book on Jonson.

*1960. *Ben Jonson and the Language of Prose Comedy*. Cambridge, Mass. Employs Croll's (1929) categories in describing Jonson's Senecan style.

Barnett, George L. 1964. *Charles Lamb: The Evolution of Elia*. Bloomington. A study of "the development of the essays through the stages of expression of the thoughts."

Baugh, Albert C. 1967. *A History of the English Language*. 2nd ed. New York.

Baugh, Albert C., *et al*. 1967. *A Literary History of England*. 2nd ed. New York.

Baum, Paull. 1952. *The Other Harmony of Prose: An Essay in English Prose Rhythm*. Durham, N.C.

Beach, Joseph W. 1926. *The Outlook for American Prose*. Chicago. Discussion of the faults and virtues of writers of the 1920's. Modern prose is generally criticized for sloppiness.

Beaumont, Charles A. 1961. *Swift's Classical Rhetoric*. Monograph No. 8. University of Georgia. Demonstrates that Swift "relied almost exclusively upon classical rhetoric as a means of creating the ironies of his essays of total ironic inversion."

Beck, Warren. 1934. "The Real Language of Men: Note on an Aspect of the Modern Short Story," *EJ*, XXIII, 731–739. Brief comment on the "one fresh aspect of the modern short story, its noticeably simple diction and style."

Bellamy, Gladys C. 1950. *Mark Twain as a Literary Artist*. Norman, Okla. Ch. 15 examines principally the travel books "because in them Mark Twain speaks in his own person."

Benstock, Bernard. 1965. *Joyce-Again's Wake: An Analysis of "Finnegans Wake."* Seattle.

Bennett, H. S. 1945. "Fifteenth Century Secular Prose," *RES*, XXI, 257–263. Qualifying R. W. Chambers' (1932) stress on religious and homiletic prose as the chief instruments of continuity, Bennett claims for secular prose an important place in the development of the main English tradition of the clear and easy plain style.

Bennett, James R. 1968a. "English Prose Style from Alfred to More: A Bibliography," *MS*, XXX, 248–259.

1968b. "Style in Twentieth Century British and American Fiction: A Bibliography," *WCR*, II, 43–51.

*Bennett, Joan. 1941. "An Aspect of the Evolution of Seventeenth-Century Prose," *RES*, XVII, 281–297. "The prose writer's new purpose was to deal with matters of fact, that could be verified." Emphasizes the influence of the Royal Society and the preaching of the latitudinarian divines on the simplifying of prose in the seventeenth century. See MacDonald (1943).

Berger, Harold L. 1963. "Emerson and Carlyle—Stylists at Odds," *ESQ*, XXXIII, 61–65. Though they were of "kindred minds," no two writers expressed their beliefs more "antithetically."

Berman, Eleanor, and E. C. McClintock, Jr. 1947. "Thomas Jefferson and Rhetoric," *QJS*, XXXIII, 1–8. Analyzes Jefferson's rhetorical principles and classical influences.

Bethurum, Dorothy. 1932a. "The Form of Aelfric's Lives of the Saints," *SP*, XXIX, 515–553. "Aelfric's translation is an astonishing feat of evoking in a Germanic language something akin to the stylistic effects of Latin."

1932b. "Stylistic Features of the Old English Laws," *MLR*, XXVII, 263–279. "They had behind them a tradition of a poetic, highly adorned prose, and in their writing they used the poetic device they knew best, alliteration."

1935. "The Connection of the Katherine Group with Old English Prose," *JEGP*, XXXIV, 553–564. First pointed out the great variety of prose styles to be found within this collection.

Bethurum, Dorothy, ed. 1957. *The Homilies of Wulfstan*. Oxford. "Wulfstan's homilies are the work of a skilled rhetorician and illustrate the teachings of the manuals of rhetoric which he must have studied."

Black, Lawrence Norman. 1959. "Samuel Butler (1835–1902) as Satirist." *DA*, XX, 2283, University of Texas. A study particularly of Butler's verbal irony: epigram, parody, juxtaposition of the incongruous.

Blake, Caesar Robert. 1959. "A Critical Study of Dorothy M. Richardson's *Pilgrimage*." *DA*, XIX, 2087, University of Michigan.

Bland, D. S. 1957. "Rhetoric and the Law Student in Sixteenth-Century England," *SP*, LIV, 498–508.

Blinderman, Charles. 1962. "Semantic Aspects of T. H. Huxley's Literary Style," *JC*, XII, 171–168. The conflict between Huxley's advocacy of simplicity, clarity, and exactness, on the one hand, and his practice of rhetorical subtlety and persuasiveness, on the other.

Bloomfield, Morton Wilfred, and Leonard Newmark. 1963. *A Linguistic Introduction to the History of English*. New York.

Bond, Harold L. 1960. *The Literary Art of Edward Gibbon*. Oxford. Ch. 4 describes Gibbon's descriptive style; Ch. 6 evaluates his use of irony; Ch. 7 examines the details of his style: syntax, metaphor, sounds, and rhythms.

Booth, Wayne. 1961. *The Rhetoric of Fiction*. Chicago.

Boulton, James T. 1963. *The Language of Politics in the Age of Wilkes and Burke*. London. Chapters on Burke, Junius, Paine, and so on.

Boulton, Marjorie. 1954. *The Anatomy of Prose*. London. "The Historical Approach" traces the fluctuations of plain and ornate since the time of Wycliffe.

Bouma, J. G. 1956. "A Study of the Prose Style of William Carlos Williams." *DA*, XVI, 1449, University of Pennsylvania.

Bowers, Fred. 1968. "An Evaluative Study of the Transformational-Generative Approach to the Syntactic Description of Thomas Deloney's Prose." *DA*, XXVIII, 3656A, University of British Columbia. The history of prose since Deloney can be accounted for through variations of the choice of interpretative transformations.

Bowman, Sister Mary Antonia. 1964. "The English Prose Style of Sir Francis Bacon." *DA*, XXIV, 4674–4675, University of Wisconsin. "The present study . . . sees a relationship between his style and the new prominence given rhetorical Memory in his program for the advancement of learning," particularly in the economy and variety of his style.

Brady, Frank. 1962. "Prose Style and the 'Whig' Tradition," *BNYPL*, LXVI, 455–463. Examines the effect of the "Whig" tradition on the style of Burke's *Reflections on the Revolution in France.*

Bredvold, Louis I., Robert K. Root, and George Sherburn. 1932. *Eighteenth Century Prose.* New York. "Introduction" contains a brief survey of the century which argues that in spite of the variety of styles one can "come to feel . . . that the century is aesthetically unified to such an extent that it is easy to recognize the excellences of such prose as deserves the label 'eighteenth-century.' "

Brewster, W. T. 1902. *Studies in Structures and Style.* New York. Anthology and analyses of seven selections from nineteenth-century writers: Froude, Stevenson, Morley, Arnold, Bryce, Ruskin, and Newman.

Brice, Marshall M. 1966. "Lincoln and Rhetoric," *CCC*, XVII, 12–14. Lincoln's revision of his 1861 inaugural address, which reveals a "master rhetorician."

*Bridgman, Richard. 1966. *The Colloquial Style in America.* New York. Ch. 1, "Parts of Speech"; Ch. 2, "Nineteenth-Century Talk"; Ch. 3, "Henry James and Mark Twain"; Ch. 4, "Copies of Misfires"; Ch. 5, "Gertrude Stein"; Ch. 6, "Ernest Hemingway." "Introduction" is included in this volume.

Brook, G. L. 1964. *A History of the English Language.* New York.

Brooke, Tucker. 1967. "The Renaissance." In Albert C. Baugh *et al.*, *A Literary History of England.* 2nd ed. New York. Pp. 315–696.

Brooks, Cleanth, and Robert P. Warren. 1958. *Modern Rhetoric.* New York.
___ 1959. *Understanding Fiction.* 2nd ed. New York.

Brower, Reuben. 1951. *The Fields of Light: An Experiment in Critical Reading.* New York.

Brown, Calvin S., Jr. 1938. "The Musical Structure of De Quincey's *Dream-Fugue*," *MQ*, XXIV, 341–350.

Brown, David D. 1961. "John Tillotson's Revisions and Dryden's 'Talent for English Prose,' " *RES*, XII, 24–39. Tillotson's influence on Dryden—clearness, dignity, and propriety of diction.

Brown, Huntington. 1966. *Prose Styles: Five Primitive Types.* Monographs in the Humanities, No. 1. Minneapolis.

Browne, Thomas Arthur. 1961. "Thomas Nashe and the Traditions of Plain-Speaking." *DA*, XXII, 1622, University of Minnesota. Places Nashe in the homiletic and comic traditions of plain-style.

Brownell, W. C. 1901. *Victorian Prose Masters.* New York. General discussions of Thackeray, Carlyle, Eliot, Arnold, Ruskin, and Meredith, including sections on the style of each.
___ 1924. *The Genius of Style.* New York. Ch. 4, "English Prose Tradition," deplores the loss of "aesthetic" style and the ascendancy of the scientific "plain" stylists during the past three centuries.

Bryan, Ralph T. 1968. "Robert Burton's *Anatomy of Melancholy*: A Study of the Style." *DA*, XXIX, 561A, University of Colorado. Creates six styles within the basic framework of the Senecan style.

Buckler, William E., ed. 1958. *Prose of the Victorian Period.* Boston. "Introduction" evaluates Allott, Elton, Culler, Svaglic. Emphasizes Pater's "style" as containing a set of critical principles for the judgment of Victorian prose, which he considers to be generally *sui generis.* Brief sections on Mill and Huxley, Macaulay, Arnold, Carlyle, Ruskin, and Newman.

Bullitt, John M. 1953. *Jonathan Swift and the Anatomy of Satire.* Cambridge, Mass. An analysis of Swift's use of rhetoric in his satirical indictments of the world.

Burke, Phyllis Brown. 1967. "Rhetorical Considerations of Bacon's Style," *CCC*, LVIII, 23–31. Questions whether the style of Bacon's *Essays* changes.

*Burke, Virginia M. 1968. "The Paragraph: Dancer in Chains." In Robert M. Gorrell, ed., *Rhetoric: Theories for Application*. Champaign. Pp. 37–43.

Challis, Lorna. 1965. "The Use of Oratory in Sidney's *Arcadia*," *SP*, LXII, 561–576. "A detailed study of the formal speeches . . . for Sidney here seems to have exploited to the full the dramatic possibilities of classical oratory."

Chambers, R. W. 1932. *The Life and Death of Sr. Thomas More, Knight, Sometymes Lord Chancellor of England, by Nicholas Harpsfield*. Oxford. Reprinted as *On the Continuity of English Prose from Alfred to More and His School*. Fair Lawn, N.J., 1932. In "Introduction" Chambers agrees with Krapp (1915) concerning the nature of the essential English prose tradition (clarity and intelligibility, simplicity and directness), but unlike Krapp, he traces this tradition back to Alfred (which Krapp thought impossible), and then forward through Aelfric and Wycliffe to More and modern prose. The prose of the eleventh century derived directly from the tenth, and the prose of the fifteenth century derived directly from the eleventh. The full revival of English prose in the fifteenth century, therefore, is the consequence of the steady development of English prose since Alfred, which was a tradition of plain and open style, typified by the *Ancrene Riwle*, and the writings of Rolle and Hilton, all of which forecast the prose of More and therefore of Bunyan, Defoe, Dryden, and modern prose. Chambers' argument has been attacked by several critics. Williamson (1951): "Chambers is content with native tradition; for him English style is like the long bow, even if Ascham required something more to write *Toxophilus*." Zeeman (1955): "It does not, in the first place, admit the interest of growth and development in the East of the country. Moreover, in failing to distinguish between widely varying kinds of prose style within the Western Group, it ignores the existence of different traditions of English devotional prose." See N. Davis (1961), Workman (1940), and R. M. Wilson (1959).

Chambers, Robert D. 1959. "Addison at Work on the *Spectator*," *MP*, LVI, 145–153. Addison's adaptation of twenty-four essays, originally intended for a volume of serious essays, into *Spectator* essays.

Chandler, Zilpha Emma. 1928. *An Analysis of the Stylistic Technique of Addison, Johnson, Hazlitt, and Pater*. University of Iowa Humanistic Studies, IV, 3. Discusses the diction and sentence structure of each author. Negatively reviewed by Elizabeth Schneider in Houtchens and Houtchens (1957): "The conclusions reached about the style of Hazlitt were obviously in the author's mind from the start and bear little visible relation to her statistical analysis. The analysis itself, moreover, is vitiated by naive unawareness of historical changes in language. . . . The book is an object lesson in how not to be scientific, for there is no 'control' study."

Chatman, Seymour. 1969. "New Ways of Analyzing Narrative Structure with an Example from Joyce's *Dubliners*," *L&S*, II, 3–36.

Chatman, Seymour, and Samuel R. Levin, eds. 1967. *Essays on the Language of Literature*. Boston.

Chisholm, William Sherman. 1965. "Sentence Patterns in *The Sound and the Fury*." *DA*, XXV, 7254–7255, University of Michigan.

Chomsky, Noam. 1965. *Aspects of the Theory of Syntax*. Cambridge, Mass.

Christensen, Francis. 1946. "John Wilkins and the Royal Society's Reform of Prose Style," *MQ*, VII, 279–290. Wilkins was principally responsible for the pertinent linguistic passages in *The History of the Royal Society* and for the appointment of the committee.

1967. *Notes Toward a New Rhetoric: Six Essays for Teachers*. New York. "A Lesson from Hemingway": What does a writer, and specifically what does

Hemingway in *The Undefeated*, add to the noun and the verb and the main clause to make a point? (Orig. pub. *CE*, 1963.) "Sentence Openers" examines the first 200 sentences from twenty recent American writers. (Orig. pub. *CE*, 1963.) "A Generative Rhetoric of the Sentence" (orig. pub. *CCC*, 1963). "A Generative Rhetoric of the Paragraph" (orig. pub. *CCC*, 1965).

Clark, Albert C. 1913. *Prose Rhythm in English*. Folcroft, Penna.

Clark, Cecily. 1968. "Early Middle English Prose: Three Essays in Stylistics," *EC*, XVIII, 361–382. Brief review of scholarship and analysis of selections from *The Life and Passion of St. Margaret of Antioch*, the *Ancrene Wisse*, and the *Anglo-Saxon Chronicle*.

Clark, Donald L. 1951. "Ancient Rhetoric and English Renaissance Literature," *SQ*, II, 195–204. An effort to show how "ancient rhetoric exerted a tremendous influence on Renaissance literature."

——— 1959. "Rhetoric and the Literature of the Middle Ages," *QJS*, XLV, 19–28. "Rhetoric did teach the poets, as well as the prose writers, to find arguments and to use an embellished and copious style."

Clark, John W. 1964. *Early English: A Study of Old and Middle English*. New York. Ch. 2 is an illuminating analysis of four versions of a passage from the New Testament: the Vulgate, Old English, Middle English, and eighteenth century.

Clark, R. 1969. "A Study of the Sermons of Henry King." *DA*, XXX, 2477A, University of Colorado.

Cleaveland, Elizabeth W. 1911. *A Study of Tindale's Genesis Compared with the Genesis of Coverdale and of the Authorized Version*. Yale Studies in English, XLIII. "It was Tindale's and not Coverdale's translation that was made the basis of the Authorized Version of 1611."

Coleman, James. 1962. "The Plain Style," *CCC*, XIII, 1–6. A protest against the excessive classroom emphasis on the plain style, with a brief historical survey of the "Plain Style bias" that focuses on a passage from *Gulliver's Travels*.

Collins, A. S. 1957. "Language 1660–1784." In Boris Ford, ed., *From Dryden to Johnson*. Harmondsworth. Pp. 125–141. A general survey of many of the influences producing useful, clear, easy, and precise communication during the age.

Conley, John. 1966. "'Aureate': A Stylistic Term," *N&Q*, XIII, 369–371. History of the usage of the term.

Connolly, Cyril. 1960. *Enemies of Promise and Other Essays*. Garden City. Discusses the "vernacular" and "Mandarin" styles. Pp. 70–80, an analysis of Hemingway and the revolt against "fine" style in the twentieth century.

Cope, Jackson I. 1956. "Seventeenth-Century Quaker Style," *PMLA*, LXXI, 725–754. Traces the increasing "plainness," or, rather, the decrease of exhortation and "incantation" of Quaker style from 1650 to 1675. Concludes that plain style owes as much if not more to the continuous theological debate as to the growth of skepticism, pragmatic theories of action, and empirical science. See Fisch (1952).

Corbett, Edward P. J. 1965. *Classical Rhetoric for the Modern Student*. New York. Excellent introduction to schemes and tropes.

——— 1966. "A Method of Analyzing Prose Style with a Demonstration Analysis of Swift's 'A Modest Proposal.'" In Gary Tate, ed., *Reflections on High School English*. Tulsa. Pp. 106–124. Reprinted in Gary Tate and Edward Corbett, eds., *Teaching Freshman Composition*. New York, 1967.

——— 1969. *Rhetorical Analyses of Literary Works*. Fair Lawn, N.J.

Costello, Donald P. 1959. "The Language of *The Catcher in the Rye*," *AS*, XXXIV, 172–181. "The language of *The Catcher in the Rye* is … an authentic artistic rendering of a type of informal, colloquial, teenage American spoken speech."

Craddock, Patricia Bland. 1965. "The Style and Construction of Gibbon's Auto-
biographies." *DA*, XXV, 4684, Yale University. "A study of the 6 drafts of
Gibbon's Memoirs and other autobiographical material reveals a progressive
polishing of style and experimentation with the genre."
　　1968. "An Approach to the Distinction of Similar Styles: Two English Historians," *Style*, II, 105–128. A comparison of one paragraph from Robertson's
History of America with one paragraph from Gibbon's *Decline and Fall*, using
methods of transformational-generative grammar.
Craig, G. Armour. 1959. "On the Style of *Vanity Fair*." In H. C. Martin, ed.,
Style in Prose Fiction. New York. Pp. 87–113. Explains how Thackeray exploits verbal complexities.
Craig, Hardin. 1936. *The Enchanted Glass*. New York. Ch. 7 is on Renaissance
rhetoric.
Craik, Sir Henry, ed., 1893–1896. *English Prose: Selections, with Critical Introductions to Each Period*. 5 vols. New York. Craik's brief introduction to each
volume generalizes about prose in each century.
Crane, Milton. 1951. *Shakespeare's Prose*. Chicago.
Crane, William G. 1937. *Wit and Rhetoric in the Renaissance: The Formal Basis of
Elizabethan Prose Style*. New York. "The emphasis placed upon the devices
of amplification by schoolmasters and literary men of the sixteenth century and
the close relationship which existed then between wit and rhetoric, throw much
light upon what was written in English between 1550 and 1700."
Croll, Morris. All of Croll's essays listed here have been reprinted in Patrick *et al.*
(1966).
　　1914. "Juste Lipse et le Mouvement Anticicéronien à la Fin du XVIe et au Début
du XVIIe Siècle," *Revue du Seizième Siècle*, II, 200–242. Although modified by
Williamson's (1951) argument that Lipsius' own style was more Tacitean than
Senecan (and by his own later concession in "Muret" [1924] that the essay
needed "revision at several points"), the essay is still standard. Recent studies of
Renaissance neo-Stoicism have confirmed its estimate of the importance of
Lipsius and philosophy to the making of seventeenth-century Senecan style.
See Dunn (1956) and Trimpi (1962).
　　1921. "'Attic Prose' in the Seventeenth Century," *SP*, XVIII, 79–129. Provides
indispensable background for Croll's earlier Lipsius essay (1914) and for his
later more detailed studies of other principal figures by relating ancient theories
of style to Renaissance prose. See J. M. Wallace's "reservations about Croll's
thesis" ("Croll's discussion oversimplifies the issue") in Patrick *et al.* (1966),
pp. 45–50.
　　1923. "Attic Prose: Lipsius, Montaigne, Bacon," *Schelling Anniversary Papers by
His Former Students*. New York. Clarifies his earlier essays (including "Muret,"
which, though dated 1924, was written prior to this essay) and furthers his general thesis that style both reflects and conditions its age, and his specific thesis
that the revolt against Ciceronianism did not become a force until the development and spread of "Atticism" ("Anti-Ciceronianism") by Muret and Lipsius.
At the end of the essay, Croll employs for the first time the term "baroque"
instead of "Attic" for this style in prose. See the comments on this essay by
Patrick and Evans in Patrick *et al.* (1966), pp. 163–165.
　　1924. "Muret and the History of 'Attic Prose,'" *PMLA*, XXXIX, 254–309. A
rehabilitation of Muret as the leader of the reaction against Ciceronianism
(followed by Lipsius, Quevedo, and Bacon) and a summary of the development
of "Attic" prose (Anti-Ciceronianism) and its relationship to the thought of
the sixteenth and seventeenth centuries. Of this and his other essays, Williamson
(1951) writes: "For a proper understanding of the [Anti-Ciceronian] movement

in general, the various studies of 'Attic Prose' by Morris Croll are indispensable." See the critique of the essay by Evans in Patrick *et al.* (1966), pp. 103–105.

1929. "The Baroque Style in Prose," *Studies in English Philology: A Miscellany in Honor of Frederick Klaeber.* Minneapolis. Pp. 427–456. Whereas in his other essays on the Anti-Ciceronian movement Croll has concentrated chiefly on the *theory* of the style, in this essay he attempts to describe the *form* of Anti-Ciceronian or, as he calls it here, "baroque" prose.

Croll, Morris, and Harry Clemons, eds. 1916. *Euphues: The Anatomy of Wit; Euphues and His England by John Lyly.* London. The introduction by Croll, "The Sources of the Euphuistic Rhetoric," is a standard reference that remains unchallenged in its main thesis—that the important roots of the Euphuistic style are found in medieval rhetoric. Faulty in omitting mention of the influence of the *cursus* and in not indicating adequately the impact of translations on English prose style. See Schoeck and Patrick's comment in Patrick *et al.* (1966), pp. 237–240.

Crompton, Louis. 1958. "Satire and Symbolism in *Bleak House*," *NCF*, XII, 284–303.

Crystal, David, and Derek Davy. 1970. *Investigating English Style.* Bloomington.

Culler, A. Dwight. 1957. "Method in the Study of Victorian Prose," *VN*, IX, 1–4. See Svaglic (1957).

Davies, H. S. 1960. "Trollope and His Style," *REL*, I, 73–85. A defense of Trollope's style.

Davis, Norman. 1955. *The Language of the Pastons.* London.

*1961. "Styles in English Prose of the Late Middle and Early Modern Period," *Langue et Littérature: Actes du VIIIe Congrès de la Fédération Internationale des Langues et Littérature Modernes.* Paris. Pp. 165–181.

Davis, Robert M. 1968. "From Artifice to Art: The Technique of Firbank's Novels," *Style*, II, 33–47. Firbank as innovator and possessor of an individual style.

Davy, F. X. 1958. "Benjamin Franklin, Satirist: The Satire of Franklin and Its Rhetoric." *DA*, XIX, 317, Columbia University.

Deen, Leonard W. 1962. "The Rhetoric of Newman's *Apologia*," *ELH*, XXIX, 224–238. Newman "used both the principles and the particular devices of classical rhetoric."

1963. "Irrational Form in *Sartor Resartus*," *TSLL*, V, 438–451. Investigates Carlyle's "use of symbolism, apparent disorder, and above all fictional 'personality' or biography as methods of correcting a rationalistic organization or interpretation of reality by an exploration and expression of the mystery and the creative vitality and disorder of experience."

Denniston, J. D. 1952. *Greek Prose Style.* Oxford.

Dill, Stephen H. 1965. "An Analysis of Some Aspects of Daniel Defoe's Prose Style." University of Arkansas Diss. Essentially an analysis of the basic elements of Defoe's prose style with historical comparisons to Addison, Johnson, Hazlitt, and Pater through the use of Lewis (1894) and Rickert (1927).

Dobrée, Bonamy. 1934. *Modern Prose Style.* Oxford. 2nd ed., 1964. Discusses more than fifty writers who wrote between 1900 and 1933. Part 4 compares Browne and William James, then examines briefly the styles of Pepys, Sidney, Shakespeare, Gosse, Stein, Woolf, Bagehot, Henry James, and D. H. Lawrence. The second edition contains material on the style of about fifteen recent writers, including Durrell, Golding, and Salinger. Impressionistic in method.

1946. *English Essayists.* London.

1949. "Some Aspects of Defoe's Prose." In J. L. Clifford and Louis Landa, eds., *Pope and His Contemporaries*. Oxford. Pp. 171–184. Describes Defoe's "staggering variety," but does find a common denominator in Defoe's best prose, "where he can moralize in the first person through the mouths of his creatures."

Doherty, Paul Colman. 1965. "The Prose Works of Robert Greene." *DA*, XXV, 5926–5927, University of Missouri. Ch. 1 deals with Greene's language and especially his syntax.

Doležel, Lubomír, and Richard W. Bailey. 1969. *Statistics and Style*. New York.

Doughty, W. L. 1955. *John Wesley, Preacher*. London. Ch. 12, "Service: Sermon: Style." Wesley a master of the plain style—lucid and direct.

Duffy, John J., Jr. 1967. "Walter Pater's Prose Style: An Essay in Theory and Analysis," *Style*, I, 45–63. Argues that describing Pater's style in musical terms cannot be easily justified. His prose clearly demonstrates at least two different sets of characteristics, of which only one is technically melody; one other is pictorial.

Duhamel, Albert. 1948. "Sidney's *Arcadia* and Elizabethan Rhetoric," *SP*, XLV, 134–150.

Dunn, Catherine. 1956. "Lipsius and the Art of Letter Writing," *SR*, III, 145–156. "I think that Lipsius wrote the *Institutio* [1591] in order to reestablish the ancient classical position of the letter, as a composition distinct from the written oration . . . offering then a consistent pattern of style in the conversational manner of spoken discourse."

Dupee, F. E. 1962. "Difficulty as Style," *ASc*, XIV, 362–365. Part of a symposium on "Obscurity in Modern Literature."

Earle, John. 1891. *English Prose: Its Elements, History and Usage*. New York. Three epochs in the history of English prose when the language culminated in a standard: the tenth, fifteenth, and nineteenth centuries.

Edel, Leon. 1950. "The Future of the Novel: James and Joyce," *Tomorrow*, IX, 53–58. James's formal perfection and analysis, Joyce's suggestiveness and virtuosity.

Emden, Cicil S. 1949. "Rhythmical Features in Dr. Johnson's Prose," *RES*, XXV, 38–54. "A constant succession of balanced phrases as an appropriate medium for the preceptor who is engaged in holding one set of moral balances after another."

Enkvist, Nils E., John Spencer, and Michael Gregory. 1964. *Linguistics and Style*. New York.

Farrell, W. J. 1961. "Rhetorical Elements in the 18th Century English Novel." *DA*, LI, 1976, University of Wisconsin. Attempts to show that there is "a significant relationship between the compositional practices" of Richardson, Fielding, Smollett, and Sterne and "the conventional techniques of traditional rhetoric."

1963. "The Style and the Action in *Clarissa*," *SEL*, III, 365–375. Describes as "oversimplified" Watt's (1957) argument that Richardson's rhetoric breaks with the traditional decorums of prose and adopts the artless accents of the familiar letter.

Feder, Lillian. 1954. "John Dryden's Use of Classical Rhetoric," *PMLA*, LXIX, 1258–1278. Emphasizes the persistence of classical rhetorical tradition in Dryden's style and thought.

Firkins, Oscar. 1924. *William Dean Howells*. Cambridge, Mass. Ch. 7 is on diction, grammar, periods, and phrases.

*Fisch, Harold. 1952. "The Puritans and the Reform of Prose-Style," *ELH*, XIX, 229–248.

Fitzgerald, Robert P. 1966. "The Style of *Ossian*," *SIR*, VI, 22–33. Macpherson's "unusual style was like nothing seen before in English prose or verse."

Follett, Robert. 1937. "The Death of the Sentence," *AM*, CLX, 503–512. Allies the crumbling of the sentence in much contemporary writing with the collapse of universal belief in an ordered world.

Forster, E. M. 1951. "English Prose Between 1918 and 1939," *Two Cheers for Democracy*. New York. Little about the technical elements of prose, but raises the problem of the extent to which writing is influenced by the period in which it is written.

Fowler, Roger, ed. 1966. *Essays on Style and Language: Linguistic and Critical Approaches to Literary Style*. New York.

Francis, J. H. 1957. *From Caxton to Carlyle: A Study of the Development of Language, Composition and Style in English Prose*. Cambridge. An anthology of prose from the fourteenth to the nineteenth century. Introductions to the chronological sections trace the development of style.

Francis, Nelson. 1965. *The English Language: An Introduction*. New York.

Fraser, G. S. 1960. "Macaulay's Style as an Essayist," *REL*, I, 9–19. "His style in the essays, in its dependence on point, balance, and abundance of not too recondite literary and historical allusion, periodic order, sharp antithesis, is essentially the old *Edinburgh Review* style."

Freeman, Donald C. 1970. *Linguistics and Literary Style*. New York.

Freeman, F. Barron, ed. 1948. *Billy Budd*. Cambridge, Mass. Pp. 97–114 of the introduction, "Convolutions and Quiddities: Melville's Style."

Freimarck, Vincent. 1952. "The Bible and Neo-Classical Views of Style," *JEGP*, LI, 507–526. The tension between neo-classical standards of sparseness of ornament and symmetry, and the often obscure, highly wrought, and irregular literature of the Bible. Generally, however, neo-classical commentators were hospitable toward Biblical style.

Friedman, Melvin J. 1955. *Stream of Consciousness: A Study in Literary Method*. New Haven. A particularly thorough analysis of the major writers, plus a stimulating chapter on "The Analogy of Music."

Frye, Northrop. 1947. *Anatomy of Criticism*. Princeton.

Fuller, John Wesley. 1959. "Prose Styles in the Essays of E. B. White." *DA*, XX, 1013, University of Washington.

Gale, Robert L. 1964. *The Caught Image: Figurative Language in the Fiction of Henry James*. Chapel Hill.

Gerber, John C. 1959. "The Relation Between Point of View and Style in the Works of Twain." In H. C. Martin, ed., *Style in Prose Fiction*. New York. Pp. 142–171.

Gerwig, G. W. 1894. "On the Decrease of Predication and of Sentence Weight in English Prose," University of Nebraska Studies, II, 17–28.

Gibson, Walker. 1958. "Behind the Veil: A Distinction Between Poetic and Scientific Language in Tennyson, Lyell, and Darwin," *VS*, II, 60–68.

*1966. *Tough, Sweet and Stuffy: An Essay on Modern American Prose Style*. Bloomington. An attempt "to describe three extreme but familiar styles in modern American prose. I call these styles Tough Talk, Sweet Talk, and Stuffy Talk. What I mean by Tough Talk is most easily discovered in works of fiction where a narrator-hero identifies himself as a hard man who has been around. By Sweet Talk I refer primarily to the blandishments of advertising. And Stuffy Talk, of course, suggests the hollow tones of officialese."

Ginsberg, Robert. 1967. "The Declaration as Rhetoric." In Robert Ginsberg, ed., *A Casebook on "The Declaration of Independence*." New York. Pp. 219–244. A searching examination of the Declaration as a work of persuasion.

Gleason, H. A., Jr. 1968. "Contrastive Analysis in Discourse Structure," *Georgetown University Monograph Series in Languages and Linguistics*, XIX, 39–63.

*Gordon, Ian. 1966. *The Movement of English Prose*. Bloomington. A sometimes successful effort to demonstrate the continuity of prose style from Alfred to the present through a focus on the sentence.

Grainger, James M. 1907. "Studies in the Syntax of the King James Version," *SP*, II, 1–60. The King James Version "summed up in many ways the transition from Late Middle to Early Modern English. It is an epitome of the development of English syntax from Tyndale's time to 1611."

Graves, Robert, and Alan Hodge. 1943. *The Reader Over Your Shoulder: A Handbook for Writers of English Prose*. New York. Chs. 5–9 present a history of English prose styles. Impressionistic.

Greene, Donald J. 1962. "Is There a 'Tory' Prose Style?" *BNYPL*, LXVI, 449–454. Questions the possibility of a "Tory" style (individuals have styles).

Greenfield, Stanley B. 1965. *A Critical History of Old English Literature*. New York.

Greenough, James B., and George L. Kittredge. 1962. *Words and Their Ways in English Speech*. Boston.

Groom, Bernard. 1934. *Short History of English Words*. New York.

Gross, Beverly. 1968. "The Poetic Narrative: A Reading of 'Flowering Judas,' " *Style*, II, 129–139. See W. Patrick (1967).

Gross, Robert Eugene. 1963. "Hawthorne's First Novel: The Future of a Style," *PMLA*, LXXVIII, 60–68. *Fanshawe* as a "Primer of Hawthorne's style."

Guerin, Wilfred L., *et al.* 1966. *A Handbook of Critical Approaches to Literature*. New York.

Gummere, R. M. 1955. "William Bartram, A Classical Scientist," *CJ*, L, 167–170. The Greco-Roman tradition as reflected in the style and content of Bartram's *Travels*.

———. 1956. "John Dickinson, the Classical Penman of the Revolution," *CJ*, LII, 81–88.

Guskin, Phyllis. 1968. "The Microcosm of the Sentence: Syntax and Tone in Swift's Prose." *DA*, XXIX, 870A, Vanderbilt University.

Halliday, M. A. K. 1962. "The Linguistic Study of Literary Texts," *Preprints of the IXth International Congress of Linguists*.

Hammond, Lansing. 1948. *Laurence Sterne's Sermons of Mr. Yorick*. New Haven. Reveals how much Sterne was influenced by the seventeenth-century divines, such as Tillotson.

Hansen, David A. 1967. "English Criticism of Prose Style: 1698–1752." *DA*, XXVIII, 195A, University of Minnesota. Defenders of eloquence in the eighteenth century.

Hargreaves, Henry. 1966. "Wiclif's Prose," *E&S*, XIX, 1–17. Uniformity in the length and construction of sentences is the chief characteristic of Wycliffe's plain style.

Harkness, Stanley. 1918. "The Prose Style of Sir Philip Sidney," *University of Wisconsin Studies*, II, 57–76. An analysis of Sidney's prose style as he adjusted it to works so disparate as the *Arcadia* and the *Apologie for Poetrie*.

Hasan, Ruqaiya. 1964. "A Linguistic Study of Contrasting Features in the Style of Two Contemporary English Prose Writers." University of Edinburgh Diss. Employs the system of grammatical description developed by Halliday (1962) to analyze *Free Fall* by William Golding and *Anglo-Saxon Attitudes* by Angus Wilson.

Hastings, George S., Jr. 1966. "Two Aspects of Style in the A B Dialect of Middle English." *DA*, XXVI, 5425, University of Pennsylvania. A study of alliteration and pronoun reference in two manuscripts by the author of the *Ancrene Riwle*: (1) *Ancrene Wisse* and (2) lives of Saints Katherine, Margaret, and Juliana, "Hali Meiðhad," and "Sawles Warde." Questions R. W. Chambers' (1932) belief that the style of the *Ancrene Riwle* was the particular one that influenced a later style.

Hayes, Curtis Wayne. 1965. "A Linguistic Analysis of the Prose Style of Edward Gibbon." *DA*, XXV, 5268, University of Texas. "This dissertation is based on the thesis that generative grammar, initially formulated by Chomsky, is a powerful tool in analyzing literary style." Throughout, Hemingway's style is analyzed as a control.

    1968. "A Transformational Generative Approach to Style: Samuel Johnson and Edward Gibbon," *L&S*, I, 39–48.

*Hayman, David. 1958. "From *Finnegans Wake*: A Sentence in Progress," *PMLA*, LXXIII, 136–154.

Hendrickson, G. L. 1905. "The Origin and Meaning of the Ancient Characters of Style," *AJP*, XXVI, 249–290. "The whole subject may be summarized by saying . . . that the grand style is rhetoric itself in the original conception of it as an instrument of emotional transport . . . the plain style a *tertium quid* intermediate between them." See Staton (1958).

Higginson, Fred H. 1960. "Style in *Finnegans Wake.*" In Thomas A. Sebeok, ed., *Style in Language*. Cambridge, Mass. P. 277 (abstract).

*Highet, Gilbert. 1949. *The Classical Tradition: Greek and Roman Influences on Western Literature*. New York. Ch. 18, "Baroque Prose."

Hilles, F. W. 1949. "Sir Joshua's Prose," *The Age of Johnson: Essays Presented to Chauncey Brewster Tinker*. New Haven. An analysis of the syntax, diction, and grammar of Reynolds' *Discourses* and three letters to *The Idler*, that discovers a basically uniform style and a close resemblance to the style of Johnson.

Hirschman, Jack A. 1962. "The Orchestrated Novel: A Study of the Poetic Devices in Novels of Djuna Barnes and Hermann Broch, and the Influences of the Works of James Joyce upon Them." *DA*, XXII, 3220, Indiana University.

Hnatko, Eugene. 1963. "Studies in the Prose Style of Laurence Sterne." *DA*, XXIII, 4685, Syracuse University. Employs traditional scholarship and approaches suggested by students of linguistics.

Hodgart, Matthew. 1962. "Politics and Prose Style in the Late Eighteenth Century: The Radicals," *BNYPL*, LXVI, 464–469. "I have time to discuss only two radical works, Tom Paine's *The Rights of Man* . . . and William Godwin's *Political Justice.*"

Holditch, William K. 1962. "Literary Technique in the Novels of John Dos Passos." *DA*, XXII, 3184–3185, University of Mississippi. Dos Passos an innovator of style.

Holland, Norman. 1965. "Psychological Depths and 'Dover Beach,'" *VS*, IX (Supp.), 5–28. Rejoinder by Wendell V. Harris, *VS*, X (1966), 70–76; reply by Holland, *VS*, X (1966), 76–82.

Holloway, John. 1953. *The Victorian Sage: Studies in Argument*. London. "Examines the rhetorical methods of Carlyle, Newman, Disraeli, Arnold, Eliot, and Hardy, emphasizing the emotional and imaginative qualities of their work."

Honan, Park. 1965. "Metrical Prose in Dickens," *VN*, XXVIII, 1–3.

Hooker, Helene M. 1944. "Father John Constable on Jeremy Collier," *PQ*, XXIII, 375–378. On Constable's *Reflections Upon Accuracy of Style* (written in 1703), which discerned a partial source for Collier's Senecan style in Sir Roger L'Estrange. See Wimsatt (1945).

Hopkins, Viola. 1958. "The Ordering Style of *The Age of Innocence*," *AL*, XXX, 345–357.

Hough, Graham. 1969. *Style and Stylistics*. London.

Houghton, Walter. 1945. *The Art of Newman's "Apologia."* New Haven. A model analysis of the relation between style and content.
    1949. "The Rhetoric of T. H. Huxley," *UTQ*, XVIII, 159–175. Argues that Huxley reinforced his arguments with rhetorical devices. See Blinderman (1962).
    1957. *The Victorian Frame of Mind: 1830–1870*. New Haven.

Houtchens, Carolyn Washburn, and Lawrence H. Houtchens. 1957. *The English Romantic Poets and Essayists: A Review of Research and Criticism*. New York.

Howell, A. C. 1946. "*Res et Verba*: Words and Things," *ELH*, XIII, 131–142. Reprinted in Bernard Schilling, ed., *Essential Articles for the Study of English Augustan Backgrounds*. Hamden, Conn., 1961. Pp. 53–65. "The pair of terms under consideration, *words* and *things*, had an interesting history during the seventeenth century because it served as a corrective comment on the heavily ornamented style of writing then in vogue."

Howes, Raymond F. 1961. *Historical Studies of Rhetoric and Rhetoricians*. Ithaca. Developments in rhetorical theory from the time of the pre-Platonic sophists to the period of William Wordsworth and his circle; a discussion of the special function of rhetorical criticism; a series of critical essays.

Humbert, Sister Agnes Margaret. 1944. "Verbal Repetition in the *Ancrene Riwle*." Catholic University of America Diss. The *Ancrene Riwle* is immediately indebted to the rhetorical systems of the time, rather than to the ornate prose of the late Old English period. See R. M. Wilson (1959), p. 487.

Humphrey, Robert. 1954. *Stream of Consciousness in the Modern Novel*. Berkeley.

Hunter, J. Paul. 1966. *The Reluctant Pilgrim: Defoe's Emblematic Method and Quest for Form in "Robinson Crusoe."* Baltimore. The Puritan background of Defoe's literary style (Chs. 1–5) and a detailed analysis of Defoe's technique in *Crusoe* (Chs. 6–8).

Jespersen, Otto. 1894. *Progress in Language; with Specific References to English*. London and New York. Describes the slow and fitful progress toward greater clearness, regularity, ease, and pliancy in English prose style.
    1948. *Growth and Structure of the English Language*. 9th ed. New York. Explains the growth and significance of those features in the structure of the English language "which have been of permanent importance."
    1949. *A Modern English Grammar on Historical Principles*. Copenhagen and London. Part 1, "Sounds and Spellings"; Parts 2 and 3, "Syntax."

Jones, Howard Mumford. 1934. "American Prose Style: 1700–1770," *HLB*, VI, 115–151. Describes the "astonishing" but "orderly development" from the style of Mather's *Magnalia* (1700) to that of Franklin's *Autobiography* (1770). Such "a remarkable revolution in style" was the result of a conscious effort to achieve the eighteenth-century ideals of lucidity and simplicity.

*Jones, R. F. 1930. "Science and English Prose Style in the Third Quarter of the Seventeenth Century," *PMLA*, XLV, 977–1009. Reprinted in *The Seventeenth Century from Bacon to Pope ... by Richard Foster Jones and Others Writing in His Honor*. Stanford, 1951. Pp. 75–110. Reprinted in Bernard Schilling, ed., *Essential Articles for the Study of English Augustan Backgrounds*. Hamden, Conn., 1961. Pp. 66–102. Shows how "consistently and emphatically the representatives of the new science from its very beginning had manifested a stylistic attitude which reached its most elaborate expression in Sprat's *History of the Royal Society*, and which profoundly influenced some of the writers of the day. The standard thus established was inspired by the materialistic nature of the experimental philosophy, and was dictated by the need which that philosophy felt for an accurate, plain, and clear medium of expression" (from Jones, 1931).

1931. "The Attack on Pulpit Eloquence in the Restoration: An Episode in the Development of the Neo-Classical Standard for Prose," *JEGP*, XXX, 188–217. Reprinted in *The Seventeenth Century* ... (see Jones, 1930), pp. 111–142. Reprinted in Schilling (see Jones, 1930), pp. 103–136. "It is the purpose of the present article to follow the new standard of prose [that is, science] as it invades an alien field, and to discuss the many and earnest efforts made to impose upon sermons the same style that had been found most serviceable to science."

1932. "Science and Language in England of the Mid-Seventeenth Century," *PMLA*, XXXI, 315–321. An extension of the same thesis propounded in Jones (1930).

1942. *Studies in Honor of Frederick W. Shipley.* St. Louis. "The Moral Sense of Simplicity" is on the simplicity of spirit and word of men like John Hales and George Herbert, which, harking back to a moderate pre-Jacobean Anglicanism, was a great influence for plainness in England.

1963. *Restoration and Eighteenth-Century Literature.* Chicago. "The Rhetoric of Science in England of the Mid-Seventeenth Century" is an effort to determine which members of the Royal Society were guilty of writing in a rhetorical and learned manner, which inspired the requirement against "amplifications, digressions, and swellings of style." Jones specifies the atomic scientists, especially Charleton and Digby.

Joseph, Sister Miriam. 1947. *Shakespeare's Use of the Arts of Language.* New York. Harbinger paperback, 1962, under the title *Rhetoric in Shakespeare's Time.* Presents "in organized detail essentially complete the general theory of composition current during the Renaissance ... and the illustration of Shakespeare's use of it." Reclassifies the more than two hundred figures distinguished by the Tudor rhetoricians according to the four categories: grammar, logos, pathos, and ethos.

*Kaluza, Irena. 1964. "William Faulkner's Subjective Style," *KN*, XI, 13 29. Offers linguistic support for the argument that Faulkner's style, rhetoric, and grammar are functional.

Karl, Frederick R. 1959. "Joseph Conrad: A *fin de siècle* Novelist—A Study in Style and Method, " *LR*, II, 565–576. "Conrad's two earlier novels absorbed the characteristic style and ideas peculiar to much late nineteenth-century poetry."

Kaula, David. 1966. "The Low Style in Nashe's *The Unfortunate Traveler*," *SEL*, VI, 43–57.

Kellner, Leon. 1892. *Historical Outlines of English Syntax.* London. A pioneer attempt to analyze the use and elaboration of subordinate clauses.

Kennedy, George. 1963. *The Art of Persuasion in Greece.* Princeton.

Kenney, William. 1961. "Addison, Johnson, and the 'Energetick' Style," *Studia Neophilologica*, XXXIII, 103–114. The mixed reaction by contemporaries to Addison's "clear, colloquial style" and to Johnson's "energy and dignity." See Reynolds (1935).

King, J. R. 1956. "Certain Aspects of Jeremy Taylor's Prose Style," *ES*, XXXVII, 197–210. Traces the Senecan and Ciceronian elements in Taylor's style and their relationship to his main themes. Draws on Croll (1929) and Williamson (1951).

King, Walter N. 1955. "John Lyly and Elizabethan Rhetoric," *SP*, LII, 149–161. Condemns the practice of ascribing a style to a writer through description of set-pieces taken out of context, and defends Lyly against Duhamel's (1948) charge that Lyly employed rhetorical frills as ends in themselves, regardless of the demands of logic.

Krapp, George Philip. 1915. *The Rise of English Literary Prose.* New York. Covers the period from the fourteenth century to the first quarter of the seventeenth. He believes that the true English prose tradition did not commence until the late fourteenth century with Wycliffe, the "father" of English prose, "the first intelligent writer of English prose." Discovers the same "spirit" in More, Tindale, Hooker, Milton, Burke, and Carlyle, indeed in "all the great masters of expositional and oratory prose in the English language." Unlike Croll (1929), he is not concerned with the Ciceronian and Attic traditions as such, nor with any general Senecan or Patristic imitation.

Kraus, Carl. 1968. *Style in English Prose.* New York.

Krause, S. J. 1958. "James's Revisions of the Style of *The Portrait of a Lady*," *AL*, XXX, 67–88. "James's late revisions show him making a consistent effort to gain clarity and concreteness, and at times greater economy and a flavor of informality in his style."

*Lannering, Jan. 1951. *Studies in the Prose Style of Joseph Addison.* Uppsala. Ch. 1, "Parallelism"; Ch. 2, "Sentence Structure"; Ch. 3, "Cadence"; Ch. 4, "Diction: Imaginative Elements."

Law, Marie H. 1934. *The English Familiar Essay in the Nineteenth Century.* Philadelphia. Compares the work of Hunt, Hazlitt, and Lamb.

Lawton, George. 1962. *John Wesley's English: A Study of His Literary Style.* London. Ranges from Wesley's Evangelical vocabulary to his aphoristic expression.

Lee, Vernon (pseud. of Violet Paget). 1923. *The Handling of Words and Other Studies in Literary Psychology.* New York. Includes "The Syntax of De Quincey," "The Rhetoric of Landor," and "Carlyle and the Present Tense."

Leech, G. N. 1966. "Linguistics and the Figures of Rhetoric." In Roger Fowler, ed., *Essays on Style and Language: Linguistic and Critical Approaches to Literary Style.* New York. Pp. 135–156.

Leed, Jacob, ed. 1966. *The Computer and Literary Style.* Kent, Ohio.

Lenz, Sister Mary B. 1963. "A Rhetorical Analysis of Cardinal Newman's *Apologia Pro Vita Sua*." *DA*, XXIII, 2518, University of Notre Dame. "A study of the various elements of style which contributed to the effectiveness of the whole; these were grouped together as 'dramatic elements' and included imagery, rhythm, sentence patterns, tone, and personalization."

Leonard, Sterling A. 1929. *The Doctrine of Correctness in English Usage, 1700–1800.* Madison. Treats the "great and increasing interest in problems of language in the eighteenth century," especially on matters of "correctness and precision."

Levin, David. 1959. "History as Romantic Art: Structure, Characterization, and Style in *The Conquest of Mexico*," *HAHR*, XXXIX, 20–45.

Levin, Gerald. 1964. *Prose Models: An Inductive Approach to Writing.* 2nd ed. New York.

Levin, Harry. 1954. "Expressive Voices: The Emergence of a National Style," *TLS*, xii–xiv. Despite the greater diversity in American literature than in English, there is an authentic American style, "not by diction or dialect, but by the whole complex of sensibility, cadence, rhythm, and structure." Impressionistic provocations for further study.

Levine, George. 1965. "The Prose of the *Apologia Pro Vita Sua*," *VN*, XXVII, 5–8.

Levine, Richard A. 1964. "Carlyle as Poet: The Phoenix Image in 'Organic Filaments,'" *VN*, No. 25, 18–20.

*Lewis, Edwin H. 1894. *The History of the English Paragraph*. Chicago. Argues that the English paragraph has increased in the number of sentences and in the quality of its structure.

Lodge, David. 1967. *Language of Fiction: Essays in Criticism and Verbal Analysis of the English Novel*. New York.

Lott, John Bertrand. 1961. "Matthew Arnold as Satirist." *DA*, XXII, 248–249, Vanderbilt University. An analysis of the devices by which Arnold accomplished his satire, through a chronological survey of his works.

Love, Glen A., and Michael Payne. 1969. *Contemporary Essays on Style*. Glenview, Ill.

Lowes, John Livingston. 1936. *Essays in Appreciation*. Boston. "The Noblest Monument of English Prose" describes how, when the translators of the Bible came to do their task, they found a medium ready to their hand: the simple, direct vigor of native English combined with the majesty and stateliness of the Latin of the Church.

Lucas, Frank L. 1960. *Style*. New York.

Lutwack, Leonard. 1962. "Melville's Struggle with Style: The Plain, the Ornate, the Reflective," *Forum*, III, 11–17. "In variety of prose styles he used as a writer of fiction, Herman Melville was exceptional for his time."

McCormick, John Raymond. 1962. "The Language of William Hazlitt: A Study of Prose Techniques in *The Spirit of the Age*." *DA*, XXII, 2384–2385, University of Alabama. A study of the diction, syntax, imagery, idiom, and minor resources.

*MacDonald, Hugh. 1943. "Another Aspect of Seventeenth-Century Prose," *RES*, XIX, 33–43. A reply to J. Bennett (1941). He stresses the persistence of a "straightforward prose," which had existed since the days of King Alfred, and "the influence which political pamphleteering and journalism had on the simplifying of prose," which he would add to the influences of the Royal Society and the preaching of latitudinarian divines stressed by Bennett.

McGinty, Sister Mary Carolyn, C.S.J. 1964. "The Jamesian Parenthesis: Elements of Suspension in the Narrative Sentences of Henry James's Late Style." *DA*, XXIV, 4193, Catholic University of America. "The parenthesis is initially isolable and identifiable as a syntactic unit, a variety of parataxis in which one form interrupts another form and is punctuationally isolated" (from Bloomfield and Newmark, 1963).

McIntosh, Angus, M. A. K. Halliday, and Peter Strevens. 1965. *The Linguistic Sciences and Language Teaching*. Bloomington.

McKeon, Richard. 1952. "Rhetoric in the Middle Ages." In R. S. Crane, ed., *Critics and Criticism*. Chicago. Pp. 260–296. Confirms the profound importance of rhetoric in the intellectual developments of the Middle Ages.

McKnight, George H. 1923. *English Words and Their Background*. Reprinted New York, 1968.

Madden, William, and George Levine, eds. 1968. *The Art of Victorian Prose*. New York. Reviewed by J. R. Bennett, *Style*, IV (1970), 177–186.

Major, John Campbell. 1944. "Matthew Arnold and Attic Prose Style," *PMLA*, LIX, 1086–1103. "An analysis of Arnold's comments on the meaning and relationships of prose style and his formulation of the qualities of an 'Attic' prose to express a sane national intelligence."

Mandeville, Sister Scholastica. 1961. "The Rhetorical Tradition of the *Sententia*; with a Study of Its Influence on the Prose of Sir Francis Bacon and of Sir Thomas Browne." *DA*, XXI, 3099, St. Louis University. "The aphoristic style characteristic of much seventeenth-century prose has been traced by Morris Croll and later scholars to the revival of Stoicism and the Senecan style at that time. This revival, however, seems to have been largely extra-academic, and it should be considered in conjunction with the academic rhetorical tradition in which *Sententia* was employed as a form of argument and a figure of style."

Manierre, W. R. 1959. "Cotton Mather and the Plain Style." *DA*, 2092, University of Michigan. A study of the style of Mather's *Magnalia Christi Americana*.

*Martin, Harold C. 1959. "The Development of Style in Nineteenth-Century American Fiction." In H. C. Martin, ed., *Style in Prose Fiction*. New York. Pp. 114–141. Discusses some changes in narrative sensibility over the course of a century from Cooper to Crane.

Matthiessen, F. O. 1931. *Translation: An Elizabethan Art*. Cambridge, Mass. Discusses Hoby, North, Florio, and Holland, with considerable analysis of style.

Mellinkoff, David. 1963. *The Language of the Law*. Boston. Treats the evolution of the legal style in England and America.

Menikoff, Barry. 1970. "Punctuation and Point of View in the Late Style of Henry James," *Style*, IV, 29–48.

Miles, Josephine. 1965. *Classic Essays in English*. 2nd ed., Boston.

*1967. *Style and Proportion: The Language of Prose and Poetry*. Boston.

Milic, Louis T. 1966. "Metaphysics in the Criticism of Style," *CCC*, XVII, 124–129. Milic's complaint against "intuitive impressionism" should be read by everyone interested in the study of style. But also read the response by D. M. Lambert, *CCC*, XVIII (1967), 49–50.

1967a. "Against the Typology of Styles." In Seymour Chatman and Samuel R. Levin, eds., *Essays on the Language of Literature*. Boston. Pp. 442–450. A needed complaint against the excessive impressionism of stylistic labels and categories. Unfortunately, the argument is vitiated by the author's choice of Sutherland's "Restoration Prose" (Sutherland and Watt, 1956) as "representative of typological *Stilforschung* in its assumptions and superior to most in originality and scholarship," but which is in reality one of the worst essays ever written on an aspect of the history of style.

1967b. *A Quantitative Approach to the Style of Jonathan Swift*. The Hague. Assuming "the unconscious nature of a mature writer's style," Milic argues that Swift's style "contains a uniform and constant diffusion of his mind and personality, expressed through certain grammatical categories which may be measured objectively."

1967c. *Style and Stylistics: An Analytical Bibliography*. New York. Reviewed by Richard W. Bailey, *Style*, II (1968), 233–238.

Miller, Perry. 1939. *The New England Mind*. New York. Devotes a chapter to the plain style of the New England Puritans, showing how their sermons were constructed according to a bold system of logical exposition with the imaginative element minimized.

Mills, Gordon. 1959. "The Influence of Darwinism on the Style of Certain American Writers," *The Impact of Darwinian Thought on American Life and Culture* (papers read at the Fourth Annual Meeting of the American Studies Association of Texas), pp. 11–26.

Mindel, Joseph. 1965. "The Use of Metaphor: Henry Adams and the Symbols of Science," *JHI*, XXVI, 89–102.

*Minto, William. 1891. *A Manual of English Prose Literature*. Boston. Detailed analyses of De Quincey, Macaulay, and Carlyle, with comparisons relating them to the history of English prose style.

Mitchell, W. Fraser. 1932. *English Pulpit Oratory From Andrewes to Tillotson*. New York. Centers on the development of prose style as related to "metaphysical" preaching. Quinn (1960) differs "fundamentally" with Mitchell.

Moloney, Michael F. 1959. "Metre and *Cursus* in Sir Thomas Browne's Prose,"

JEGP, LVIII, 60–67. "The peculiar genius of Browne in its final development found expression . . . in the rhythm of the great dramatists [the native tradition] adjusted cunningly to the fall of the classical oratorical cadences."

Moore, Geoffrey. 1955. "American Prose Today." In *8th Mentor Selection, New World Writing*. New York. Pp. 47–70. "American 'expositional prose' is much weaker than American creative prose."

Morgan, Edwin. 1951. " 'Strong Lines' and Strong Minds; Reflections on the Prose of Browne and Johnson," *CJ*, IV, 481–491. An impressionistic but brilliantly suggestive contrast of Browne's expressive, "involved and metaphysical" writings (*Urn Burial* and *Garden of Cyrus*) to Johnson's "lifeless" almost "soporific" but "absolutely intelligible" *Rasselas*. Morgan's general argument is that "after 1660 there was a broadening tendency for matter to outweigh expressiveness."

Morgan, Margery M. 1952–1953. "*A Talking of the Love of God* and the Continuity of Stylistic Tradition in Middle English Prose Meditations," *RES*, III–IV N.S., 97–116. An analysis of the Latin and vernacular underlying the style of the *Wooing of Our Lord*, the *Orison of God Almighty*, and *A Talking*.

Muir, Lawrence. 1935. "Influence of the Rolle and Wycliffite Psalters upon the Psalter of the Authorized Version," *MLR*, XXX, 302–310. "It may well be that an English 'Psalter tradition' extends back even farther than the fourteenth century, into the Old English Period. One of the continuous threads of English prose, connecting the time of Alfred with the time of Thomas More, may be the thread of English Biblical translation."

Munson, G. B. 1929. *Style and Form in American Prose*. Garden City. Ch. 15 complains about the decline of American prose.

Natanson, Maurice. 1957. "The Privileged Moment: A Study of the Rhetoric of Thomas Wolfe," *QJS*, XLIII, 143–150. "The present essay cannot claim to be a study of Wolfe's style or an anatomy of his language. Rather, I am here concerned with his rhetoric as a single, though crucial facet of a phenomenology of language."

Nichols, Ann E. 1965a. "A Syntactical Study of Aelfric's Translation of Genesis." *DA*, XXV, 5270–5271, University of Washington. "The Genesis translation . . . exemplifies these major syntactical devices: construction classes (subject and predicate), syntactical classes (positional classes defined by the occurrence of grammatical classes), government, concord, and word order."

1965b. "Syntax and Style: Ambiguities in Lawrence's 'Twilight in Italy,' " *CCC*, XVI, 261–266.

Nichols, James W. 1965. "Julian Huxley: The Specialist as Rhetorician," *CCC*, XVI, 7–13.

Nist, John. 1966. *A Structural History of English*. New York. Brief section called "Formal Stylistics" on each historical period.

Ohmann, Richard M. 1962. *Shaw: The Style and the Man*. Middletown, Conn.

*1965. "Methods in the Study of Victorian Style," *VN*, XXVII, 1–4. Reprinted (enlarged) in William Madden and George Levine, eds., *The Art of Victorian Prose*. New York, 1968. Pp. 289–313. Compares a passage by Arnold with one by Burke.

1966. "Literature as Sentences," *CE*, XXVIII, 261–267.

Oliver, H. J. 1945. "Izaak Walton's Prose Style," *RES*, XXI, 280–288. Controverts MacDonald (1943) and others who have argued that Walton wrote in a straightforward, limpid, and easy style. On the contrary, "he was struggling with the more ornate, balanced prose of a previous age."

Ong, Walter J., S.J. 1958. *Ramus, Method, and the Decay of Dialogue*. Cambridge, Mass. The authoritative book on Ramus (1515–1572), his significance in the history of Western ideas, sensibility, and prose style (plain).

———. 1965. "Oral Residue in Tudor Prose Style," *PMLA*, LXXX, 145–154. "Latin sustained the rhetorical—which is basically oratorical and thus oral—cast of mind. The stress on *copia* which marked Latin teaching and which was closely associated with rhetorical invention and the oral performer's need for an uninterrupted supply of material favored exploitation of commonplaces. The use of these in turn made for the 'adding' or 'rhapsodic' style which survives in so much Tudor writing as it had in medieval 'amplifications.' "

Ordoněz, Elmer Alindogan. 1963. "The Early Development of Joseph Conrad: Revisions and Style." *DA*, XXIII, 4362, University of Wisconsin. "In his early years as a writer of fiction (from *Almayer's Folly* [1893] to *Typhoon and Other Stories* [1903]), Joseph Conrad deliberately and conscientiously developed a system of verbal patterns which may be called his early style."

Partridge, Eric. 1950. *Slang Today and Yesterday*. 3rd ed. London.

Patrick, J. Max, Robert O. Evans, John M. Wallace, and R. J. Schoeck, eds. 1966. *Style, Rhetoric, and Rhythm: Essays by Morris W. Croll*. Princeton. A major source book for the study of seventeenth-century prose style.

Patrick, Walton R. 1967. "Poetic Style in the Contemporary Short Story," *CCC*, XVIII, 77–84. Makes a distinction between "lyrical" and "mimetic" stories and briefly examines the lyrical qualities of stories by James, Porter, Capote, and Welty. See B. Gross (1968).

Paulson, Ronald. 1960. *Theme and Structure in Swift's "Tale of a Tub."* New Haven.

Perrin, Porter. 1959. *Writer's Guide and Index to English*. 3rd ed. Chicago.

Pickett, Calder M. 1961. "Mark Twain as Journalist and Literary Man: A Contrast," *JQ*, XXXVIII, 59–66. A comparison of Samuel Clemens' Holy Land letters for newspaper publication and *The Innocents Abroad* shows a transition from journalist to literary writer.

Poirier, Richard. 1966. *A World Elsewhere: The Place of Style in American Literature*. New York.

Pollard, A. W. 1926. *The Beginning of the New Testament Translated by William Tyndale, 1525*. Oxford. In the introduction, Pollard estimates that the King James Version of the New Testament, "alike in language, rhythm, and cadence," is fully 90 per cent Tyndale's.

Polsky, Ned H. 1950. "Literary Background of *Finnegans Wake*," *CR*, III, 1–8. The satirical influence of Swift, the stylistic influence of Sterne.

Postman, Neil, *et al.*, eds. 1970. *Language in America*. New York. Reviewed by Richard M. Ohmann, *Style*, V (1971).

Potter, Simeon. 1965. *Our Language*. Rev. ed. Baltimore. "The Sentence" describes the historical continuity of the English sentence and distinguishes the loose, the balanced, and the periodic sentences.

Pretzer, Wallace Leonard. 1963. "Eighteenth-Century Literary Conventions in the Fictional Style of John Pendleton Kennedy." *DA*, XXIV, 731–732, University of Michigan. Studies mainly Kennedy's domestic novel, *Swallow Barn* (1832), and his two historical novels, *Horse-Shoe Robinson* (1835) and *Rob of the Bowl* (1838), "in the light of Fielding's and Sterne's styles," particularly "Kennedy's greater similarity to Fielding than to Sterne."

Price, Martin. 1953. *Swift's Rhetorical Art: A Study in Structure and Meaning*. New Haven. Ch. 1, "The Rhetorical Background" (from which Swift evolved his style); Ch. 2, "The Plain Style."

Prins, A. A. 1952. *French Influence in English Phrasing*. Leiden. Makes the case against R. W. Chambers (1932) that modern English is a gradually evolved, "harmoniously interwoven" blend of Anglo-Saxon, French, and Latin, the strands "equally present in vocabulary, phraseonomy and style." The Prayer Book of 1549 is a good exponent of this resulting style.

Purdy, Strother B. 1967. "Language as Art: The Ways of Knowing in Henry James's 'Crapy Cornelia,'" *Style*, I, 139–149.

Pyles, Thomas. 1952. *Words and Ways of American English*. New York.

Quinn, Dennis. 1960. "Donne's Christian Eloquence," *ELH*, XXVII, 276–297. Donne's "eloquence—style, structure, images, psychology, wit—proceeds from" the Bible.

Raleigh, John Henry. 1963. "Style and Structure and Their Import in Defoe's *Roxana*," *UKR*, XX, 128–135. Partly about the "Protean range of Defoe's middle way."

Randolph, Gerald Richard. 1963. "An Analysis of Form and Style in the Prose Works of Thomas Nashe." *DA*, XXIII, 3890–3891, Florida State University. "Nashe is an experimentalist in style.... He works in many genres, and he changes his style for each genre."

Rantavaara, Irma. 1960. *Virginia Woolf's "The Waves."* Helsinki. "Language and Style," pp. 36–91.

Read, Herbert. 1928. *English Prose Style*. Boston. 2d ed., 1952. "Unity" erroneously considers Dryden the "starting point of the main traditional style in English," believing that before Dryden there was "no corporate literary sense."

Reynolds, W. V. 1935. "The Reception of Johnson's Prose Style," *RES*, XI, 145–162. Discusses "the various opinions of the contending parties on Johnson's prose style" primarily during the eighteenth century.

Rickert, Edith. 1927. *New Methods for the Study of Literature*. Chicago.

Riedel, F. C. 1969. "A Classical Rhetorical Analysis of Some Elements of Stevenson's Essay Style," *Style*, III, 182–199.

Riffaterre, Michael. 1959. "Criteria for Style Analysis," *Word*, XV, 154–174.

1960. "Stylistic Context," *Word*, XVI, 207–218.

Rigg, A. G., ed. 1968. *The English Language: A Historical Reader*. New York.

Ringler, William. 1938. "The Immediate Source of Euphuism," *PMLA*, LIII, 678–686. Argues in favor of the Latin prose of John Rainolds, providing a definite connection between medieval schematic prose and the development of Euphuism and supplementing Croll's thesis (Croll and Clemons, 1916). See Toor (1966).

Ringler, William, and W. Allan. 1940. *John Rainolds' Gratio in Laudem Artis Poeticae*. Princeton. Works out a thorough analysis of the Latin counterpart of Euphuism and demonstrates the heritage of Euphuism postulated by Croll and Clemons (1916).

Roberts, Edgar. 1969. *Writing Themes about Literature*. 2nd ed. Englewood Cliffs, N.J.

Robertson, Stuart, and F. G. Cassidy. 1954. *The Development of Modern English*. 2nd ed. Englewood Cliffs, N.J.

Rodgers, Paul C., Jr. 1965. "Alexander Bain and the Rise of the Organic Paragraph," *QJS*, LI, 399–408. Bain's contribution of the "first systematic formulation of paragraph theory," with the result that he is partly responsible "for placing twentieth-century paragraph rhetoric in a deductive cage, from which it has yet to extricate itself."

1966. "A Discourse-Centered Rhetoric of the Paragraph," *CCC*, XVII, 2–11.

*Roellinger, Francis X. 1957. "The Early Development of Carlyle's Style," *PMLA*, LXXII, 936–951. Carlyle "first mastered a rather conventional style, a mildly Johnsonian mode, as typical of the prose of the late eighteenth and early nineteenth centuries as the heroic couplet is of the poetry of the same time"; but with *Sartor* there is a sudden "break too radical to admit the description of its style as a mere exaggeration of a former manner."

Rooney, William J. 1962–1963. "John Donne's 'Second Prebend Sermon'—A Stylistic Analysis," *TSLL*, IV, 24–34. Describes the style of this "alogical" sermon as "baroque" and compares it to El Greco's *St. Andrew and St. Francis*, "where the divisions in the canvas ... are made quite clear, only to have the symmetry exploded by startlingly excessive emphases."

Roth, Russell. 1951–1952. "The Centaur and the Pear Tree," *WR*, XVI, 199–205. On Faulkner's rhetorical devices, especially in "The Spotted Horses."

Saintsbury, George. 1892. *Miscellaneous Essays*. London. "English Prose Style."
1912. *A History of English Prose Rhythm*. London. A sometimes difficult book, as reflected in the criticism by Lucas (1960): "Much as I admire Saintsbury's *History of English Prosody*, I can make little of his *History of English Prose Rhythm*. I do not believe the ordinary reader attaches the slightest importance (even if he knows what they are) to all these amphibrachs and molossi, dochmiacs and paeons. And, in practice, I am often baffled by Saintsbury's scansions." Baum (1952) agrees with Lucas: "Saintsbury has many fine qualities and his book on prose rhythm is indispensable, but one may say without straining that his principles were wrong and his method false. His ear was good, however, and his taste generally sound." It is the judgment of A. C. Clark (1913) that the "most disconcerting feature in his book is the lack of positive results."

Sanders, Charles E. 1957. *Lytton Strachey: His Mind and Art*. New Haven. Ch. 12, "Some Comments on Style"; Ch. 13, "Style in Action."

Sankey, Benjamin. 1965. "Hardy's Prose Style," *TCL*, XI, 3–15. An analysis of general qualities as well as specific passages from the novels.

Schlauch, Margaret. 1950. "Chaucer's Prose Rhythms," *PMLA*, LXV, 568–589. Describes how Chaucer adapted the tradition of cadenced Latin prose to English usage, stressing the artful appropriateness of his style to purpose and reader.
1952. "Chaucer's Colloquial English: Its Structural Traits," *PMLA*, LXVII, 1103–1116.
1955. *The Gift of Language*. New York. Ch. 8 offers a short, coherent account of the development of English diction, grammar, and syntax from their origins to the present.
1964. *The English Language in Modern Times, Since 1400*. 2nd ed. Fair Lawn, N.J. Sections on the styles of various historical periods.

Schorer, Mark. 1941. "The Background of a Style," *KR*, III, 101–105. Hemingway.
1949. "Fiction and the 'Matrix of Analogy,'" *KR*, XI, 539–560. A study of critical method (especially of metaphor), with special reference to *Persuasion, Wuthering Heights*, and *Middlemarch*. Criticism of the novel "must begin with the base of language, with the word, with figurative structures, with rhetoric as skeleton and style as body of meaning."

Schuster, Sister Mary Faith, O.S.B. 1955. "Philosophy of Life and Prose Style in Thomas More's *Richard III* and Francis Bacon's *Henry VII*," *PMLA*, LXX, 474–483. Following the approach suggested by D. C. Allen (1948) in seeking the relationship between style and "philosophy of life," the author argues that the styles More and Bacon employ in their histories are appropriate to the philosophy of each writer.

Scott, Fred N., and Joseph V. Denney. 1894. *Paragraph-Writing*. Boston.

Scott, Izora. 1910. *Controversies over the Imitation of Cicero as a Model for Style*. New York.

Scott, John H., and Z. E. Chandler. 1932. *Phrasal Patterns in English Prose*. New York. Ch. 17 is a survey from Wycliffe to Swinburne, showing the growing complexity of style.

Seaman, John. 1968. "Style and Perspective in Anticommunist Polemic," *L&S*, I, 49–61.

Serjeantson, Mary S. 1936. *A History of Foreign Words in English*. New York.

Shear, Walter L. 1961. "Thoreau's Imagery and Symbolism." *DA*, XX, 860, University of Wisconsin. Chapters on Thoreau's esthetic theory and individual works—"A Winter Walk," "Slavery in Massachusetts," and *Walden*.

Sherman, Lucius A. 1892. "On Certain Facts and Principles in the Development of Form in Literature," *University of Nebraska Studies*, I, 337–366. Furnishes evidence that the English prose sentence had decreased in average length by half from Chaucer to Emerson, each individual author writing in "a consistent numerical sentence average." See also Sherman's "Some Observations upon the Sentence Lengths in English Prose," *University of Nebraska Studies*, I (1888), 119–130. In the opinion of Milic (1967b), "The defect of these methods (from Sherman to Edith Rickert) is that they seem to represent a mere emulation of the outward aspect of the sciences. The mathematical and statistical aspects were only half understood and the results were negligible."

1893. *Analytics of Literature: A Manual for the Objective Study of English Prose and Poetry*. Boston. Discusses the stages through which English prose has passed: coordinative, subordinative, "suppressive," and steady decrease in predication. Some useful analysis of the nineteenth-century sentence.

Short, R. W. 1946. "The Sentence Structure of Henry James," *AL*, XVIII, 71–88. Considers the sentences of the novels from *The Sacred Fount* (1901) to *The Golden Bowl* (1904).

Simon, Irène. 1963. "Dryden's Revision of the *Essay of Dramatic Poesy*," *RES*, XIV, 132–141. A comparison of the two versions of the *Essay*, which reveals "the process by which the conversation of gentlemen can become 'slightly formalized.'"

1965. "Dryden's Prose Style," *RLV*, XXXI, 506–530. "His distinction as a prose-writer lies in the happy blend of the aristocratic virtues of ease and negligence with sense, in the alliance of grace and reasonableness."

Smith, Henry Nash. 1962. *Mark Twain: The Development of a Writer*. Cambridge, Mass. "The book considers first the problems of style and structure Mark Twain faced at the outset of his career, and then traces his handling of these problems in nine of his principal works."

Smith, Logan Pearsall. 1936. *Reperusals*. "Fine Writing" is a very general discussion of plain-ornate prose and a plea for ornate ("fine") writing in modern prose. In the opinion of Connolly (1960), "the most convincing attack on the realism of the thirties."

Spencer, John, and Michael Gregory. 1964. "An Approach to the Study of Style." In Nils E. Enkvist, John Spencer, and Michael Gregory. *Linguistics and Style*. New York. Pp. 57–105.

Spingarn, J. E. 1908. *Critical Essays of the Seventeenth Century*. Oxford. Part 4 of the Introduction contains a general survey of the "trend toward simplicity" during the seventeenth century as reflected in the sermon. "This long campaign of good sense against the figures of rhetoric."

Spitzer, Leo. 1948. *Linguistics and Literary History*. New York.

Sprott, S. E. 1955. "Cicero's Theory of Prose Style," *PQ*, XXXIV, 1–17.

Stathis, James John. 1964. "Swift and the Rhetoric of Reason: A Study of the Sermons." *DA*, XXV, 2988–2989, University of Wisconsin. "The term 'plain,' most often used by critics to describe Swift's sermon style, is clearly inadequate and misleading."

    1967. "Swift and the Rhetoric of the Anglican Via Media." In Robert Gorrell, ed., *Rhetoric: Theories for Application*. Champaign. Pp. 75–81. Swift, sharing the "new stylistic ideal of reasoned discourse" in the interpretation of Christian doctrines, "depends mainly upon such devices of logical proof as aetiologia, definition, and enthymeme. . . . It is not plainness but this quality of forcible reasoning that best characterizes Swift's sermons and the rhetoric of the seventeenth-century Anglican *via media*."

*Staton, Walter F., Jr. 1958. "The Characters of Style in Elizabethan Prose," *JEGP*, LVII, 197–207.

Stauffer, Donald Barlow. 1964. "Prose Style in the Fiction of Edgar A. Poe." *DA*, XXIV, 2912, Indiana University. "I first describe, classify, and define his style, and find those elements of style which are characteristic of all his creative efforts in prose. This descriptive approach, in which I have tried to isolate the predominate characteristics of all of Poe's fictional writing, is followed by a second, analytic, approach, in which I closely analyze the relationship of style to meaning in four different tales."

    1967. "The Two Styles of Poe's 'Ms. Found in a Bottle,'" *Style*, I, 107–120. "Plausible" and "arabesque" styles.

*Stedmond, J. M. 1959. "Style and *Tristram Shandy*," *MLQ*, XX, 243–251. Places Sterne in the Anti-Ciceronian tradition of the loose style and its reaction against formality of procedure and the rhetoric of the schools.

Steinberg, Edwin R. 1968. "Introducing the Stream-of-Consciousness Technique in *Ulysses*," *Style*, II, 49–58. See Friedman (1955) and Humphrey (1954).

Steuert, Dom Hilary. 1944. "The Place of Allen, Campion and Parsons in the Development of English Prose," *RES*, XX, 272–285. An effort to revive these "unjustifiably neglected" Catholic writers as important upholders of the "prose of plain statement" during the sixteenth century.

Stevenson, Lionel. 1958. "Meredith and the Problem of Style in the Novel," *ZAA*, VI, 181–189.

Stevick, Philip. 1965. "Familiarity in the Addisonian Familiar Essay," *CCC*, XVI, 169–173. Focuses on the tenth *Spectator*.

Stokes, Edward. 1959. *The Novels of Henry Green*. London. Ch. 6, "Styles and Manners": "I shall here be concerned chiefly with vocabulary, syntax and sentence structure."

Stone, Robert K. 1963. "Middle English Prose Style: Margery Kempe and Juliana of Norwich." *DA*, XXIV, 288–289, University of Illinois. Compares *The Book of Margery Kempe* with *Revelations of Divine Love*, mainly emphasizing Kempe.

Strainchamps, Ethel. 1961. "Nabokov's Handling of English Syntax," *AS*, XXXVI, 234–235.

Strauss, Albrecht D. 1959. "On Smollett's Language: A Paragraph in *Ferdinand Count Fathom*." In H. C. Martin, ed., *Style in Prose Fiction*. New York. Pp. 25–54. Analysis of the vocabulary and syntax of one paragraph confirms Strauss's belief that "there is no such thing as one kind of Smollett."

Summers, W. C., ed. 1910. *Select Letters of Seneca*. New York.

Summersgill, Francis L. 1951. "The Influence of the Marprelate Controversy upon the Style of Thomas Nashe," *SP*, XLVIII, 145–160. "The Marprelate tracts bring many of the elements of popular literature into the arena of learned disputation, and a balancing of the academic with the popular is a fundamental characteristic of Nashe's style." After participation in the Marprelate controversy, Nashe "achieved a conversational ease and offhand brilliance hitherto unknown in English prose."

Sutherland, James R. 1957. *On English Prose.* Toronto. London, 1958. An extremely impressionistic study of the history of English prose style.

Sutherland, James R., and Ian Watt. 1956. *Restoration and Augustan Prose.* Los Angeles. Sutherland's "Restoration Prose" argues that "Restoration prose is, in the main, a slightly formalized variation of the conversation of gentlemen." Watt's "The Ironic Tradition in Augustan Prose from Swift to Johnson" contains provocative generalizations, such as "The analyzing, generalizing tendency of the eighteenth-century vocabulary may itself be regarded as ironigenic." See Milic's (1967a) attack on Sutherland.

Svaglic, Martin J. 1957. "Method in the Study of Victorian Prose: Another View," *VN*, XI, 1–5. Mainly a critique of Culler's (1957) argument.

"Symposium on the Paragraph." 1966. *CCC*, XVII, 60–87. Christensen, Becker, Rodgers, Miles, and Karrfalt.

Taylor, Ivan E. 1963. "Mr. Pepys' Use of Colloquial English," *CLAJ*, VII, 23–36.

Teets, Bruce E. 1964. "Two Faces of Style in Renaissance Prose Fiction." In Natalie Lawrence and J. A. Reynolds, eds., *Sweet Smoke of Rhetoric: A Collection of Renaissance Essays.* Coral Gables. Pp. 69–81. Treats two manners of writing, "*estilo culto*, an artificial mode of expression traced back to Gorgias" (Lyly and Sidney), and the native, more realistic prose tradition existing in England from medieval times (Greene, Nashe, and Deloney).

Tempest, Norton. 1939. *The Rhythm of English Prose.* Cambridge.

Thomas, Owen. 1965. *Transformational Grammar and the Teacher of English.* New York.

Thomas, Patricia. 1962. "A Note on Wyatt's Prose Style in *Quyete of Mynde*," *HLQ*, XXV, 147–156. "*Quyete of Mynde* (1528) stands in the plain prose tradition."

Thompson, Elbert N. S. 1935. "Milton's Prose Style," *PQ*, XIV, 1–15. An analysis of Milton's syntax and "splendid diction." His "rather heavy and involved" syntax in *The Liberty of Prophesying* is contrasted to Jeremy Taylor's smoother rhythm and quicker movement in *Holy Dying.* The "graphic power" of his diction is compared to Carlyle's and Swift's.

Thompson, J. A. K. 1956. *Classical Influences on English Prose.* London. Chs. 9 and 10 treat the plain and ornate styles; Ch. 16, the classical rhetorical background.

Tilley, A. A. 1933. "The Essay and the Beginning of Modern English Prose." In *The Cambridge History of English Literature*, Vol. 8: *The Age of Dryden.* New York. P. 446. Covers such topics as "Growing Plainness and Simplicity of Pulpit Oratory" and "Dryden's Influence on English Style."

Tindall, William Y. 1959. *A Reader's Guide to James Joyce.* New York.

Toor, Sidney D. 1966. "Euphuism in England Before John Lyly." *DA*, XXVI, 4642, University of Oregon. Traces Euphuism back to King Alfred. "I maintain in this study that euphuism was not imported into England during the Renaissance from Continental models, but that it made its first appearance in the earliest literary prose in the language, based on classical rhetorical models."

Townsend, Francis G. 1957. "Newman and the Problem of Critical Prose," *VN*, XI, 22–25.

Trimpi, Wesley. 1962. "Jonson and the Neo-Latin Authorities for the Plain Style," *PMLA*, LXXVII, 21–26. Offers another reason for the popularity of Senecan style during the early seventeenth century by showing how Lipsius and others widened the scope of the familiar epistle for the discussion of subjects formerly reserved for other genres.

Tuell, Anne K. 1930. "Creed of the Concrete: A Counterblast," *SeR*, XXXVIII, 210–216. A defense of the "abstract noun" against the modern penchant for the concrete.

Ullmann, Stephen. 1957. *Style in the French Novel.* New York.
    1963. *The Image in the Modern French Novel.* New York.
    1964. *Language and Style.* New York.
Umbach, Herbert H. 1945. "The Merit of Metaphysical Style in Donne's Easter Sermons," *ELH*, XII, 108–125. "Shows specifically where Donne is metaphysical as a preacher": the "frequent use of strange figures of rhetoric," the "ingenious straining after wit," the "exaggerated importance given to certain words and expressions," the "packing of authorities," and the "numerous, sometimes illogical, and often unnecessarily detailed divisions and sub-divisions." Donne's sermons, Umbach believes, "have the merit of not being extremely metaphysical."

Vallins, G. H. 1957. *The Pattern of English.* Baltimore. "The developments in the construction of the English prose sentence from the earliest times to the present day."
Van Kranendonk, A. G. 1932. "Notes on the Style of the Essays of Elia," *ES*, XIV, 1–10. On the relation between Lamb's "ornateness" and his complex vision, especially the variety of his effects. See the reply in the same year by T. B. Stroup (XIV, 79–82), which emphasizes Lamb's informal manner.
Vickers, Brian. 1968a. *The Artistry of Shakespeare's Prose.* London. Reviewed by Joanne Altieri, *Style*, IV (1970), 159–162.
    1968b. *Francis Bacon and Renaissance Prose.* New York. Reviewed by Robert Adolph, *Style*, III (1969), 200.
Visser, F. T. 1941, 1956. *A Syntax of the Language of St. Thomas More: The Verb.* 3 Pts. in 2 vols. A detailed analysis of one feature of the language of More, "namely, the verb, its meaning and functions."
    1963, 1966. *An Historical Syntax of the English Language.* 2 Pts. Pts. 1 and 2: *Syntactical Units with One Verb.*

Walcutt, Charles C. 1962. *An Anatomy of Prose.* New York.
Walker, Hugh. 1966. *The English Essay and Essayists.* Mystic, Conn.
Wall, Carey Gail. 1965. "Faulkner's Rhetoric." *DA*, XXV, 5947, Stanford University. The title derives from Booth's *The Rhetoric of Fiction* (1961) and designates not only mannerisms of style but also matters of structure and dramatization.
Warburg, Jeremy. 1965. "Idiosyncratic Style," *REL*, VI, 56–65. A sampling of highly individual styles from Lyly to Faulkner.
Warner, Alan. 1961. "English Without Bones," *English* (Oxford), XIII, 136–139. The decline in present-day prose style.
Warren, Austin. 1951. "The Style of Sir Thomas Browne," *KR*, XIII, 674–687. Following a brief discussion of the nature of style, Warren emphasizes the variety of Browne's styles. "Browne has at least three styles—a low, a middle, and a high—the low represented by *Vulgar Errors*, the high by the *Garden of Cyrus*, the medium by *Religio* and (in decadent form) by *Christian Morals*."
Watson, Melvin. 1946. "The *Spectator* Tradition and the Development of the Familiar Essay," *ELH*, XIII, 189–215.

Watt, Ian. 1957. *The Rise of the Novel: Studies in Defoe, Richardson, and Fielding*. Berkeley.

——— 1960. "The First Paragraph of *The Ambassadors*: An Explication," *EC*, X, 250–274. A minute examination of James's vocabulary and syntax in one paragraph, which reveals a "narrative texture as richly complicated and as highly organized as that of poetry."

Webb, Howard W. 1960. "The Development of a Style: The Lardner Idiom," *AQ*, XII, 482–492.

Webber, Joan Mary. 1962. *Contrary Music: The Prose Style of John Donne*. Madison. Ch. 11 analyzes Donne's sentence patterns.

——— 1965. "Celebration of Word and World in Lancelot Andrewes' Style," *JEGP*, LXIV, 255–269. In praise of the "metaphysical" style in prose and of Andrewes, "the greatest of all the metaphysical preachers."

Wellek, René, and Austin Warren. 1942. *Theory of Literature*. Rev. ed. New York.

Wells, Rulon. 1960. "Nominal and Verbal Styles." In Thomas A. Seboek, ed., *Style in Language*. Cambridge, Mass. Pp. 213–220.

Wendell, Barrett. 1891. *English Composition*. New York.

White, Eugene. 1960. *Fanny Burney, Novelist: A Study in Technique*. Hamden, Conn. Ch. 5, "Style."

White, Mother Elizabeth Stuyvesant, R.S.C.J. 1963. "A Study of the Symmetrical and Asymmetrical Tendencies in the Sentence Structure of Sir Thomas Browne's *Urne Buriall*." *DA*, XXIV, 733, Catholic University of America. "The two-fold tendency towards and away from symmetry that characterizes Browne's sentence structure in this work."

Wilcox, Stewart C. 1943. *Hazlitt in the Workshop*. Baltimore.

Williamson, George. 1935. "The Rhetorical Pattern of Neo-Classical Wit," *MP*, XXXII, 55–81. The development of couplet rhetoric and the relation of this rhetoric to Senecan prose.

——— 1951. *The Senecan Amble: A Study in Prose Form from Bacon to Collier*. Chicago. An outstanding work of scholarship, indispensable to the study of prose style. "This is not a history of prose style in the seventeenth century, but an account of its most incisive pattern—the Senecan." Fisch's criticism (1952): "It is hard to agree with him that this [Senecan, or Anti-Ciceronian, style] was a determining factor in the sphere of literary prose of more importance than the factual style of the scientists—a point which is in dispute between him and Professor R. F. Jones.... Mr. Williamson sees the Senecan influence everywhere, even in the Royal Society itself, a distorted view which springs from his concentration on this one phenomenon."

Wilson, Herman Pledger. 1956. "Chaucer as a Prose Writer." *DA*, XVI, 2154, University of Tennessee.

Wilson, John. 1956. *Language and the Pursuit of Truth*. New York.

*Wilson, R. M. 1959. "On the Continuity of English Prose," *Mélanges de linguistique et de philologie Fernand Mossé in memoriam*. Paris. Pp. 486–494.

*Wimsatt, W. K., Jr. 1941. *The Prose Style of Samuel Johnson*. New Haven. Chs. 1–4 discuss the elements of his style; Chs. 8 and 9 place him historically according to antecedents and effects.

——— 1945. "Further Comment on Constable and Collier," *PQ*, XXIV, 119–122. Indicates Senecan resemblances among Collier, Rymer, Bacon, and the character writers. Suggests that such a style (sententious, brief, antithetic, pointed, asymmetrical) "should be viewed not as a branch of plain style but as a recrudescence of more extravagant Senecan style."

——— 1948. *Philosophical Words: A Study of Style and Meaning in the "Rambler" and "Dictionary" of Samuel Johnson*. New Haven. This book is "a development of several pages of my earlier study, *The Prose Style of Samuel Johnson*, and diverges from the whole of that study in placing a greater emphasis upon origins."

Winterowd, Walter. 1965. "The Poles of Discourse: A Study of Eighteenth-Century Rhetoric in *Amelia* and *Clarissa*." *DA*, XXVI, 65–7860, 360–361, University of Utah.

Woodring, Carl. 1961. *Prose of the Romantic Period*. Boston. "Introduction."

Woods, Samuel H., Jr. 1956. "The Literary Mode of Goldsmith's Essays and of *The Vicar of Wakefield*." Yale University Diss.

*Workman, Samuel K. 1940. *Fifteenth Century Translation as an Influence on English Prose*. Princeton.

Wright, Joseph. 1898–1905. *The English Dialect Dictionary*. New York.

Wyld, Henry C. 1936. *A History of Modern Colloquial English*. Oxford. New York, 1937. Ch. 2, "Dialect Types in Middle English and Their Survival in the Modern Period"; Ch. 3, "The English of the Fifteenth Century."

Wyly, R. D., Jr. 1966. "The Travel Books of Norman Douglas." *DA*, XXVI, 3967, Ohio State University. Traces the evolution of Douglas's style "from a mannered, artificial, rococo expression in *Siren Land* to a modern, conversational, informal idiom in *Alone* and *Together*."

Yoder, Samuel A. 1941. "*Dispositio* in Hooker's *Laws of Ecclesiastical Polity*," *QJS*, XXVII, 90–97. Hooker employed the "method fixed by the common public disputation as it came to be modified by the rediscovery and influence of classical rhetoric, particularly the *Rhetoric* of Aristotle."

Young, Philip. 1952. *Ernest Hemingway*. New York. The last chapter traces modern prose style back to *Huckleberry Finn*.

Zandvoort, R. W. 1963. "What is Euphuism?" *Mélanges de linguistique et de philologie Fernand Mossé in memoriam*. Paris. Pp. 508–517. Contrasts Sidney's *Arcadia* with Lyly's *Euphues* to make clear the basic symmetry of euphuism (isocolon, parison, paromoion) and examines the reliability of handbooks on euphuism in the past half-century.

Zeeman, Elizabeth. 1955. "Nicholas Love—A Fifteenth Century Translator," *RES*, VI, 113–127. "His rendering of the pseudo-Bonaventuran *Meditationes Vitae Christi*, which he called *The Mirror of the Blessed Life of Jesu Christ*, was one of the most popular books of the fifteenth and early sixteenth centuries, and contains some of the finest English prose of any time. There are, in fact, few texts which can claim to . . . point so clearly the contribution made by Medieval translators to the general development of English prose style." Zeeman emphasizes that Love, like other writers in the East of England (Hilton, Dame Juliana of Norwich), writes in the tradition of vernacular prose first established by King Alfred, rejecting sustained alliteration, elaborate cadence, and accumulation of imagery.

1956. "Continuity in Middle English Devotional Prose," *JEGP*, LV, 417–422. Primarily an analysis of *Vices and Virtues* as "the first large-scale prose work to come from the East of England."

ABBREVIATIONS USED IN THE BIBLIOGRAPHY

AJP	American Journal of Philology	KN	Kwartalnik Neofilologiczny
AL	American Literature	KR	Kenyon Review
AM	Atlantic Monthly	LR	Literary Review
AQ	American Quarterly	L&S	Language and Style
AS	American Speech	MFS	Modern Fiction Studies
ASc	American Scholar	MLR	Modern Language Review
BNYPL	Bulletin of the New York Public Library	MLQ	Modern Language Quarterly
		MP	Modern Philology
CCC	College Composition and Communication	MQ	Musical Quarterly
		MS	Mediaeval Studies
CE	College English	NCF	Nineteenth Century Fiction
CJ	Cambridge Journal	N&Q	Notes and Queries
CLAJ	College Language Association Journal	PMLA	Publications of the Modern Language Association
CR	Chicago Review	PQ	Philological Quarterly
DA	Dissertation Abstracts	QJS	Quarterly Journal of Speech
EC	Essays in Criticism	REL	Review of English Literature
EJ	English Journal	RES	Review of English Studies
ELH	Journal of English Literary History	RLV	Revue des Langues Vivantes
		SEL	Studies in English Literature
ES	English Studies	SIR	Studies in Romanticism
E&S	Essays and Studies	SP	Studies in Philology
ESQ	Emerson Society Quarterly	SQ	Shakespeare Quarterly
GR	Georgia Review	SeR	Sewanee Review
HAHR	Hispanic American Historical Review	SR	Saturday Review
		TCL	Twentieth Century Literature
HLB	Huntington Library Bulletin	TLS	Times Literary Supplement
HLQ	Huntington Library Quarterly	TSLL	Texas Studies in Literature and Language
JC	Journal of Communication	UKR	University of Kansas Review
JEGP	Journal of English and Germanic Philology	UR	University Review (Kansas City)
JHI	Journal of the History of Ideas	UTQ	University of Toronto Quarterly
JQ	Journalism Quarterly	VN	Victorian Newsletter

VQR	Virginia Quarterly Review	WR	Western Review
VS	Victorian Studies	ZAA	Zeitschrift für Anglistik und
WCR	West Coast Review		Amerikanistik (East Berlin)

INDEX OF STYLISTS CITED